The American Teacher

"*The American Teacher* is impressive in the way the chapters are organized, the content is chosen, and the theoretical scenarios and critical thinking activities are selected, making this a user friendly book. This text provides students with a solid foundation in conceptualizing the education process."

—P. Masila Mutisya, Professor of Education, Department of Curriculum Instruction & Professional Studies, School of Education, North Carolina Central University

The American Teacher is a comprehensive education foundations text with an emphasis on the historical continuity of educational issues and their practical application in the classroom. Aspiring teachers enter the classrooms with an innate optimism, and the challenge of *The American Teacher* is to engage them and to provide meaningful direction to channel their idealism. By reconnecting individuals with their society, community, and workplace, this engaging text provides education students with a grounding in their profession and an understanding of how important social and political issues affect educational practice.

Special Features Include:

- "Portfolio Activities" that promote reflection and journaling
- "Wisdom of Teachers" sections that introduce students to the advice and insights of experienced, progressive educators
- "Links to the Past" that provide thoughtful connections between historical teaching trends with ones used today
- "Praxis Alerts" that help students prepare for their licensure exams
- Access to the companion website provides additional resources and further ways to engage with the material presented in the chapters: http://www.routledge.com/textbooks/9780415963879/

Donald H. Parkerson is Distinguished Professor of Teaching and Professor of History at East Carolina University.

Jo Ann Parkerson is Professor Emeritus of Education at Methodist University.

The American Teacher

Foundations of Education

Donald H. Parkerson and
Jo Ann Parkerson

Routledge
Taylor & Francis Group

NEW YORK AND LONDON

Please visit the companion website at
www.routledge.com/textbooks/9780415963879

First published 2008
by Routledge
270 Madison Ave, New York, NY 10016

Simultaneously published in the UK
by Routledge
2 Park Square, Milton Park, Abingdon, Oxon OX14 4RN

Routledge is an imprint of the Taylor & Francis Group, an informa business

© 2008 Taylor & Francis

Typeset in Sabon and Gill Sans by EvS Communication Networx, Inc.
Printed and bound in the United States of America on acid-free paper by Edwards Brothers, Inc.

Library of Congress Cataloging in Publication Data
Parkerson, Donald Hugh.
The American teacher : foundations of education / Donald H. Parkerson and Jo Ann Parkerson.
p. cm.
Includes bibliographical references and index.
ISBN 978-0-415-96386-2 (hb : alk. paper) — ISBN 978-0-415-96387-9 (pb : alk. paper) — ISBN
978-0-203-89512-2 (ebook) 1. First year teachers—In-service training—United States. 2.
Teaching—United States. 3. Education—United States—History. I. Parkerson, Jo Ann. II. Title.
LB2844.1.N4P37 2008
371.100973—dc22
2007051054

ISBN 10: 0-415-96386-9 (hbk)
ISBN 10: 0-415-96387-7 (pbk)
ISBN 10: 0-203-89512-6 (ebk)

ISBN 13: 978-0-415-96386-2 (hbk)
ISBN 13: 978-0-415-96387-9 (pbk)
ISBN 13: 978-0-203-89512-2 (ebk)

To Our Students

Contents

SECTION 5
The Noble Profession   **203**

Acknowledgments

We wish to acknowledge the contributions of many people in the development of this manuscript. We thank our family, friends, and colleagues for their support and encouragement, especially Mike Palmer, Gerry Prokopowicz, Carl Swanson, Ken Wilburn, and Cathy Maahs Fladung.

We appreciate the valuable insights and suggestions from the teachers who responded to our NBPTS Survey, especially: Jan Swanson, Debbie Metcalf, Jill Ripley, Jennifer Yazawa, Gregory Bouljon, Matthew Kingsley, John Altounji, and Shelly Wilfong.

The editorial staff at Routledge Press was extremely helpful during the editing and production process. Catherine Bernard, Senior Editor, provided valuable encouragement and Elizabeth Renner devoted many hours to the development of the manuscript and provided thoughtful suggestions for revisions. Anonymous reviewers of the manuscript also provided important insights.

Lastly, we are grateful for the inspiration and enthusiasm from thousands of students at East Carolina University, Methodist University, University of Illinois at Chicago, Columbia College, University of Puget Sound, University of Washington, and Hawthorne, Hammerschmidt, and Fairview elementary schools to whom this book is dedicated.

The American Teacher

Chapter 1

The American Teacher

Welcome to teaching! As the first generation of teachers of the 21st century, you have inherited a proud tradition. The spirit, excitement, and hard work of countless teachers in the past will inform you and help provide you with a virtual bridge to the classrooms of the new millennium. You are truly the critical link in the chain of civilization. Without your enthusiasm and strong commitment to the children of America, that chain would be broken. Congratulations!

THE AMERICAN TEACHER

In chapter 1, we introduce each of the chapters in this book as well as the focus boxes that will help clarify ideas and themes that are presented in the text. As you begin your exciting journey into the classroom, this book will be your guide. Chapter 1, will help you understand your important role in society and, in turn, what society expects of you. Together we will explore the dramatic changes that our country has experienced over time and how teachers have responded to those changes. The core of chapter 1 is an overview of the material that will be presented in this book. Use it as a general introduction to familiarize yourself with the book's overall structure.

TEACHING IN THE 21ST CENTURY

In Section 2: Teaching in the 21st Century, we begin by addressing the major philosophical ideas that will shape your teaching experience. We then turn to the new multicultural classroom and focus our attention on issues of gender, race, ethnicity, and exceptionalities. Finally, we introduce the noble profession of teaching, discuss how we can help children learn and conclude with a discussion of salaries and lifestyles.

Philosophy and Education

In chapter 2, we survey classical and educational philosophies in a way that demonstrates the evolution of ideas rather than simply presenting a "grab bag" of seemingly conflicting views and confusing terms. We examine the philosophies that are important to teachers and explore their relationship to the primary branches of classical philosophical thought. These ideas are presented as part of an evolutionary process that demonstrates our transition to a more secular world, the importance of assuming individual responsibility for our actions, and a worldview that values our diverse multi-cultural society.

Multicultural Classroom

Our new multicultural society represents both a challenge and opportunity for American teachers of the 21st century. In chapter 3, "Multicultural Classroom," we discuss how American teachers can help our nation overcome some of its parochial attitudes and move toward a more open and democratic society. While we must treat all children equally, we cannot simply ignore the differences that divide us. As we will see, our nation has a heritage of misunderstanding based on racial and ethnic differences. By recognizing this heritage rather than simply ignoring it, we position ourselves to deal effectively with our social problems and promote human rights. Moreover, by acknowledging diversity within the classroom and by building lessons around the experiences of diverse students, we can focus on individuals rather than group stereotypes.

Finally, we must remember that in addition to the growing ethnic and racial diversity of our classrooms, American teachers must also be aware of other important subcultures that make up our multicultural classrooms. These include gender, class, religion and culture, geography, and exceptionalities. As a new teacher you will be at the cutting edge of these changes, helping to overcome the parochial and superficial differences that have separated us in the past.

By celebrating both our differences as well as our common culture and by modeling tolerant open attitudes in our classrooms, we can literally change the world, one student at a time.

Just Outside the Classroom

In chapter 4 "Just Outside the Classroom," we profile our profession and discuss some of the reasons we become teachers. With literally millions of Americans involved in education today, we represent one of the largest and most influential professions in the country. We examine how teachers, parents, the general public, and students perceive our schools today and suggest ways that we can improve parent–teacher relations, reach out to the community and enrich our instruction in the classroom. Finally, we discuss the important issues of teacher salaries and benefits and how we compare to other professions; discuss the freedom and autonomy we enjoy as teachers and then point to the bright employment future of our profession. The time to become a teacher has never been better!

OUR EDUCATIONAL HERITAGE

While each chapter in *The American Teacher* will provide you with an historical perspective to understand changes in education, in Section 3: Our Educational Heritage, we

---

Wisdom of Teachers

One teacher, Jan Swanson of Bath, North Carolina, offers this insight to new teachers:

> Children are beautiful human beings. And if you've made a difference in the life of one child, then your own life is that much more precious. And the children are fun. They keep the child in us alive.

Source: NBPTS Survey, 2002 Jan Swanson,
Elementary School Counselor, Bath, NC

examine the deep historical roots of education. First, we consider the global history of our profession, followed by an examination of American educational history. We conclude this section by turning to an historical perspective of diversity in American society.

Classical and Global Roots of Education

Our tour of educational history begins with chapter 5, "Classical and Global Roots of Education." First we discuss the roots of education in a number of ancient civilizations. We then turn to the Western model with a discussion of the Socratic method, the contributions of Plato and Aristotle as well as the Roman tradition of the Latin school. Attention then shifts to the so-called Dark Ages in Western society during which religious bigotry eclipsed secular education for nearly a millennium! Next, we turn to the slow revival of education during the Renaissance and Reformation. Finally we shift our focus to the educational ideas that emerged from the Age of Reason and Enlightenment when individuals such as John Locke, Jean Jacque Rousseau, and Johann Pestalozzi revolutionized our understanding of childhood and the importance of early education.

American Educational History

In chapter 6, "American Educational History," we address the history of education in this country beginning with New England's Puritan schools, the religious schools of the middle colonies, and "home schooling" tutors of the colonial south. We then turn to the "common school" of the 1800s—what Horace Mann called "the greatest experiment of man." And indeed it was! For the first time in world history, education was—theoretically—within the reach of all. The results of this great experiment were stunning and led to a literacy rate more than twice as high as those in Western Europe! The central figures in this important shift toward universal education were the young schoolteachers of America. These courageous men and women brought culture and learning to every corner of the new nation.

Next we discuss the "graded schools" that emerged in the late 1800s and early 1900s and the "educational ladder" of primary, junior high schools, and high schools. We also introduce a number of great progressive reformers of the early 20th century including Francis Parker, Johann Herbart, John Dewey, and Maria Montessori.

We conclude our historical journey with a brief look at our contemporary system of education examining the process of school consolidation as well as the growing presence of the federal government in education as well as the effect of the Supreme Court as an agent of reform and reaction. Finally, we examine the new age of accountability and how this new "reform impulse" impacts American teachers.

Links to the Past: Maria Montessori (1870–1952)

Maria Montessori was one of the first educators to reach out to poor children who were mentally and physically handicapped. She started a school for 60 children that focused on the use of manipulatives (objects that children can touch) as the basis of learning.

Source: Retrieved July 17, 2007,
from http://www.webster.edu/~woolflm/montessori.html

America's Diverse Society

In chapter 7, "America's Diverse Society," we examine the old myths associated with race, ethnicity, and gender and focus on your role in the monumental struggle to open our schools to people of all colors, races, genders, and beliefs. We have a great deal to be proud of as Americans, but there is still much to do. As teachers we must remind our students that our country has always been a multicultural nation. From the beginning of our nation's history, distinctive ethnic communities were prominent features of settlement. This rich diversity has provided the foundation upon which our multicultural nation was born. At the same time, African slaves were brought to this country in bondage. Their struggle for equality was a central feature of our nation's social and political history and their contributions have added an important element to our diverse culture.

Today's immigrants may appear to be different but are in fact part of the same historical pattern that has made this nation great. Gone are the boatloads of European immigrants and trainloads of African Americans from the South. Now Asian and Hispanic (Spanish-speaking) people have become the centerpiece of the new immigration. The changing face of immigration provides both challenges as well as great opportunities for American teachers. By embracing the new multicultural curriculum we can help transform America into a more open and tolerant society.

RESHAPING OUR WORLD THROUGH TEACHING

Once we have surveyed our important educational history, we are ready to step inside the classroom! In section 4 we address the curricular, instructional, and disciplinary ideas that will guide you in your journey and give you practical direction to help you succeed in your first classroom.

School Curriculum

In chapter 8, "School Curriculum," we begin with a discussion of the typical curriculum of public schools today by focusing on the core curriculum and multicultural education. In addition we examine the democratic and authoritarian curricular approaches as well as different forms of curriculum evaluation.

Finally, we examine how the changing composition of schools has impacted today's curriculum recognizing that the traditional "one size fits all" approach of the past cannot meet the needs of today's diverse student bodies. Rather, we must embrace the total environment that includes the explicit and implicit curriculum as well as the extracurricular programs to facilitate student learning.

Instruction and Discipline

In chapter 9, "Instruction and Discipline," we turn to a discussion of instructional strategies and disciplinary techniques and how they have evolved over time to accommodate both the changing curriculum and a more diverse student body. First, we explore the important ideas of educators that focus on both the planning and delivery of instruction. Then, we turn to the importance of defining both general objectives of learning as well as specific learning outcomes. Recognizing that not all children learn in the same way, we focus on the primary domains of learning that include cognitive, affective, and psychomotor. Finally, we examine a number of approaches to learning including whole-class instruction, cooperative learning, and discovery learning.

With this general introduction to theories of learning we turn to the actual delivery of instruction with special emphasis on what educational researchers call the "hierarchies of instruction." These range from lecture and recitation to guided discovery to individual inquiry. We also emphasize more recent developments in teaching methods such as effective teaching and invitational education.

Our ideas regarding student discipline have also changed greatly since the early years of our nation's history. During the American colonial era, children were seen as inherently corrupt and routinely were whipped and administered other severe punishments.

By the early 1800s however, these traditional attitudes toward children had begun to change. Gradually young people came to be seen as either inherently good, though sometimes corrupted by society (Rousseau), or as a blank slate (*tabula rasa)* that could be scripted through vigorous intervention (Locke). These new approaches emphasized the importance of providing incentives and rewards for good behavior and achievement as well as shame and humiliation for misbehavior, laziness, or poor grades.

By the 1900s, society's attitudes toward children had changed once again. Children were now seen as individuals having unlimited potential and as a result, discipline gradually became more democratic in focus, based on mutual respect while recognizing the importance of developing self-esteem in children.

Today, teachers maintain classroom discipline through preventative disciplinary methods based on effective communication and by creating an environment where students understand the consequences of their actions. Moreover, as teachers have helped students balance their individualism with a sense of community, discipline in the classroom has improved. We conclude this section by presenting specific examples of corrective and preventative disciplinary strategies that have been successfully implemented in the classroom with attention to the self-perpetuating nature of a positive classroom environment and a democratic classroom.

THE NOBLE PROFESSION

As we settle into our 2nd millennium, we have a unique opportunity to look back and examine what is right and what is wrong with American education. In section 5, The Noble Profession, we focus on the organization, funding, and legal foundations of American schools. We then conclude with a discussion of our noble profession by examining the issues of professionalization, certification, accountability, support networks, and getting that first job.

Organization and Funding of Schools

In chapter 10 we examine the organization of American education. We will see that early American schools typically were controlled by local communities and funded through property taxes. Community members shared responsibility for the construction and

---

Links to the Past: Changes in Discipline
Go online to http://library.thinkquest.org/J002606/Discipline.html (retrieved July 9, 2007) and compare disciplinary techniques used in the Canyon View Elementary School today with those during the Colonial period and 19th century.

Links to the Past—Unpleasant living Conditions

The following story, drawn from the writings of Laura Ingalls Wilder, illustrates some of the unpleasantness and jealousy that young school teachers who boarded were forced to endure:

> Laura had just crawled under the blankets in her bed (the sofa in the living room that was separated by the rest of the house by a curtain across the doorway) when she overheard her landlady, Mrs. Brewster arguing with her husband. She said "she'd not slave for a hoity-toity snip that had nothing to do but dress up and sit in a schoolhouse all day" and that if Mr. Brewster "did not put Laura out of the house, she'd go back east without him." She continued quarreling with her husband.

Source: Laura Ingalls Wilder (1971). *These Happy Golden Years*

---

maintenance of schoolhouses and often boarded teachers. (Yes, incredibly, teachers in the past actually lived in the homes of their students—we have come a long way!)

Reflection

Why do you think that Mrs. Brewster referred to Laura as a "hoity-toity snip?" Do attitudes towards teachers such as these persist in society today? Why?

The administrative organization of these schools was simple. Elected school officials, sometimes called trustees, were responsible for the hiring, firing, and the annual examination of both children and teachers.

As our educational needs grew however, control of schools gradually was assumed by the states, with shared responsibility for funding through state tax revenues and local property taxes. With state money, however, came the call for greater accountability and schools adopted what some educators have called the corporate or bureaucratic model of school administration. This system is typically organized with state or municipal (city) superintendents of education and school boards defining educational policy and directing the curriculum of the schools. While local boards of education continue to monitor the actions of states, their power has gradually become more indirect.

Today, the needs of education have changed. As a result of the increasing demand for more rigorous accountability standards for teachers and students, as well as the growth of federal funding of specific educational programs, some control of the schools began to shift to the national level.

For example, national academic standards have begun to shape the school curriculum and teachers are monitored through credentialing standards defined by national organizations such as National Council for the Accreditation of Teacher Education (NCATE). Moreover, as you move forward in your teacher training in the next several years, you may be required to pass several professional examinations in the Praxis series.

Praxis Alert: The Praxis Series

Detailed information regarding Praxis I, II, and III state requirements, registration information, and preparation booklets (Tests at a Glance) are available at the Praxis Web site: http://www.ets.org/portal/site/ets (retrieved June 5, 2007).

We encourage you to go online and familiarize yourself with these important national exams.

Links to the Past—Centralized Control of Schools

Andrew Draper was a turn-of-the-century educational reformer who sought to centralize the administration of the public schools. He argued that:

> Efficient schools can be secured only by providing suitable buildings and appliances and by keeping them in proper order on the one hand, and on the other hand, by employing, organizing, aiding, and directing teachers, so that the instruction shall have life and power to accomplish the great end for which schools are maintained.

> To ensure efficiency in these departments, there must be adequate authority and quick public accountability.

Source: Andrew S. Draper, "Organization for City Schools Systems." National Education Association, Report of the Committee of Fifteen, (1895: Washington, D.C.) Retrieved February 23, 2008, from http://www.archive.org/details/addressespapersb00draprich

---

The Educational Testing Service, a national licensure examination organization, developed the Praxis exams. In addition, the No Child Left Behind Act (NCLB) passed in 2001 has had a profound impact on American schools.

Reflection

Why was Andrew Draper so concerned about "directing teachers?" How would Draper's ideas be seen today? What do you think?

The NCLB Act has increased accountability for teachers and schools. As a result of this federal legislation, states are required to administer End of Grade Tests:

- In grades 3 through 8, End of Grade Tests are administered to determine if students are achieving at grade level in reading and math.
- In the 10th grade students must pass the End of Grade tests in both reading and math as part of their high school graduation requirements.

By defining what subjects are most important and linking those subjects to high stakes testing, the NCLB has begun to dictate the content of the school curriculum and it has placed increased emphasis on reading and math at the expense of other subjects. Although reading and math are important, a balance of the curriculum is essential for the development of the child.

States and local communities, of course, continue to direct school policy and administer credentialing standards. However, their role has gradually changed from direct control to advocacy. The 300-year shift from local to state to national control of the schools appears to be an emerging reality.

Rights, Responsibilities, and the Law in American Schools

As the first generation of teachers in the 21st century, we can see how the law has changed American public schools over the years. And while these changes may seem bewildering, there are a number of clear patterns. In chapter 11, "Rights, Responsibilities and the Law," we examine some of these patterns and themes. One of the most important of these is the ongoing struggle of minorities against policies constructed by local majorities.

Links to the Past—Satire of Female Degrees

During the 19th century, some felt that an education was neither necessary nor even desirable for young women. The following newspaper article reflects such views.

Female Degrees—Yesterday we gave some accounts of the degrees conferred in the Young Ladies College in Kentucky. In addition to those, we would recommend the following, which we think will be of more use—namely—M.P.M. (Mistress of Pudding Making), M.D.N. (Mistress of the Darning Needle), M.S.B. (Mistress of the Scrubbing Brush), and especially M.C.S. (Mistress of Common Sense).

Source: "Female Degrees," Springfield, MA. *Republican and Journal*, March 14, 1835

Journaling Activity

Although this article was written nearly 170 years ago, it reflects some attitudes toward women that still exist in our society. Have things changes since 1835? Have some things remained the same? Discuss.

Reflection

During the 1800s many states in the South passed laws against teaching slaves. Why do you think that these democratic majorities passed such laws? What does this tell you about the power of education?

For all our celebration of local democracy, we sometimes forget that local majorities have often imposed their religious beliefs and prejudices on the public schools. They have segregated and excluded on the basis of gender, ethnicity, and race, and sometimes they have acted irresponsibly in the hiring and firing of teachers and school employees.

The legal history of public education in the United States, therefore, has often been a struggle with local and sometimes state level majorities to ensure the basic rights of individuals and groups who occupy a minority position in their communities and schools.

Local communities and states should have an important role in influencing the direction and operation of schools. However, over the years we have learned that local and state power must be monitored and limited to prevent discrimination. Of course, the same holds for federal power as well. In short, changes in school law in the last 50 years are not just another chorus of regulations and restrictions that have been arbitrarily imposed on teachers, administrators, and students. Far from it!

By recognizing these important realities, you will be in a better position to understand the direction of school law and discern its underlying progressive nature. You will see that school "rules and regulations," for the most part, are designed to correct historical inequities and they often provide a positive good for our society and our schools.

And yet there may be danger on the road ahead. A number of recent court rulings on school desegregation and minority access to schools suggest that courts may have begun to abandon their proactive role in the protection of minority and student rights. As teachers we must be alert to these changes. Rather than continuing our efforts to embrace diversity these decisions may result in resegregation of our classrooms and send the wrong message to students.

Links to the Past—The Public Prayer Decision, 1962

The *Engel v. Vitale (1962)* Supreme Court decision ended required prayers in public schools. As Justice Black noted:

> The First Amendment tried to put an end to governmental control of religion and of prayer, [but] it was not written to destroy either. It is neither sacrilegious nor antireligious to say that each separate government in this country should stay out of the business or writing or sanctioning official prayers and leave that purely religious function to the people themselves.

Source: The U.S. Supreme Court, *Steven I. Engel et al. vs. William J. Vitale, Jr., et al.,* 1962, 370 U.S., 421-460. Decision rendered by Justice Black.

Reflection

What did Justice Black mean when he wrote that the government "should stay out of the business of sanctioning official prayers"? What are the negative effects of prayer in schools considering our emerging multicultural society?

The Noble Profession

In chapter 12, "The Noble Profession," we turn to the issue of professionalism in education. We begin by discussing the evolution of teaching from the "schoolmarms" of the early republic to our positions as professionals today. Central to this discussion, of course, is the question of teacher accountability and we will review the increasingly rigorous standards that teachers have achieved over the years. In addition we will focus on the new Praxis exams that have become the standard assessment measures for today's teachers.

We also will examine the vast professional support network that exists for teachers. It begins at the local school and includes teacher aides, counselors, and administrators. In addition this network includes professional organizations serving specialty areas and national organizations such as the American Federation of Teachers and the National Education Association. We even have international teacher organizations such as the Phi Delta Kappan. You are not alone as a teacher but part of a large network of professionals that can assist you with your career and provide you with information and training.

Journaling Activity

Go online to the National Education Association Web site (http://www.nea.org) and review some of the programs offered by this organization. Why is the NEA so important for teachers?

We then discuss the importance of maintaining a portfolio and provide specific examples of how you can begin this important process. We also detail a number of strategies you can use to obtain your first teaching position. These include the preparation of your resume, getting the most out of job fairs, and even some hints on how to develop a network during your student teaching assignment. We then turn to the master teachers of our profession—those who have achieved National Board Certification—and discuss the process by which you too can become part of this prestigious group of educators. Finally, we conclude with a discussion of becoming a professional.

National Board of Professional Teaching Standards

The Web site for the National Board for Professional Teaching Standards contains information about state requirements and procedures for the certification process. Go online and review these important requirements at http://www.nbpts.org/ (retrieved June 7, 2007). Remember, however, that these are for Master Teachers at the top of our field.

THE AMERICAN TEACHER FOCUS BOXES

Your journey into the classroom is an adventure! This book will be your guide and will help you achieve your goal of becoming a teacher. In order to make this process more productive and enjoyable, we have included a series of Focus Boxes that will explain, examine, and clarify the issues and ideas that are presented in the text. In addition to *Journaling Activities* and *Reflections*, these Focus Boxes include: *Situations and Solutions, Links to the Past, Wisdom of Teachers,* and *Praxis Alerts.*

Situations and Solutions

In *Situations and Solutions* you will be presented with a common situation that you may face in the classroom, hallway, or on the school playground. A veteran teacher will then recommend creative solutions to these problems. Situations will range from dealing with student disciplinary problems and communicating with parents to providing external support for a student in the midst of a domestic crisis. The insights provided in these boxes will help you to do well on the Praxis II exam and make a successful transition to the classroom.

Wisdom of Teachers

Wisdom of Teachers focus boxes provide you with teaching tips, helpful hints, and successful teaching strategies from some of America's finest educators, including certified teachers on the National Board of Professional Teaching Standards (NBPTS). For example we include: "Ways to Reach Out to Bilingual Students," "Working with Learning Disabled Students," and "Creating an Inviting Classroom Environment." Taken together, the *Wisdom of Teachers* will give you a wealth of information, distilled from the insights of America's most successful teachers.

Praxis Alerts

Praxis Alerts focus on the three Praxis Exams that you may be required to pass for licensure. In these Alerts you will be directed to material to help you prepare for these exams, such as the general pedagogical knowledge in Praxis II. Other alerts and content in the curriculum and instruction chapters will help you prepare for your Specialty Area Examinations. Finally, the Alerts give you general tips and strategies to prepare for the Praxis exams.

Links to the Past

Throughout the text you will notice two different kinds of *Links to the Past* Focus Boxes. The first will provide you with insights of how teachers in the past dealt successfully with their problems. Drawn from diaries and letters of actual teachers, these boxes will demonstrate the historical continuity of the teaching profession and provide you with a perspective to understand some of the dilemmas you may face as a teacher. For example, you will be introduced to "Dress Codes of a 19th Century Teacher," "He Didn't Whip 'em Enough," and "Getting Paid." Taken together, *Links to the Past* will help you place our profession into historical context. In addition, *Links to the Past* will also draw your attention to key arguments, ideas, and points of view of some of the great educators in the past as well as some of the important historical documents in education. These insights will help you understand our noble profession, direct you to the historical education literature, and help you prepare for your Praxis II exams.

An Invitation to Teaching

In addition to the Focus Boxes that are included *The American Teacher*, chapters include summaries, discussion questions for review, journaling activities, reflection opportunities, and portfolio development, including INTASC activities.

As teachers, we understand some of the difficulties you may encounter on your journey into the classroom. We have designed this book to be "user friendly" to help you succeed in your chosen career. Good luck to you and welcome to the noble profession!

Teaching in
the Twenty-First Century

Chapter 2

Philosophy and Education

Danger, danger! A discussion of philosophy will follow! While this intimidating subject might send some "running for the hills," philosophy is really a very simple set of ideas that provides us with a way of understanding our world. Actually the word philosophy is derived from the Greek philos, or love, and sophos, or wisdom. In other words, philosophy refers to the "love of wisdom." As lovers of wisdom, teachers are at the heart of the enterprise of philosophy. Teachers take their love of learning and pass on a small part of it to their students.

In this chapter 2 we will explore both classical and modern philosophies in a historical framework that focuses on the process of human intellectual development. Rather than seeing these philosophies as fixed and unrelated, we will explore them as sets of ideas that have evolved over time to define our world. These evolutionary ideas involve a shift from spirituality to secularism, from passivity to individual responsibility, and from the acceptance of universal, unchanging truths to a more relative vision of our world. In addition we will address a number of alternative and non-Western philosophies that reflect the multicultural realities of our world.

We conclude this chapter by addressing the major educational philosophies that have emerged over the years and examine their affect on our classrooms. In so doing we will develop a better appreciation of the diversity of our world and our classrooms. Moreover we will also get a better sense of how our own developing philosophies (yes, we have them!) will affect our choice of curriculum, methods of instruction, and disciplinary techniques.

THE THREE BRANCHES OF WESTERN PHILOSOPHY

In order to understand philosophy we present three simple questions that represent the three branches of philosophy. The first is, what is real? The second is, how do we know what is real? And the third is, what is valuable? These three questions are the cornerstones of philosophy.

Metaphysics: What Is Real?
Epistemology: How Do We Know?
Axiology: What Is Valuable?

Metaphysics: What Is Real?

Metaphysics forms one of the primary branches of philosophy and addresses the question: What is real? As teachers we can restate this question as what knowledge do students need to know or, said another way, what subjects shall we teach our students? In its most direct form, then, the question of metaphysics involves the curriculum of the school. The curriculum, of course, is central to the educational experience of our students by defining their course of study.

Over time, we have seen a dramatic shift in our metaphysical perspective regarding education. Traditional societies, for example, perceived religion as the most important subject and as a result most early schools focused on religion as the basis of learning. As our society has become more secular-oriented toward worldly, individual human experiences, the curriculum has begun to reflect those changes. Today however, the growing emphasis on End of Grade Exams (EOGs) and the rigid tenets of the No Child Left Behind (NCLB) in the schools has tended to restructure the curriculum by emphasizing the subjects that are tested—especially math and reading. This sort of policy is danger-ous. While these subjects are important, other subjects such as science and social studies, not to mention art, music, and physical education, are often neglected. In short, the cur-riculum is gradually shifting from the teacher to the testing instrument.

Epistemology: How Do We Know?

While metaphysics asks, what is real, epistemology examines how do we know? Once again, this question can be refashioned for students and teachers to ask: How do we learn or how shall we teach the subjects that we see as most important? Here we are dealing with a basic educational issue—our methods of teaching.

Over the years, we have seen some important changes in the way we teach. In tra-ditional societies we assumed that we obtained information from divine revelation or personal intuition. Today, we occasionally gain spiritual insight or have a "gut feeling," but as educators, we recognize that learning is more complex and involves hard work, reason, and scientific experimentation. This shift in thinking represents a fundamen-tal evolution of our understanding of learning and teaching. Once again however, the recent emphasis on high stakes testing—as required by the NCLB—represents a return to more traditional epistemological (instructional) approaches. By requiring students to take multiple-choice exams as the exclusive measure of learning, and whether a "school is fail-ing," instruction is moving away from understanding back to memorization. This trend is troubling because it turns its back on decades of educational research that promotes critical thinking and evaluation skills over simple parroting of facts.

Axiology: What Values Are Most Important?

Metaphysics and epistemology then focus on questions of what subjects should be taught and how we teach them. The final branch of classical philosophy—axiology—asks the question: What values are the most important and how do we teach those values?

While there is some overlap between the questions of axiology and the two other primary branches of philosophy in terms of what we should teach and how we teach it, axiology is distinctive because it deals with fundamental questions of social, religious, and moral values.

In more traditional societies, values were seen as absolute and unchanging. For Chris-tians, Jews, and Muslims these values were summarized in the Ten Commandments and clearly outlined in biblical scriptures and the Koran, respectively. In our culturally diverse and complex society today, however, we embrace a more relativistic set of values that reflect different cultures and worldviews. Similarly, while traditional approaches to teaching required students to memorize lists of values and then recite them to the teacher, teachers today focus more on the understanding of those values.

In terms of axiology, there has been a shift from absolutes to a more relative perspective on the values of society and in terms of teaching those values, a shift from memorization and recitation to understanding. Rather than simply reciting the pledge of allegiance to the American flag, the teacher might lead a discussion concerning the nature of our democratic government and the role of patriotism.

The recent movement toward EOGs mandated by the NCLB however has disrupted and misdirected this shift towards understanding. First, values are not considered to be essential to "academic" achievement, and because of this, axiology is generally being ignored in today's classrooms. In addition, the persistent return to memorization over understanding has made it more difficult for teachers to discuss the complex issues and inherent values that students and teachers face today.

EDUCATION AND PHILOSOPHY

Metaphysics
What subjects shall we teach our students (the curriculum)?
Epistemology
How do we learn? How shall we teach (teaching methods)?
Axiology
What values are most important and how shall we teach them (values education)?

CHURCH AND STATE

Our world and philosophical orientations have changed dramatically over time. At the heart of this transformation is a growing secularization of society and a recognition that "church and state"—as we sometimes refer to it—operate on different levels. Therefore when we discuss philosophical changes over time from say, absolutes to relative values, as previously discussed in relation to axiology, we are recognizing the ancient divisions between religious and secular values, and the need to understand each of them as central components of our complex world.

Having said this, it is also important to remember that as individuals we will have different philosophical perspectives and values. This is a natural part of our diverse society! Our hope, however, is that as intelligent thinking teachers we will recognize that our philosophical orientation and values are not universal. Consider this point well. If you do not agree—if you feel that all your students must accept your values—perhaps you should choose another career path.

MODERN WESTERN PHILOSOPHIES

In this section we will examine four modern Western philosophical orientations and how each addresses the three basic questions or branches of philosophy. These include idealism, realism, pragmatism, and existentialism. These four modern philosophies represent distinctive positions with regard to understanding our world. As we will discuss later in this chapter, idealism and realism generally are part of a more traditional philosophy associated with the authoritarian approach to education. Pragmatism and existentialism on the other hand, typically represent a more contemporary, democratic philosophical approach to education that is embraced by most teachers today.

THE FOUR MODERN WESTERN PHILOSOPHIES

Idealism
Realism
Pragmatism
Existentialism

Idealism

Idealism is a philosophical orientation that was first articulated by Plato in ancient Greece. At its heart, idealism centered on the notion that there exists an unchanging set of ideas that form the core of our society. For the American teacher pondering questions of metaphysics, epistemology, and axiology, idealism has distinctive answers. As to the subjects that are most important to teach (metaphysics) the idealist would argue that the classics and the study of the ancient languages (Greek and Latin) should form the basis of the curriculum. Students learn best (epistemology) through rigorous development of their minds, achieved through memorization and recitation. Finally in terms of axiology, the idealists would argue that values are absolute and unchanging and that the best way to teach them would be through memorization of specific sets of rules or oaths. The idealist, for example, might argue that values inherent in religion are absolute and should be memorized in order to become a good person.

Realism

While the idealist embraced a very traditional perspective on curriculum, methods of teaching and values, the realist had a different perspective. While quite similar to the idealist in terms of axiology (values), the realist represented a distinctive historical shift in thinking in the areas of metaphysics and epistemology. Realism developed as philosophers of the 1600s and 1700s pondered the seeming paradoxical relationship between religion and science. The fundamental question these philosophers asked was: How do we reconcile the existence of an all-powerful god God with a new science that demonstrates an order to our world that can be understood and measured by humankind?

The more traditional position of course was that only god God understood the mysteries of the universe and that humans were incapable of comprehending nature. (This notion may remind you of the contemporary debate over including "intelligent design" in the curriculum.) As scientists rediscovered the ancient wisdom of the Greeks—especially the scientific approaches of Aristotle—they began to "solve" these mysteries. As a result, many enlightenment philosophers of the 1700s such as Voltaire and Gibbons rejected biblical interpretations as mere superstition.

Given this new worldview, the philosophical tradition of realism began to flourish. Realists embraced the study of science, mathematics, and the environment as the proper subjects to be studied (metaphysics). Similarly they held that the development of skills to understand the natural laws of our world was the appropriate method of instruction (epistemology).

The evolution of philosophy from idealism to realism therefore represented a clear recognition of the world of science. Through natural law, God and science were reconciled and humankind was now actively engaged in the process of learning and discovery. We had moved from a very passive understanding of the world to a more active one. With this shift moreover, science and the scientific method of investigation became an important component of the curriculum and instruction.

Pragmatism

By the 1800s our philosophical evolution continued as society became more secularized and the spheres of church and state became more distinct. Pragmatism represented a shift in thinking about the importance of separating religion from the worldly activities of humankind.

Pragmatism was a new philosophical approach to our world. For the pragmatist the primary metaphysical questions (what subjects should be taught) were the major problems facing society. In a world that had seemingly been turned upside down by the market and industrial revolutions, the growing problems of poverty and increasingly deadly wars, pragmatists desperately sought answers through this problem-solving approach.

Unlike the idealists who sought to train student's minds through rigorous study of classic literature and language, or the realists who saw mathematics and science as the keys to unlocking the secrets of the universe, the pragmatists sought to use our growing body of knowledge to make our world a better place.

In terms of teaching methods (epistemology), pragmatists represented a distinctive shift from the abstract to the concrete, from the theoretical to the practical. Educational philosophers such as John Dewey, for example, argued that abstract, theoretical learning simply did not work. Students learned best "by doing," not by listening or memorizing. Rigorous repetition was all well and good but students often forgot lessons because they were learned "out of context" and had no direct connection to their lives. For example, simply reading about how to perform well in a sport such as baseball by practicing the skills of running, throwing, and hitting is only one part of the learning experience. Actually "playing" baseball is important because each of the skills is integrated into the context of the game itself.

John Dewey and other pragmatists understood this concept well. Dewey sought to channel students' interests through projects that engaged them at a number of levels in order to ponder real-life problems and to offer solutions to solve them. This was often done in the context of group work where teamwork and cooperation was favored over individual competition.

While these new methods were different from traditional curricular and teaching methodologies, pragmatists departed from their colleagues in the area of axiology (values and how to teach them). For centuries, idealists and realists argued that values were universal and absolute. Pragmatists however asserted that these values are relative. Similarly while idealists and realists believed values are best learned through memorization of rules, pragmatists argued that students should be encouraged to develop skills to make appropriate choices and understand the full consequences of those choices. Pragmatists noted that while memorizing rules might generate good behavior—temporarily—rules are often inadequate in guiding complex decision-making in our modern world.

Existentialism

Our whirlwind tour of modern philosophies has taken us from the ideas of Plato, Locke, James, and Dewey. Our final stop brings us to the present day and the philosophy of existentialism. Idealists and realists focused their attention on the unchanging ideas and natural laws associated with an all-powerful god God who governed our world. Pragmatists centered their attention on society and the major social and economic problems we face today.

Existentialists are different. Their attention is on the individual and the world of individual relationships. In one sense the evolution of philosophical thought from idealism

---

The Existential Moment

Jean Paul Sartre (1905–1980) is often recognized as one of the leading lights of existentialism. He argued that in the lives of all young people there is an "existential moment" where one recognizes that they are accountable and must take personal responsibility for their future. An example of this existential moment might be that moment of insight when you begin to understand that you are in school to develop skills for your future career and not simply to make your parents happy.

    This idea contrasts sharply with the more conservative vision that we are in God's hands and everything we do is for him.

---

to existentialism represents a change in the philosophical focus from the almighty to the individual.

    In a metaphysical sense the existentialists recommended a humanities curriculum that addresses the questions of human existence, relationships and an understanding of success and failure—tragedy and triumph. Additionally the existentialist emphasized the development of individual self-esteem and human motivation. In a world where individualism and self-improvement are central concerns, existentialism represents an important philosophical tradition (Greene, 1988).

    Because the individual is the primary focus of the existentialist, questions of epistemology or what is the best way to teach, center on achieving personal insight through journaling and autobiography. By responding to different intellectual dilemmas through personal writing, students find relevancy in what appears to be an abstract and detached world. Teachers use empathy and encouragement to help students make personal choices and realize the ramifications of those choices. For the existentialist, the ultimate goal of education is for students to understand the importance of individual responsibility.

    Finally, in the area of axiology (values and how to teach them) values are not only relative (similar to the pragmatists) but students have a role in choosing them. The existentialist teacher uses empathy and understanding to guide students to embrace a life that is ethically responsible. Rather than directing students through lists of behaviors and prohibitions, they explore the full range of individual choices and discuss options.

Journaling Activity

Have you had an existential moment? If so, discuss that moment and how it has affected you as an individual.

ALTERNATIVE PHILOSOPHIES AND NON-WESTERN PHILOSOPHIES

Our discussion of the three branches of philosophy and the four modern philosophies are derived from the Western tradition. This tradition has emerged over the years from the historical experiences of the Greeks and Romans through the development of ideas in Europe and the Americas. This Western tradition is important and central to our understanding of culture and philosophy.

    Over the years however, our world has become more diverse as we embrace the global economy and experience a growing multicultural presence in our daily lives. Today our schools clearly reflect that diversity. The result is a greater awareness of alternative and non-Western philosophies. Therefore, a brief look at Middle Eastern, Native American,

Asian, and African philosophies and cultures will give us some important multicultural insights.

Judaism, Christianity, and Islam

Since the events of September 11, 2001, we have begun to recognize how little we know about Middle Eastern cultures and philosophies. The Middle East, of course, is the birthplace of civilization and the origin of a number of religions including Judaism, Christianity, and Islam.

Each of these religions, however, embraces a number of distinctive interpretations and sects. These range from progressive, inclusive denominations to more conservative, fundamentalist divisions to cults. As teachers we need to understand these differences and how they may impact learning. For example, progressive Christians, Jews, and Muslims will generally be more open to diversity and the separation of church and state and a relative understanding of values in our society. More conservative, fundamentalist divisions, on the other hand, may tend to be less open to diversity of thought, more dogmatic in their understanding of science, and more oriented towards a belief in absolute values. By recognizing these differences within these religions we can identify problems, adapt our instructional methods and content in order to help all students learn.

Native Americans

In addition to the religious-based cultures of Christianity, Judaism, and Islam are other alternative and non-Western cultures. Some Native American cultures, for example, place special emphasis on living in harmony with the land (rather than the Western tradition of development) and cooperation with members of the community (rather than individualism and competition). The Navajo's idea of "Walking in Beauty," for example, illustrates this search for harmony and peace. Other Native American cultures embrace the important contributions of elders as a primary source of knowledge.

These values, however, may conflict with traditional instruction in the classroom. Since competition is the cornerstone of most forms of evaluation, Native Americans may have difficulty adjusting to examinations and competitive games such as spelling and math bees. By adjusting your teaching methods to include cooperative learning and other forms of evaluation such as portfolios and performance, we can help these children learn (Villegas, 1991; Wilson, 1994).

Asians

Similarly, many Asian cultures embrace the values of harmony within the family and community. This philosophical and cultural tradition is reflected in their respect for elders and authority with special emphasis on politeness and devotion to tradition. Many Japanese, for example have embraced Shinto, a fusion of Confucian, Buddhist, and Taoist beliefs. Others have turned to Zen Buddhism, which emphasizes an introspective, intuitive search for wisdom and knowledge. Once again, by adjusting our methods of instruction to include cooperative learning and noncompetitive forms of evaluation, we will position ourselves to help these children learn.

African Americans

Finally, for some African cultures, introspective thought and strong family relationships represent crucial ways of learning and understanding while art and music provide an important outlet of expression and communication. These traditions were reinforced in this country when millions of Africans were enslaved on southern plantations, (1607–1865). Prohibited from education and sometimes practicing their religion, family relationships became the centerpiece of slave life with music and art as one of the few outlets of personal expression. In this case, culture was reinforced by the realities of slavery (Nieto, 1996).

The Danger of Stereotyping

As teachers we need to recognize these cultural attributes and respond to them. Remember, however, that not all Native Americans, Asian American, and African Americans are the same. This may seem obvious, and we hope that it is, but sometimes in our attempt to understand cultural differences among people we begin to think in terms of stereotypes. This is dangerous. Moreover, it is important to understand these cultural and philosophical differences are not excuses for poor or even extraordinary performance in the classroom. Rather, this diversity serves to remind us of the complexities of teaching and the importance of developing a curriculum that both empowers and takes into account our diverse culture.

EDUCATIONAL PHILOSOPHIES

In our discussion of the four modern Western philosophies—idealism, realism, pragmatism and existentialism—we have made direct connections to the world of education. Over the years, however, educators have built on this foundation and developed a number of educational philosophies that sometimes parallel directly one of the four modern philosophies and sometimes borrow ideas from these and other alternative philosophies.

This should be expected. As teachers, we must be flexible and able to adjust our curriculum, methods of teaching, and even our perspective on values to meet the needs of our students. One philosophical approach might work well with a group of children who have had the benefits of a variety of cultural experiences and a solid educational background. Children though, who have had few meaningful cultural experiences and minimal education, might need a different educational philosophy. Students from different cultures may require different approaches as well. In short, the educational philosophies that we will discuss must be seen as strategies that can be cobbled together to create successful experiences in the classroom.

Two Philosophical Schools of Thought

Even a brief examination of any book on educational philosophy or even a chapter on this subject in a textbook will reveal a confusing number "isms." These "isms" are often presented systematically but they tend to numb the mind as we attempt to sort out their complex definitions, not to mention understand their similarities and differences. Don't worry! (Okay, you can worry a little.) In order to make sense of this seemingly overwhelming subject, we have organized all the educational philosophies into two categories or schools of thought. These schools of thought are the Authoritarian and the Democratic (sometimes called "nonauthoritarian"). Let's take a look at each.

The Authoritarian School of Thought

The authoritarian school is a traditional educational approach. It is rooted in the philosophies of idealism and realism and is derived, in part, from the ideas of philosopher John

---

The Authoritarian School of Thought

- Rooted in idealism and realism
- Derived from writings of John Locke–Blank Slate
- Stressed the products rather than the process of learning
- Favored a subject-centered curriculum
- Embraced convergent thinking (inside the box)
- Perennialism, essentialism, behaviorism, and positivism

Locke (1632–1704). Locke argued that students were essentially blank slates (tabula rasa) that must be scripted by the teacher. Since students brought little knowledge or understanding to the classroom it was the job of teachers to provide them with the information they needed and thus the products of learning were the key element in the educational process.

Finally, the authoritarian school favors convergent thinking or what might be seen as "thinking inside the box." Students are expected to provide exact solutions to particular problems in math or science, exact definitions of words and precise (and accepted) answers to questions in literature or history. The authoritarian approach to education is typically embraced by supporters of the NCLB and EOGs as the sole measures of student learning and school accountability.

The Democratic School of Thought

The democratic school of education (sometimes called the nonauthoritarian) is a more contemporary orientation. Rooted in the philosophies of pragmatism and existentialism, it offers a dramatic alternative to the authoritarian approach. The Democratic School is derived, in part, from the writings of Jean Jacque Rousseau (1712–1778) who held that students were not blank slates but came to the classroom with experiences and ideas, however undeveloped.

The role of the democratic teacher, therefore, is to build on these experiences and to emphasize the process of learning, not just its outcomes or products. This approach favors an experience or student-centered curriculum where learning is achieved through a dialogue between teacher and student. Discussions and projects rather than exclusive reliance on lectures provide the core of learning. Finally, the democratic method embraces divergent thinking or "thinking outside the box." This approach encourages students to provide unique and creative solutions to problems rather than reciting fixed and memorized answers to questions.

The Democratic School of Education

- Rooted in pragmatism and existentialism
- Derived from writings of Jean Jacque Rousseau
- Stressed the process rather than the products of learning
- Favored an experience-centered or student-centered curriculum
- Embraced divergent thinking (outside the box)
- Progressivism, humanism, constructivism, postmodernism, reconstructionism

---

THE AUTHORITARIAN SCHOOL OF EDUCATION

The educational philosophies that we discuss in this section are representative of the authoritarian school and include perennialism, essentialism, behaviorism, and positivism. Each will be related to the three basic branches of philosophy as well as a number of important questions associated with teaching.

Perennialism

The most traditional educational philosophy associated with the authoritarian school is referred to as perennialism. This philosophy, rooted in ideas of idealism and realism has been the cornerstone of education for centuries and continues to fascinate politicians and some educational administrators because of its standardized approach to education and the "Great Books" curriculum.

Great Books of the Western World, Selected Books from the 20th Century

Philosophy and Religion

> James. *Pragmatism*
> Bergson. *An Introduction to Metaphysics*
> Dewey. *Experience and Education*
> Whitehead. *Science and the Modern World*
> Russell. *The Problems of Philosophy*
> Heidegger. *What is Metaphysics?*
> Wittgenstein. *Philosophical Investigations*
> Barth. *The Word of God and the Word of Man*

Imaginative Literature

> James. *The Beast in the Jungle*
> Shaw. *Saint Joan*
> Conrad. *Heart of Darkness*
> Chekhov. *Uncle Vanya*
> Pirandello. *Six Characters in Search of an Author*
> Proust. *Remembrance of Things Past. "Swann in Love"*
> Cather. *A Lost Lady*
> Mann. *Death in Venice*
> Joyce. *A Portrait of the Artist as a Young Man*
> Woolf. *To the Lighthouse*
> Kafka. *Metamorphosis*
> Lawrence. *The Prussian Officer*
> Eliot. *The Waste Land*
> O'Neill. *Mourning Becomes Electra*
> Fitzgerald. *The Great Gatsby*
> Faulkner. *A Rose for Emily*
> Brecht. *Mother Courage and Her Children*
> Hemingway. *The Short Happy Life of Macomber*
> Orwell. *Animal Farm*
> Beckett. *Waiting for Godot* (Adler, Fadiman, & Goetz, 1990)

Perennialists argue that since nature is constant, so too should the curriculum be constant and unchanging. Perennialists are similar to the idealists who emphasize the importance of teaching what they see as the enduring ideas of humankind. Perennialists also embrace the ideas of the realists who have traditionally focused their attention on the instruction of the natural laws of nature and the physical universe. Both of these philosophical traditions then, provide a component of the perennialist educational philosophy.

At its heart, perennialism favors a standardized curriculum that aims to develop student's academic capabilities. The relevancy of that curriculum, however, is not important. The perennialist teacher favors the top down teacher-centered, or subject-centered, method with lectures or lessons delivered to silent, passive students. Students memorize the information given to them and are assessed with regular objective (often multiple choice) examinations such as EOGs.

A good example of the perennialist curriculum can be found in Mortimer Adler's classic *The Paideia Proposal* (1982). In this work, Adler rejected much of the progressive and neo-progressive approaches to education that had been embraced during the 1960s and 1970s. Like many conservative educators of the time he argued that these curricular approaches were not challenging students nor developing their intellectual capacity.

As a result, he argued that radical changes must be instituted. In his *Paideia Proposal* he wrote that all students must be exposed to a standard curriculum of mathematics, science, history, geography, literature, and fine arts. The primary goal of this "one size fits all" curriculum was to develop the intellect of students. Conservative educators throughout the country eagerly embraced this approach.

While Adler's curricular focus centers on a standardized, fixed curriculum, he does propose a variety of teaching styles. Factual knowledge, he argued, was best taught through direct instruction and practice, while an understanding of ideas and values could be achieved through the Socratic Method. Thus, while Adler's teaching methods were more flexible, his curricular approach was clearly perennialist.

Mastery Learning

Central to the revival of the perennialist curriculum in recent years is the concept of "Mastery Learning." The basic idea here is that given a well-defined, standard curriculum, adequate time and resources, all students can "master" the academic material presented to them. The focus of mastery learning is to provide administrators, parents, and politicians with evidence of mastery through systematic testing. The NCLB is a reflection of this idea.

Reflection
Can all students learn with a standard curriculum? Discuss your ideas on this subject.

On the surface, perennialism appears sound. What possibly could be wrong with a standard curriculum that would help all students develop their intellectual capacity? But critics of perennialism argue that these approaches are elitist. They note that while this curricular method might work well with the highest achieving, highest ability students, who would probably do well with any curriculum, it is not appropriate for slower students, those with few cultural experiences or those with limited educational backgrounds. Some students simply learn more slowly than others. They may have learning disabilities or physical impairments such as visual or hearing problems. Others may have never visited a museum, art institute, or a play. Each of these considerations will impact on learning and many of these children may not respond well to the "one size fits all" curriculum.

Moreover, critics argue that perennialism is much too abstract and formulaic for some students. Classic literature, for example, can be difficult for low achieving students. While there is nothing wrong with reading William Shakespeare—in fact, there is a great deal to recommend him—students with limited educational backgrounds often find "the Bard," as Shakespeare is sometimes called, too remote and lacking relevancy to their lives.

Similarly, the teaching method inherent in perennialism calls for a top-down approach with little student interaction. Low achieving students who are not engaged by the instructor, however, often remain passive and simply do not learn. These critics argue that active discussion, student–teacher interaction and hands-on learning is much more effective teaching method for these students (Ozmon & Craver, 1995).

Essentialism

Like perennialism, essentialism is a traditional educational philosophy rooted in the beliefs of the idealists and realists and part of the Authoritarian School of education. But while the perennialists seek to train the intellect through exposure to the enduring ideas of the past, essentialists focus more on the development of essential skills for the future— especially the workplace.

Reflection
Are there subjects that are not essential? What are these subjects and why are they not essential?

The essentialist argues that there is a core of information that all students must learn. Students must be exposed to this core—often referred to as basic skills—and then be required to master those skills. Similar to the perennialist, the essentialist favors a top-down learning environment of lecture and questioning with frequent rigorous assessment through multiple choice and essay exams. Essentialists therefore generally embrace the NCLB and EOGs as central to the learning experience.

Like perennialists, essentialists suggest that the public schools have failed. They argue that the curriculum is not rigorous and therefore "dumbs-down" students. They are also critical of modern educational efforts to develop self-esteem among students (Ravitch, 2000).

If the contemporary focus of the essentialists is the "back to basics" movement, its guiding centerpiece has been *A Nation at Risk* published in 1983. This controversial publication warned the American people that the skills of American students had deteriorated dramatically over the years and that radical changes in education were needed if the nation was to maintain its position as the leader of the world.

The Essential Schools Movement

In recent years, essentialism has been revitalized by the demands of the business community and has found expression in the essential schools movement championed by Theodore Sizer. Sizer favors a "striped-down" educational approach that eliminates what he sees as unimportant subjects. In his influential Horace's *Compromise*, published in 1984, Sizer criticized the curriculum of public high schools in America, arguing that they had failed to provide an essential core of knowledge for students.

Privatization of Public Schools: The Edison Project

In response to criticism of public schools, including *A Nation at Risk*, President George H. W. Bush introduced his America 2000 initiatives. As part of those initiatives he brought business leaders together to form the New American Schools Development Corporation (NASDC). The purpose of this organization was "to unleash America's creative genius to invent . . . the best schools in the world . . . to achieve a quantum leap in learning" (NASDC, 1991).

This group, composed almost exclusively of businessmen, was convinced that they could create a "privatized" system of schools that would outperform any public institution in the country. To that end Christopher Whittle, the chairman of the group, launched the Edison Project, so called because these schools would be superior to public schools as a light bulb was to a candle. This project was to create hundreds of private schools that would quickly demonstrate their superiority to public institutions (Kozol, 1992). Of course, the initial enthusiasm for this plan quickly faded when students did not outperform their counterparts and often did more poorly than students in public institutions on standardized exams.

Critics of essentialism, however, reject both the tone and findings of *A Nation at Risk*. They argue that at best this report represented a naïve exaggeration of the problems facing education today. At worst, it was a deliberate attempt to frighten the American people and promote a conservative agenda to privatize American schools.

Behaviorism

Behaviorism is an educational philosophy of the Authoritarian School that has its roots in psychology, especially the writings of William James (1842–1910), Edward Thorndike (1874–1949), John Watson (1878–1958), and B. F. Skinner (1904–1990). James established the concept of "stimulus response" in learning while Thorndike is considered the father of the standardized test. Watson and Skinner extended this research into the classroom. Watson's early experiments with infants, for example, led him to conclude that the environment was more important than heredity and that, through training, all students could achieve in the classroom. Skinner carried this research even further, arguing that students learned more quickly when given rewards. His work in this area became the basis of "programmed learning."

Behaviorism has become popular among some educators in the last few decades both as a method of discipline and as the foundation of computer-aided instruction. As part of the authoritarian model of education, it assumes that students are essentially blank slates when they arrive in the classroom and that they can be "manipulated" through a rewards system to learn. Moreover, behaviorism embraces the idea that the products of learning, the facts, if you will, as well as convergent thinking, must be the focus of education.

Positivism

The final educational philosophy in the authoritarian school is positivism. Positivism is derived from the writings of Auguste Comte (1798–1857) who promoted a different metaphysical (what is real) and epistemological (how do we know) approach to understanding. Comte argued that reality existed only as observable fact. In other words, belief

---

**William James and Edward Thorndike: Behaviorism,
Intelligence Testing and Educational Psychology**

William James (1842–1910) is considered one of the fathers of Behaviorism. His early work on this subject involved the concept of "stimulus-response" published in his *Principles of Psychology* in 1890. His experiments involved a baby who reached for a candle's flame as a result of a normal reflex. When the baby's fingers were burned, however, she learned not to repeat that behavior because the consequences were too painful. From this insight James reasoned that all learning was similar to the baby burning its finger and developing the habit of not doing it again (James, 1890).

Edward Thorndike (1874–1949) was James's student and he applied some of James's theories to the classroom. Thorndike also focused his attention on the measurement of student's progress and developed some of the first standardized intelligence tests. Thorndike is sometimes referred to as the father of educational psychology because of this work. In his classic statement on learning published in Educational Psychology in 1913, Thorndike argued that intelligence was a product of "connectionism" or the connections between "stimulus-response." The more often a child made the connection between stimulus and response and the more gratification he or she achieved by choosing the correct responses, the greater the learning. This "fundamental law of change" was the basis of his learning theory (Thorndike, 1913).

---

and faith were not real; in fact they were fantasy. Moreover, he felt that we could know only through direct observation and that intuition, gut feelings, and revelation were inadequate ways of knowing. This positivism, as it is called, was based on empirical (observable) science.

As an educational philosophy, therefore, positivism is the basis of empirical observation and experimentation. It is consistent with the authoritarian school in that it embraces a curriculum based primarily on science and math with rigorous assessment of specific knowledge. It favors convergent thinking in that there are precise facts and an exact method of understanding the basics of math and science. Although empirical observation and experimentation are important components of some educational philosophies in the democratic school—namely progressivism—the general orientation of positivism is usually seen as part of the authoritarian school.

DEMOCRATIC SCHOOL OF THOUGHT

If the authoritarian philosophies of perennialism, essentialism, behaviorism, and positivism occupy one end of the educational philosophy spectrum, then the democratic philosophies of progressivism, humanism, constructivism, reconstructionism, and postmodernism are firmly embedded at the other end of that spectrum. Moreover, while the authoritarian philosophies embrace a more traditional metaphysical and epistemological approach to education, reminiscent of the 19th century and before, the democratic philosophies have emerged from the 20th and 21st centuries.

Progressivism

The educational philosophy of progressivism emerged from the school of pragmatism pioneered by Charles Pierce (1839–1914), William James, and John Dewey. Like many other philosophers and scholars of the early 1900s, the pragmatists were concerned about the enormous problems facing the United States as we moved from a traditional to a more modern society. The growing problems of poverty, crime, pollution, materialism; the disappearance of the skilled craftsman, the rise of industrialization, and the decline of the spirit of community all suggested that we must aggressively deal with these problems. And today this philosophy seems even more relevant. The general philosophical solution embraced by the pragmatists was to recognize these problems and then search for realistic solutions that work.

John Dewey applied the general ideas of pragmatism to create an educational philosophy that eventually became known as progressivism. Dewey argued that traditional forms of American education (rooted in perennialism and essentialism) were simply too authoritarian, too abstract, and had failed to deal with the rapidly changing realities of our society.

He noted, for example, that our society had become fragmented because of the rise of industrialism and individualism. In a more traditional economy, he wrote, Americans understood the interconnectedness of society. From this knowledge came an understanding as well as an appreciation—of the importance of the community in these individual's lives.

Dewey argued that schools were ideally suited to deal with the problem of fragmentation and could help students understand their interconnections with members of the community in which they lived. As a result he favored an "open classroom" environment in which students worked in groups, learned to cooperate with one another, and grappled with real social problems. Today, of course, cooperation in the workplace clearly is a high priority and is embraced by small businesses and corporations alike.

In his famous "lab school" established with his wife Alice Chipman Dewey, young students might work together on household projects such as preparing their own breakfast. Later they might establish a simulated grocery store to learn cooperation as they developed their skills in math and reading. Others would build a farmhouse and barn from blocks and would "play" farmer to learn the importance of the agricultural community. Others became weavers or printers. Whatever the role students played, the key was to help them understand the limits of their own individualism and recognize the importance of the larger community in which they lived (Dewey, 1899, Dewey & Dewey, 1915; Dworkin, 1959).

While contemporary progressives and neo-progressives embrace a variety of curricular approaches and methods of teaching, they do share a common set of ideas. First, in a metaphysical sense, most would agree that the curriculum should address the major problems facing society and not the abstract (and often elitist) approaches of the perennialists and essentialists. Issues such as global warming, the globalization of the economy, the corporation, immigration and foreign policy, as well as the problems of racism, they would argue, must be incorporated into the curriculum.

Similarly the progressives would agree that, in an epistemological sense, the best way to learn and teach is a problem-solving approach that focuses on student interests, group work, and hands-on learning. In this way, students are introduced to the ideas of cooperation in addition to individual competition. Moreover, most progressive educators promote the learner-centered or student-centered curriculum that involves students more actively in the learning process (Lambert & McCombs, 1998).

George S. Counts

In 1932, with a single address to the Progressive Education Association (PEA), George Counts became the most discussed educator in the United States. His speech—"Dare Progressive Education be Progressive?"—articulated the anxieties and ambitions of professional educators during the Depression. Calling American teachers to arms, he demanded that they put their talents to work not only as educators but as economic reformers and political activists. Insisting that only education could advance the cause of social reform without revolution, Counts challenged educators to take an increased role in the leadership and government and to impart to their students a sense of progressive politics.

Early supporters including George Counts, for example, called for the creation of a new international social order founded on democratic principles. The role of the reconstructionist educator, therefore, was to help transform society (Counts, 1932).

In the last two decades, there has been a growing conservative criticism of progressives and their general approach to education. These critics—usually perennialists and essentialists who have embraced such policies as the NCLB and EOGs—argue that the alleged failure of education today is a result of the "warm and fuzzy-touchy feely" educational approaches of the progressives—especially their emphasis on the development of self-esteem among students and their focus on the relevancy of the curriculum (Ravitch, 2000).

Of course, some progressive educators over the years may have placed more emphasis on self-esteem and relevancy and less on traditional curricular content, just as some conservative educators have ignored the importance of developing self-esteem among students. For the most part, however, progressives are dedicated educators who have effectively integrated innovative approaches to education with a solid curricular foundation and rigorous measures of assessment.

Reconstructionism

Reconstructionism is a progressive-based educational philosophy firmly embedded in the democratic school. It emerged during the 1930s at a time when the country was experiencing the difficulties of the Great Depression. Whereas progressivism centered its attention on reconnecting students with the greater society through purposeful activities and group projects, reconstructionism was more political.

Reflection
What was Counts advocating for education? Are his ideas relevant for education today?

Today, reconstructionists such as Henry Giroux challenge teachers to become "transformative intellectuals" and provide students with a "critical pedagogy" that empowers them to become agents of social change. For example, as a teacher you might incorporate a lesson on contemporary American foreign policy into your discussion of history with your students. You could lead a discussion of how our policies in the Middle East have affected citizens of Iraq and the United States. When the class reaches a consensus on these matters and perhaps develops a number of alternative policies to consider, it might

---

Dare Progressive Education Be Progressive?

In choosing the title for my address this evening I have had no desire to be sensational or unnecessarily critical. On the contrary, I am merely registering a genuine concern regarding the future of what seems to be this most promising movement above the educational horizon. This movement holds out so much promise that its friends must insist on high accomplishment. The Progressive Education Association includes among its members more than its share of the boldest and most creative figures in American education. My hope is that it will not dissipate its energies or fail to measure up to its great opportunities. But, if it is to fulfill its promise it must use some of this easy optimism and prepare to deal more fundamentally, realistically, and positively with the American social situation than it is has done up to the present moment (Counts, 1932).

---

draft a resolution or write a letter to the president and local representatives and then track the responses to their ideas. By engaging students in a proactive way, learning is enhanced and perhaps change is initiated (Giroux, 1985).

Reconstructionism may appear radical to some conservative educators. However, reconstructionists would argue that by challenging the status quo we are in fact strengthening our democracy.

Journaling Activity
Should a teacher challenge the political, social, or economic policies of the government or simply accept those policies? In your journal, discuss some of the issues that are important to you.

Humanism

Humanism is an educational philosophy of the democratic school that most closely embodies the ideas of Jean Jacque Rousseau. As you recall, Rousseau believed strongly that students were not empty vessels or blank slates that could be scripted by a teacher. Rather, they were endowed with a basic goodness at birth that was often diminished by society.

Emile, Jean Jacque Rousseau (1712–1778)

As Rousseau noted in the opening line of his famous educational treatise *Emile*: "God makes all things good; man meddles with them and they become evil" (Rousseau, 1974).

Reflection
What do you think of Rousseau's opening line of *Emile*?

Johann Pestalozzi, Humanist Educator

Johann Pestalozzi is widely considered one of the leading lights of humanistic education. He felt strongly that teachers must use nurturing love in the classroom to be successful. Moreover he recommended that teachers use familiar objects to help children learn. Many of his ideas were incorporated into the Kindergarten movement of the 19th century and continue to influence early primary education.

Pestalozzi presented his ideas concerning education in two novels: *Leonard and Gertrude* (1781/1894) and *How Gertrude Teaches Her Children* (1799–1804/1894). Briefly, these novels centered on how Gertrude used everyday items as the basis of learning and the importance of the teacher's love in learning. In his first novel, for example, Gertrude taught children arithmetic by having them count the number of steps from one end of the room to the other, the threads while spinning, and the number of turns on the reel when they wound the yarn into skeins.

Reflection
Can Gertrude's methods be applied in classrooms today?

The essence of humanism, therefore, is to nurture the individual spirit without imposing external ideas on the student. In other words, the humanist educator allows students to formulate their own answers to questions and solutions to problems without attempting to persuade them or indoctrinate them. This is perhaps the ultimate form of divergent thinking, to allow students to find their own way, to think outside the box, and to employ the creative impulses that are part of the uncorrupted human spirit.

Since the 1960s, the humanistic approach to education has been very popular. Charles Silberman's *Crisis in the Classroom*, for example, set the tone for a variety of new humanistic approaches to education including greater emphasis on the individual. He argued forcefully that: "learning is likely to be more effective if it grows out of what interests the learner, rather than what interests the teacher" (Silberman, 1970).

This learner-centered or student-centered approach is at the heart of the democratic school of education. For example, you may have planned a lesson in science that focused on the weather. The day before however, the school had a speaker on global warming and its consequences for the environment. Before class you notice that many students seem to be interested in this subject. You respond by altering your lesson slightly and allowing the students to discuss the environmental effects of global warming. You then integrate your original lesson on the weather into those discussions. In so doing you have drawn on the interests of your students and improved your lesson (Silberman, 1970).

While critics may find humanism incomprehensible and dismiss it as an extreme form of "warm and fuzzy" democratic education, humanism is actually at the heart of the nurturing educational experience. Empowering students to employ their own creative ideas, intuitions and feelings to learn, is a noble educational goal. Of course, not all educational approaches are appropriate for all students. One size does not fit all! But for some students, especially those who are creative and independent minded, the humanistic approach can bear fruit. Moreover, as we shall see, the essence of this nurturing, humanistic approach can be successfully integrated into a number of other educational approaches.

Constructivism

Closely related to humanism is the educational philosophy of constructivism. While humanism focuses on individual development through a nurturing approach to teaching, the goal of constructivism is to provide students with hands-on activities that will allow them to "construct" their own frames of thought and develop critical thinking skills. This democratic approach to education emphasizes divergent thinking and stresses the process of learning rather than the products of learning. In other words, constructivist educators favor the understanding of large, complex ideas rather than the mastery of facts.

Constructivist educators call for a fundamental reconceptualization of the curriculum with greater emphasis on understanding our changing, multifaceted world and less on the memorization of arcane detail and facts of that world. As such, constructivists are at odds with the current emphasis on "mastery learning" and accountability as envisioned in such programs as NCLB. Constructivists argue that preparing students for the global economy and the realities of our changing world requires that we help them develop critical thinking skills and perspective rather than simply memorizing facts. As a constructivist educator you might introduce a lesson on the complexities of the emerging global economy. Rather than presenting this material as an abstract concept focusing on "bottom line" issues of profit and expanding economies, you could help students investigate the complexities and consequences of "outsourcing." A class project might consist of interviewing workers (and their families) from a local mill or factory who have been laid off because the company moved their manufacturing facilities to another country. As part of the project, students might investigate how the local community coped with the lay offs, and how other businesses in the community were effected. By incorporating the personal realities of globalization into a discussion of changing economic policies, students will learn a great deal about the complexities of our world.

Postmodernism

Our final stop on this survey of the leading educational philosophies of the democratic school is postmodernism. Postmodernism is by far the most contemporary of the educational philosophies that we have examined thus far, and one of the most controversial. Its philosophical foundation is existentialism but its development owes a great deal to the upheavals of society beginning in the 1960s and 1970s.

The basic goal of postmodernism is to understand power relationships within society. Postmodernists believe that those in power use the institutions of government, culture, and school to maintain their positions within society. They argue that American society has marginalized women, workers, people of color, as well as cultural and religious minorities. Although the actual mechanisms of this "marginalization" are complex and certainly not a part of a vast conspiracy, postmodernists argue that it exists nevertheless.

In the schools, for example, postmodernists argue that the curriculum focuses too much on classic literature or the "Great Works." As a result there is little room left for the works of women, people of color, and ethnic writers. Similarly, in the area of history, a narrative that centers almost exclusively on the contributions of the so called "great men" of the past leaves little room for the equally important history of everyday people, including ethnic and cultural minorities and women. The effect of this "virtual exclusion," postmodernists argue, is that students are unaware of the intellectual and historical contributions of other groups and individuals in our diverse society and as a result, assume that they played marginal roles at best in the development of our society (Martin, 1985).

What do postmodernists mean by "marginalization and virtual exclusion?" Do these problems exist? If so, how might you remedy the situation in the classroom? Record some strategies that you might use.

The goal of postmodernists in the area of metaphysics, then, is to carefully examine power relationships within our society and the role that institutions play in reinforcing the prestige and position of those in power. By including works of "marginalized" people in literature, history, and other subjects, students will have a better appreciation of the contributions of other members of our diverse society.

In terms of epistemology or methods of teaching, postmodernists employ a student-oriented approach with an emphasis on questioning and understanding. Like their existential cousins, postmodernists recommend the use of journal writing as they examine the power relationships within our society. The goal, of course, is to help students recognize the accomplishments of individuals and groups that have been traditionally excluded from our literature and our history. In so doing an appreciation of diversity will naturally follow.

As you might expect, conservative educators have criticized postmodernists on a number of grounds. They argue that they are attempting to exclude classic literature and traditional history from the curriculum. Moreover, they claim that postmodern educational approaches promote radicalism and disrespect for the status quo.

Postmodernists have responded to this criticism by pointing out that blindly maintaining the status quo should not be the goal of education and that a healthy skepticism about the nature of power is at the heart of a democratic society. Finally they make the case that since our world is becoming more diverse and thus more multicultural, and as women, people of color, and ethnic cultures play an ever-increasing role in our world, we must begin to embrace their contributions and understand their perspectives if we are to grow and thrive as a free nation.

Journaling Activity
Compare and contrast the educational philosophies of reconstructionism and postmodernism. In your entry consider the areas of culture and politics.

AXIOLOGY AND EDUCATION: CHARACTER AND MORAL EDUCATION

There are significant differences between the educational philosophies of the authoritarian and democratic schools of education in terms of the structure of the curriculum (metaphysics) and the methods of teaching (epistemology). And, as you might expect, there are also important differences in the area of axiology (values and how to teach them). The primary distinction between them centers on the question of character versus moral education in the schools.

While the idea of character or moral education may seem to be a new idea, it actually has had a long history in this country. From the Colonial period until quite recently it has been a central part of the curriculum of American private and public schools.

In fact, training children to be good people has been a preoccupation of civilizations for thousands of years. The question of how one becomes a good person, for example,

---

Moral Education

- Assumes that students are undeveloped
- Focuses on the development of moral reasoning
- Consistent with the democratic school
- Embraces progressivism, reconstructionism, humanism, and postmodernism

---

has been a reoccurring theme in the writings of the ancient Egyptians, Babylonians, Hebrews, Greeks, Chinese, Indians, Anglo–Saxons, and Americans. The common values promoted by each of these cultures include kindness, honesty, loyalty to parents and family, as well as an obligation to the poor, sick, and less fortunate.

Yet, while most educators agree that children should be taught to become good people, there have always been two central questions: the first is should schools venture into this area at all; and secondly, if they do, should they emphasize character or moral education. These of course are the central questions of axiology.

Although we often use the terms character and moral education interchangeably, there is an important difference. Proponents of character education argue that specific values such as honesty and patriotism should be emphasized, taught, and rewarded. Moreover, character educators favor the memorization of oaths and pledges as the primary method of learning these specific values. As such, character education is consistent with the authoritarian school of educational philosophy.

Moral education, on the other hand, emphasizes the development of students' moral reasoning without establishing a preset list of values that learners should acquire. Morals educators typically favor programs such as "values clarification" where students make choices and decisions about complex issues such as racism, gender discrimination, war and peace. Democratic philosophies of progressivism, reconstructionism, humanism, constructivism, and postmodernism are consistent with this approach (Raths, Harmon, & Simon, 1966).

Character educators assume that students are unsocialized, blank slates and need discipline in terms of values. Moral educators, on the other hand, see students as undeveloped and need stimulation to construct more mature moral views. Character education emphasizes the transmission of unambiguous moral values into behavior while moral education attempts to be value free and emphasizes the student's moral reasoning.

Clearly, while the debate over the curriculum (metaphysics) and methods of teaching (epistemology) continue to dominate our field, questions of axiology, character versus moral education in the schools, will also be an important part of this philosophical discussion.

Character Education

- Students are blank slates
- Favors the transmission of "unambiguous moral values"
- Consistent with the authoritarian school
- Embraces perennialism, essentialism, behaviorism, and positivism

---

PHILOSOPHY AND POLITICS

We've nearly made it! We are almost there! There is just one final matter to consider before we close—the role of politics. As you might know, in the last few years there has been a philosophical and political disagreement over the direction of education brewing on the national stage. This disagreement—what some have called the "culture wars"—is a fierce ideological debate between conservatives and progressives. Generally speaking, conservatives ally with the authoritarian school of education—the perennialist, essentialist, or behaviorist philosophies while progressives can be found in the progressive, humanistic, constructivist, or postmodern camp.

Over the last 20 years or so, progressive educational policy—in place for many years in the public schools—has been challenged and ridiculed by conservatives. In response, progressives have lashed out against conservative plans to reshape or even privatize public schools.

Whatever your political persuasion, and as educators we come in all stripes, remember that the vitriolic rhetoric of politics has no place in the classroom. Do not be influenced by misguided political attacks on teachers, educational policy, or the presumed failures of education over the last few decades. Instead, develop your teaching strategies based on what is best for your students. Choose a curriculum that meets the needs of your diverse classroom and base it on solid educational research.

Finally, consider the individuals who criticize public education and teachers. Are they self-serving politicians who have never set foot in a classroom or are they educators who are attempting to improve the quality of education for your students? Do they base their criticisms of education on the changing whims of politics or public opinion polls or are their recommendations grounded in the careful research from the educational community? As educators we must be able to tell the difference. Our students are counting on us.

SUMMARY

As we have seen, the term philosophy is derived from the Greek and refers to a love of wisdom. As teachers, we embrace this love of wisdom and pass on a small part of it to our students. This chapter explores the fundamentals of philosophy by examining its three branches: metaphysics, epistemology, and axiology; the four modern philosophies: idealism, realism, pragmatism, and existentialism; and the four primary educational philosophies: perennialism, essentialism, progressivism, and postmodernism.

The Three Branches of Philosophy

The three branches of philosophy represent the basic intellectual questions that we grapple with as humans. They include metaphysics or what is real; epistemology or how do we know; and axiology or what is of value. For educators these basic questions can be restructured to provide understanding of the educational process. The question of metaphysics—what knowledge is most important or more directly, what subjects shall we teach our students? On the other hand the basic questions of epistemology can be restated as how do we learn or how shall we teach the subjects that we see as the most important? Finally, the concerns of axiology center on the questions of what values are the most important and how do we teach them? In very simple terms then, metaphysics deals with the curriculum of the school, epistemology deals with teaching methods and axiology focuses on character or moral education.

The Four Modern Philosophies

While the three branches of philosophy represent the basic questions posed by humankind, the four modern philosophies focus on the answers to those fundamental questions. While there are many modern schools of thought the four primary modern philosophies are idealism, realism, pragmatism, and existentialism.

Idealism was a traditional Western philosophy that held that there is an unchanging set of ideas that formed the core of our society.

Realism embraced a curriculum that emphasized science and mathematics but used traditional methods of teaching to achieve their ends.

Pragmatism favored a problem-solving curriculum that emphasized group work to develop the spirit of cooperation among students.

Finally, existentialism represents the most modern of our philosophies. Existentialism favors a more individualized curriculum that focuses on the humanities and teaching methods that center on journal writing and autobiography to achieve personal insight.

Authoritarian and Democratic Educational Philosophies

Over the years, educators have also created their own unique set of philosophies that are related to the four modern philosophies discussed above but are focused more directly on the persistent issues facing education. The nine educational philosophies can be seen as part of either the authoritarian or democratic schools.

The authoritarian school is a traditional educational approach. It is rooted in the philosophical traditions of idealism and realism and derived, in part, from the ideas of philosopher John Locke. The authoritarian school favors convergent thinking or what might be seen as "thinking inside the box." Educational philosophies in the authoritarian school include perennialism, essentialism, behaviorism, and positivism.

The democratic school of education is a more contemporary orientation. Rooted in the philosophies of pragmatism and existentialism, it offers a dramatic alternative to the authoritarian approach. The democratic school is derived, in part, from the writings of Jean Jacque Rousseau who felt that students were not blank slates but came to the classroom with experiences and ideas. The democratic approach embraces divergent thinking or "thinking outside the box." Educational philosophies of the democratic school include progressivism, reconstructionism, humanism, constructivism, and postmodernism.

Axiology in the Classroom: Character and Moral Education

There are two distinct philosophical schools of thought regarding the teaching of values in the classroom. The first, rooted in the authoritarian school favor character education while educators in the democratic school typically embrace moral education.

Character educators argue that students are unsocialized and need values discipline in the form of memorizing oaths or lists of behaviors and values. Moral educators, on the other hand, see students as undeveloped and need stimulation to construct mature and reasoned moral views through discussion and individual introspection.

Philosophy and Politics

As educators we must be aware of the "culture wars" that are raging in our society. While these wars are little more than the age-old liberal/conservative debate, in recent years that war has reached the schools.

Politics disguised as philosophy has begun to negatively impact our students. Educators now face ideological challenges from politicians who use the schools and important issues of education to promote their own agenda and careers.

As educators we must remember that politics has no place in the classroom and that the curriculum and methods of teaching are best determined by educators and not politicians. Our best advice is to choose a curriculum and teaching method that promotes diversity and allows all students to learn. The future depends on it.

DISCUSSION QUESTIONS

1. What are the three branches of philosophy? Discuss their classic meaning.
2. How can the three branches of philosophy be restated for the educator? Briefly restate each.
3. What are the four modern Western philosophies? Discuss the basic ideas associated with each.
4. Discuss some of the important non-Western philosophies. Why is it important that teachers be familiar with these ways of thinking? Give an example.
5. Discuss the difference between the authoritarian and democratic schools of educational philosophy. What are the primary attributes of each? Summarize each of these schools in a sentence or two.
6. Discuss the differences between character and moral education.
7. What are the culture wars? How have they impacted education?
8. Given this general introduction, define your own personal philosophy. (It may be a combination of several) Make a list of the characteristics of a good teacher and next to each characteristic write the philosophy associated with that characteristic.

Chapter 3

Multicultural Classroom

American teachers of the 21st century work in classrooms that are very different from those of just a few years ago. The dramatic surge of immigrants since the mid-1960s has changed the composition of American classrooms and has redirected its curriculum. In addition to the expansion of English as a Second Language (ESL) and other programs designed to help immigrant children, the general curriculum has also continued to change. New reading material reflective of the cultural diversity of America has become commonplace, expanding the core of material that now defines our literary cannon. Similarly, this diversity requires new curricular approaches that help students celebrate both their differences as well as the common culture that binds the nation.

OPPORTUNITIES OF THE MULTICULTURAL CURRICULUM

The developing multicultural curriculum represents a great opportunity for American teachers to overcome parochial, superficial differences towards a pluralistic, multicultural, democratic society. Developing this curriculum will consist of a wide variety of teaching strategies that embrace the diverse cultures in the classroom. Moreover as teachers, we will need to continually critique teaching methods and instructional material to determine bias and carefully monitor all students in the classroom to assure that their diversity is valued.

CHALLENGING THE STATUS QUO: SUBCULTURES IN THE CLASSROOM

In addition to establishing awareness of ethnic diversity, American teachers must also acknowledge various cultures and subcultures. These include gender, race, class, religion/culture, geography, as well as exceptionalities. Finally, as teachers, we need to be able to recognize intragroup cultures such as being a black woman, a poor immigrant, or a young man with a learning disability as these intersections create specific needs to address. It is because of these specific needs that teachers have to be sensitive and understanding to successfully teach.

Why Celebrate Diversity?

But why is it important for American teachers to be aware of the growing diversity of our nation? Can't we just treat all our students equally without reference to the differences between them? These are excellent questions and the simple answer to them is yes and

---

Creating an Authentic Multicultural Classroom

There are six steps teachers can take to create an authentic multicultural classroom:

- Use multicultural books and materials
- Show an appreciation of cultural, racial and ethnic differences
- Avoid stereotypes
- Acknowledge differences in children
- Discover the diversity within the classroom (know your students and their backgrounds)
- Accept and embrace all of your students

Source: McCormick & McCormick, 1992, retrieved June 15, 2007, from http://www.edchange.org/multicultural/papers/buildingblocks.html

---

no. As role models, teachers need to treat all children equally, but treating equally does not mean ignoring the differences that are part of us. In fact, teachers need to be sensitive to and aware of the innate differences among students to ensure all receive appropriate instruction. Chapter 7 discusses the historical period of cultural misunderstanding which was based on prejudice and discrimination. By learning from this heritage rather than ignoring it, we will be in a better position to deal with our social problems and promote human rights. Acknowledging diversity in the classroom and building lessons around the experiences of diverse students encourages children to focus on individuals rather than stereotypes.

Gender Equality

One of the most basic differences that exist between individuals whether they are black, white, native or foreign born, is gender. In fact, the struggle for gender equality has been one of the longest in American history. For years, women were seen as second-class citizens and until relatively recently, have not had the basic rights enjoyed by men. During the early 1800s, young girls were excluded from public elementary schools and when they finally were admitted they often were required to attend segregated facilities. Women also lacked political rights until the passage of the 19th Amendment to the U.S. Constitution when they were guaranteed the right to vote. And in 1973, with the *Roe v. Wade* decision of the U.S. Supreme Court when women were granted the right to reproductive freedom.

Journaling Activity

Carefully examine this list of characteristics. Do they seem accurate or are they simply stereotypes? As a young man or women were you "socialized" differently than those of the opposite sex? If so, did that socialization limit what you could or could not do? What can American teachers do about this problem in the classroom?

Gender Differences

These differences between males and females listed below are not true for all individuals and are based on stereotypical images held by society.

Personality Characteristics

Males	Females
Aggressive	Not aggressive
Strong	Weak
Not domestic	Domestic
Not nurturing	Nurturing
Dominating	Submissive
Suppress emotions	Emotionally expressive
Vent anger	Peaceful

Schooling and the Gender of Students in the Primary Grades

Males

More often retained.
More likely to be labeled ìlearning disabledî or placed in remedial classes
Short attention span
Restless, hyperactive

Females

- More likely to do well in school in primary grades
- More likely to learn to read earlier
- More attentive
- Typically more focused on work

Schooling and the Gender of Students in High School

Males

- Score higher on math and science on the SAT and ACT
- More likely to be involved in serious disciplinary actions
- More often placed in remedial classes

Females

- Receive higher grades in writing
- More likely to do their homework
- Less likely to enter careers in engineering or computer science

Differences between Men and Women

There are, of course, physical differences between men and women. Besides the biological functions associated with childbirth and child nurture, females tend to be smaller than males, and reach full maturity earlier in life. Otherwise, most differences between males and females are a result of society. Historically, young boys were socialized as warriors and protectors of the family and society (not the nurturers). They were supposed to be strong (not weak), competitive (not cooperative), and assertive (not passive). Moreover, they were often encouraged not to display emotions such as empathy, sympathy, or fear. It was assumed that boys were healthier and stronger physically and because of this, boys were expected to succeed at physical tasks.

Wisdom of Teachers—Treatment of Female Students

High school science teacher Matthew Kingsley offered the following suggestions regarding the treatment of female students:

> I try to provide topics that will attract and hold their attention for science. For example, I hold a "Women in Science" Symposium every other year. At this event I have 4–5 women scientists come in and give their stories. I have them talk about how they got into science, what classes they took in school, and their current research projects. More importantly, I have them relate any types of prejudice that they encountered while in school. I also utilize research to provide a classroom environment that is conducive to the female learning style.

Source: NBTS Survey. Matthew D. Kingsley, High School Chemistry, Biology, and Physical Science, Floyds Knobs, Indiana

---

Reflection
What other ways can teachers encourage all their students to learn?

Young girls, on the other hand, were socialized to be nurturing (not warriors), passive (not assertive), and were encouraged to display emotion and sentiment. Over time, young men and women internalized these signals, accepted their stereotypes and began to see them as part of the "natural order of things." As a result, these gender role identities have been deeply embedded in our society and have provided the foundation of prejudice and discrimination.

Differences Due to the Environment

Early educational research reinforced these prejudices because there were significant differences between boys and girls standardized math, verbal, and spatial skills examinations. However, more recent research has demonstrated that these measured differences are beginning to disappear. For example, we now know that there are no quantitative differences on standardized tests between boys and girls until the age of 10 and after that, differences are slight. Similarly, while men do better in high school, those differences have begun to disappear as women improve their scores in mathematics. At the same time, spatial organization and verbal ability differences between males and females are declining as well (Sadker, Sadker, & Klein, 1992). In short, perceived ability differences between males and females are being discovered as not biologically determined, as we once assumed.

Challenging Female Stereotypes

A good example of all this was the change in attitude towards athletics among women since the early 1970s. At that time, because female athletic programs weren't encouraged or funded, women rarely participated in sports. When the federal government mandated that women receive equal funding under Title IX of the education amendments in 1972, this all changed. Women were provided access to intramural sports, club sports, and even competitive interschool sport activities. As a result, their interests and skills in these sports immediately began to grow. Today it is socially acceptable for women to be athletic and succeed in a wide variety of sports.

The Role of Teachers in Gender Stereotyping

As American teachers we contribute to the struggle for gender equality. Research has demonstrated that in the past some teachers bought into gender stereotypes and assumed that boys had a "natural" superiority in subjects such as math and science. Young boys were called on first to answer questions in class and given verbal and nonverbal encouragement. At the same time young girls often went unnoticed. As teachers we need to recognize the powerful role we play in the classroom, and avoid gender stereotyping. This will promote a classroom environment that encourages both males and females to excel and participate in all subjects (Sadker et al., 1992).

RACIAL PREJUDICE AND DISCRIMINATION

While gender discrimination is based on perceived differences between men and women and often the presumed superiority of males, the basis of prejudice against other groups in society often emerges as a result of power relationships that develop as part of the socialization process. As young people grow they often search for personal identity. The perennial question of course is: Who am I? While many young people (and some older ones too) may not be able to answer that question, they often learn quickly "who they aren't." This sense of "otherness" can lead to feelings of either domination or submission; pride or even shame based on the embedded stereotypes and prejudices projected by their family, friends, community, society, the media, or even teachers. It is part of your job as a teacher to inform children of the rich cultural history of America, stressing the importance of all ethnic groups and races to America.

The "Cycle of Poverty"

A good example of how these power relationships are reinforced through societal and cultural stereotypes can be seen in the context of Black–White relationships. Educational research has demonstrated that African American children often come to accept the beliefs and values of the dominant White society. This often includes negative stereotypes about their own race. In 1944, for example, Gunnar Myrdal published his now famous study *An American Dilemma*. This powerful work, which provided the impetus for the famous "War on Poverty" during the mid-1960s, focused on race in American society. Myrdal argued that African Americans often were caught in a "cycle of poverty" that we now understand is reinforced by negative stereotypes. He pointed out that many poor African Americans had little access to quality education. This limited their employment options, which in turn led to more poverty and a lifestyle of hopelessness. As a result, the pernicious stereotype of the "lazy African American" was reinforced and further strengthened the cycle of poverty. Important programs such as Head Start and Affirmative Action provide assistance to those enrolled and are instrumental in leveling the playing field. As teachers, we need to remember to create classroom environments void of these stereotypes (Myrdal, 1944).

Reflection

What is the cycle of poverty and what can American teachers do to break that cycle?

Breaking the Cycle: The Role of American Teachers

For their part, Whites often reinforce this cycle of poverty by buying into the stereotypes of Blacks, Hispanics, Asians, and other groups. Many young children are unaware of themselves as part of a racial group and as a result are relatively "color blind." As they enter school, however, some begin to identify themselves as part of the "in group," distinct from others who may look different in terms of skin color, hair texture, language, or cultural behavior. It is at this critical juncture that American teachers must create an inclusive classroom. Rather than reinforcing these potentially racist dynamics through inaction, teachers need to help students develop an appreciation of the diversity of America. By teaching students to value the histories of all people and their cultures that make up the identity of America, we will achieve the goal of democratic classrooms and help all children learn and succeed.

In short, children begin to be socialized to act in certain ways toward others. While they may not know who they are, they begin to define themselves by who they are not. Typically very young children see themselves as either male or female, black or white, dark or light, young or old, speakers of English or not. As children get older they begin to recognize other "differences" between themselves and others. These include class, religion, culture, exceptionalities, geography, and sexual orientation. As American teachers, we can celebrate our differences by creating a multicultural classroom. One way to do this is to select books that discuss in a positive manner the working class, women, racial and ethnic groups, individuals with disabilities, and people who have different lifestyles. As a teacher and a role model, demonstrate tolerance and acceptance of all people. In so doing you will create democratic classrooms that are tolerant and sensitive to the differences among us.

CLASSISM: THE BLIGHT OF MATERIALISTIC CULTURE

As children begin to mature, they often recognize differences in the class position (or family income) of their schoolmates. Some children are often looked down upon as being "low class," and what this actually means is that they are poor. In our culture, which emphasizes the importance of material wealth, individuals from working-class or even lower-middle-class families may be discriminated against. Because they do not have the resources to purchase name brand clothing or new clothes for various occasions, they are regarded as uncool or worse. The media plays a powerful role in this regard. Through advertising, children are programmed to think that, in order to fit in, they must wear a particular brand of clothing or have a particular logo on their backpack or wear a certain brand of running shoes. These particular brands and logos are often expensive and impractical for many families.

Reflection

What can teachers do to minimize the differences in socioeconomic status among students? Why is it important to lessen these differences?

Pervasiveness of Poverty

Although the United States is the wealthiest nation in the world there are large segments of our population that are either marginally poor, sometimes referred to as the working poor, or living below the poverty line as defined by the U.S. government. In fact using government figures, the number of Americans living in poverty today is an astounding 40 million or nearly 15% of our entire population! Today about 30% of all African Americans, 28% of Hispanics and 31% of Native Americans are living below the poverty line (U.S. Census Bureau, 2000a).

In a nation that boasts the highest *average* standard of living in the world, traditional myths concerning poverty persist. The most persistent of these myths is that those who are poor do not work. Yet, many people living in poverty are employed in low paying, full-time jobs. Unfortunately, many of these people are caught in a cycle of poverty. They are willing to work, but they lack the education and skills necessary to get higher paying jobs. As is sometimes the case, their parents may have received little education as well and had difficulty getting a good job themselves.

Researchers have shown that nearly 2 million people living below the poverty line work full time. Another 7 million living in poverty are employed part time. The hardest fact to accept about these statistics is the number of children who are living in poverty. As innocent victims of poverty they have few resources at home such as computers, books, and other reading material that might to help them do well in school. Moreover, their parents may have little education themselves and therefore are unable to prepare them for school or help with assignments. As teachers, we need to help parents and children access free resources, such as the public library, Boys and Girls Clubs, and in-school and special programs. Above all we need to encourage these children, help to build their self-esteem and try to break the insidious cycle of poverty (U.S. Census Bureau, 2000a).

Children in Poverty: International Comparisons

A study by the relatively conservative magazine *U.S. News and World Report* has shown that despite our great wealth, the percentage of children in the United States living in poverty is well above every other industrialized nation in the world. Even when welfare payments are considered, more than 1 in 5 children in the country—21.5%—are living in poverty. This figure compares to 6.8% for West Germany, 6.5% for France, and 9.9% for Great Britain. Sweden boasts of a child poverty rate of only 2.7%. The article went on to say that while wealthy U.S. children are richer than the wealthiest children anywhere in the world, "Poor children have less to live on—than those in all [industrialized countries] but Ireland and Israel" (*U.S. News and World Report,* 1995, p. 24).

Reflection
How does the United States compare with other industrialized nations in regard to child poverty? What can we as teachers do to help our students living in poverty?

While these figures are overwhelming, the data on homeless children are even more alarming. Concrete statistics are difficult to calculate, but it has been estimated that on any given day, the number of homeless children in the United States ranges from over 65,000 to nearly 500,000. Add to these numbers the nearly 14 million children who now reside in some form of foster care, we can recognize the enormity of this problem (Jencks, 1994; Sandham, 2001).

Often overlooked by teachers, this classism is one of the most vicious forms of discrimination in the classroom. As American teachers we must recognize the power of materialism in our society and work to minimize its discriminatory aspects. Like sexism and racism, classism can be a potent form of exclusion, ridicule, and prejudice.

What Can American Teachers Do?

As American teachers we can play a major role in minimizing classism both in the selection of curricular materials and in our own actions in the classroom. Carefully choosing reading materials that emphasize the accomplishments of working class or poor people in history can certainly be helpful. Historical references to the labor struggles of working people in the past can also be useful. Frank discussions about the power of advertising that lead us to purchase products that we truly don't need might also demonstrate the shallowness of material obsession. And of course, as with all forms of discrimination, American teachers must be positive role models who value performance, cooperation, and achievement over materialism. This will send a positive message to children.

RELIGIOUS AND CULTURAL PREJUDICE

While classism is often an open form of discrimination in the classroom, prejudice based on religion and culture is usually more subtle and guarded. Its impact, however, can be just as potent in excluding individuals from the "in group" or making individuals vulnerable to ridicule.

"Invisible" Cultural Preferences

Religious and cultural preferences may be virtually invisible in the classroom during most of the school year, but can appear during holiday celebrations or in their ambivalence towards them. The Jewish celebration of Hanukkah, the Muslims' Ramadan, Roman Catholics celebration of All Saints Day and Lent as well as the Baptist's objection to a Halloween parade might trigger feelings of "otherness" which can encourage prejudice on the part of those in the dominant culture. Similarly, the yarmulke of the Jew, the plain dress of the Amish and Mennonite or even the Crucifix, as opposed to the simple cross, of the Roman Catholic might signify otherness as well and lead to exclusion or prejudice. These are just a few examples of how religion and culture might serve as grounds for discrimination both inside and outside the classroom.

Reflection

How would you create some activities based on the culture of your classroom that would align with your curriculum?

Wisdom of Teachers—Raising Cultural Awareness in the Classroom

Debbie Metcalf, Special Education Teacher, explained how she raises cultural awareness in her classroom:

> I try to include my families in developing interdisciplinary unit/lesson plans. I use standard course of study objectives and fit them to the culture of my classes. For example, when I had a student from a Jewish family, I chose books that helped students learn about their faith/culture. We learned songs and dances and—a father came in and made potato latkes—we had a book about that as well. We also made dreidels and learned to play with them.

Source: NTBS Survey: Debbie Metcalf, Special Education Teacher, Farmville, NC

Wisdom of Teachers—Celebrating Diverse Cultures

Once again, Debbie Metcalf explains how she celebrates cultural diversity:

My classrooms have always been diverse, so I have always had to adapt to my environment to create a classroom community. My first assignment was teaching ESL students in a US/Mexico boarder town. I spoke Spanish frequently, learned how to make tortillas, spent time with the families of my students at "cumpleano" parties (birthday) and other special occasions.

Source: NBTS Survey: Debbie Metcalf, Farmville, NC, Special Education Teacher

---

Journaling Activity

This teacher obviously enjoyed her experience. Can you think of other ways you might connect with the community if you were in this situation? Record your ideas in your journal.

Minimizing Religious and Cultural Prejudice

As American teachers, we must recognize these potential problems and be resourceful in order to overcome them. Once again, by including content inclusive of all cultures, both ethnic and religious into the curriculum, you can be an effective role model and simply by showing interest in and enthusiasm about the diverse cultures you present in your classroom. Also, by discussing various cultures in engaging ways, your students will find them intriguing as well. A clear and simple message is relayed to your students if you ignore or tacitly dismiss these cultures—your students will be encouraged to do the same.

GEOGRAPHY, SEXUAL ORIENTATION, AND EXCEPTIONALITIES

Beyond ethnicity, gender, race, and religion are other cultures that the American teacher must understand and address. These include students from different regions or types of communities, those with different sexual orientations and students with exceptionalities.

Geography

While racism, ethnic hatred, and misogyny (hatred of women) are classic and easily identifiable dimensions of prejudice, more subtle differences in speech or dress due to our region or community can also be the basis of prejudice in the classroom. In our mobile, multicultural society, students hail from communities and regions all over the country. Differences in students' accents, speech patterns, or even regional cultural attitudes can make them a target for prejudicial remarks. American teachers must prevent the possibility of alienation and intervene quickly to address problems should they arise.

Sexual Orientation

Similarly, individuals with sexual orientations that do not conform to the majority of society can also be targets of prejudice. While you may not have gay or lesbian students

---

Gay and Lesbian High School Students

Gay and lesbian high school students have a number of difficulties as a result of their sexual orientation.

- Suicide—gay and lesbian students are 2 to 3 times more likely to attempt suicide
- Drop out—28% of the gay and lesbian high school students drop out of school, primarily because of harassment
- Isolation—80% of these students suffered social and emotional isolation
- Violence—45% of the males and 20% of the females were subject to verbal harassment and or physical violence
- Homeless—26% of the students were forced to leave home because of their sexual orientation
- HIV/AIDS—By the time students were age 20–29, 20% were infected. Most of them were infected as teenagers
- Student attitudes—97% reported hearing homophobic remarks from other students
- Staff attitudes—57% overheard homophobic comments from school staff
- Health issues—68% of the males and 83% of the females use alcohol
- 44% of the males and 56% of the females use other drugs
- Depression—students have 4 to 5 times the incidence of depression

Source: GLSEN's 2005 National School Climate Survey. April 26, 2006. GLSEN: Washington, DC

---

in your class, there may be references to gays or lesbians in literature or in the media. If homophobic attitudes result, you need to deal with it frankly and openly. Help your students recognize that gays and lesbians are no different than heterosexuals, that they do not represent a threat and that they are part of the multicultural society. Most importantly, demonstrate through your own actions that toleration for different attitudes, behaviors, and lifestyles is essential in being a productive member of society (Sears, 1991, Sears & Williams, 1997).

Students with Exceptionalities

Since the early 1980s, students with exceptionalities have increasingly been mainstreamed into regular classrooms throughout the nation. Today there are more than 6 million students in the United States who are considered "exceptional." These include individuals identified as mentally retarded, learning disabled, visually or speech impaired, hearing impaired, emotionally or behaviorally disturbed, or physically impaired. In recent years, the federal government has implemented a policy of inclusion for students with exceptionalities. This policy offers students with physical handicaps and learning disabilities an opportunity to meet and interact with nondisabled children and gives them exposure to both the regular and special curriculum of the school. Moreover, nondisabled students benefit from this policy as well. Many develop a sensitivity and understanding of students with disabilities and carry values of toleration throughout their lives (Office of Special Education and Rehabilitative Services, 2006).

Ten Suggestions for Teachers to Reduce Homophobia in Your School Environment

1. **Make no assumption about sexuality.** Do not assume all of your students are heterosexual. Use neutral language such as "Are you seeing anyone?"
2. **Have something gay-related visible in your office.** A sticker, a poster, a flyer, a brochure, a book, a button. This will identify you as a person who is open and accepting to all students. SAFE ZONE campaign stickers and resources can provide this visibility.
3. **Support, normalize, and validate student's feelings about their sexuality.** Let them know that you are there for them. If you cannot be supportive, please refer them to someone who can be. Then work on your own biases by reading, learning, and talking to people comfortable with this issue.
4. **Do not advise youth to come out to parents, family, and friends as they need to come out at their own safe pace.** Studies show as many as 26% of gay youth are forced to leave their home after they tell their parents.
5. **Guarantee confidentiality with students.** Students need to know their privacy will be respected or they will not be honest with you. If you cannot maintain confidentiality for legal reasons, let students know this in advance.
6. **Challenge homophobia.** As a role model for your students, respond to homophobia immediately and sincerely. Encourage in-service trainings for staff and students on homophobia.
7. **Combat heterosexism in your classroom.** Include visibly gay and lesbian role models in your classroom.
8. **Learn about and refer to community organizations.** Familiarize yourself with resources and call them before you refer a student. Also, refer to gay-positive books.
9. **Encourage school administrators to adopt and enforce anti-discrimination policies for their schools or school systems which include sexual orientation.**
10. **Provide role models.** Gay and straight students benefit from having openly gay teachers, coaches, and administration. You, as teachers, can help by making gay and lesbian students feel more welcome.

Source: Compiled by Youth Pride, Inc. Source: Retrieved February 23, 2008, from http://www.youthpride.org/home.html

Reflection

In recent years the numbers of students with learning disabilities, physical impairments—visual, speech and hearing—mental retardation, and emotional and behavioral disorders have increased. Discuss how the policy of inclusion benefits all your students.

On the other hand, while inclusion programs have been very successful, they also can be a source of prejudice and discrimination within individual classrooms. Some children can be insensitive, if not brutal. They can perceive exceptional children as inferior, dumb, or just "weird."

This presents a real challenge for American teachers. To begin with, most classrooms are not designed with exceptional children in mind. Blackboards are too high for students confined to wheelchairs and most desks will not accommodate them. Elevators are rare in most schools, as are access ramps. Some schools, though, have made extraordinary efforts

---

Wisdom of Teachers—Raising Awareness of Hearing Impairment

Special Education teacher Debbie Metcalf discussed how she raised awareness of the hearing impaired in the classroom:

> One year, when I had a child with a severe hearing impairment, the whole class did a unit on hearing/sound. We read about Helen Keller and Louis Braille and did research on other people with similar challenges. The whole class learned sign language, developed a computer slide show of Helen Keller, and studied the science of sound. For a culminating activity, we constructed a large ear canal that we placed in the hallway outside our classroom. The students constructed an outer ear and the outer ear parts with big paper stuffed with newspaper. The inner ear parts were suspended from the ceiling—large black cloth was added to create a "tunnel" effect. We invited other students to walk through our "Earie Canal." Some of my students wore lab coats and had flashlights . . . giving tours of the ear canal . . . once inside the room, we had centers for them to visit—to learn sign language, learn about Helen Keller, learn tips on how to talk with people with hearing disabilities . . . and how to use a TDD/TTY machine (which the telephone company hooked-up for free).

Source: NTBS Survey. Debbie Metcalf, Special Education Teacher, Farmville, NC

---

to provide amplification equipment and special computers, and reconfigured blackboards to facilitate learning. Other schools provide a positive learning environment for exceptional children by matching a special education teacher with a regular classroom teacher and a teacher's aide. This individualized, team-teaching approach can be very effective.

Beyond these efforts, as an American teacher you must create a classroom environment that is positive, open, and understanding of the problems and possibilities of exceptional children. Like those without learning disabilities, exceptional children need love, friendship, acceptance, and a place to learn like everyone else. By being a positive role model for your students, by exhibiting openness, acceptance, and understanding, you can help students learn the valuable lessons of inclusion and tolerance.

AMERICAN TEACHERS CHANGING THE WORLD

American teachers can change the world! By recognizing the true nature of prejudice, by understanding the long history of intolerance in this country, and by taking a proactive stance within each of our classrooms, we can make a difference—child by child.

Remember that prejudice in its many forms slowly emerges from the consciousness of young children as they search for their own identity. As they develop, they desperately seek for acceptance among their peers and often find that membership in a group often comes at the expense of others. This is where you can make a difference. By assertively challenging negative stereotypes in both formal lessons and informal discussions with your students, by developing policies of inclusion, by demanding tolerance in the classroom, by celebrating our diversity, and most importantly by modeling behavior that is open and inclusive, we can change the world—one student at a time!

Wisdom of Teachers—Avoiding Prejudice in the Classroom

Below is a simple exercise for establishing an inclusive classroom.

1. Have students brainstorm names they have heard people call others.
2. Write all of these words on the board.
3. Assign categories: racial, ethnic, sexual, or religious bias.
4. Discuss them.
5. Make students aware that all name calling involves prejudice and disempowerment and is harmful to the person being oppressed.
   - State that none of the listed names is acceptable in your classroom.
   - Make it clear that you will not tolerate any form of name calling.
   - Help class participants to establish classroom rules and to brainstorm/agree upon the social consequences of breaking this rule.
   - React immediately to any transgressions to make sure that students will feel safe in the classroom.

Source: Virginia Uribe, Fairfax High School, LosAngeles Unified School District, founder and director of PROJECT 10. www.members.tripod.com/~twood/guide

---

SUMMARY

Our New Multicultural Classrooms

American teachers of the 21st century will work in classrooms that are very different from those of just a few years ago. This diversity will require new curricular approaches that will help students celebrate both their differences as well as the common culture that binds the nation. The developing multicultural curriculum therefore represents a great opportunity for American teachers to help our nation overcome parochial, superficial differences and truly move toward a pluralistic, multicultural, democratic society. By teaching students to value the histories of all people and their cultures that make up the identity of America, we will achieve the goal of democratic classrooms and help all children learn.

Subcultures in the Classroom

In addition to our growing ethnic diversity, American teachers must also be aware of a number of other cultures or subcultures that exist in our diverse nation. These include gender, race, class, religion/culture, geography, as well as exceptionalities. In addition, American teachers must also recognize intragroup cultures (such as being a black woman, a poor immigrant, or a young man with a learning disability). Each of these complex intragroup subcultures must also be understood as well.

Gender

As American teachers, we can help continue the struggle for gender equality by recognizing the powerful role we play in the classroom. First, we must recognize that gender role identities are deeply embedded in our society and have laid the foundation of prejudice and discrimination against women. Then, by avoiding gender stereotyping we can promote a classroom environment that encourages both males and females to excel in all subjects.

Race

While gender discrimination is based on perceived differences between men and women and often the presumed superiority of males, the basis of prejudice against other groups in society often emerges as a result of power relationships that develop as part of the socialization process.

In addition we must understand the "cycle of poverty" among various groups within our society. Poor African Americans, for example, often have little access to quality education, which limits their employment options, which in turn leads to more poverty and a lifestyle of hopelessness. As a result, the pernicious stereotype of the "lazy African American" is reinforced and further strengthens the cycle of poverty. While programs such as Head Start and Affirmative Action have helped to break the cycle of poverty, it is clear that as teachers we have a long way to go!

Class and Poverty

Although the United States is the wealthiest nation in the world, there are large segments of our population that are either marginally poor—sometimes referred to as the working poor—or living below the poverty line as defined by the U.S. government. In fact, using government figures, the number of Americans living in poverty today is an astounding 40 million or nearly 15% of our entire population! Of course, poverty is more common among certain groups in society. Today about 30% of all African Americans, 28% of Hispanics, and 31% of American Indians are living below the poverty line.

As teachers, we need to help parents and children access free resources, such as the public library, Boys and Girls Clubs, and schools and special programs. Above all we need to encourage these children, help to build their self-esteem and try to break the insidious cycle of poverty.

We also can play a major role in minimizing the pernicious aspects of classism both in the selection of curricular materials and in our own actions in the classroom. Carefully choosing reading materials that emphasize the accomplishments of working class or poor people in history can certainly be helpful.

Finally, we can become a positive role model by valuing performance, cooperation and achievement over materialism. This will send a positive message to children.

Changing the World—One Child at a Time

As American teachers, we must recognize each of these potential problems and be resourceful in order to overcome them. By paying close attention to the curriculum, being an effective role model, and showing interest in and enthusiasm about the diverse cultures present in your classrooms, your students will usually find them intriguing as well. On the other hand, if you ignore these cultures or tacitly dismiss them, your students will do the same. With regards to curriculum, religious or cultural holidays can be a wonderful opportunity to create a new multicultural mindset among your students.

American teachers can change the world! By recognizing the true nature of prejudice, by understanding the long history of intolerance in this country, and by taking a proactive stance within each of our classrooms, we can slowly make a difference—child by child.

DISCUSSION QUESTIONS

1. What is the "cycle of poverty?" How does this cycle affect a child's learning? What can you do as an American teacher to help break this cycle?
2. Should we celebrate diversity in the classroom or simply ignore it? Why?
3. What is Title IX of the education amendments in 1972? Why is it important?
4. What is the poverty rate among children in the United States? How does this rate compare with other industrial nations? What can American teachers do about this problem?
5. What is mainstreaming? How does this policy affect teaching in the classroom?

Chapter 4

Just Outside the Classroom

There are over 3.3 million public school teachers in the United States today. Just over half teach in elementary schools while the remaining teach in high schools. In addition, there are more than 235,000 school administrators, and over a quarter million teachers in private schools throughout the country. Add to these numbers about 1.2 million college professors and over a million men and women in education-related jobs in government, the private sector, and the military and you can see that education is one of the largest and most influential professions in the country (National Center for Educational Statistics, 2003).

WHY WE TEACH

Why are so many people interested in education? Why do nearly 300,000 new teachers enter the classrooms of the nation each year? In chapter 1 we suggested one important reason: teachers represent a critical link in the chain of civilization. We are essential for the survival of humankind! Beyond this noble idea however, hundreds of thousands of young men and women enter the profession each year for a variety of personal and professional reasons (National Center for Educational Statistics, 2003).

Working with Young People

As you might expect, the most common reason that we choose to become teachers is to work with young people. In fact, over the years, 7 in 10 teachers enter the profession because of this single reason. Moreover, the vast majority of teachers remain in the classroom because of their desire to work with and improve the lives of children (National Education Association (NEA), 2003).

Job Security

And yet, there are a number of other reasons that we enter teaching. For some of us job security is an important factor. While the private-sector job market for managers, administrators, sales personnel, accountants, and marketing executives may appear stable, during periods of economic slowdown many of these jobs are lost. As the economy slows, businesses often "downsize" in order to improve profits. And despite your skills, determination, and work ethic, if your company is doing poorly, the chances are, you may be let go.

Wisdom of Teachers—Why Did You Become a Teacher?

Teachers enter the profession for a variety of reasons. Here are some of the reasons that teachers mentioned in a recent survey:

- I love working with children.
- I want to make a difference in a child's life.
- Teaching is a calling, like being a minister or a priest.
- Teaching provides a service to society. You are not exploiting anyone.
- You have a great deal of independence in the classroom. No one is looking over your shoulder.
- You have a lot of time off: all holidays and every summer.
- You are a professional and have a position of respect in the community.
- I love helping young people.

From: NBPTS Survey, teacher respondents, Fall 2002

Teaching is different. Once you achieve tenure, you will have long-term job security even if the economy slows. You may not receive the hefty raise you were hoping for but you will in all likelihood keep your job. Education is, as they say, "recession proof."

The Influence of Former Teachers and Family

In addition to job security, some of us enter teaching because of the influence of a former teacher or family member. There always seems to be one teacher that has touched us in a special way; perhaps a teacher who introduced us to a subject that we would like to pursue as a career or a teacher who changed our lives. Many teaching careers have begun because of these special teachers.

In addition, some teachers choose our profession because they have grown up among teachers. Their mother or sister may have been a teacher. Their father or brother may have taught in the past. Growing up with a professional, recognizing their dedication to young people, or just hearing stories of their classroom work may have had a profound effect on your decision to carry on the tradition and become a teacher yourself.

Wisdom of Teachers—Teachers in the Family

Many teachers enter the profession because of the influence of a parent. One teacher noted the influence of her father and grandfather:

Perhaps I should have realized that I might have a calling for teaching since my father was a special education teacher and my grandfather taught high school English.

Source: NBPTS Survey, Debbie Metcalf, Fall 2002

Optimism

For many others, optimism is the primary motivating factor. Let's face it, teachers are optimistic. Most of us want to give something back to society, make a difference, and perhaps even change the world in some small way. Many of us also recognize that working in the field of education provides us with an unrivaled opportunity for intellectual and professional development. The world of education is a world of wonderful and exotic ideas, a boundless world of books and information, and a world of continually growing knowledge.

Autonomy and Freedom

And finally, some teachers enter our profession because of the great autonomy and freedom that it offers. Teachers have rules and restrictions imposed by state and local administrators, but inside the classroom, you are in charge. You direct learning and discipline. You make decisions. There is no supervisor literally looking over your shoulder, though under the provisions of NCLB you are accountable for your students' performances on End of Grade tests. Moreover, once you complete the school year, you have a long summer vacation (usually about 2 months!) to pursue your interests, to read, to relax, to travel, to take classes, to care for your children, or to do whatever you want. This freedom and autonomy has drawn many teachers into the field. And why not?

Journaling Activity
Discuss some of the reasons that you would like to become a teacher. When did you first think that a teaching career might be the right choice for you?

Wisdom of Teachers—Interesting Perspectives on Entering Teaching

High school social studies teacher Shelly Wilfong noted:

> I entered teaching because I love to learn. I like the challenge of getting students to take an interest in government and becoming active citizens.

On the other hand, special education teacher Jennifer Yazawa, recalled:

> I entered teaching accidentally. I had an opportunity to go to Europe and do a semester in comparative educational practice serving students with special needs. I saw the importance of what I learned there and finished my B.S. in Elementary Education and Behavioral Disabilities.

Source: NBPTS Survey, 2002, Shelly Wilfong, High School Social Studies & U.S. Government, Goshen, IN; Jennifer Yazawa, 8th Grade Humanities and Special Education, Albuquerque, NM

WHO ARE WE?

Teachers in public schools today are a diverse group of individuals, although the number of racial and ethnic minority teachers is still too small. According to the National Center of Education Statistics, nearly 83% of all teachers are white with about 17% from a minority group. This figure includes African Americans (8%) and Hispanic (6%). Over one third of all public school children are either African American or Hispanic (Spanish speaking), and more should be done so that the diversity of the faculty reflects the diversity of the classroom. In fact, schools of education throughout the country are attempting to address this by vigorously recruiting minority teachers (National Center of Educational Statistics, 2003–2004).

Reflection
Most public school teachers today are White. What are colleges, schools, and departments of education doing to recruit African-American and Hispanic teachers? Why is this recruitment important?

Age and Education

The average age of teachers today is about 43 years with nearly 1 in 6 in their 20s. However, in the next few years, many teachers who started their careers in the 1960s will retire. As a result, our profession will become much "younger" as millions of new American teachers enter the classrooms of the nation (NEA, 2003).

In terms of education, nearly all public school teachers have earned their bachelor's degree from a college or university with 90% having received training in colleges, schools, and departments of education throughout the country. In addition, the majority of teachers today have completed some post-graduate work. In fact, about 50% of all teachers today can boast of having achieved an advanced degree in their specialty area (U.S. Department of Education, National Center of Educational Statistics, 1994).

Reflection
Teachers today have achieved the highest levels of education in history. What does this tell you about teachers' pursuits of lifelong learning?

Men and Women as Teachers

Both men and women enter teaching for similar reasons, but there are some differences in their preferred specialty areas. For example, in the elementary grades, more than 8 in 10 teachers are women (84%). Women also represent a majority of all special education teachers and a majority in some high school specialty areas such as English/language arts (80%). On the other hand, in areas such as social studies, the majority of teachers are men (62%). Finally, in specialty areas such as math and science there are roughly equal numbers of men (52%) and women (48%) (National Center of Educational Statistics, 2003–2004).

ENLISTING THE HELP OF PARENTS

As teachers, we are a pretty happy lot, generally satisfied with our work. Nevertheless, as professionals, we have identified a number of persistent problems. Interestingly however, recent Phi Delta Kappan polls of teachers demonstrate that public perceptions of problems in schools today do not match those of teachers. These surveys show that it was *not* the use of drugs (teachers see alcohol abuse as a more serious problem); it was *not* the supposed lack of moral standards among students; and, with the exception of some inner city school teachers, it was *not* the alleged violence, gangs, or fighting in the schools that concerned teachers. Rather, the most serious concerns of teachers today center on issues associated with parents, the home environment, and the community's support of education (Langdon, 1999).

REASONS FOR THE LACK OF PARENTAL SUPPORT

For teachers, the most pressing problem facing education today is the lack of interest and support of parents. In the mid-1980s, over a third of all teachers saw this as the biggest problem facing schools; and while there has been some improvement in this area over the years, nearly a quarter of us continue to see parental apathy as one of the central problems facing schools today (Langdon, 1996, 1999).

Decades of educational research has demonstrated that the home is the first place of learning and that attitudes toward school are shaped there long before the child enters the classroom. As teachers we understand this reality and recognize that for some students who are doing poorly in school, they would benefit dramatically from greater parental support (Langdon, 1999; Parkerson, 1989).

Reflection

Many teachers think that a lack of parental support is a key problem for education. Moreover, parental interest in their child's schooling seems to decline by high school. What can we do as teachers about this problem?

Of course, there are many reasons for parents' lack of involvement in their child's education. Among the most important of these are financial problems, domestic upheavals, cultures of educational failure, language difficulties, and parental naïveté regarding education.

Financial Problems

For many years, the ideal image of the American family presented in fiction, film, and television has been the two-parent household with a working father and a stay-at-home mother raising the children. In fact, in many families today both parents work and some find it necessary to work several jobs in order to make ends meet. And of course, there are many single-parent households today. This compounds these financial problems considerably. After a hard day at work single parents have little time or energy to help their children with homework, encourage them to achieve, or even to monitor their television viewing. Their top priorities are basic needs like shelter, food, and clothing.

Reflection

The divorce rate in the United States has increased significantly in the last 140 years. It has also skyrocketed in the last generation. How do you think that this has affected children? As teachers, what can we do to help children who come from single parent households?

Domestic Problems

Domestic upheavals can also cause parents to be distracted from their child's education. Today, domestic violence is a common feature of family life and many children grow up in dysfunctional, violent environments. Even more alarming is the abandonment of children altogether, because of parental incarceration, drug addiction, or alcoholism. This forces children into foster homes, group homes, or into the care of a family member. While many of these care givers provide warmth and love, the memories of domestic violence are difficult for children to overcome. Moreover, when physical safety and emotional security are the caregiver's top priorities, the child's education may be overlooked (U.S. Bureau of the Census, 2001).

Reflection

Why do you think that there are more cases of child maltreatment today than a generation ago? What can you do to help children who are victims of domestic upheaval?

A Culture of Educational Failure

In addition to financial problems and domestic crises are the negative attitudes toward their children's education brought on by a culture of educational failure. Many parents were poor students themselves and they remember their school days painfully. This may

---

Situations and Solutions: The Parent Facilitator and the Wake-up Call

To help bridge the communication gap between teachers and parents, the Cumberland County School System in North Carolina employs parent facilitators in their schools. The parent facilitator at one school is an African American woman by the name of Anna Moore. In her school more than 80% of the students are African Americans, while the teachers are predominately White. She is able to effectively work with the teachers and relay information clearly and frankly to parents in order to help solve problems.

For example, one child named Rishan missed a great deal of school. Rishan's teacher, Ms. Green, was especially concerned about his absences because he was doing poorly in school. Ms. Green asked Anna to help resolve Rishan's absenteeism. Ms. Moore called Rishan's mother and discovered that she frequently overslept and since she did not have a car, when Rishan missed the school bus, she had no way to get him to school. Ms. Moore bought an alarm clock for the household. When this failed to bring the desired result, Ms. Moore called the household with a wake-up call each morning. Although Rishan's mother was not very excited about being aroused by a phone call, Rishan's attendance and grades improved.

Source: Anna Moore, Teacher Facilitator, Cumberland County Schools, NC, personal interview, April 20, 2001

be difficult for us to understand since we typically "loved" school and fondly look back on our school days. Some parents may place little value in their child's education because they did not value it when they were in school. These negative attitudes can foster poor attitudes among their children who may end up habitually truant and/or lack self-discipline in the classroom. Moreover, parents who see no value in education will not actively help their children learn and may even discredit the value of them going to school.

Journaling Activity

What do you think of the idea of a "parent facilitator"? What other things might a parent facilitator do to help children learn?

Language Difficulties

In addition to these problems, language difficulties can also be a major cause of parental apathy. While many bilingual students can communicate well in the classroom and at home, some parents cannot speak English. Whether they simply have no time or interest in learning a new language, parental language barriers can be devastating to the child's education. These parents cannot effectively monitor their child's progress nor can they help them with homework. Moreover, when parents have limited knowledge of English, your use of educational jargon when communicating with them, such as references to hyperactivity, behavioral disorders or individualized education plans, can be frustrating and even infuriating. Always keep this in mind.

Parental Naïveté

Finally, even in households where there are no apparent financial, domestic, cultural, or language problems, there can be a great deal of parental naïveté regarding their child's education. Many parents assume that learning occurs *only* in the classroom and that their job is to "raise their children" and that the teacher's job is to teach them. When compounded with other problems, it can severely limit the achievement of their children.

WHAT CAN TEACHERS DO?

While these problems may seem impossible to overcome, there are things that we can do as teachers to help parents help their child learn. Educational research has shown that even in the poorest, most dysfunctional families, parents can still play a positive role in their child's education. The most important things they can do are to encourage learning, demonstrate support for their teachers, and show interest in their child's schooling. In addition, if parents make sure that their child's homework is completed on time and that they have a quiet place for them to study, learning and achievement test scores improve. Parents also can help their child learn and achieve by regulating their television viewing and not allowing homework to be done while they watch television. Finally, parents can help their children learn by reading to them when they are young and by reading themselves. By demonstrating that reading is not only an important part of life but also a lot of fun, children will learn and achieve in school.

Wisdom of Teachers—Reading Aloud to Children

Experienced teachers recognize the power of reading aloud to children. Here is what one teacher suggested for parents:

- Begin reading to the child at approximately 3 months of age
- Hold or cuddle the child while you are reading
- When you read aloud you are building the child's vocabulary because children imitate what they see and hear
- Select books to read that are interesting
- Use books with pictures
- At first, keep the readings short to fit with the child's short attention span
- Gradually, lengthen the time spent reading as the child's attention span grows

Source: NBPTS Survey, Fall 2002. Jill Ripley, Elementary teacher, Indianapolis, IN

Journaling Activity

In early March to celebrate Dr. Seuss' birthday, Read Across America sponsors a series of Read Aloud programs in schools, libraries and bookstores. Volunteer with Read Across America and record your experiences in your professional journal. Go online to http://www.nea.org/readacross find out more about this important program. Make sure you list your participation on your resume as well.

Sharing Learning Strategies with Parents

Some parents seem to intuitively understand the enormous impact they have on their child's learning, but others require the help of a teacher to develop a supportive learning environment in the home. In fact, one of the most frequently asked questions by parents during parent–teacher conferences is, *How can I help my child?* American teachers should have a variety of specific strategies on hand to share with parents. For example, first, suggest the parent read to the child for 20 minutes each evening. Second, recommend that the parent and the child take turns reading aloud to each other. Third, encourage parents to be supportive of their child's reading even if it is at a low level. Make clear to the parent that they should not be critical of the child. Additionally, it's not so important what they read, but that they read regularly. Reading the sports page of the daily newspaper will help just as well as a book specifically designed for children. Finally, suggest that parents have a set time and place for doing homework such as after school at the kitchen table or while preparing dinner.

Turn off the Television!

And by all means, teachers must encourage parents to reduce the amount of television viewing of the child and closely monitor the shows that the child watches. Young children spend far too much time watching television. This should be discouraged. Recommend instead that parents and children use some of this time (perhaps just an hour to begin with) to read either individually or as a family. When families do watch television, you might encourage parents to help their children develop their oral communication skills by

---

Distractions in the Home Environment

Television, video games, computers, and other forms of electronics create distractions in the home. These take away from time children might spend doing homework or reading. Consider these realities:

- Ninety-nine percent of homes have at least one television set
- The average household has 2–3 television sets
- The television is turned on in each home approximately 7 hours per day
- Children ages 3–10 spend approximately 30 hours per week watching television. (This figure does not include time spent watching videos or DVDs.)
- Ninety-nine percent of homes own a VCR and/or a DVD player
- Seventy percent of children and teenagers have their own television in their bedrooms
- Forty-five percent have their own VCR and/or DVD player

Source: Adapted from Trelease (1995)

---

watching programs together and then discussing those shows with the child. The key here is that parents should listen to the child and allow them to express themselves.

American teachers clearly have their work cut out for them. Most parents simply do not understand their critical role in their child's learning. In fact, the Phi Delta Kappan survey discussed above showed that only 5% of parents saw their lack of interest as a problem facing education today. Rather, as we have seen, it was the behavior of students that concerned parents the most.

Reflection

Given the many distractions in the home today, how can we help parents help their children learn?

EDUCATION AND THE PERCEPTION GAP

In addition to a general lack of parental support for their child's education, is an alarming perception gap between teachers and the general public regarding education. For example, national surveys have consistently demonstrated that more than twice as many teachers as parents perceive "lack of proper financial support" as an important problem facing schools today. In fact, only 5% of parents in the Phi Delta Kappan survey perceived low teacher salaries as a problem facing education today and only 9% saw a lack of financial support as a problem or concern. This compares to nearly a quarter (22%) of all teachers who saw a lack of financial support as a problem. Clearly the issue of a fair salary and educational funding will continue to be a concern of teachers as long as the public remains indifferent or uninformed about these issues (Langdon, 1999; National Education Association, 2002).

School Choice and Vouchers

Another example of these differences in perceptions has to do with the issue of "school choice" and vouchers. According to most surveys of public opinion, the vast majority of teachers today (78%) oppose the concept of "school choice," that is, allowing students and parents to choose a private school to attend at public expense through a "voucher" plan. This educational reform emerged in the early 1980s and for some, has become a favored "solution" to virtually all the problems facing schools today. For many teachers, however, this issue continues to strike a nerve. Many feel that vouchers are unworkable, while others see them as yet another conservative "reform" designed to privatize public schools. As one of our the teachers we surveyed noted: "I think if we spent more time, energy, and resources on the existing public schools, it would lessen the public's desire for alternative schools" (Langdon, 1999; NBPTS Survey, 2002).

But while teachers recognize both the political nature and inherent problems associated with school choice and vouchers, nearly half of the American public (44%) has embraced this reform as a viable option for our schools. As presented in the national media school choice may *sound* like an excellent reform for education. (The word "choice" seems to resonate well with us.) However, charter schools do not have a good track record. Their students do not perform better than average on standardized tests. Moreover, a recent study found that in fourth and eighth grade mathematics, students in charter schools scored lower than students in public schools. When Americans are faced with the reality of this reform, their attitudes often change dramatically (National Assessment of Educational Progress, 2006).

Problems with School Vouchers

Goodwin Liu (2002), former special assistant to the deputy secretary of education, recently detailed some of the problems with school vouchers: "In some school districts high poverty and low performance are so pervasive that choice makes little difference" (Liu, 2002, p. B-7). Simply giving students in one low performing school the choice of moving to another low performing school is not the solution. Liu went on to point out that schools' participation in these voucher plans is voluntary and that suburban schools seldom participate. As a result, school choice is really no choice at all. Once again, teachers' understanding of these issues is grounded in the realities of education while the public is often influenced by the grab bag of reforms regularly paraded by politicians and the media.

Accountability and Standardized Tests

One final example of the perception gap between the public and teachers is the issue of accountability and the use of standardized tests as the exclusive measure of school effectiveness. Phi Delta Kappan poll results on this controversial issue have demonstrated that public school teachers have little faith in the multiple choice examination as the sole measure of school effectiveness. In fact, only 15% of American teachers see these standardized examinations as viable in this context. As one of the teachers we surveyed noted, "Testing day is awful—some teachers are literally sick to their stomachs. So are the students. It's an enormous amount of pressure. I don't think teachers are teaching any better because of the standardized examinations—I think they do more harm than good." Indeed decades of educational research has shown that no single measure of student achievement or "school effectiveness" is adequate. Rather, while multiple measures, including written essays, exams, grades, and portfolios may seem more time consuming and expensive, they are a superior method of evaluation (NBPTS Survey, 2002, Jan Swanson, School Guidance Counselor, Bath Elementary School, Bath, NC).

Despite these realities, 50% of the American people see these standardized, multiple-choice examinations as a key measure of how well schools are doing. Clearly it has been some time since they personally have faced the reality of "high stakes testing." Moreover, their position on this issue has been influenced neither by the realities of the classroom nor the research in this area but rather the current "feel good" notion of accountability. Their source of information about the schools, as usual, is the media (Langdon, 1999).

Why do the American public and teachers see things so differently? The public's ideas about today's schools are often shaped by the sensationalism and exaggeration of the nightly news. Teachers' perceptions, on the other hand, are grounded in the realities of the classroom and decades of educational research.

Perhaps the clearest example of this is how Americans perceive schools at the national, community, and local level. When asked to grade schools around the country, they were very critical. In fact, less than a quarter, 24% of the general public and 21% of parents, gave the nation's schools marks of "A" or "B." When they graded their community schools they gave higher marks—about half, 49% public, 56% parents—gave these schools these high grades. However, when these same individuals were asked to rate their local schools, about two thirds of parents graded them as "A" or "B." Generally, people are pleased with the schools their children attend and the schools in the community. The closer Americans get to public schools, the better those schools appear to them. Teachers must act as their own advocates, promoting the benefits and successes of public education in America (Langdon, 1999).

THE ROOTS OF THE PERCEPTION GAP

But there is much more to this issue. At the heart of the problem is the tendency among both educators and their critics to make a common cause of denouncing American public education. Educators sometimes focus their attention on the problems in education in an attempt to get more money for schools. At the same time educational critics, often politicians who call themselves reformers, exploit the widespread anxiety of the American people over the nature and purpose of education in our society and characterize the public schools as inadequate or failures.

A number of educational historians have made this point over the years. For example, Gerald W. Bracey in his *Setting the Record Straight* recently has demonstrated that at least since the end of World War II, many educational "reformers" have been critical of public education. For Bracey the reason is "nostalgia and amnesia." These reformers often look to a nostalgic past, to a "golden age of education" that never really existed. They then collectively, and conveniently, forget that the state of education today is far superior to what it was in the past (Bracey, 1997, 2002).

Education and the Cold War

In the 1950s, numerous reformers bemoaned the public school's alleged failures. For example, Arthur Bestor in his popular book, *Educational Wastelands,* argued that the schools had staged a "retreat from learning" and he harkened back to a golden age of education at the turn of the 20th century. While many Americans were alarmed by Bestor's arguments, he failed to mention that during his "golden age of education" only 50% of the student age population was enrolled in any school and that the overall graduation rate from high school was an appalling 7%! By contrast, in the early 1950s the vast majority of American children were enrolled in schools and high school graduation rates were well over 60% (Bestor, 1954).

Nevertheless, this sort of criticism continued. Several years later in October 1957, when the Soviet Union launched its first satellite—Sputnik—Admiral Hyman Rickover lashed out at American public education. He blamed schools for what he saw as the failure of the United States in the "Space Race." The following year, *Life* magazine published a 5-part series of articles entitled *Crisis in Education* that were extremely critical of the public schools. And yet, no one seemed willing to give the public schools credit when 11 years later, the United States put a man on the moon and secured its place as the leaders in space technology. Educational "failure," it seemed, made headlines while the great success of schools was often ignored! The sensationalist nature of the news media tends to focus attention on perceived problems rather than the slow but consistent progress of public schools. In turn, some politicians build their careers by promising simple solutions to these complex problems. (*Life* magazine, 1958).

A Nation at Risk?

The general criticism of public education continued throughout the 1960s and 1970s when schools were characterized either as hotbeds of political radicalism or nests of drug users. Then, during the severe recession of the early 1980s, President Ronald Reagan lashed out at American schools and held them responsible for our faltering economy. Reagan was ideologically opposed to the expansion of public education at the national level and to the creation of the Department of Education in 1977 during the presidency of Jimmy Carter. Finally, Reagan was attuned to the persistent criticism of public schooling by ultraconservatives such as Rickover, Bestor, and others (Parkerson & Parkerson, 2001).

A Nation at Risk

Findings from *A Nation at Risk* (1983) report created a heated debate about education that lasted for years. Following are recommendations from the report:

- **Content**—High school graduation requirements should consist of: (a) 4 years of English; (b) 3 years of mathematics; (c) 3 years of science; (d) 3 years of social studies; and (e) one-half year of computer science. For the college-bound, 2 years of foreign language in high school are strongly recommended in addition to those taken earlier.
- **Standards and Expectations**—Universities adopt more rigorous and measurable standards, and higher expectations, for academic performance and student conduct, and that 4-year colleges and universities raise their requirements for admission.
- **Time**—*Significantly* more time be devoted to learning the New Basics. This will require more effective use of the existing school day, a longer school day, or a lengthened school year.
- **Teaching**—This recommendation consists of seven parts. Each is intended to improve the preparation of teachers or to make teaching a more rewarding and respected profession. This included increased teacher salaries, 11 month contracts and a career ladder.
- **Leadership and Fiscal Support**—That citizens across the nation hold educators and elected officials responsible for providing the leadership necessary to achieve these reforms, and that citizens provide the fiscal support and stability.

Source: Retrieved June 2, 2007, from http://www.ed.gov/pubs/NatAtRisk/recomm.html

---

He appointed a commission to study the "rising tide of mediocrity" in education, and in 1983 that commission published *A Nation at Risk*. This report was one of the most damning assessments of American education in history.

But while this influential report painted a bleak picture of public education in America, some educators questioned its selective use of statistics, its exaggeration, and its politically conservative agenda. For example, the report paid a great deal of attention to the decline of science achievement scores among 17 year olds between 1969 and 1977. But when examined more closely, this was the *only* area where systematic declines in test scores could be found. As Bracey notes, "Of nine trend lines, only one supported the crisis rhetoric—[and] that was the one the commission reported" (Bracey, 1997).

While educators should have been more critical of the report, many were not. Some passively accepted the findings of the commission as fact. That was a mistake. Others reasoned that if the American people understood the problems in education, they would be willing to put more money in the schools. They were wrong! Rather than encouraging greater funding of schools, the report was used as the basis of Ronald Reagan's conservative national "educational policy." This program called for the abolition of the Department of Education—which recently had been elevated to cabinet status under Democratic President Jimmy Carter—and the use of tuition tax credits and educational vouchers to "reform" American public schools. Once again, the politics of nostalgia for a "golden age of education" that never existed and a collective amnesia about the actual state of education had created a crisis mentality that we still deal with today.

Since then, the American media has had a field day criticizing education. On the nightly news and in our daily newspapers we have been inundated with lurid stories about the violence, drug use, and discipline problems in schools throughout the nation. Reporting problems in schools has become a national obsession. Moreover, in our media-saturated "24/7" environment, where radio, television, and newspapers desperately compete to get the highest ratings of viewership or readership, there is a constant search for stories about schools that will intrigue, horrify, and perhaps even anger their listeners and readers.

Educational Reform

The National Commission on Teaching and America's Future

Since the publication of *A Nation at Risk* in 1983 (which we have referred to as the most critical assessment of education this century) many "reform" commissions and task forces have been established to study education. The National Commission on Teaching and America's Future was created to study teaching in America and its work should be considered by all teachers. It is composed of 26 public officials including business people and educators. The NCTAF has recently published a number of recommendations for teachers:

- Get serious about standards for both students and teachers
- Reinvent teacher preparation and professional development
- Overhaul teacher recruitment and put qualified teachers in every classroom
- Encourage and reward knowledge and skill
- Create schools that are organized for student and teacher success

Source: The National Commission on Teaching and America's Future. Retrieved June 8, 2007, from http://www.nctaf.org

With a steady diet of this sort of "news" it's no wonder that Americans often get the impression that our schools are on the verge of self-destruction. They are not!

HOW CAN WE CLOSE THE PERCEPTION GAP?

As teachers, what are we to make of all of this? Our survey results suggest that we must reach out to parents and the community in general in order to communicate both the needs and realities of education today. We must get the true story of public education to the American people! Developing a rapport with the parents of your students is the first

---

Parent–Teacher Conferences

Parent–teacher conferences are an important time to communicate with parents and elicit their help with the child.
    Prior to the conference:

- Send a note to parents with a suggested conference time
- Have parents confirm the conference appointment
- Reschedule any parent conferences with conflicts
- Make sure parents know how to contact you in case they have to cancel the appointment
- Make a folder for each child
    - Record their academic progress
    - Note their behavior, work habits, social skills
    - Include both good and constructive comments
    - Use the "sandwich" approach: begin with the positive, squeeze-in some suggestions for improvement, and conclude with positive comments
- During the conference:
- Establish rapport—You appreciate the parent helping with the child's homework, volunteering to help, going on field trips, etc.
- Ask questions: Does the parent have any questions or concerns?
- Address problems: academic, behavioral, etc.
    - Discuss these in a calm, objective manner
    - Have a plan in mind
    - Ask for parents input
    - Suggest how they might help
    - Schedule a follow-up conference or a specific way to stay in touch (phone, email, etc.)
- Conclude the conference by reviewing, restating plan and **end with a positive comment regarding the child**

After the conference:

- Record the outcome—Plan, insights, and agreed upon methods of communication with parents

For information to share with parents regarding preparation for parent–teacher conferences, see the National PTA Web site, http://www.pta.org

step in this process. Written and oral communications in the form of notes, phone calls, emails, and face-to-face conferences are essential in developing a positive relationship with parents. Formal parent–teacher conferences are very important but alone they are not enough. In the elementary grades most parents, about 80% will attend parent–teacher conferences. On the other hand, that means that 20% do not attend these conferences, usually, the parents of those who need the most help are the ones that don't attend. Perhaps these parents feel alienated from school or are overwhelmed with working several jobs to support their family. Whatever their reasons, the percentage of parents attending these conferences declines over time and by high school, you can expect fewer than 50% of all your students' parents to attend (U.S. Department of Education, National Center of Education Statistics, National Household Education Survey, 1999).

In addition to formal parent–teacher conferences, most schools require interim grade reports for all students as well as end of term report cards. Schools also schedule a number of open houses during the year to allow greater communication among parents, administrators, and teachers. In addition to these formal methods of communication, the National Parent Teacher Association (PTA) has developed a number of standards to promote parent–teacher communications. These standards are critical to effective relations with parents. Take a moment to study them. (National Parent Teacher Association Standards for Parent/Family Involvement Program; retrieved February 27, 2008, from http://www.pta.org/dadsandschools_landing.html.)

Newsletters

These standards demonstrate that beyond the formal avenues of communication, teachers can reach out to parents in a number of ways. Some teachers publish a class newsletter and distribute it at the beginning of the year to let parents know what is going on in the classroom. These newsletters, whether they are hard copy or electronic, might explain your disciplinary policies, homework assignments, your expectations for students, as well as your grading criteria. You might also include some suggestions for parents to help their child learn. If one of your students comes from a home where English is a second language or is not spoken, have the letter translated. A colleague or student might help you with the translation.

Throughout the school year, you should regularly send student work home to parents, to be examined and then returned. In addition, you might send personal notes to parents

---

Wisdom of Teachers—Communicating with Parents

To close the perception gap with parents, these National Board certified teachers employ a variety of strategies.

Here are some of the ideas they suggested:

- Send out Good-News Memos
- Invite parents into the classroom
- Ask parents for their advice on managing their child
- When talking with parents, use "we" instead of "I" or "you"
- Send out midterm reports

Source: NBPTS Survey, Fall 2002, Jennifer Yazawa, Humanities Ninth Grade, Albuquerque, NM and Gregory Bouljon, Eighth Grade, Language Arts and Literature, Berttendorf, IA

praising their child's achievement or suggesting ways that they might help them improve. Similarly, you might personally invite parents to visit your classroom and give them your school phone number to call if they have questions or concerns. By demonstrating to parents that you care about their child and that you are enlisting them to help their child achieve, you will be surprised at how cooperative they will become.

Reflection

These teachers use a variety of strategies to reach out to parents. Can you think of other ways we can close the perception gap?

Be Proactive

Moreover, these sorts of formal and informal communication can help to avert problems before they begin. Clearly, it is better to anticipate potential criticisms and problems through proactive communications with parents rather than waiting for problems to occur.

For example, one of the teachers we surveyed was given the responsibility of presenting a unit on sex education to eighth-grade girls. Recognizing the potential problems of such a unit, she took action. Before the class began she formally invited all the parents to a meeting where she described the curriculum, answered questions, and allowed parents to examine the curricular materials. She then had parents sign a consent form giving their permission for their child to participate in the class. While this comprehensive approach may seem a bit extreme, given the controversial nature of this topic, she had clearly taken a wise course of action.

Some parents may object to topics in the curriculum other than sex education, such as those that may have religious or political content. For example, as a teacher, some parents might object to you assigning the popular *Harry Potter* books in class. Their main criticism might be that these books focus on magic and wizards. You can head off this criticism by presenting parents with a list of all the books that their child will read during the school year and alert them to potentially controversial materials. By explaining to the parents why you selected this book, (the children love them) your perspective on magic and wizards (these books are fantasies and not intended to glorify witchcraft), and how the book relates to the other subjects in the curriculum (they are examples of a particular literary genre that the students are studying) you can avoid problems. And, as an added bonus, by communicating directly with parents, they will know the real story of education.

Communicate with the Community!

But we need to do more. As professionals we must reach out to the wider community to explain the realities of public education. Rather than focusing exclusively on the *problems* of education today—and there are problems—educators must work with our national leaders to change the public's perceptions of the schools. Join the National Education Association (NEA) and the American Federation of Teachers (AFT) and encourage these organizations to promote a more positive image of public schools to the American people. After all there are many things that we can be proud of as teachers. The AFT, for example, publishes a weekly column in the *New York Times* that conveys a positive message about the nature of education today. More of this sort of communication is necessary. Write your congressman and send him or her a positive message about education.

Situations and Solutions

Political Action Committees (PACs)

Over the years, teachers have found that the most effective method of informing the American people about the needs of education and encouraging our elected officials to support public education is through political action committees. PACs are lobbying organizations that support and promote public education in this country.

The political action committee for the AFT is the Committee on Political Education (COPE), while the National Education Association has NEA-PAC. Each of these groups monitors the voting records of our elected officials. This information can help us choose a candidate to support on election day.

As a teacher, you should understand whether or not your elected officials are supportive of public education and vote accordingly. In the past both the NEA and the AFT have supported candidates from the Democratic Party but occasionally they will endorse others.

Also support politicians who are friendly to public education. And don't support those who are actively trying to dismantle public education in the name of "reform."

As a teacher, you need to be a spokesperson for education. Explain to your friends and family the real needs of education today and avoid the tendency to complain about the schools. Think of education as "your family." Work within the family to improve the schools but avoid the tendency to share "horror stories" (the educational version of urban legends!) with individuals outside "the family." They may misinterpret your meaning and see the schools as on the verge of collapse. If we are to change the public's opinion about schools today it will take consistent effort. And, as an American teacher, you must take the lead.

HELPING ALL CHILDREN LEARN

Clearly, parents, the general public, and teachers perceive what is happening in the classroom very differently. But how about the students? How do they see their schools, their education, and their teachers? The answers to these questions, as we might expect, are mixed. According to a recent Metropolitan Life Survey of the American Teacher conducted by Lou Harris and Associates, about two thirds of students in grades 7–12 were satisfied with their schools and 70% felt that teachers were doing a good job. An even greater percentage felt that their teachers were competent in their professional fields and typically helped students learn. We received lower grades on "making learning interesting." Only 50% of the students surveyed felt that their teachers made learning interesting inside the classroom, while a stunning 72% wrote that teachers did not provide them with interesting experiences outside the classroom, presumably in the form of homework assignments (Louis Harris and Associates, 1996).

THE CHALLENGE OF TEACHING TODAY

Of course, some of what is revealed in this survey must be subjected to a great deal of scrutiny. Nevertheless, the survey suggests that we are doing a pretty good job as teachers but that we have much more to do in the future. Certainly we know our subject matter and we have mastered our fields of expertise. The question is, however, can we take this knowledge and present it to our students in a way that is both meaningful and interesting? As teachers today we must recognize that we have to compete with cell phones, movies, radio, television, video games, and the Internet for the attention of our students. The passive lecture or lesson that may have captured the attention of students a generation or two ago is no longer adequate. Students expect more from their schools and their teachers today.

Enriching Classroom Lessons

This does not mean that we have to present our lessons in a music video format but it does mean that simply requiring students to complete worksheets in class will not do. These have been boring to students for generations! However, using the available technology in the classroom such as videos, PowerPoint presentations, or even the overhead projector creatively can help improve students' interest.

Using Technology Wisely

If you have access to the appropriate hardware and software, you could present a Power-Point lecture on the American Revolutionary War and include maps, portraits of political leaders, soldiers and sailors, as well as the common folk of the period. These images can be imported from the Internet or scanned from a book into a file and included in your presentation.

For elementary students there are a number of computer software programs that can help generate interest in reading. For example, "Reader Rabbit" is fun and will help students develop their basic phonics skills. Similarly, the Accelerated Reader program encourages students to read stories independently and then answer comprehension questions on the computer. Their scores then can be recorded on a data management program. As a teacher, you can encourage your students' reading by keeping track of these scores on a bulletin board or poster and by providing individual incentives for achievement such as printed certificates that students can bring home to show parents. To further encourage and challenge students, you could recruit top readers to help others through "partner reading."

Be sure to remember, however, that while competitive programs such as Accelerated Reader may motivate some students to achieve, it may have the opposite effect on others. Students who have learning disabilities or are slower to learn may feel left out or consider themselves failures in a highly competitive environment. A cooperative learning approach might be more appropriate in these cases. Group success rather than individual success then becomes the focus. For example, when the entire class has achieved a certain level of reading you might reward them with a pizza party or popcorn party or by taking them out to lunch or on a picnic. You can enlist the help of a parent or your teacher's aide for these kinds of activities.

"Low Tech and No Tech" Ideas to Enrich Lessons

For those who do not have these technological capabilities, or access to computers in your classrooms, lectures and lessons can still be enriched. For instance, break your class up into small groups to examine photographs from one of your college textbooks or books from the library. Also something as simple as a wall map, available in most classrooms, can be used to improve student interest. In addition, most textbooks today include maps, charts, and photo transparencies as part of the Instructor's Guide package. By presenting these images on an overhead projector, as part of your lecture or lesson, students will be drawn into the subject matter.

For middle grades and high school literature classes, you could introduce a particular selection by showing a video. For example, the video *O* can help to motivate students and introduce them to the basic plot of Shakespeare's *Othello*. In fact, depending the grade level and maturity of your students, there are hundreds of films on video that can be used to *introduce* and stimulate interest in a piece of literature. Your school library may have these videos or you could borrow them from your local library. These films, of course, are no substitute for reading but they can help motivate students to read and provide them with a more concrete background to the reading selection.

The key here is to use the technology that is readily available to provide a visual component to your oral presentation. As we have seen, students today have grown up in a world of constant visual stimulation. As a result, they usually respond well to visual images integrated into your lectures and lessons.

Cooperative Learning

Beyond technology however, there are many other ways to enrich your lesson. Decades of educational research have demonstrated that encouraging cooperative learning in groups can engage your students. Begin by grouping students according to their interests in a history or civics project such as the 1960s and have them work together in role interdependence. Then have the individual groups focus on topics such as the Civil Rights Movement, The Moon Landing, the Vietnam War, or the Women's Movement. Individuals in each group might focus on a particular aspect of their topic—such as the Civil Rights Movement—and then conduct research on Rosa Parks, Martin Luther King, Jr., The Civil Rights Bill of 1964, The Voting Rights Act of 1965, or the Black Panther Party etc. Afterwards, have each group organize an overall presentation of the material and each student could present his or her own individual research.

Another way to enrich your lessons is to tie your particular curricular topic to a discussion of an important contemporary issue or event of the day. For example, you might use the attacks of 9/11 to examine how such events both shape our patriotic attitudes and generate anti-immigrant feelings. Finally, remember that students respond more enthusiastically to varied instructional techniques such as lectures, videos, discussions, and skits that are rotated throughout the semester.

Enriching Homework Assignments

Similarly, homework that simply requires rote or repetitive work is not very effective. The rule of thumb is that homework assignments should challenge students with work that cannot be done in the classroom. Have students use materials around the home, resources in the community, or conduct library or Internet research. For example, you could have children in Kindergarten and first grade make a list of objects in the home that begin with the letters "A," "B," or "C" and so on. The class can then share these lists during lessons on reading. You can probably get through most of the alphabet in the course of a semester. Students could also collect pictures cut from magazines and newspapers that represent different phonetic sounds, assemble them in a collage and then put them on the classroom bulletin board.

Activities for Elementary Students

As a teacher in the second, third, and fourth grades, have students bring photographs of themselves from home and write a paragraph about why they are special. On the bulletin board, place photos of their favorite sport activities or perhaps a family vacation. This assignment will help them develop a sense of self and give them a chance to write about their favorite subject: themselves! You could also have students bring photos of a special holiday or cultural celebration and describe these in a paragraph or two. Bring these photos to the attention of the class on a lesson about African American history month, Hanukkah, Ramadan, Christmas, or Cinco de Mayo, or include them as part of lessons that celebrate our cultural diversity.

In addition to homework assignments that emphasize our cultural differences, students might also collect magazine photographs that focus on important events in our national culture, including Martin Luther King Jr. Day, Labor Day, Independence Day, Veterans Day, or Patriot's Day (September 11). You can then help your students understand that while we may be very different we have a rich national culture that ties us together as a people.

Enriching Homework in Middle Grades and High School

Homework assignments for students in middle grades and high school, of course, will have a specific disciplinary focus. As a social studies teacher, have students interview grandparents, aunts, uncles, or neighbors regarding a particular historical event that they are studying in class. This might include the Great Depression, World War II, the assassination of John F. Kennedy, the moon landing, the bicentennial celebration, the War in Vietnam, the Gulf War, or the assassination of Martin Luther King Jr., etc. Have students transcribe interviews or use them for a written report or oral presentation.

They could also interview family members about their culture or history to be presented as part of a lesson on our multicultural history or they might describe how a recent historical event might have affected them and their family. Again, with these assignments, involve family and community members, and celebrate both our differences as a people as well as our similarities.

As a teacher, have students in middle grades or high school science work in teams to develop a science project for a school science fair. You could even have your own classroom science fair. Have students demonstrate each project to the class and write an essay describing its importance. Use problem-solving projects in the context of homework assignments. Give students a problem facing our society or community and have them work in teams to solve that problem. For example, a unit on global climate changes might include a project where teams of students design a recycling center for the community, or a newspaper-recycling receptacle. Have students present their findings to the class and write an essay on how they addressed and solved a particular problem.

Situations and Solutions—Homework Assignments for Elementary Students

Homework doesn't have to be boring. Give students assignments that require more creative thought. Do not give worksheets as homework.

Use your creativity. Ask your colleagues for good ideas. Look for ideas in books, teachers' magazines, like *Instructor*, and teachers' Web sites such as www.theteacherscorner.net. Choose assignments that are fun and educational.

Literature students in middle grades and high school could write different endings to classic literary pieces or even compose different scenarios of contemporary films. Students might also write a parody of a novel, short story, or a television commercial. Writing and presenting commercials about items in the school (cafeteria "mystery meat," for example) can be fun and engage them in creative writing as well.

In chapter 9 we will explore other instructional strategies that have been successfully implemented in the classroom. However, the key to challenging homework is to recognize the resources that your students have available to them outside the classroom and then utilize those resources as the focus of your assignments. Whether it's collecting specimens for science class, interviewing family members or leaders of the community for a history or civics class, researching a project for a sociology class, or using a variety of newspapers to trace changing economic conditions, creatively designed homework assignments can make learning more interesting for your students.

SALARIES AND LIFESTYLE OF TEACHERS

As teachers we are concerned with reaching out to parents and the community to communicate to them the real story about education today. We also want to enrich the classroom and homework experiences of our students. Beyond these important concerns, however, are issues of our salaries and lifestyles. And as we noted, there never has been a better time to become a teacher.

In the last decade teacher salaries have risen sharply. Nevertheless, many of us feel that they should be higher still considering the years of education, clinical experiences, and certification requirements we must complete before we enter the classroom. While the national average teacher salary today is over $47,600 (2006), beginning salaries are about $32,000. Some states such as Alaska and New York pay beginning teachers more ($38,600 in Alaska and $37,300 in New York; 2004), while others such as North Dakota and Mississippi offer beginning salaries that range from about $24,872 to $28,200 (2004; American Federation of Teachers, 2004–2005).

Salary Supplements and Incentives

Of course, there are a number of other important factors beyond beginning salary figures that we need to consider. The first is the cost of living. In states such as Alaska and New York, for example, the costs of housing, taxes, and entertainment are much higher than in the Dakotas or Mississippi. And yet some communities will supplement the salaries of their teachers to offset the higher costs of living. In one North Carolina community, for example, the 2001–2002 entry-level teacher salary began with the state rate of $25,000 per year. In addition, however, each teacher in the district receives a $2,000 "local supplement" and up to $1,500 in "Sign-on-Bonuses" depending on your specialty area. For example, if you are a math, science, foreign language, special education, or technology specialist hired in this community, you can expect a $1,500 supplement. On the other hand, if you specialized in elementary education, media, or vocational education your bonus will be $1,000 (Cumberland County Schools, 2001).

In addition to these local and sign-on bonuses, the state of North Carolina provides a supplementary bonus if you teach in a "low performing" school or one that has achieved an "exemplary" rating. In short, the beginning salary of a teacher in special education at a low-performing or exemplary school can expect $30,000 in their first year. And if he/she has earned a graduate degree, his/her salary would increase to $32,700 the first year (Cumberland County Schools, 2001).

New Teacher Incentives

Many communities throughout the nation offer new teachers various other incentives. These include waiving rental security deposits and the opportunity to receive low mortgage rates to purchase homes. Similarly, security deposits for utilities are often waived for new teachers and there are even guaranteed discounts from local department stores (Cumberland County Schools, 2001).

For example, in the summer of 2001, the Dallas school board announced a starting salary for teachers of $34,000 with signing bonuses up to $4,500; a good insurance plan and they even threw in a free laptop computer! Sensing that this was not enough, the school board raised the starting salary another $3,000 to $37,000! These sorts of aggressive bonus plans are quite common in communities where teachers are in great demand (*Daily Reflector*, 2001).

Finally, in addition to these bonuses, incentives, and packages, we should also remember that most teachers are married and that our "household incomes" compare very favorably with others in our communities. Similarly, as mentioned, the average *individual* teacher salary in this country is over $47,000 per year—up from $32,600 in 1989–90. This figure is $13,000 higher than the national average *household* income (American Federation of Teachers, 2004-2005).

Teacher Salaries Compared to Other Professionals

But how do our entry-level salaries compare with those in other professions? The answer here is mixed. According to recent surveys from the U.S. Department of Labor, for example, financial managers earn about $20,000 as they begin their careers, accountants begin at about $27,000, chemists earn $29,000, mathematicians earn about $30,000, and registered nurses earn about $31,000. Clearly, each of these occupations offers entry-level salaries that are comparable with those of teachers. On the other hand, attorneys and physicians earn significantly more than teachers at the entry level, though lawyers and doctors must complete at least 3–10 years of post-graduate education and training. Attorneys earn an average of $37,000 when they begin their careers but most experienced attorneys have incomes that average over $115,000. Similarly, physicians earn $30,000 to $40,000 when they enter their profession but they can anticipate much greater incomes if they remain in their fields and specialize. For example, doctors in family practice earn about $110,000 per year while surgeons average $225,000 annually (U.S. Department of Labor, 2002).

In short, teacher's salaries vary considerably by state, community, and region of the country. They also differ when we consider sign-on bonuses and local supplements that are offered by many communities. Our entry-level salaries compare favorably with many other professionals but in relation to those of doctors and lawyers, they are lower. However, if a teacher is willing to stick it out, get an advanced degree and remain in the profession for a few years, both average individual incomes and household incomes compare quite favorably with the general population of the United States.

Quality of Life

One other factor should be considered when we compare our salaries as teachers with those of other professionals. That factor is the quality of life. While the work of teaching can be difficult, we are engaged with optimistic young people, we work fewer hours and fewer days, and we have more vacation time than any other profession. Think about it for a moment. Doctors and nurses typically work with sick and dying people as well as those with severe injuries who are often in terrible pain. We deal with young, healthy, and generally happy children. Attorneys must deal with people in trouble, hardened criminals, as well as people with financial and personal difficulties. We work with students who have their lives before them and who are often excited about their futures which are full of promise. Many office professionals work in isolation, spend the majority of their time in small cubicles, and are subjected to the uncertainty of layoffs due to changes in the economy. We are engaged with classrooms full of children and adolescents and, if we do our jobs well, we have lifelong job security.

Make no mistake about it—as teachers, we spend a great deal of time with our students, preparing our lessons, and grading papers and other assignments. Nevertheless, we still work fewer hours than most other professionals. While the typical professional outside of teaching works about 250 days per year, we spend about 160 days in the classroom. And because of the decentralized nature of "local schools" we often are able to live closer to our places of employment than other professionals. The typical school day (though it may seem longer sometimes) is from 9 a.m. to 3 p.m. We can be home, preparing our dinner, playing with our children and pets, or working in our gardens, hours before other professionals even begin to consider their long commute home. Moreover, while they yearn for their 2-week vacation each year, we often have 2 months or more off each summer!

Of course, we work very hard as teachers. After all, we are devoted to our students. Sometimes we spend time outside of the classroom with after-school activities such as academic clubs or sport teams and occasionally we are called upon to return to our schools in the evenings for conferences or special events. Nevertheless, the quality of our lives is excellent. Indeed one of the best-kept secrets is that teaching is a wonderful occupation that is rewarding, interesting, and never boring. This, above all, should be kept in mind when pondering the complexities of teaching salaries.

Higher Salaries

And there is even better news. Teacher salaries are on the rise and will continue to rise in the future. There are two important reasons for this. The first is that as accountability in education has become an important national issue, more and more Americans are willing to pay higher teacher salaries in order to get quality teachers for their schools. Thus, as requirements for teacher licensure and certification have become more rigorous, salaries have improved considerably. We will consider the issue of teacher certification in chapter 12, but it is important to remember that the bright side of the accountability movement in education is that it will help to improve teacher salaries.

The second major reason that teacher salaries are improving is the simple economics of "supply and demand." Like everything else in the American free market economy, teachers' salaries are determined in part by the forces of "supply and demand." When the numbers of students attending elementary and secondary schools increased dramatically during the 1950s and early 1960s, teachers were in great demand and salaries climbed considerably. Following the "baby bust" of the so-called Generation X, the numbers of school age children declined from over 42.6 million to 40.4 million. As a result, fewer teachers were needed and salaries stalled. By the early 1990s however, the so called "baby boom echo," children of late baby boomers and early Generation Xers began to enter school in great numbers, 42.8 million in 1993, and climbed to nearly 50 million by the year 2000. This increase in the number of students led to a growing demand for teachers and with it came steady increases in teacher salaries.

Population projections suggest that demand for teachers will be strong at least for another generation and as a result, teacher salaries should continue their upward track.

The National Center for Educational Statistics has estimated, for example, that in 2006, over 2 million new elementary and special education teachers were hired by school districts across the nation. Add to that number another 1.4 million jobs in secondary education and we can see that the demand for teachers will continue throughout your careers. These figures, of course, do not include those teachers who will be hired to replace ones that retire. And when we consider the fact that "baby boomers" have begun to retire during this decade, those numbers should be enormous (National Center for Educational Statistics, 2005).

Region, Community, and Specialty Areas

In addition, there will be regional, community, and specialty area variations in the demand for teachers. Generally speaking, the greatest regional demand will be in California and the Pacific Northwest where a 10% increase in new teachers is expected. In the South and the West, increases for new teachers will range from 5–10% and only in the upper Midwest and in the Northeast will demand either remain the same or decrease slightly. Keep in mind, however, that even in areas where there is no expected increase in new teachers, millions of teachers will be hired each year to replace those who will retire or who simply leave teaching for other jobs.

In addition to these regional variations, larger metropolitan areas such as Chicago, New York, Los Angeles, Atlanta, Charlotte, Raleigh, Seattle, and Dallas (to name just a few) will have the greatest demands for teachers and typically will offer the largest salaries in the country. While the cost of living in these cities is higher than in other areas, the greater availability of cultural and educational experiences, dining, entertainment, and professional sports is a very exciting prospect and will certainly add an important dimension to the quality of your life.

Specialty Area Variations in Demand

Finally, remember that there will be specialty area variations in the demand for teachers as well. One important publication that we recommend that you examine as you plan your teaching career is *The Job Search Handbook for Educators*. The recent edition of the handbook estimates that specialty areas of greatest demand—that is, those where the greatest numbers of new jobs will be created over the next few years—will be in special education, bilingual education, speech pathology, the sciences, mathematics, computer science, and foreign languages such as Spanish and Japanese. Areas such as elementary education, music, journalism, physical education, art and dance education, English and driver's education, on the other hand, will experience less new growth but because of the normal turnover in these fields, millions of jobs are expected in these areas as well (American Association for Employment in Education, 2000).

Consider one final matter. While these figures concerning new job growth in certain regions, urban centers and specialty areas are important in understanding changes in our profession over the next decade, do not use them as your sole guide in selecting either your specialty area or where you should apply for a teaching position. The most important consideration in determining your specialty should be your interests and not where the market for jobs is the greatest. Jumping into a specialty area simply because "there are lots of jobs" can be a big mistake. Your career decision should be made on the basis of deliberate planning with your professors, discussion with your parents, and most of all your own interests. Remember that even in areas such a elementary education where the growth in "new jobs" will be less than in other specialty areas, there will be millions of teaching positions opening as a result of the natural process of turnover.

IT'S UP TO YOU!

Similarly, carefully select the region of the country and type of community in which you would like to live. Do your research: go online or to the library to investigate the quality of life in different kinds of communities in this country. Most communities have extensive Web sites with a wealth of information. Use the resources in *The Job Search Handbook for Educators* to contact various state departments of education either through the internet or more traditional methods such as the telephone or mail. Talk to your professors, friends, or relatives who may have lived in other areas of the country or who may have important insights about life in a distant region or city. Through careful planning you can take charge of your own future. You can decide whether to stay near your hometown or move to California, Florida, Washington, Arizona, North Carolina, or to live and teach in one of the country's great cities such as New York, Chicago, Los Angeles, or Atlanta. It's up to you!

SUMMARY

A Profile of Teaching

Each year nearly 300,000 new teachers enter the classrooms of the nation. The most common reason that we choose teaching as a career is to work with young people but job security, autonomy, freedom, and optimism are also factors. We are an extremely well educated group of professionals. Nearly 50% of us have achieved advanced degrees in our specialty areas.

Enlisting the Help of Parents

For teachers, the most pressing problem facing education today is the lack of interest and support of parents. While there are many reasons for this lack of support, we must use a variety of methods to reach out to parents to help them help their children learn.

Education and the Perception Gap

Teachers must also recognize that the general public is often misled about what is really happening in our schools. As teachers we must become more proactive in order to communicate the real story about education today.

Helping All Children Learn

As teachers today we must compete with cell phones, movies, radio, television, video games, and the Internet for the attention of our students. Nevertheless, we can enrich both classroom lessons and homework assignments by drawing on available technology and using techniques of cooperative learning.

Salaries and Lifestyles of Teachers

There never has been a better time to become a teacher! Our salaries are on the rise and as a result of the growing demand for new teachers they will continue to increase in the future. The quality of our lives is also excellent. We typically work fewer hours and have longer vacations than other professionals. We also work with the best that society has to offer—young children. Through careful planning you can take charge of your own future and live and work in virtually any community in the country. It's up to you!

DISCUSSION QUESTIONS

1. Discuss the importance of teaching in our modern society.
2. Why do some parents seem to be disengaged from their child's education? As teachers how can we reengage parents?
3. Discuss the impact of *A Nation at Risk*, (1983) on the public's perception of education today. How have educators perceived this report? Do you feel that it is a fair representation of education? Compare this work with the writings of Gerald Bracey.
4. What can we do as professional educators to improve the public's perception of education?
5. What strategies can we use as teachers to engage students in both classroom instruction and homework?
6. Discuss the role of "supply and demand" in terms of the availability of teaching positions and teachers' salaries. How do our prospects look for the next decade?

Section 3

Our Educational Heritage

Chapter 5

Classical and Global Roots of Education

The history of our profession is an ancient and noble one, standing on the broad shoulders of some of the most remarkable figures of the past. It reaches deep into antiquity and represents contributions from our rich multicultural heritage.

EDUCATION IN EARLY SOCIETIES

Humankind has existed for perhaps 1 million years, though our present form, that of Homo sapiens, emerged about 37,000 years ago. Only relatively recently, however, have we developed a distinctive human culture. When early humans discovered that it was more effective to hunt with stones rather than their bare hands; when they found that fire could keep them warm and cook their food, the basis of human society, culture, and economy began to emerge. The transmission of this knowledge from one generation to the next through education signals the beginning of our history (Bowen, 1972).

Gradually, early humans emerged from caves and trees and began to control their environment. They constructed dwellings that would provide shelter from the elements; they domesticated animals and learned to plant crops for their survival; they began to make cloth from animal skins; and they began to use gestures, signs, and symbols to communicate.

At the heart of this gradual transition from primitive savagery to a human culture that is recognizable to us today, was education. Over the centuries, millions of men and women passed on the collective knowledge and skills they had learned to the next generation. These were the first teachers and their lessons were the basis of our civilization.

The foundation of this early human culture was the kin, or family group, clan, or tribe. This unit was our first social institution. It emerged because of our need for protection and survival. As these kin groups grew in size and complexity, informal rules of behavior gradually emerged. These rules typically specified the accepted relationships between men and women, children and parents. They defined power relations and the need for loyalty to leaders and elders. Gradually these cultural rules would develop taboos regarding the consumption of certain foods, the accepted interpretations of natural phenomena such as the reasons for seasonal change and natural disasters and would provide the basis of primitive religions. Culture bearers, whether they were called priests, witch doctors, or voodoo queens, were responsible for understanding and promoting the tribe's rules of culture. These individuals were our first real teachers and their lessons represented the primitive "curriculum" of the time.

As these groups established permanent agricultural communities and grew in size, they created more complex forms of social organization. About 6000 BCE, the first permanent human societies were established in an area that historians call the "fertile crescent."

This small area in Asia Minor between the river valleys of the Tigris and the Euphrates is located in present-day Iraq. It was here that written language took form.

Babylonia

As the population of the fertile crescent grew and people moved to nearby regions, so did the competition between groups for control of scarce resources and land. This competition led to conflict and the consolidation of political power into small states. Among the most important of these early states was Babylonia. Under Hammurabi, the most powerful king of the Babylonians, a formalized system of laws was created. The Hammurabi Code, as it is called, recognized the concept of private property and established the idea of economic class.

During these years a system of education, for the wealthy, was established. This system served to reinforce the existing political, social and economic structure of Babylonia and was controlled by the priestly class. These early teachers closely guarded some of the most sacred secrets of their religion, but passed on information that allowed the maintenance of society through the training of scribes. These young men represented the educated class of the Babylonian Empire. As the empire expanded during the 2nd millennium BCE, this model of education developed as well. In a world where religion was the intellectual and cultural center of life, clergymen were the font of all knowledge. As a result, religion was the primary reason that education existed.

The Emergence of Written Language

Throughout this period, written language gradually emerged as a new form of communication. Prior to the "invention" of writing, all communication was oral and all customs, beliefs, and cultural rules had to be committed to memory and then transmitted to others in order to survive. At first, writing consisted of primitive symbols. Gradually, these symbols were organized and became the basis of a formal alphabet.

Links to the Past: The Training of Scribes

In ancient Babylonia scribes wrote letters, legal documents, religious documents, and kept tax records and accounts. Writing was very difficult, because there were hundreds of symbols that were laboriously etched on clay tablets or parchment. (Classical Babylonian script had between 600–700 symbols.) A young scribe might begin his training in childhood, and it consisted of several stages. In the first stage, he was trained in basic literacy through group instruction in a school called the Tablet House. The student would copy and memorize "prepared lines" from the teacher called the "tablet writer." The student would copy the lines directly below on a clay tablet. Then the work was "corrected" by the teacher and the student would recopy his work. When the lesson was finished, the clay tablet was rolled up and pressed back out for more writing lessons. In the next stage, the student would specialize in one branch of government—law, medicine, trade, military, teaching, or the temple. He received individualized instruction in script appropriate for his specialization. Later he would serve as an apprentice. During their training, scribes often received severe treatment. Ironically, in ancient Egyptian, the word "teach" also meant "beat".

Source: J. Bowen (1972). *A History of Western Education: Volume 1*

In Babylonia and Egypt, early written language took the form of pictograms. The earliest records of this writing consisted of accounts, lists of assets, legal documents, letters, itineraries of leaders, and medical formulas. The Babylonians also used written language to commemorate their great leaders while the Egyptians (using the papyrus plant for their paper) employed written language to record their religious ideas and communicate stories and songs that were part of their culture.

Written language transformed education. It gradually shifted instruction from an informal one-on-one oral transmission of cultural beliefs and survival skills to a more formal system based on books and written symbols. With writing, ideas could be codified, memorized, and retained. This provided more precision and allowed individuals to accumulate more useful knowledge.

On the other hand, by writing down ideas and stories, they lost a great deal of the spontaneity and flexibility. Within the oral tradition these tales could be adapted to the events of the day and thus could be made more relevant to students. When they were written down, however, they became static and unchanging. Gradually they became more and more abstract and difficult for new generations of students to understand. In short, with the advent of written language, teaching became more important and at the same time, became more difficult.

EARLY MULTICULTURAL ROOTS OF EDUCATION

As societies throughout the world became more complex and organized around formal governments and religions, and as written language became more sophisticated, education became a central part of the ancient world. From various multicultural threads, the basis of our educational history has gradually emerged. These threads come from the ancient Egyptians, Jews, Indians, Chinese, and pre-Columbian American cultures.

Egypt

From the Egyptians we see the first example of formalized education in the West. In order to reinforce their writing skills and achieve a better understanding of the values of

---

The Good Life: Instruction in Wisdom from Ptah-Hotep

The Good Life was a lesson or instruction book attributed to Ptah-Hotep. He was the Vizier of the Fifth Dynasty King approximately 2450 B.C. It was customary for lessons to be presented as advice from the father or elder to his son. The following is an excerpt from the text:

> In instructing the ignorant about wisdom and about the rules of good speech [is an] advantage to him who will harken and [is a] disadvantage to him who may neglect them.
> Let not thy heart be puffed-up because of thy knowledge: be not confident because thou art a wise man. Take counsel with the ignorant as well as the wise. The (full) limits of skill cannot be attained, and there is no skilled man equipped to his (full) advantage. Good speech is more hidden that the emerald, but it may be found with maidservants at the grindstones (Carroll Jr., Embree, Mellon, Schrier, & Taylor, 1961, p. 14)

society, students were required to copy, verbatim, the writings of respected leaders and scholars.

Reflection

What does the phrase "puffed-up" mean? Is there a message for teachers today in dealing with students and their parents?

One of the first examples of such an exercise was the Instruction in Wisdom of the Vizier Ptah-Hotep: The Good Life (see above). In books made of papyrus, students copied the words of the great Vizier who ruled Egypt around 2450 BCE. Later, when students had mastered the language, they read stories and tales of morality that were designed to reinforce the values of Egyptian society. A good example of this literary form was the Book of the Dead. This book taught students about the afterlife and the moral precepts of Egyptian society. Other educational materials such as the Rhind Mathematical Papyrus helped Egyptian students learn the basics of mathematics. And yet, there was little room for creativity in Egyptian schools; the primary emphasis was on memorization and absolute adherence to the religious precepts of society.

Since the Egyptians left few historical records of their own civilization, we do not know much more of their system of education. However, we can clearly see its result. The great advances in commerce among the Egyptians made arithmetic, not to mention accounting, a necessity for this society. Similarly the building of roads and, of course, the great pyramids and temples required extensive knowledge of geometric principles and engineering. Knowledge of astronomy also helped the Egyptians navigate and predict the annual floods of the Nile while there also is evidence of a large class of physicians in Egypt who experimented with surgery and pharmaceuticals. Finally, the incredible sculptures, engravings, and rich artifacts created by this society cannot be overlooked. In short, while we have little information on the existence of schools in Egypt, their great achievements demonstrate that formal education was a central part of the Empire.

The Jews

While the Egyptians used education to venerate their secular and religious leaders and to help build their great empire, the ancient Hebrews saw education as the key to unifying the culture and religion of their people. In fact, the Jews were the first to record their own history in order to provide their descendents with a story of their past struggles and a plan for the future.

During the Babylonian Captivity (the period of the exile of the Jews, 597–538 BCE) the distinctive cultural identity of the Jewish people nearly disappeared. During this time however, Jewish scribes slowly reassembled their spiritual literature and in so doing gained great prestige within the Hebrew community in exile. When the Jews returned to Palestine, they were determined to reinforce their language, culture, and religion. They did so through education. The primary focus of Jewish education, therefore, was the history and traditions of Jewish culture and religion. As a result, the Synagogue became both a place of education and worship. The result of this educational movement was that their oral traditions were recorded and became what we know as the Old Testament of the Bible.

During this period (c 530–500 BCE) Scribes became an important part of the Jewish community as arbiters of Hebrew law. As a result their position became powerful and scholarly; learning became an activity revered by the community. Scribes also taught classes and the basis of their instruction was memorization. Strict and severe discipline

---

The Hitopadesa

Regarding education, the ancient Hitopadesa, Sanskrit text, said: "Among all things, they say, knowledge is truly the best thing. Knowledge gives prudence, from prudence one attains fitness for work—thus arises happiness." (Ulrich, 1950, p. 10)

---

was typical of Hebrew schools as it was in most other schools during this period. Some of the older students would continue with their studies focusing on biblical literature, ciphering (basic arithmetic), and sacred music. The ultimate goal of many of these students was to become Scribes themselves.

While it is clear that the Hebrew civilization was not as powerful as the Egyptians, Persians, or Babylonians before them, the Jews contributed greatly to the intellectual and educational history of our world.

India

Like the Egyptians and Jews, Indian religion, culture, and education were closely tied together. While we know little of the actual schools of ancient India, we get some sense of the importance of education in this society from their sacred writings. In fact, from the ancient Hindus we see the appearance of the central idea that knowledge was of great value both in the spiritual and secular world. For these people, the path to Nirvana was an educational journey to understand the true character of the human soul.

But while education was central to one's spiritual journey, it was important in the secular world as well. The sacred Hindu religious figure "guru," for example, is translated as the "destroyer of darkness." As such the guru was both a holy man and a teacher (Ulrich, 1950, p. 10).

China

The Chinese also grappled with the question: what is the purpose of education? And like the Indians, they saw education as useful in both the spiritual and material worlds. Two ancient Chinese philosopher/educators, in particular, dealt with this question and their writings provide us with some insight into their evolving educational philosophy and their system of education.

Lao Tse

The two basic themes of Chinese education were Taoism and Confucianism. Taoism focused on the development of the individual while Confucianism centered on the practical question of developing good citizens. The first theme, Taoism, comes from Lao Tse in the 6th century BCE. His writings reinforce the mystical or spiritual foundation of education—that which creates a good individual. But rather than using education to reinforce a particular religious sect or glorifying a particular set of spiritual leaders, Lao Tse's intended approach to education was to cultivate the goodness of humankind.

In *The Tai Teh King*, Lao Tse focused on understanding the self. "Without going outside his door, one understands all that takes place under the sky. The farther that one goes out from himself the less he knows." He continues by noting that "He who knows other men is discerning; he who knows himself is intelligent." In short, Lao Tse's teachings emphasize the self-synthesis of information. He taught that understanding comes from within through enlightenment rather than formal memorization of creeds or catechisms (Ulrich, 1950, p. 17–18).

Confucius

The second theme of Chinese education—Confucianism—is represented by the great philosopher/educator Confucius (550–478 BCE). Confucius saw education in a very practical sense. His philosophy focused on developing good citizens and the critical role of the teacher in this process. Confucius wrote in his *Record on the Subject of Education* that if the ruler wishes to "transform the people and to perfect their manners and customs, must he not start from the lessons of the school?" For Confucius, the perfection of the state began in the classroom (Ulrich, 1950, p. 19).

Confucius also described the highly organized system of education in ancient China. He noted that for local families "there was the village school; for the neighborhood there was the hsiang, for the larger district there was the hsu and in the capitals there was the college" (Ulrich, 1950. p. 19).

He also wrote that colleges gave "competitive examinations" to all students every other year. These exams determined whether they could "read the texts intelligently—that they were attentive to their work—and whether they could discuss the subjects of their studies" (Ulrich, 1950, pp. 19–20).

The course of study he described took 7 years to complete. Confucius concluded his description of college life with his typical metaphorical imagery: "The little ant continually exercises the art of amassing" (Ulrich, 1950, p. 20). In short, 2,500 years ago Confucius described what we now know as the "educational ladder" complete with higher education and a series of competitive examinations.

Pre-Columbian Educational Forms in the Americas

In the Americas, other forms of ancient education emerged in the Aztec and Incan civilizations. The Aztecs promoted a mandatory and public system of education for young boys and girls while the Incas developed an elite system of mathematics and engineering education.

Aztecs

The Aztecs were a Pre-Colombian (predating the arrival of Columbus) Mesoamerican (central American) people who built an impressive empire that controlled the region from the 1300s until the arrival of the Spanish Conquistadors and Hernando Cortez in the early 1500s.

The educational system of the Aztecs was unique in several ways. At age 15, all boys and girls—irrespective of class—were required to attend school. Boys memorized a collection of "sayings of the old" (huehuelatolli) while young girls were instructed in domestic tasks, childrearing, and religion. In fact, Aztec women played an important role in religion and often became priestesses.

When Aztec boys completed their basic education, they would attend either a "telpochcalli" to receive military training, or the "calmecac" where they would focus on academic subjects such as astronomy, statesmanship, and theology (Holmer, 2005; Leon-Portilla, 1990).

The Incas

The powerful Incan Empire, to the south of the Aztecs, was located along the Andean Mountains in what is now Peru, South America. The Incas dominated this region for about a century from the early 1400s until the Spanish Conquistadors under Francisco Pizarro destroyed it in the early 1500s.

Unlike the Aztecs, Incan education was neither public nor mandatory. And yet, there is evidence that some noble women did attend Incan schools that the Spanish considered a kind of nunnery. The unique contribution of Incan education, however, was their training in advanced mathematics and engineering.

Young men of promise were chosen to attend "houses of knowledge" (Quechua) around age 13. Students received a general education in Incan history, religion, government, and moral philosophy. But more importantly they learned the Quipuóa mathematical system that employed knotted strings and provided the basis of record keeping and civil engineering. It also allowed the creation of a complex road system, water fountains, rope bridges, and elaborate irrigation methods for which the Incas are still known today (Cobo, 1983; De Diaz Canseco, 1999).

The Aztec concepts of mandatory public education and the Incan emphasis on advanced studies in mathematics and engineering would become powerful models for education. These forms would be adapted by the Spanish and eventually would make their way into the southwestern areas of the future United States.

ANCIENT GREECE

The roots of our Western education tradition therefore are both multicultural and global. They reach from the Middle East, Northern Africa, to India, China, and the Americas. They benefit from the collective wisdom and determination of millions of teachers in the past that passed on the traditions of culture and learning from one generation to the next.

As these roots of educational thought and experience were taking hold, two new cultures were beginning to emerge in the Mediterranean that would eventually transform Western civilization as well as our ideas about learning and education. These new cultures were that of the Greeks and the Romans.

The Greeks and the Romans were descendants of Indo-European tribes that had migrated from the Black Sea and Caspian Sea region during the 2nd millennium BCE. The first group pushed into the area we now know as Greece, eventually establishing the ancient city of Mycenae. Settlers then pushed south and occupied the interior portion of the peninsula and the many islands that surround the mainland.

Meanwhile, the other group of migrants pushed further west and eventually settled the Italian peninsula. Some established a community in the fertile land of the Po River valley while another occupied the lower valley of the Tiber River and eventually founded the city of Rome.

While these two civilizations—Greek and Roman—had not yet developed a culture that was equal to that of Egypt or the Persians before them, each was able to thrive because of their unique location along the Mediterranean Sea. Each developed a maritime culture and participated in the growing trade of the region. This connection to other civilizations, moreover, provided them with a more cosmopolitan perspective and saturated the area with new ideas from all over the world. At the same time, the Mediterranean provided a natural barrier from invading tribes and states and allowed them to flourish in relative peace.

As both the Greeks and Romans developed over the centuries that followed, they each recognized and gloried in their cultural uniqueness from the rest of the world. In Greece, the hero as outlined in some of their earliest literature, including the *Iliad* and the *Odyssey* by Homer mythologized the heroic deeds of great men. These in turn became the

---

The Greek Alphabet

The ancient Greek alphabet improved until by the year 403 BCE, the older Attic version was replaced by the Ionic version that became the standard. The Greek alphabet was phonetic; each sound had its own symbol and shape. There were 24 letters in the alphabet, writing was done from left to right and later the letters were connected in cursive style. Unfortunately, little remains of many of the Greek accounts, loans, or receipts because writing was done on either papyrus or clay tablets which were reused, and sometimes calculations were done quickly in the dust (Bowen, 1972).

---

basis of a new individualism—the Greek Ethos or character. Similarly, the Romans eulogized their great mythic heroes made famous in the *Epics of Virgil*—such as the Aeneid. Eventually, the warrior hero became the mythological symbol of Rome.

But heroes were only part of the legacy of these two great civilizations. In fact, it was here that the intellectual foundations of Western civilization and the conception of modern education began.

Reflection

Do you see any similarities between the Greek alphabet as described above and our English alphabet?

From the Greeks, two traditions in education would emerge. The first, from Sparta, was the training of the patriot warrior. The second, emerging from Athens, was the training of the democratic citizen.

Spartan Education

Around 800 BCE, Sparta emerged as the most powerful city–state on the Greek Peninsula. As Sparta expanded its influence, leaders recognized the importance of maintaining a strong army. Gradually they developed a system of education that emphasized the virtue of valor.

Other than military training, Spartan boys received little formal education. There was some emphasis on memorization, especially the epic poetry of Tyrtaeus, which idolized

---

Plutarch's Description of Spartan Education

While we know few specifics of Spartan education, Plutarch (an important Roman historian) has provided us with some details. He wrote that:

> Their training was calculated to make them obey commands well, endure hardships, and conquer in battle. Therefore as they grew in age their bodily exercise was increased; their heads were close clipped and they were accustomed to going bare-foot and to playing for the most part without clothes. They slept together in troops and companies on pallet-beds which they collected for themselves, breaking off with their hands—no knives allowed—the tops of rushes which grew along the river Eurotas. (Bowen, 1972, p. 72)

Links to the Past: Learning to Read

Dionysius of Halicarnassus wrote this description of learning to read in the 1st century BCE:

> When we learn to read, we first learn the names of letters, then their shapes and values, then the syllables and their properties, after this the words and their inflections—their longer and shorter forms and their declensions . . . Then we begin to read and write, slowly at first, and syllable by syllable. When, in due process of time, the forms of words are fixed in our mind, we read easily and get through any book handed to us without stumbling, with incredible ease and speed. (Bowen, 1972, p. 81)

---

the virtues of bravery and showed distain for cowardice. But there was little in the way of academic training. When a Spartan man reached the age of 30 years, he could elect to leave the military and retire to a life of leisure.

Women, on the other hand, were trained for motherhood. As part of that training, Plutarch noted, they were expected to develop themselves physically and "exercise their bodies in running, wrestling, casting the discus and hurling the javelin in order that the fruit of their wombs might take root in vigorous bodies and come to better maturity." Like Spartan boys, there was little emphasis on academic pursuits. As a result, illiteracy in Sparta was extremely high (Bowen, 1972, pp. 55–56).

Athens

While the model of the patriot warrior was well established in Sparta, in Athens the tradition of academic learning and democratic citizenship began to emerge. In the 4th century BCE (400–500) the idea of education—what they called paideia—took shape in Athens. Early on, Athenians saw education primarily as a function of government. Its purpose was to develop individuals who could serve the state. Gradually, however, Athenian leaders recognized that an educated people were essential to the maintenance of a democracy.

The Athenian system of education began with mandatory primary and secondary education of boys beginning at age seven. The curriculum included reading, writing, and "reckoning" (math), as well as music and physical training. Eventually, three distinct kinds of teachers emerged to meet the educational needs of Athenian youth. These were the teachers of letters or grammatistes, teachers of music (kitharistes), and physical training instructors or poidotribes.

Students often were assigned a slave to attend to their educational needs and escort them from one learning environment to another. In the earliest stages of learning, students might attend school in the home of one of their teachers or in a rented building. They normally were issued a wooden tablet coated with darkened wax (6 inches by 4) and practiced their alphabet by scraping out letters with a stylus. When they had mastered the alphabet, they turned to syllables and then simple words.

Reflection

In some schools today, children learn to read first by recognizing letters, making the letters, then learning their sounds, and eventually blending sounds into words. What are the similarities between this method and the one described above?

Once a student had learned to read, he proceeded to the study of music and physical fitness. As Plato noted, teachers put into the students' hands "the works of great poets which he reads sitting on a bench at school; in these are contained many admonitions and many tales—which they learn by heart" (Bowen, 1972, p. 82).

Later they would learn to play the lyre and set poems to music. According to Plato, this was done so that students would become "more gentle and harmonious and rhymical—for the life of man in every part has need of harmony and rhythm" (Bowen, 1972, p. 82).

To meet the needs of higher education, a new group of intellects emerged in Athens known as the sophists (derived from the word sophia which means "wisdom"). The sophists were the first professors of higher education and were responsible for bringing a relatively sophisticated level of learning to the Athenian people.

There were no formal universities in Athens, and as a result, the sophists traveled from place to place, lecturing as they went. Among the most important subjects they taught was rhetoric—the art of public speaking. Since this skill was an important part of Athenian democracy, especially in the court, rhetoric was highly prized.

Socrates

The greatest of all the sophists was Socrates, who lived from 469–399 BCE. His father was a sculptor and his mother was a midwife. As a result, his family never had a great deal of money. Perhaps it was this humble beginning that led Socrates to reject materialism as the basis of life and to live frugally. In fact, as a teacher he avoided the common sophist practice of taking fees for teaching, and lived simply on the generosity of his students and close friends.

The Socratic Method

While Socrates is often seen as Athens' greatest teacher, he offered no systematic body of knowledge or curriculum to his students. Rather, his approach was one of critical analysis based on logical argumentation. This process is what we call the Socratic Method—what he called maieutic—a word drawn from the art of midwifery (Bowen, 1972).

In other words, Socrates felt strongly that he was not presenting knowledge to his students, but in a sense was helping to give birth to knowledge. He encouraged students to understand moral and ethical behavior by challenging their preconceived ideas and perceptions. Once Socrates revealed the faulty logic of their assumptions, he would guide them to a better understanding of the question through suggestions.

Despite his great contributions to education, Socrates became embroiled in bitter partisan politics. In 399 BCE, he was charged by the state of impiety toward the gods and

---

Socratic Method

One of the most important contributions of Socrates is the dialectic method of inquiry, referred to as the Socratic Method. It involves answering a question with a question. In this method, a series of questions are posed to help a person or group determine their underlying beliefs and the extent of their knowledge. The Socratic Method is designed to help students eliminate contradictions in their thinking. It encourages them to examine their own beliefs regarding concepts such as justice and virtue.

"corrupting the youth of Athens." We now know that these charges were completely false and baseless, designed to force him into exile. But during his trial Socrates infuriated the judges with his logic and his rhetorical skills. As a result, the judges not only convicted him, but also sentenced him to death. As Plato later explained in the *Phaedo* and the *Apology*, Socrates could easily have escaped and avoided his death sentence. But rather, as an act of courage and conscious, he accepted his punishment, drank poison hemlock, and died. In so doing, Socrates became the first real educational martyr in history.

Plato

Much of what we know about Socrates comes from his brilliant and noted student, Plato (427–347 BCE). This is because Socrates neither recorded his dialogues with students nor did he write. In fact, Socrates did not trust the written word. As a result, the philosophical writings of Plato, as well as those of Xenophon and Aristophanes, are our only record of the great teacher's ideas and methods.

Unlike Socrates, who came from rather humble origins, Plato was an aristocrat. His early education was typical of other wealthy Athenian boys and at the age of 22 he began 6 years of study with Socrates. Plato was profoundly influenced by his mentor and was changed forever when Socrates was tried, convicted, and sentenced to death. Plato actually attended the famous trial and later he recorded in the *Apology*, the words of Socrates to his judges.

The great travesty of justice against Socrates influenced Plato in two ways. First, it gave him a profound distrust of popular democracy, leading him to the idea that social and political harmony was best secured by justice administered by enlightened men, not necessarily ones that were popularly elected. Secondly, it led him to reject a career in politics and gave him an interest in teaching.

Following the trial in 399 BCE, Plato spent a year traveling. When he returned he taught at a school called the Academy located outside of Athens. Several years later Plato adopted that name—the Academy—for his own school that he established in 387 BCE. The Academy eventually became the centerpiece of formal education in Athens. Plato's form of instruction at the Academy was based on the Socratic Method, what he called the dialectic, but we also know that he grudgingly gave a few lectures to his students as well (Bowen, 1972).

Plato's Dialectic

Plato's dialectic, however, was at the heart of his teaching. In *The Republic*, Plato noted that the dialectic was the highest form of education which involved oral questioning and student responses. Like Socrates before him, Plato felt that this method of instruction allowed the unfolding of knowledge, what he saw as universal ideas that were already present in the mind. In addition we know from the writings of Aristotle, one of Plato's greatest students, that the curriculum of the Academy also included studies in mathematics, especially geometry and number theory. As a critic of contemporary politics, however, Plato rejected the study of rhetoric and as such did not include it as part of the Academy's curriculum.

Aristotle

While the ideas and methods of Socrates and Plato revolutionized education in Athens and provided us with the basis of modern philosophy, it was Aristotle who significantly expanded his mentor's ideas. Not only was Aristotle responsible for catapulting philosophy and modern educational ideas outside of Greece as tutor to Alexander the Great, but he was also the first to conceptualize the basis of the empirical method and the idea of causality. In a real sense, it was Aristotle who provided the basis of the scientific method.

Aristotle's Education

Aristotle was born in 384 BCE in the Greek city of Stagira. At the age of 18 he traveled to Athens to attend Plato's Academy, where he studied for the next 20 years until the death of Plato in 347 BCE. For several years he wrote and taught at the court of Hermeias (near Troy) and then spent a year conducting zoological research on the island of Lesbos. In 342 BCE, Aristotle was invited to serve as a tutor of Alexander (later known as Alexander the Great), son of Philip II of Macedon. This experience elevated Aristotle's reputation as a great teacher and expanded the educational ideas of Socrates and Plato beyond Athens into the worldwide Macedonian empire.

Aristotle's Lyceum

In 335 BCE, Aristotle returned to Athens and opened his famous Lyceum, an institution of higher learning that would eventually rival Plato's Academy. It was during this time that Alexander sent back to his former tutor an enormous amount of information about the people and territories that he had conquered. This included plant and animal specimens and a bounty of written records from civilizations that were virtually unknown to the Greeks at the time. For the next decade, Aristotle and his students carefully studied this material, categorized it, and used it to expand significantly the knowledge of the ancient world.

Aristotle and the Scientific Method

It was from these studies that Aristotle's conception of empirical analysis emerged. Unlike his mentor, Plato, who argued that knowledge was present in the minds of individuals, only to be unfolded through the process of the dialectic, Aristotle wrote that knowledge was the product of intellectual activity, specifically learning through observation. For Aristotle, learning began with simple perceptions that would be linked together by the mind into more complex patterns. These patterns would eventually provide the basis of universal generalizations about the nature of our world. In other words, knowledge was the product of direct observation.

But empirical observation alone was not enough to produce useful generalizations about the world in which we live. In addition, Aristotle argued that observations must be subjected to an ordering of facts derived from these observations into cause and effect relationships if they are to become generalizations or laws. For example, if we heat water to a certain temperature, it will boil and steam will always be produced. Aristotle's conception of the Four Causes—material, formal, efficient, and final—is at the heart of scientific method.

In short, Aristotle argued that we expand our body of knowledge through empirical observation. We then search for cause and effect relationships in order to gain universal generalizations and more fully understand our world.

Aristotle taught at the Lyceum for 12 years and established the institution as the preeminent school in Athens. In 323 BCE, however, Alexander the Great, his former student and powerful supporter, died and Aristotle's political fortunes abruptly changed. Because of a growing anti-Alexander sentiment of politicians throughout Greece, Aristotle was implicated by association and eventually was charged with impiety. He fled the city to Chalcis and died there one year later.

Aristotle's contributions to philosophy, science, and education in general, however, continued. In the years following his death more schools of higher education were built on the model of the Lyceum and the Academy—each with their unique philosophical perspective such as Stoicism and Epicureanism. Education moreover became more systematized and standardized curriculums were established providing the basis of learning throughout the Western world.

ROME

The culture of the Greeks (referred to as Hellenistic) was powerful. With the conquests of Alexander amounting to a world empire that included Persia and Egypt, the colonization of Iberia and Gaul (modern day Spain and France), the influence of the Greeks was astonishing. In addition, however, the Greeks had a powerful influence on the Romans through their system of education.

Greek Influences on Roman Education

As early as the 1st century BCE, most Romans saw the Greek form of education as the best. Educated Greek slaves were sought by wealthy Romans to teach and Roman children learned the Greek alphabet and used the Greek method of writing on wax-coated boards discussed earlier. Similarly, the writings of Homer, especially the *Iliad* and *Odyssey,* became the standard literature read by Roman children.

Greek higher learning also made its way into Rome. In 167 BCE, for example, the Stoic philosopher Crates of Mallos visited Rome and while he was recuperating from an accident in the city, delivered a series of lectures on Stoic grammatical theory. By this time Stoicism had become the chief philosophical doctrine of Greece. One of those attending the lectures was Scipio Africanus, a prominent Roman aristocrat. It was through Scipio that other Stoics were invited to Rome, establishing the influential Scipionic Circle. And while there was some resistance—especially from the influential Cato who demanded that the Stoics be expelled—the educational influences of Greeks continued to grow.

Cicero

The critical link between Greek and Roman education, however, was made possible by Cicero (106–46 BCE). Cicero was perhaps the most important figure in Roman intellectual life during his lifetime and his influence persisted until the end of the Roman Empire, 6 centuries later. Cicero was a product of Greek schooling and throughout his life he embraced and promoted the Greek model of education. Although he rejected some aspects of Greek culture as inconsistent with the Roman experience, he argued that Greek education should be the model for Rome.

In the preface of his classic treatise on education, *De oratore*, Cicero noted: "[A]s we go to our fellow countrymen for examples of virtue, so we—turn to the Greeks for models of learning" (Bowen, 1972, p. 179). Written in 55 BCE, the three-volume *De oratore* became the basis of Roman education—namely Oratory or public speaking. Like the Stoics before him, Cicero argued that public speaking was the cornerstone of higher education and *De oratore* became the standard treatise on the subject.

The Maturing of Roman Education

While Greek would remain the primary language of scholarship and education throughout much of the early history of Rome, Latin gradually made its way into the literature.

During the 1st century BCE, Cicero and others promoted the use of Latin in education and Latin became the language of choice among poets such as Virgil.

Meanwhile, a formal system of Roman education took shape during this period. Gradually it developed four components: basic elementary education, the grammar school, military service, and higher education.

Roman Elementary and Grammar School

The vast majority of Roman boys went to elementary school know as the ludus. There also is evidence that a few girls attended these schools and a number of women taught in Roman elementary schools. The elementary school teacher or Litterator instructed children between the ages of 7 and 12 in reading and writing using the wax covered tablet or tabella, introduced by the Greeks centuries before. Students sat in a circle with their tablets on their laps and like the Greeks before them, learned the letters of the alphabet, then syllables, short words, words of two or three syllables, and finally sentences. Once a student had learned to read he began to memorize lines from poets and the speeches of great orators. This general method of memorization, repetition, and recitation would persist in elementary schools well into the modern era (Bowen, 1972, p. 183).

Mathematics

Some of the more talented students also would study reckoning with an instructor called the Calculator. Children were taught to use their fingers to count and there is some speculation that this was the basis of the shapes of Roman numerals. In addition, students used pebbles to help them count and later they would be introduced to the Roman abacus for simple calculations. Because of the cumbersome nature of the Roman system of numbers, however, reckoning was difficult and instruction in it was limited. It would be up to the Arabs, centuries later, to introduce a number system that could support the development of higher mathematics.

The Seven Disciplines

Young boys in their 12th year progressed to the grammar school instructed by the Grammaticus. Roman grammar schools typically focused on literature, but according to Cicero, some schools also embraced the traditional seven disciplines of grammar, logic, rhetoric, music, astronomy, geometry, and arithmetic. Cicero also noted that some schools taught history and oratory as well as physical education.

Upon completion of their studies in the grammar school, students went through the important formal ceremony of Liberalia. Later this ceremonial passage was shortened into its more familiar commencement exercise of graduation. At this point, most students proceeded to their military service and later, advanced students received higher education

---

Quintilian

Marcus Fabius Quintilianus (circa 35–95 CE), was a Roman orator and rhetorician (meaning that he was skilled in the art of oral persuasion). He was born in Spain and was sent to Rome for his education. He later opened a school of rhetoric where he taught for many years. This great educator wrote a multi-volume textbook on rhetoric, titled *Institutio Oratoria*.

in rhetoric conducted by the Rhetor. Here they prepared for a career in law or politics and learned the skills of Roman oratory. In addition, some students studied the philosophy of Stoicism or Epicureanism.

Quintilion

While Roman education closely resembled the Greek model at all levels, the work of Marcus Fabius Quintilianus (35–90 CE) represents the first major reform of elementary education in the classical world. Quintilian, as he is referred to, was one of the most distinguished professors of rhetoric in the Roman Empire.

His *Institutio Oratoria* or *The Education of the Orator* written during the 1st century CE was the most important teachers' training text of this period, focusing on the aims, methods and content of elementary education. While Quintilian's work was written in the tradition of Cicero's *De oratorio*, he departed from the great master by emphasizing the role of the teacher.

Quintilian argued, for example, that children should be placed in school before their 7th year because by then they would have developed poor habits. He felt strongly that teachers should not only be scholarly but must also have good moral character. This combination would provide an excellent role model for children. As part of this approach Quintilian rejected corporal punishment as ineffective, favoring instead encouragement and praise for successful completion of work.

One of his most important educational ideas was the developmental level of the child. He felt strongly that teachers must carefully choose assignments that were appropriate for them. He wrote, "Vessels with narrow mouths will not receive liquids if too much be poured into them at a time, but are easily filled if the liquid is admitted in a gentle stream or, it may be, drop by drop." Related to this idea was his concept of plasticity, the ability of a child to learn a variety of subjects simultaneously rather than learning those subjects in separate years, as had been the common practice in the classical world (Bowen, 1972, p. 186).

Quintilian had a powerful effect on Roman education. In contrast with the more abstract theories of some of his contemporaries, Quintilian's ideas were intuitive and his advice was direct and understandable. Rather than simply having children memorize and recite the letters of the alphabet, he developed the idea of "letter blocks." He recommended that letters of the alphabet could be carved from ivory and then used by children in play. In so doing, they would be able to touch the letters and learn their names. Similarly he recommended that letters should be cut into a tablet so that children could trace them. As a result, they would experience the sensation of actually writing their forms.

The Decline of Roman Education

The great reforms of Quintilian ironically signaled the end of a "golden" era of classical education in Rome. The Roman Republic had passed into history with the elevation of Julius Caesar to Emperor a generation before and Rome had entered a period characterized by some as one of self-satisfaction and materialism secured by military conquest. Quintilian himself feared for the future of education, noting a tendency of his generation to spurn "the direct simplicity of Cicero—considering our own mannered productions to be superior even though they have lost all precision and clarity" (Bowen, 1972, pp. 204, 205).

Support for education also declined during this period as did the general status and salaries of teachers. The great Roman historian Tacitus argued that at the heart of the problem was the change in child rearing techniques. He noted that during the Roman

---

Criticisms of Teachers in the 1st Century

By the beginning of the 1st century CE, teachers had lost a great deal of their status in Rome. The satirist, Juvenal, for example, listed the occupations of painter, animal trainer, ropedancer, and teacher as comparable. Another writer by the name of Petronius noted that "teachers nowadays are not worth even two brass farthings." With regards to teacher's pay, Juvenal wrote: "Pay indeed? Why, what have I learnt?" asks the scholar. "It is the teacher's fault, of course, that the Arcadian youth feels no flutter in his left breast when (the teacher begins a lesson)" (Bowen, 1972, pp. 204–205).

Republican era, parents raised children by themselves. With the growth of the Roman Empire, however, slaves began to perform that function. As the Empire spread throughout the ancient world through military conquest, educated slaves were brought to serve the Roman people and they often worked as tutors and nurses. Over the years, it appears that children became accustomed to being served and, as a result, many lost their intellectual discipline. For Tacitus, this was the root cause of the intellectual decline of Rome.

In short, there were a number of reasons for the gradual decline of Roman education. First, there was growing lack of support for education in the late Roman Empire as well as a growing chorus of unfair criticism aimed at Roman teachers. Second, as the Roman Empire became more powerful over the years because of its awesome military, the Roman people became more self-satisfied and materialistic, leading to a general lack of intellectual vigor at all levels of society. And finally, the growing wealth of the Roman people led to fundamental changes in child-rearing practices especially the custom of allowing slaves to provide more and more of the basic child-care and education. This overindulgence encouraged general laziness and deteriorated the traditional Roman work ethic.

THE LEGACY OF THE CLASSICAL TRADITION

We should, however, keep these changes in perspective. Certainly it is true that education in the late Roman period may not have had the intellectual vigor it once had during the republican era. And it is also clear that the growing materialism of the Roman Empire had eroded the basic values of the Roman people. Nevertheless, the model of education that had been created by the Greeks and then expanded by the Romans would endure. The great classical tradition of learning had a profound influence on the world and made possible the great achievements of the Roman Empire.

The Fall of Rome

In his classic *History of the Goths* written in 551 CE, Jordanes recounted this pivotal moment in world history.

> When they finally entered Rome, by Alaric's express command they merely sacked it and did not set the city on fire, as wild peoples usually do, nor did they permit serious damage to be done to the holy places. Thence they departed to bring like ruin on Campania and Lucinia. (Carroll et al., 1961)

The Decline of the Roman Empire

Although Edward Gibbons saw the rise of Christianity as one cause of the fall of Rome, there were many others. He noted:

> The Decline of Rome was the natural and inevitable effect of immoderate greatness. Prosperity ripened the principle of decay; the cause of the destruction multiplied with the extent of conquest; and, as soon as time or accident had removed the artificial supports, the stupendous fabric yielded to the pressure of its own weight. The story of the ruin is simple and obvious; and instead of inquiring why the Roman Empire was destroyed, we should rather be surprised that it had subsisted so long. (Gibbon, 1909, pp. 173–174)

The Fall of Rome and the Dark Ages

The Roman Empire was truly awesome. No other empire in world history had done so much, had so much power and wealth, and had lasted so long. It seems almost inconceivable then that a barbarian invader by the name of Alaric could invade and sack the imperial city of Rome in the year 410 CE. And yet that is exactly what happened.

The sacking of Rome and the ultimate collapse of the political apparatus of the Roman Empire dramatically changed the course of Western civilization. For centuries, the mighty Roman Empire had provided cohesion for most of Western Europe and the Mediterranean basin. But now that great empire was broken into thousands of small states, principalities, kingdoms, and territories, each controlled by local warrior princes. The unifying theme of Roman education also was shattered. Secular (nonreligious) education virtually collapsed and literacy plunged.

Gradually, the system of feudalism emerged in Europe. Under that system leaders consolidated their power, claimed land, and established quasi-legal relationships with their people. These relationships were based on protection. The nobles, as they were called, provided military security for the people (the peasants) and in return, these farmers worked the land of the noble. Formal education virtually ceased to exist. Some nobles were very wealthy; others were extremely poor. Sometimes their kingdoms were as little as a square mile or two; sometimes they were enormous. But whatever their power or wealth, this new class of leaders—collectively—would rule Europe for the next 1,000 years.

St. Augustine's Rejection of Greek Philosophy—Book III, *The Confessions*

In Book III of *The Confessions*, St. Augustine provides us with a good example of his rejection of the great philosophy of the ancients.

> Beware lest any man spoil you through Philosophy and vain deceit after the tradition of men, after the rudiments of the world, and not after Christ." He went on to say "so that what book so ever was without that Name (Christ) though learned, political and truly penned, did not altogether take my approbation." (pp. 44–45)

In other words, the erudite Augustine ignored all books that did not focus on the life of Christ or his teachings.

The Role of the Church

The one remaining element of the Roman Empire, however, was the Christian Church: the Roman Catholic Church. Through all the chaos following the breakup of Rome and the establishment of the new political and economic order of feudalism, the Church endured. In fact, since the central secular (political) authority of the empire had collapsed, the church's influence became even stronger. It solidified its position within society by aligning itself with the new feudal leaders across Europe and then demanded that the people accept its absolute power and the authority of the noble class.

The Church also became more conservative during this period and demanded absolute adherence to its doctrines. As a result, intellectual freedom gradually faded as open criticism of Church teachings literally became more and more dangerous. The Church not only ignored the secular teachings, ideas, and philosophies of the ancient Greeks and Romans such as Socrates, Plato, and Aristotle, they openly ridiculed these ideas because did not align directly with Christian theology.

Reflection

What do you think was the effect of Augustine's condemnation of secular literature? Why was the church so determined to undermine all secular teachings?

Given this new, repressive, intellectual environment, secular education all but disappeared. What had been the lifeblood of the ancient world was now but a distant memory. There were, of course, a handful of secular institutions that persisted during this period, such as Plato's Academy. But even this institution eventually was forced to close its doors after 900 years of operation because it was out of step with the new Christian order that had spread across the West. The intellectual vigor associated with secular Greek and Roman education was gone and nearly forgotten.

The Monastery

As secular education in the West collapsed with the decline of Rome, a new institution emerged that would have a profound effect on Christian education for centuries to come. That institution was the monastery. By the 5th century CE (400s) dozens of monasteries had been founded by three of the greatest "church fathers": Basil, Jerome, and Augustine. The purpose of these institutions was to preserve the traditions of the Roman Catholic Church and to prepare young boys for the priesthood. It was now up to the church to preserve the slender thread of education in Western society.

As the chaos of society associated with the fall of Rome continued during the late 400s and early 500s CE, monasteries became havens and retreats for pious monks seeking refuge from a violent world. Many of these monasteries were so isolated from Rome, however, that they developed their own theology and way of life, often based on the interpretation of the scriptures of the founder of the order itself. It was in the midst of this chaos that in 529 CE Bishop Benedict created his monastery at Monte Cassino and established the so-called Rule of Benedict.

The Rule of Benedict

The Rule of Benedict established the Benedictine Order and provided the model upon which most other monastic orders were built in the future. The Rule, moreover, clearly defined the social order of the monastery, the activities of the monks, the distribution of property, and perhaps more importantly, the education of aspirants (Bowen, 1972, p. 330).

The "Venerable Bede"

The Benedictine model of Christian education spread among Monks from Italy throughout Europe, during this period. In fact, it reached as far north as England, with the establishment of monasteries in Wearmouth (674 CE) and Jarrow (682 CE). It was at Jarrow, for example, that the famous Bishop Bede (sometimes known as the venerable Bede) wrote his classic *A History of the English Church and People* as well as *On Orthography* during the early 700s CE. Bede also taught in the Monastic school, later to known as the Cathedral School of York.

After Bede's death in 735 CE, this scholarship was carried on by his finest student, Egbert, later the Archbishop of York. Egbert maintained the York school, established rigorous standards of scholarship, and expanded the curriculum beyond religion to include the liberal arts. It was in this growing intellectual environment that monks from all over England, Ireland, and beyond studied. Later, these scholars would return to their own monasteries to preserve the traditions of learning and scholarship. In addition, it was at York that the great scholar Alcuin studied, taught, and wrote.

Charlemagne and Alcuin

As we have seen, the fall of Rome had a dramatic impact on the level of secular scholarship, learning, and education in Western society. Moreover, the gradual fragmentation of the European continent under feudalism had eliminated virtually all remnants of the once powerful Empire. For a brief moment in history, however, the Franks—under their powerful ruling family, the Carolingians—expanded their influence throughout much of present-day Europe. The greatest of the Frankish kings was Charlemagne.

Charlemagne was a brilliant military leader and a devout Christian. He extended his small empire in the late 700s CE, first by conquering the Lombards, defeating the Saxons, and then forcibly converting them to Christianity. He then defeated the warlike tribes of the Avars, the Wends, and the Slavs and pushed his kingdom as far east as present-day Germany. The Church was so grateful to Charlemagne that he was coronated as King of the Franks by the Pope on Christmas Day, 800 CE.

Under the Christian king Charlemagne, some of the grandeur of the Roman Empire returned and with it there was a revival of Western culture and education. He encouraged the Church to establish village schools throughout Christendom; called for improved education in the monasteries themselves, and he engaged scribes to copy the Bible for distribution throughout the empire. In fact, for the next century, Charlemagne's court at Aachen became the center of what some scholars call the Carolingian Renaissance.

Charlemagne's most important intellectual achievement, however, was to recruit Alcuin of York—the great educator from England—to his court. Alcuin became Charlemagne's personal tutor and later he was placed in charge of the impressive palace library. Alcuin soon became the Abbot of the School at Tours, which developed into the intellectual center of Charlemagne's Empire.

Byzantium

Despite the contributions of the monastic movement and the brief "Carolingian Renaissance" fostered by Charlemagne and Alcuin, much of Western Europe had remained in intellectual darkness since the fall of Rome in the 400s ce. And yet, within this gloom there was a beacon of intellectual light and hope in the East. This was Byzantium. The Byzantine Empire, with its capital in Constantinople (now Istanbul) had been an important part of the Roman Empire for centuries. In fact, the emperor of Byzantium was

---

The Capitol School in Constantinople

The Capitol School was to have:

> Three orators and ten grammarians, first of all among those teachers who are commended by their learning in Roman oratory. Among those professors who are recognized as being proficient in facility of expression in Greek (oratory), there shall be five sophists in number and likewise ten grammarians. Since it is our desire that our glorious youth should be instructed not only in such arts, we associate authorities of more profound knowledge and learning with the aforesaid professors. Therefore it is our will that to the other professors, one teacher shall be associated who shall investigate hidden secrets of philosophy, two teachers also who shall expound the formulas of the law and statutes. (Bowen, 1972, p. 295)

---

referred to as the Basileus Rhomanian—King of the Romans. Moreover, the culture of the Byzantine Empire was Hellenistic, steeped in the rich traditions of the Greeks.

Byzantium was independent of the Roman Empire. The primary language of Byzantium was not Latin, but Greek, and its form of Christianity (Catholicism) was Eastern Orthodox, not Roman. Moreover, the growing independence and power of the Byzantine Empire beginning in the 5th century (late 400s CE) alienated church leaders in Rome and eventually led to a great schism (1053 CE) between the Roman Catholic and the Eastern Orthodox churches. As a result, the people of the West were not able to benefit directly from Byzantine's traditions of education and intellectual development.

The Flicker of Light in the East

Nevertheless, the Byzantine Empire became one of the last vestiges of Western civilization during the long and dark ages of Europe. For centuries, a series of powerful Byzantine emperors maintained the empire from barbarian invaders, internal strife, and eventually from the growing presence of the Persians and then the Muslims to the east. Moreover, the Byzantine Empire maintained a powerful economy, especially as the center of trade between East and West.

This relative prosperity allowed Byzantine scholars to maintain an intellectual curiosity and freedom that had all but disappeared in Europe because of the collapse of Rome and the traditions of Roman education. Byzantine scholars studied the ancient classics; expanded the contours of secular knowledge and writing, and they maintained the traditions of classical education.

The Rise of Islam

Meanwhile a new powerful religion was rising in the East. According to Muslim scholars, Islam emerged during the early 600s when an Arab from Mecca by the name of Muhammad (570–632 CE) had a revelation from Allah (God) and was commanded to reveal the three truths and go among the people to preach. His message was simple: "There is no God but Allah and Muhammad is his prophet." The religion spread rapidly and within a decade of Muhammad's death, Arab Muslims had conquered Syria and Palestine, Egypt, and most of the Persian Empire. By 750 Muslims also controlled most of northern Africa and had pushed into what is now Spain.

The Intellectual Contributions of Islam

While Muslim warriors spread Islam and the Arabic language throughout their conquered territories, they also synthesized many of the intellectual ideas and cultural elements from them. For example, Islamic scholars translated a great deal of classical Greek literature and philosophy into Arabic. They also translated Persian, Indian, and Chinese science and philosophy and built a powerful intellectual tradition on this foundation.

Muslims created an impressive numerical system adopted from the Indians and later developed algebra, geometry, and trigonometry based on the writings of Greek mathematicians. They used Chinese technology of papermaking and adapted it to produce their own manuscripts. They developed the study of astronomy based on the works of Persian and Hindu science and provided an important link to the scientific revolution in Western Europe beginning in the 1600s. Finally, they expanded the frontiers of medicine based on the works of Greek and Alexandrian scholars. In short, while the West was in chaos and secular education based on the Greek and Roman model had virtually collapsed, Islamic scholars preserved, promoted, and expanded these ancient traditions.

The Crusades

While the rise of Islam provided an intellectual tradition that would preserve much of the scholarship and educational ideas of the ancients, it also represented a powerful challenge to Western civilization and Christianity. Arab warriors, and later, tribesmen from central Asia who were converted to Islam, were imbued with a messianic desire to spread their faith. This led to the conquest of most of the Mediterranean world including the Holy Lands of Palestine.

Many Christians saw this occupation as unacceptable and their resentment eventually led to a series of Crusades that pitted Christian armies from France, Germany, and England against Islamic forces and others.

These Crusades, alas, were a pathetic period in the history of the world. They led to devastations, massacres, and genocide, and left the worlds of Christendom as well as Islam more militant, warlike, and aggressive. For more than 400 years—from the onset of the first Crusade in 1095 to Pope Pius II's final attempt to raise yet another army for a Crusade in 1464—the world was engulfed in ongoing and crippling wars.

The Renaissance

Ironically, these bloody crusades became the catalyst of change that would eventually lead to a renaissance or rediscovery of the wisdom and ideas of the ancients.

Links to the Past: Petrarch, "Renaissance Man"

Francesco Petrarca—or Petrarch—was a man of many titles. These included the arbiter of the 14th century, the mainspring of the revival and the initiator of the Renaissance. He was also the first modern man. Petrarch challenged many of the educational institutions of the medieval world including monasticism and scholasticism.

Petrarch was a scholar of the ancient Greeks and Romans. He especially admired Cicero and Virgil and collected their works. He also promoted a rediscovery of the wisdom of the ancients and has been seen as ushering in the revival of learning that we call the Renaissance.

As we have seen, for nearly 1,000 years—between the fall of Rome in 410 and the end of the Crusades in the mid 1440s—Europe had been mired in intellectual darkness. There were, of course, important intellectual traditions coming from the Byzantine Empire and from the scholarship of Islamic Arabs. Moreover, Roman Catholic monks in secluded monasteries from Italy to Ireland were able to maintain a degree of intellectual wisdom, learning, and education. In fact, it was this tradition that led to the creation of a number of universities beginning in the 1000s.

But beyond these important threads of education, the West had clearly declined from the "grandeur of Greece" and the "glory of Rome." Secular learning and education had become a distant memory, replaced instead by a narrowly focused religious educational tradition. And even here only a few men who aspired to the priesthood were able to receive this form of training. Literacy among the common folk had plummeted and with a few exceptions, the intellectual environment of Europe had become a wasteland.

The Rise of Humanism

While it is difficult to identify the specific "moment" in history when the Renaissance began, it appears that the first rumblings of change occur in the 1300s in Florence, Italy. It was in this thriving commercial city that Francesco Petrarch (1304–1374) widely referred to as the "father of humanism," lived, wrote, and taught.

In many ways, Petrarch was an important link between the medieval and modern worlds. He embraced a philosophy that was centered on religion but was also rooted in the classics. He was said to have carried copies of both St. Augustine's *Confessions* and a volume of work from the great pagan, Cicero.

This new humanism was the heart and soul of the Renaissance. It focused on the importance of the individual and looked to the ideas of the Greeks and Romans for intellectual nourishment. At the same time it recognized the Church and its teachings. Humanism was rooted in the emerging commercial world and market economy of the 1300s and 1400s but by seeking to reconcile religion with the new sensibilities of the day, it clearly embraced a new vision for the future.

In the area of education, humanism flourished during this period. Under the influence of Giovanni Pico della Mirandola (1463–1494), for example, a new school of Christian Platonism was established in Florence. This new school of thought (sometimes referred to as Neoplatonic or "new Plato") successfully reconciled the classic teachings of Plato and Socrates with the Church. This new vision reemphasized the importance of education and like Petrarch and others, looked to the classics for intellectual sustenance.

The humanists were instrumental in building a bridge between the Medieval Christian world and the nearly forgotten teachings of the classics. Slowly, Europeans began to rediscover the importance of the long lost ancient world and marveled at their knowledge, learning, art, and scholarly traditions. What began as a quest for a greater understanding of the ancient past eventually became an obsession. Artists were in awe at the great paintings, sculptures, and architecture of Greece and Rome and copied their style and form. Scientists studied the medicine, astronomy, and mathematics of the ancients, often derived from Islamic or Byzantine writers, and built a new science on that foundation. And of course, scholars and teachers read the classic poets and philosophers and passed on that knowledge and excitement of learning to their students. The Renaissance had reawakened the Western world from darkness.

Humanism, of course, was not confined to Italy, but rather was part of an intellectual movement throughout Europe during this period. Desiderius Erasmus (1466–1536), like other Christian Humanist scholars of this era, was a product of scholastic training in the medieval university but was also influenced profoundly by the writings of classical poets

An Appeal for Universal Education—*A Letter to the Mayors and Aldermen* by Martin Luther

Therefore, I beg you all, in the name of God and of our neglected youth, not to think of this subject lightly, as many do who do not see what the prince of this world intends. For the right instruction of youth is a matter in which Christ and the entire world are concerned. If we must annually expend large sums on muskets, roads, bridges, dams, and the like, in order that the city may have temporal peace and comfort, why should we not apply as much to our poor, neglected youth (Binder, 1970).

and philosophers. Like his Humanist colleagues, Erasmus was a virtual bridge between the medieval world of Christianity and the ancient wisdom of the Greeks and Romans. In addition, however, Erasmus represented the spirit of reform that would eventually lead to Luther, Calvin, and the great Reformation of the mid-1500s and beyond.

As we will see, the Reformation was the beginning of the modern era. The uncontested power of medieval Christianity—formally embodied in the Roman Catholic Church—would be broken. The cement that held feudalism together, the institution of Christianity, would begin to erode and a new era would emerge. This new era in the West would still be profoundly Christian but would begin to reconcile the ancient "pagan" teachings of the Greeks and Romans with the beliefs of Christianity. Moreover, as this intellectual door opened slightly, the light of a new era of science and philosophy would gradually illuminate the darkness of Europe. The long sleep was at an end and a new era was about to begin.

The Reformation

As we have seen, in the early 1400s, Christian Humanists such as Erasmus had begun to challenge the power, materialism, and worldliness of the Roman Catholic Church. This reform tradition would grow over the years and eventually lead to a major schism within the Catholic Church itself.

Martin Luther

One of the first theologians to officially break from the church was Martin Luther. By criticizing some the basic teachings of Roman Catholicism, he indirectly launched the Protestant Reformation.

Luther was important not only because of his role in the Protestant Reformation, but also because of his revolutionary educational ideas. For Luther, education was essential so that individuals could read and interpret the Holy Bible. Luther and his colleague Melanchthon gradually embraced the idea of universal elementary education. In his *Visitation Articles* written in 1528, for example, Melanchthon argued that education should be provided for all children regardless of their economic status or gender. He also felt that education should be compulsory (Binder, 1970).

In his A Letter to the Mayors and Aldermen of All the Cities of Germany, Luther also recommended a state-supported system of universal education that would focus on the study of Greek and Latin, mathematics, science, history, and physical education. A new and exciting chapter in the history of education was beginning to unfold. While the future United States would not adopt a national organization of public education, Luther's ideas

---

The "Ratio Studiorum" of the Jesuits

Since it is one of the weightiest duties of our society to teach men all the branches of knowledge in keeping with our organization in such a manner, that they may be moved thereby to a knowledge and love of our Creator and Redeemer, let the Provincial hold it as his duty, to provide with all zeal that the results, which the grace of our vocation demands, abundantly answer to our manifold labors in education (Binder, 1970).

---

of a state-supported system, a unified curriculum, and compulsory education would persist and have a profound effect on our educational systems (Binder, 1970).

The Jesuits

As the Reformation spread throughout Europe in the 1500s, a new educational reform movement also developed within the Roman Catholic Church itself. The most important example of this reform was the Society of Jesus, or Jesuits, established by Ignatius Loyola.

The Jesuits represented a new kind of religious order with a mission that was focused on rigorous teaching. Over the next several centuries, they established hundreds of schools throughout Europe and through the work of Spanish missionaries brought education to the Southwestern United States. They also reinvigorated secondary and higher education within the Catholic Church. Their influence continues to the present day (Pavur, 2005).

Meanwhile, many of the new Protestant sects of this era either directly or indirectly embraced the educational ideas of Luther and Melanchthon. These Protestant reformers argued that reading the Bible and interpreting the scriptures was at the heart of religion. This belief further strengthened the idea of universal public education—though it would retain its religious focus.

The *Great Didactic* (1632)—John Amos Comenius (1592–1670)

Following in the footsteps of nature we find that the process of education will be easy:

- If it begin early before the mind is corrupted.
- If the mind be duly prepared to receive it.
- If it proceed from the general to the particular.
- And from what is easy to what is more difficult.
- If the pupil be not overburdened by too many subjects
- And if progress be slow in every case.
- If the intellect be forced to nothing to which is natural bent does not incline it, in accordance with its age and with the right method.
- If everything be taught through the medium of the senses.
- And if the use of everything taught be continually kept in view.
- If everything be taught according to one and the same method.
- These, I say, are the principles to be adopted if education is to be easy and pleasant. (Binder, 1970)

The great theologian and educator Comenius (1592–1670) was important in this tradition of public education. Comenius lived during a difficult period of the Thirty Years' War in Germany that ravished the country for over a generation. As a Bishop of the Moravian Brethren, a Protestant denomination that emerged during this period, he had seen the extremes of human cruelty and religious fanaticism. And yet he maintained a strong belief in the perfectibility of humankind through education.

For much of his life, Comenius focused his attention on the education of children. As part of that effort he wrote a number of books that would have a dramatic effect on the development of education for generations to come. His *Great Didactic*, for example, was an extraordinary treatise that focused on the importance of education in society.

The *Great Didactic* is considered the first modern statement on the discipline of education. In the area of instruction, his most important contribution was the *Orbis Pictus*. This illustrated textbook was designed to help young students learn to read, and his concept of combining reading lessons with pictures revolutionized elementary classroom instruction (Binder, 1970).

John Calvin and the Puritans

Other Protestant sects were also being formed in the 1500s. One of the most important of these was Calvinism. John Calvin, a Frenchman living in Switzerland, broke from Catholicism and began preaching his new religion in the 1530s. So successful was his new denomination that he was able to establish a kind of "theocratic" state in Geneva—a government run by the faithful.

Calvin's unique form of Protestantism focused on the purification of religion and inspired thousands to convert.

Among those many converts were the Puritans, one group of which eventually made their way to the new world and established the colony of Massachusetts Bay. In the next chapter we will explore the educational revolution that these settlers initiated.

SUMMARY

Our profession is an ancient and noble one standing on the broad shoulders of some of the most remarkable men and women of the past. The collective educational wisdom of our world, moreover, reaches deep into antiquity and represents diverse contributions from our rich multicultural heritage.

The Emergence of Education

The evolution of humankind from primitive savagery to a human culture that is recognizable to us today was the result of education. Over the centuries, millions of men and women passed on the collective knowledge and skills they had learned to the next generation. These were the first teachers and their lessons were the basis of our civilization. During the 2nd millennium BCE, the Babylonians experimented with various forms of religious education but it was the Egyptians who established the first formalized educational experience in the West. The Jews were the first to record their own history of their physical and spiritual struggle and pass on that knowledge to their children. The Indians and Chinese also established early forms of education to help students develop an appreciation and understanding of their particular religious orientation.

Ancient Greece

While religious education was the focus of early civilizations, the Greeks were the first to establish secular schools. Spartan education, for example, had little academic orientation but focused on physical training—especially for the military. In Athens, however, the tradition of academic learning and democratic citizenship began to emerge. In the 4th century BCE (400–500) the idea of education—what they called paideia—took shape. The system that eventually emerged began with mandatory primary and secondary education of boys beginning at age seven with a curriculum that included reading, writing, "reckoning" (math), as well as music and physical training. Athens' greatest teacher was Socrates. His teaching method was based on critical analysis and logical argumentation between him and his students. This process is what we call the Socratic Method. Socrates most famous student was Plato. Plato's method of involved the oral questioning and student responses on questions of philosophy. Like Socrates before him, Plato felt that this method of instruction allowed the unfolding of knowledge (what he saw as universal ideas) that was already present in the mind. Plato's student, Aristotle, was responsible for not only transmitting modern educational ideas outside of Greece as tutor to Alexander the Great, but he was also the first to conceptualize the basis of the empirical method and the idea of causality. In a real sense, it was Aristotle who provided the basis of the scientific method. Moreover, his famous Lyceum became the standard of secondary education for the next several centuries.

Roman Education

It was the Roman educator and orator Cicero (106–46 BCE) that was the link between Greek and Roman education. Cicero was the most important intellectual in Rome and his influence persisted until the end of the Roman Empire—six centuries later. He received a Greek education and throughout his life he promoted the Greek model of education with an emphasis on oratory (public speaking). The vast majority of Roman boys went to an elementary school (know as the Ludus). Some girls also attended, but they were the exception rather than the rule. Like the Greeks before them, students sat in a circle with their tablets on their laps and learned the letters of the alphabet, and then syllables, short words, words of two or three syllables, and finally sentences. Once they learned to read, they began to memorize lines from poets and speeches.

Some of the more talented students would also study reckoning or math with an instructor called the Calculator. Young boys in their twelfth year progressed to the grammar school—instructed by the Grammaticus—where they typically focused on literature, but according to Cicero, some schools also embraced the traditional seven disciplines of grammar, logic, rhetoric, music, astronomy, geometry, and arithmetic. Cicero also noted that some schools also taught history and oratory as well as physical education.

While Cicero was the vital link between the Greek and Roman forms of education, the work of Marcus Fabius Quintilianus (35–90 CE) represents the first major reform of elementary education in the classical world. Quintilian, as he is referred to, was one of the most distinguished professors of rhetoric in the Roman Empire. He rejected corporal punishment as ineffective, favoring instead encouragement and praise for successful completion of work. One of his most important contributions was recognizing the developmental level of the child. He felt strongly that teachers must carefully choose assignments that were appropriate for them. While the "golden age of Roman education" declined after Quintilian the classical model of education that had been created by the Greeks and then expanded by the Romans would endure. The great classical tradition of learning—

with all its problems—had a profound influence on the world for the next two millennia. That tradition came to an abrupt end with the fall of Rome during the mid-400s CE.

The Dark Ages

The sacking of Rome and the ultimate collapse of the Roman Empire dramatically changed the course of Western civilization. For centuries, the mighty Empire had provided cohesion for most of Western Europe and the Mediterranean basin. But now Europe was shattered into thousands of small states, principalities, kingdoms, and territories each controlled by local warrior princes. Classical education was, for the most part, replaced by sporadic forms of religious education. As a result we also see the rapid decline of education and a dramatic rise in illiteracy. The church not only ignored the secular teachings, ideas, and philosophies of the ancient Greeks and Romans such as Socrates, Plato, and Aristotle, they openly ridiculed these ideas because did not align directly with Christian theology. Given this new, repressive, intellectual environment, education all but disappeared. What had been the lifeblood of the ancient world was now but a distant memory.

Waking from Intellectual Slumber

During these years of intellectual slumber, however, the monastery movement and the great work of Charlemagne saved education in the West. A small number of Roman Catholic monks from Italy to Ireland literally hand-copied some of the great works of classical Greece and Rome as well as the Bible itself. Moreover, during the 9th century CE (the 800s) the Franks under Charlemagne expanded their influence throughout much of present-day Europe and reinvigorated education. During this "Carolingian Renaissance," Charlemagne recruited Alcuin of York—the great educator from England—to his court. Alcuin became Charlemagne's personal tutor and later he was placed in charge of the impressive palace library. Alcuin soon became the abbot of the school at Tours, which develop into the intellectual center of Charlemagne's empire. Nevertheless, much of Western Europe remained in intellectual darkness throughout this period. Within this gloom there was a beacon of intellectual light and hope in the East. This was Byzantium. The Byzantine Empire prospered throughout much of this period and promoted education. Byzantine scholars maintain an intellectual curiosity and freedom that had all but disappeared in Europe. They studied the ancient classics; expanded the contours of secular knowledge and writing, and they maintained the traditions of classical education. In addition to the intellectual contributions of the West, Islamic scholars translated into Arabic a great deal of classic Greek literature and philosophy. They also translated Persian, Indian, and Chinese science and philosophy and built a powerful intellectual tradition on this foundation. The Muslims also created an impressive numerical system adopted from Indians and later developed algebra, geometry, and trigonometry based on the writings of Greek mathematicians. They used Chinese technology of papermaking and adapted it to their own needs. They also developed the study of astronomy based on the works of Persian and Hindu science and they expanded the frontiers of medicine based on the works of Greek and Alexandrian scholars.

Renaissance and Reformation

While it is difficult to identify the "moment" in history when the Renaissance began, it appears that the first rumblings of change occur in the 1300s in Florence, Italy. It was in this thriving commercial city that Francesco Petrarch (1304–1374), widely referred to as the "father of humanism," lived, wrote, and taught.

In many ways, Petrarch was an important link between the medieval and modern worlds. He embraced a vision that was centered on religion but was also rooted in the classics. He was said to have carried copies of both St. Augustine's Confessions and a volume of work from the great pagan, Cicero. Humanism sought to reconcile religion with the new sensibilities of day but clearly it embraced a secular vision for the future. While Italian humanistic scholars such as Petrarch and Machiavelli embraced the emerging secular world and looked to the ancient past to understand and improve the future, others, like Sir Thomas More were more skeptical of the direction of modern society. These Christian Humanists were concerned about the new commercial economy and the growing individualism associated with capitalism. In many ways the Humanists represented the first step toward the Reformation where the uncontested power of the Roman Catholic Church would be broken. The cement that held feudalism together would begin to erode and a new era would emerge. This new era in the West would still be profoundly Christian but would begin to reconcile the ancient "pagan" teachings of the Greeks and Romans with the beliefs of Christianity. Moreover as this intellectual door opened slightly, the light of a new era of science and philosophy would gradually illuminate the darkness of Europe. The long sleep was nearly at an end and a new era was about to begin.

DISCUSSION QUESTIONS

1. Why is education central to the development of civilization? Who were the first teachers?
2. Discuss the development of formal writing. How did it impact education both positively and negatively?
3. Compare Spartan and Athenian educational forms.
4. Discuss the Socratic Method. How could you use this method in the classroom?
5. Discuss Aristotle's scientific method. Why is it important?
6. Discuss the contributions of Cicero and Quintilian to the development of educational thought.
7. Why did Roman education begin to decline? What is the Dark Ages?
8. Discuss the educational role of the Roman Catholic Church during the middle ages.
9. Discuss the role of the Byzantium and Islam in the maintenance of education during the middle ages.
10. Discuss the role of the Reformation in the development of education.

Chapter 6

American Educational History

The history of education is both global and rooted in antiquity. From the early writings of Indian and Chinese scholars, the classical education of the Greeks and Romans, to the work of obscure medieval monks, education developed erratically in the years prior to the settlement of America.

The link between European educational forms and American education, however, was the Reformation of the 1500s and 1600s. It was this religious upheaval that directly led to the settlement of the Puritan colony of Massachusetts Bay and the American educational revolution that followed.

AMERICAN COLONIAL EDUCATION

The Puritans developed a system of nearly universal primary education in the Massachusetts Bay colony. In 1642, leaders of the colony enacted the first education law in America. This law directed town leaders to determine whether their children were receiving an adequate education at home, especially learning "to read and understand the principles of religion" (Hillway, 1964, p. 20).

They were not. Since the leaders felt strongly that the ability to read the Bible would help thwart the delusions of Satan, they passed a series of educational laws including the colony's first compulsory education law—what is called the "Old Deluder Law of 1647."

This successful model of public education gradually would be adopted in other New England colonies over the next century and it then spread west as New Englanders migrated to New York and the upper Midwest in the 1700s. It also endured as New England gradually became more diverse and abandoned its theocratic basis of government.

The Old Deluder Law of 1647

It being one cheife project of ye ould deluder, Satan, to keepe men from the knowledge of ye Scriptures . . . it is therefore ordered, yt evry township in this jurisdiction, aftr ye Lord hath increased yr number to 50 householders, shall then forthwith appoint one within their towne to teach all such children as shall resort to him to write and reade. (Hillway, 1964, p. 20)

Education in the Middle Colonies

The schools that developed in the middle colonies during the colonial period reflected the rich ethnic and religious diversity of this region. In New York City, for example, members of the Dutch Reformed church were active in providing education for their children. These schools were taught in Dutch until the eve of the American Revolution in 1772. In addition to these primary schools, the Dutch Reformed church established a handful of "secondary" schools using the Latin School Model (Cohen, 1974).

The German Lutherans followed the lead of the Dutch Reformed church and focused on religious training, learning the catechism, and memorizing its rules of religious and moral behavior. These schools provided a basic model for many German-speaking groups in Pennsylvania.

The Quakers also had a long tradition of education in Europe and brought these ideas with them to America. The Quakers were also among the first to accept both women and African Americans as students. They also pioneered new instructional techniques in the context of religious education.

In Roman Catholic settlements like those in Pennsylvania and New York, a private elementary school tradition gradually developed. Typically organized and controlled by the parish priest with the help of local community members, Catholic schools developed during the 1700s. Like their Lutheran counterparts, these schools were oriented toward religious education and used a catechism as the basis of instruction. Their primary goal was to prepare younger students for their first communion (Burns, 1969).

Christopher Dock—Mennonite Teacher

The Mennonites of Pennsylvania placed a great deal of emphasis on education. This selection comes from an exchange between a "newcomer" and an "inhabitant" and reveals the importance of education to these people.

Newcomer: A matter that is of very treat importance to me is, that, in Germany, one is able to send his children to school to have them instructed in reading and writing. Here it is well nigh impossible to get such instruction; especially where people live so far apart. O, how fortunate are they who have access to a good teacher by whom the children are well taught and trained.

Inhabitant: It is true. On that account many children living on our frontiers grow up like trees. I do recall two schoolmasters—Ludwig Hoecker and Christopher Dock—who have many good qualities. The one (Hoecker) spent most of his time in secret prayer and heartfelt sighing that God might keep the hearts and minds of his pupils. He taught them their letters faithfully. He observed also their natural dispositions. If he found the child ambitious, he would praise it so that it learned its lessons fairly well.

I remember still another one (Dock) who, out of love of God, loved his pupils as if they all were his own children. They in turn loved him dearly. Whenever he was obligated to reprove the children for ill behavior, he did so with grievous words coming from his wounded heart, so that he frequently softened their hearts. The children of the poor he taught willingly without pay as he taught others for pay. Those who learned to write he induced to correspond with one another. (Brunbaugh, 1908, pp. 18–20)

Finally, in more self-contained religious settlements, such as the Mennonites in Pennsylvania, the primary school became a central part of community life. School attendance was required in these settlements and teachers within the faith instructed young boys and girls in basic reading, arithmetic, and religious instruction (Cohen, 1974).

In short, the rich ethnic and religious diversity of the middle colonies was reflected in a wide range of educational experiments, each of which centered on religious and moral education. Since there was little organized political structure at the community level and virtually no commitment to secular public education at this time, individual churches often established schools to instruct children in their set of religious beliefs. The quality of these schools varied dramatically from community to community and they often appeared and then disappeared as a result of individual and local interest. In some towns they thrived for generations. Other communities provided virtually no formal primary schooling for children, preferring that families provide them with a basic education of reading and writing.

Education in the Colonial Southwest

In addition to the Roman Catholic communities in the Northeast, were the Spanish colonial settlements in the Southwest. In areas extending from present day Santa Fe, New Mexico (1689) through San Diego, California (1769) and Los Angeles, California (1781), Jesuit education flourished. In these communities, Jesuit priests established hundreds of primary and secondary Catholic schools. This tradition continues to the present day.

Education in the Southern Colonies

While settlers in the middle colonies embraced a variety of primary educational experiments, the South adopted a laissez-faire approach to education that was typical of England. In these communities, private schools and in-home tutoring for the wealthy planter class was the norm. Beyond apprenticeship and minimal reading education in charity schools, however, there were few opportunities for poor children (Craven, 1949).

For African Americans, free or enslaved, formal education was extremely rare. Prior to the 1800s, a few charity schools had been established to provide education for black slaves with religious groups taking the lead. Moreover, the Quakers were persistent in their support of African American education throughout this period.

Philip Vickers Fithian—Tutor on a Virginia Plantation

Plantation masters in the South often hired young tutors—frequently from the North—to teach their children. The following selection comes from a letter of Philip Fithian (tutor) to his friend the Reverend Enoch Green of New Jersey.

> I set out from home the 20th of October and arrived at the Hon: Robert Carters of Nominy, in Westmorland County, the 28th. I began to teach his children the first of November. He has two sons, and one Nephew; the oldest Son is turned of seventeen and is reading Salust and the Greek grammar; the others are about fourteen, and in English grammar, and Arithmetic. He has besides five daughters which I am to teach English, the eldest is fifteen, and is reading the Spectator; she is employed two days in every week in learning to play the Forte-Piano, and Harpsichord. The others are smaller, and learning to read and spell. (Williams, 1900, pp. 278–280)

An Enlightened View of the Intellectual Abilities of African Americans—Late 1700s

During the late 18th century, it was commonly held that African people were inferior to whites. This belief in the inferiority of black men and women helped justify the system of slavery. Not all Americans had these views however. The selection from the letter below was written by Mr. McHenry regarding the accomplishments of a "free Negro" by the name of Benjamin Banneker. With the publication of *Banneker's Almanac*, Mr. McHenry hoped to demonstrate the innate intelligence of African American people.

> Benjamin Banneker, a free Negro, has calculated an ALMANACK for the ensuing year, 1792 which being desirous to dispose of, to the best advantage, he has requested me to aid his application to you for that purpose. Having fully satisfied myself, with respect to his title to this kind of authorship, if you can agree with him for the price of his work, I may venture to assure you it will do you credit, as Editors, while it will afford you the opportunity to encourage talents that have thus far surmounted the most discouraging circumstances and prejudices.
>
> I consider this Negro as fresh proof that the powers of the mind are disconnected with the colour of the skin or in other words, a striking contradiction to Mr. Hume's doctrine that "the Negroes are naturally inferior to the whites and unsusceptible of attainments in arts and sciences." (Cohen, 1974c, p. 600)

A good-hearted master might allow the plantation tutor to teach the sons and daughters of house slaves to read. And occasionally a member of the plantation household might instruct a precocious black slave. Frederick Douglass, the great black abolitionist, for example, was taught to read by his owner's wife. Moreover, some slaves were self-taught and passed on those skills to their children. Typically, however, the education of slaves was viewed as dangerous and was forbidden by law and custom.

African American slaves did have a thriving oral culture, complete with their own morality tales, rich folklore, and music handed down from generation to generation. In addition, thousands of African Muslim slaves struggled to maintain both their literacy and their religion in the face of oppression. Finally, many slaves learned trades that were useful to the plantation owner. These included masonry, blacksmithing, carpentry, cooking, and bookkeeping. Later these skills would provide the economic foundation of free black communities throughout the South. Formal schooling however, would have to wait until after the American Civil War (Diouf, 1998; Morgan, 1995).

In short, access to formal education during the colonial period varied by ones economic class, gender, religious denomination, race, and region. It represented both the best intentions as well as the greatest neglect, and it reflected the rich ethnic, religious, and geographic diversity of the emerging nation.

THE COMMON SCHOOL

But good intentions were not enough and neglect was much worse. As Americans attempted to create a new Republic, following the Revolution, it became clear that the diverse forms of education available to their children during the colonial period were inadequate for the new nation. Children needed a common set of cultural and social experiences in order to appreciate the concepts of nationhood and civic responsibility. Although the decentralized religious and haphazard approaches to education seemed to work during the colonial period, those experiments were simply too uneven and too narrowly centered on religious training.

Early on, founding fathers such as Benjamin Rush, Thomas Jefferson, and Noah Webster began to call for some form of "common school" experience. In fact, for statesmen like Rush, the common school was the only avenue to a unified republic. Thomas Jefferson, on the other hand, recognized the importance of a "common school" as a defense against power-hungry politicians (Rudolph, 1965).

These important leaders understood that an educated citizenry was critical to the success of the American republic. Citizens needed to make responsible decisions about their elected leaders and the issues that faced them (Rudolph, 1965).

While it would take over a generation to realize the educational dreams of these and other reformers, the common school movement took root and began to grow in the first half of the 1800s. Tireless advocates of public education such as Horace Mann of Massachusetts set the course for the development of common schools throughout the country. Many of these common schools were little more than converted sheds, barns, or abandoned cabins, though the romantic image of the "little red schoolhouse" continues to this day. Whatever the schoolhouse may have looked like, countless common school teachers during this period quietly pursued the vision of the founding fathers and embraced a curriculum that would teach students the basics of reading, writing, and arithmetic—the three Rs—and nurture a passionate patriotism among their young charges. While these schools would continue to include some religious materials, they represented the first secular curriculum in American education.

For young Americans of diverse ethnic and religious backgrounds, the road to a unified nation began with the development of the idea of "civic virtue." By first developing the idea that there was something greater and more important in the world than your own ethnic and religious interests, teachers were then able to instruct young children as to the importance of the nation and help them transcend their own cultural orientation. When primary Readers such as the McGuffey series became available in the late 1830s, lessons on patriotism and civic virtue became the mainstay of reading instruction (Parkerson & Parkerson, 2001: Rudolph, 1965).

Thomas Jefferson's Call for Schools—Bill introduced into the Virginia Legislature in 1789

Thomas Jefferson called upon the Virginia legislature to establish schools in the state to "guard the sacred rights and liberties of their fellow citizens." He then went on to describe these schools.

At every of those schools shall be taught, reading, writing, and common arithmetick, and the books which shall be used therein for instructing the children to read shall be such as will at the same time make them acquainted with Graecian, Roman, English and American history. At these schools all the free children, male and female, resident within (the community) shall be entitled to receive tuition gratis, for the term of three years and as much longer, at their private expense, as their parents guardians, or friends think proper. (Hillway, 1964, p. 20)

The Market Revolution: The Emergence of Capitalism

Providing a common political culture for the emerging nation was one important pillar of the common school movement; the other was the preparation of students for the new market economy. Not only did the new nation demand a sense of patriotism from its citizens, but fundamental changes in the American economy called for a new secular culture as well. In response, the common school created a curriculum that prepared young Americans to negotiate and succeed in its new market economy. In short, the common school was the catalyst that transformed the nation from a culture based on ethnicity and religion to one centered on capitalism and materialism (Sellers, 1991).

The Examination

It was in this environment that the examination gradually developed as an instrument to stimulate competitive instincts and to measure student achievement in relation to others. At first, the "exam" was oral and a little more than a recitation of memorized verses or poems before the schoolmaster. Later, spelling and ciphering "bees" became important measures of success as well as a form of community entertainment. By the mid-1800s, however, the written examination had become an important tool to measure student achievement and soon the dreaded "report card" detailed a student's success or failure to their parents. As the stakes of achievement became clearer and more emphasis was placed on the examination, students realized that only through hard work and determination could they compete successfully.

Slowly and quietly through the early years of the 1800s, American teachers promoted a new political and economic culture. On the one hand, their reading instruction helped develop a fervent patriotism and a civic virtue among students. On the other hand, their methods of instruction stimulated competitive instincts and a desire to achieve through hard work and determination. These were the unique values that 19th century American teachers promoted to unite the diverse religious and ethnic people into a nation.

Fear of Foreigners (Xenophobia) During the mid-19th Century

During the mid-19th century, many American were alarmed with the rising numbers of immigrants to this country. This selection represents the extreme reaction to immigration—nativism—fueled by xenophobia. Does this statement have a contemporary ring to it?

America for the Americans, we say. And why not? Didn't they plant it and battle for it through bloody revolution—and haven't they developed it, as only Americans could, into a nation of a century and yet mightier than the oldest on earth? Why shouldn't they shape and rule the destinies of their low land—the land of their birth their love, their altars and their graves; the land red and rich with the blood and ashes and hallowed by the memories of their fathers? Why not rule their own, particularly when the alien betrays the trust that should never have been given him and the liberties of the land are thereby imperiled? (Cohen, 1974c, pp. 997–998)

**New York City's Common Council's Book Committee Requests
Changes in Public School Reading Material (1840)**

The following represent some of the changes that were recommended in the reading materials of public school children that were seen as offensive by Roman Catholics.

New York Reader, Page 205, erase last paragraph

English Reader, Page 51, strike out paragraph: the "Queens bigoted zeal," to "eternal welfare." Page 152, "the most credulous monk in a Portuguese convent."

Sequel Murray's, The whole article "Life of Luther"

Putnam's Sequel, Erase the article "John Huss." (Cohen, 1974c, p. 1139)

Reflection

While the nature of these changes cannot be determined from these simple requests, they do indicate that the New York Public Schools were responding to criticism of the reading curriculum by Roman Catholics. What sorts of material might be seen as objectionable to ethnic or religious groups today?

Religious and Cultural Conflict

But while the common school sought to encourage national unity and develop the values of the marketplace among its students, its curriculum still reflected elements of Protestantism. Because books were rare, children often brought their King James Bibles to class and reading lessons often revolved around the scriptures. Moreover, teachers were sometimes required by the local community to promote values that were unique to Protestantism, such as temperance. Finally, since many immigrant children did not speak English, they were often alienated in the classroom and could not achieve. Each of these problems would eventually cause problems for the common school as our society became more diverse.

As Irish, German, and then Southern and Eastern Europeans migrated to America during the 1800s, the Protestant-oriented common school curriculum became a growing source of conflict. Although most new immigrants enthusiastically supported their new adopted country and often were the most fervent patriots, many objected to the recitation of Protestant prayers and references to drinking as evil. Many Roman Catholics opposed these prayers and values lessons in the primary school curriculum. In Philadelphia, for example, this led Catholics to demand the use of the Roman Catholic Bible (The Vulgate Bible) for instruction in public schools that were primarily Catholic in composition. The outrage over this demand spawned a series of "Bible riots" that left 13 dead and many Catholic churches in ruins (Higham, 1988; Kaestle, 1983).

In New York City there was a similar anti-Catholic riot in 1842. This violence finally ended when some Roman Catholic wards were given the right to choose their own curriculum. But this compromise was short-lived and Roman Catholics eventually were forced to create their own separate school system (McCluskey, 1964).

Excerpt from the First Plenary Council on the subject of Catholic Schools (1852)

Roman Catholic children and their parents felt isolated from their religion when they attended public schools. The schools used Protestant prayers and the curriculum included anti-Catholic messages, like temperance. The Catholic Church called for parents to establish their own schools as noted in the excerpt from the First Plenary Council below:

> Encourage the establishment and support of Catholic schools; make every sacrifice which may be necessary for this object: spare our hearts the pain of beholding the youth whom, after the example of our Master, we so much love, involved in all evils of an uncatholic education, evils too multiplied and too obvious to require that we should do more than raise our voices in solemn protest against the system from which they spring. (Guilday, 1932)

While the debate over the content of curriculum was central to the Roman Catholic/Protestant school controversies of the 1800s, there were other important cultural battlegrounds between the public schools and new immigrants during this period. Europeans from many countries, for example, rejected the values of temperance and prohibition that had become an important component of the public school curriculum. For these new Americans, this moral focus conflicted with their cultural beliefs. This of course was a major source of irritation between ethnic families and the public schools of this era.

In the Southwest this situation was different. Since these communities typically had larger Spanish-speaking, Roman Catholic populations, these tensions were often diffused more effectively. In New Mexico, for example, state-supported Spanish-speaking schools taught by Roman Catholic priests were established in the 1800s.

English Only Instruction

Finally, since virtually all instruction at the primary and secondary level was given in English, many immigrants suffered. German-, Polish-, Russian-, and Italian-speaking

Solutions to the German Language Question (1870)

German immigrant children who were not fluent in English had difficultly attending English-only speaking schools. Teachers and other students perceived them as "dumb" because of language differences.

Below are excerpts from a letter dealing with this issue:

> Whenever a sufficient number of German families had settled, elementary schools were founded by them. [After a series of meetings they established the German-American Teachers' Association]. The German settlers are far from wishing to be a separate people; they want to be Americans in the most extended meaning of the word. The Germans can offer no better contribution—than an improved system of education.

Source: Letter from William Steffen to John Eaton, in the U.S. Bureau of Education, Annual Report of the Commissioner of Education for 1870 (Washington, D.C., 1871), pp. 437–438

immigrants, for example, resented English-only instruction that often branded their children as deficient and even ignorant because they had difficulty speaking English. On the other hand, when young immigrant students attempted to assimilate quickly into the dominant American culture, this caused tension within their own families and sometimes fueled resentment of the public schools. Again, this is a problem that we continue to see today among many immigrants.

AFRICAN AMERICANS

While the cultural conflict between the dominant Protestant population and other Christian and non-Christian people would continue to rage in the common schools throughout the 1800s, the question of race would ultimately have a deeper and more lasting impact on public education in this country.

As the common school blossomed during the 1800s and provided an education for hundreds of thousands of white children, African Americans, enslaved or free, often did without. In the colonial South, as previously mentioned, slave children had very few opportunities for education other than the good will of a master or the occasional charity or Sunday School. By the early 1800s things had gotten even worse. Following the Denmark Vessy slave rebellion of 1822 and the Nat Turner uprising a few years later, many southern states passed laws that made the education of slaves illegal.

In the North, educational opportunities for free black children existed during the 1800s, but were limited. A few communities allowed integrated schools, though most would remain segregated throughout this period.

More often than not, free blacks themselves played the greatest role in the primary education of their own children during this period. Black preachers sometimes doubled as teachers following their Sunday sermons and often established schools in their own churches.

The turning point for African-American education, however, was the Civil War. When slavery officially ended in 1865, a new era of educational reform swept the South with the establishment of the Freedmen's Bureau. This agency established by the federal government, settled land disputes and also attended to the educational needs of former slaves by creating The Freedmen's Bureau Schools. These schools fostered what Booker T. Washington called "a veritable fever" for education. Thousands of idealistic, young men and women from the North came south to teach in Freedmen's Bureau schools. At its peak in 1869, there were over 9,000 such teachers in these schools. Their impact was dramatic.

The Backlash during Reconstruction

The Freedmen's Bureau Schools were quite successful. But as a central part of the plan of Reconstruction, they were opposed and resented by many White southerners. In fact, throughout the entire period of Reconstruction (1865–1877), states in the South fought desperately to bring back their conservative governments, destroy the Freedmen's Bureau and generally return things to the way they were prior to the war.

The tactics of intimidation worked well and when Reconstruction ended in 1877, each of the former confederate states returned political power and social control to the "old guard" planting class under newly rewritten state constitutions. While white Southerners called this "victory" redemption, for freedmen and their fragile experiment in education, it seemed more like revenge (Parkerson & Parkerson, 2001).

Education Following Reconstruction

Following Reconstruction most Southerners recognized the pressing need for public education but states typically adopted a system of segregated schools with limited state funding based on a per-capita basis, awarded to individual counties. Under this system wealthier counties received the vast majority of state monies for public education and most of that money went to white schools. Poor "back country" counties, on the other hand, typically received little state funding and blacks received even less (Foner, 1988).

Despite the promise of the 13th, 14th, and 15th Amendments to the U.S. Constitution (the 13th freed the slaves; the 14th provided for the civil rights of the freedmen; and the 15th gave black men the right to vote), the social and economic position of former slaves clearly deteriorated after 1877. In just 35 years, the educational experiment of the Freedmen's Bureau schools had been effectively subverted. Capped with the infamous Supreme Court decision of *Plessy v. Ferguson* (1896) segregated educational facilities were given the false legitimacy of the federal government. It would take another half century until the dark legacy of this era would begin to change.

Despite the lack of support by the federal government and the hostility on the part of state governments throughout the South, African Americans supported their own schools and promoted both primary and secondary education. As we have seen, African American preachers used their churches as make-shift schools that were supported by the local black community. This tradition of self-help was essential for the survival of African American education and later would be embraced by reformers such as Booker T. Washington and W. E. B. Dubois (Anderson, 1995).

EUROPEAN EDUCATIONAL REFORMERS

While problems would continue to plague the common school and its curriculum, new ideas emerging from the reformers of the European enlightenment of the 1700s would begin to energize American education and transform it into a modern system of instruction. These ideas gradually made their way to America by the 1850s. Perhaps the most important influences on American education during this period can be found in the writings of John Locke, Jean Jacque Rousseau, and Johann Pestalozzi. These reformers emphasized the development of the intellect among children and proposed new, humane methods of discipline.

Locke, Rousseau, and Pestalozzi

In his classic work, *Some Thoughts Concerning Education* (1705/1968), John Locke revolutionized our ideas concerning child rearing. Religion influenced traditional views of discipline, nurture, and education such that children were perceived as products of "original sin." The implications of this were that they needed to be saved, were naturally prone to sin, and required strict instruction to correct their wayward minds. Locke, on the other hand, argued that the child's mind was like "white paper void of all characters"— what some have called the *tabula rasa* or "blank slate" (Locke, 1705, p. 199).

As a result, Locke felt that parents and teachers could literally script a child's values and behavior through education. Locke wrote that the most effective method of instruction was to provide powerful incentives of praise for good behavior and achievement but shame and humiliation for those who misbehaved or failed through inattention. In addition, he rejected corporal punishment as the "the most unfit of any to be used in education" (Locke, 1705, p. 201).

Some Thoughts Concerning Education—1693 John Locke

I think I may say, that, of all the men we meet with, nine parts of ten are what they are, good or evil, useful or not, by their education. It is that which makes the great difference in mankind. The little, or almost insensible impressions on our tender infancies, have very important and lasting consequences; and there it is, as in the fountains of some rivers, where a gentle application of the hand turns the flexible waters into channels, that make them take quite contrary courses; and by this little direction, given them at first, in the source, they receive different tendencies and arrive at last at a very remote and distant places. (Binder, 1970)

In his influential work *Emile* (1762), Jean Jacque Rousseau also challenged the prevailing attitudes toward children and education. But while Locke perceived young people's minds as a *tabula rasa* that could be scripted by teachers and parents, Rousseau felt that children had innate intelligence, were born without original sin, but were corrupted by society (see chapter 3.).

Since children brought experiences and ideas to the classroom, Rousseau felt that primary education should be based on the child's experiences and on his or her need to know and understand. Rather than forcing a student to memorize reading passages at a young age, Rousseau argued that reading instruction should begin when the child saw it as necessary. Only then would it be successful. Rousseau's ideas provided the foundation of the learner-centered approach to education as we discussed in chapter 3. Here, the needs of students are central to both the curriculum and instructional methods.

This learner-centered vision was also the basis of Johann Pestalozzi's humanistic approach to education. Like Rousseau, he argued that children were inherently good at birth and that early education should focus on the "objects" and activities of the real world presented to them with love and nurture.

Pestalozzi's instructional methods were simple and he presented them in two novels: *Leonard and Gertrude* (1794) and *How Gertrude Teaches her Children* (1804). In each, Gertrude used everyday items to teach her children. She taught arithmetic by counting the number of steps from one side of the room to another or by counting the panes in a window. She also focused on the critical importance of loving and nurturing children in order for them to learn (Pestalozzi, 1794, 1804).

Pestalozzi's ideas were popularized in this country by a number of educators. During the early 1800s they were successfully adapted by Charles Mayo, who employed them in his "infant schools," and later they were embraced by Froebel as the basis of Kindergarten instruction. By the late 1850s, Edward Sheldon, the founder of the Oswego State Normal School in New York, adopted Pestalozzi's methods of teacher education. Moreover, for the rest of the century, Pestalozzi's ideas were popularized in a series of public lectures known collectively as the Oswego movement (Silber, 1960).

By 1900, the use of familiar "objects" both inside and outside of the classroom had become an accepted part of the primary school curriculum. Map reading, for example, had become a standard component of the history and geography curriculum. Moreover, primary grade teachers typically used physical objects such as desks, chairs, and windowpanes to help children learn.

Similarly, nature walks where students identified plants and animals often supplemented traditional biology texts. Finally, as we shall see, Pestalozzi's nurturing approach to education (the role of love) gradually was accepted as an important instructional and disciplinary model in public schools and forms the core of humanism.

Pestalozzi's School at Yverdon—1818

According to John Griscom's account of Pestalozzi's school in October 1818:

> Very few books are used. . . We saw the exercises of arithmetic, writing, drawing, mathematics, lessons in music and gymnastics, something of geography, French, Latin and German. The teacher (is) constantly with the child, always talking, questioning, explaining and repeating. The pupils, however, by this process, are brought into very close intimacy with the instructor (and) this gives him an advantage which cannot possibly be gained in the ordinary way in which schools are taught. (Binder, 1970)

THE REVOLUTION IN EDUCATION

Building on the enormous contributions of Locke, Rousseau, and Pestalozzi, American educators transformed the schools of late 1800s and the early 1900s. While these reformers represented a variety of different perspectives and advocated a number of different teaching methods, they collectively transformed our ideas on education. Among the most important of these was Herbart and his lesson plan; Kilpatrick and his "project method"; Thorndike and educational measurement; and John Dewey with his enormous contributions of the "laboratory school" and concepts of "learning by doing" to name just two. Each of these powerful figures in their own way contributed to this revolution in teaching.

Herbart and the Lesson Plan

Johann Herbart (1776–1841) was a psychologist who introduced the idea of the structured lesson plan—a template that outlined the five steps of instruction:

- Preparation
- Presentation
- Association
- Generalization
- Application

The Formal Steps of Instruction—Johann Friedrich Herbart

In teaching we need to have:

- **Clearness** in the presentation of specific facts, or the elements of what is to be mastered
- **Association** of these facts with one another
- **Systematic ordering** so that our knowledge will be more perfectly unified
- **Methodical application** in exercises that call forth the vigorous self activity of the pupil

Source: Binder, 1970, adapted from: Herbart, 1835/1970, *"Outlines* of Educational Doctrine," p. 235

Herbart was a disciple of Pestalozzi, especially with his emphasis on learning through the senses and the use of objects. Very simply, Herbart argued that when the interests of the child were stimulated, learning would take place. Today the lesson plan is a central component of instruction (see chapter 9).

William Heard Kilpatrick

During the late 1910s and early 1920s, William Heard Kilpatrick's "project method" became extremely popular among educators. Very simply, the project method involved student learning by means of a "socially purposeful act." Like most progressive educators of this period, Kilpatrick felt that modern world had fragmented the lives of Americans. We had become disconnected from the larger society. The answer to this dilemma was to reestablish those connections through the schools. By involving students in projects like making a dress or putting out a newspaper from start to finish, teachers could direct student learning to socially useful ends and strengthen their connection to the larger society (Kilpatrick, 1933).

William James and Edward Thorndike

While progressives such as Herbart and Kilpatrick revolutionized our ideas of instruction, William James (1842–1910) introduced the concept of "stimulus-response" to explain *how* children learned. As a proponent of what we now call "behavioral psychology" or behaviorism, James argued that children learned by developing habits in response to external stimulation. His classic example of this process involved a baby who reached for a candle's flame as part of a normal reflex. When the baby's finger was burned, however, she learned never to repeat that behavior because the consequences were too painful. While learning did not have to involve pain, according to James, it did involve the use of external stimulation and the development of habits (James, 1890/1950).

Edward Thorndike (1874–1949) expanded on James' ideas. He recommended that all instruction be based on the scientific method and evaluated by scientific instruments. Rigorous educational testing would help teachers choose the most effective instructional methods and direct students to their "most useful role" in society. Thorndike is often considered the father of academic evaluation.

John Watson and B. F. Skinner: Behaviorism

While James and Thorndike pioneered the use of the scientific method in educational research, instruction and testing, John Watson (1878–1958) and B. F. Skinner (1904–1990) popularized educational psychology by broadening its appeal. Their approach called behaviorism has had an enormous impact on education. Watson's research with infants, for example, demonstrated that the *environment was more important than heredity* in regard to achievement. He showed that through proper education and training, any normal child could become an athlete or a doctor. This notion appealed to many educators.

B. F. Skinner, on the other hand, focused on the effect of rewards in the learning process, which became the basis of "programmed learning." While many humanistic scholars have criticized these approaches, behaviorism has had a major effect on the development of educational research and teaching in the last half century (Skinner, 1951).

Characteristics of the Newer Basal Reader Series

1. Many of the stories include a variety of genres and are often pieces of high-quality literature written by famous authors and illustrators.
2. The basal units are composed of integrated themes that can be incorporated into content subjects as well as the language arts.
3. The lessons allow opportunities for listening, speaking, and viewing in the classroom, as well as reading and writing.
4. Emphasis is placed on tapping into students' prior knowledge about a story concept.
5. The teacher's manual gives suggestions for extended literature reading for a particular theme.
6. The manuals give suggestions on promoting parental involvement.

Source: "The Basal is not the Enemy," 1998:
http://www2.selu.edu/Academics/Education/TEC/basal.htm

THE BASAL READER

While each of these ideas certainly did not make their way directly into every classroom in the nation, their collective influence can be seen in reading instruction, especially with the development of basal readers in the early 1920s. These basal readers represented a revolution in reading instruction. They incorporated Pestalozzi and Herbart's ideas of distinctive developmental levels through the use of a controlled vocabulary in conjunction with Pestalozzi's concept of "objects" in the form of vivid illustrations of everyday life. Incorporated as well was Kilpatrick's idea of drawing on the interests and experiences of students by providing familiar settings for the readers. Herbart's idea of the lesson plan in terms of the presentation and review of materials were also utilized. Borrowed as well was the concept of measuring the progress of student comprehension from Thorndike and they drew on Herbart's concepts of sequencing reading materials. The basal readers were the first textbooks to be based on scientific educational research.

What are Basal Readers?

Basal readers are textbooks used to teach reading and related skills to children. Frequently referred to as "reading books," they are usually anthologies that contain previously published short stories, selections from longer pieces of literature, and other selections. Typically, a basal series contains individual student books, a "teacher's edition," and an assortment of workbooks, worksheets, activities, and tests.

Dick and Jane

As the early readers of McGuffey and others were replaced with "basal readers," like the classic "Dick and Jane" series, the gradual shift from memorization to comprehension was nearly complete. Basal readers provided students with graded reading and spelling material accessible for each developmental level. Rather than a first grade student being required to read (and memorize) a passage from Shakespeare, materials were "graded" so that students actually understand what they had read.

Links to the Past: Dick and Jane

Dick and Jane were the main characters in the popular basal readers that were used to teach primary children to read. Originally published in the 1920s, their popularity peaked during the 1950s when 80% of first graders used these books. The stories centered on Dick and Jane, brother and sister, their mother and father, Sally, the baby sister, Spot, the dog and Puff, the cat. The books focused on sight reading and repetition, and did not use phonics.

It is interesting to note, that first editions of these books are now valuable and contemporary memorabilia such as T-shirts, magnets, and calendars are currently available.

THE PROGRESSIVES

As the basal reader gradually made its way into the classrooms of America beginning in the 1920s, socially progressive educators were also introducing other innovative reforms. While there were dozens of important progressives that had an impact on education, John Dewey stands alone. Although the educational community did not always adopt Dewey's enormous contributions during his early career, his work can be seen as a critical link between the ideas of Rousseau and Pestalozzi, the progressives of the early 1900s, the instructional and curricular innovations of the 1960s, and some of the more innovative programs of today (Dworkin, 1959).

John Dewey clearly was influenced by Johann Pestalozzi especially his use of "objects" in the classroom as an instrument of learning. Like Pestalozzi, Dewey felt that learning

Various Progressive Education Plans

John Dewey, the father of progressive education, contended that: schools should reflect society; students should learn by working on projects that relate to their own interests; and learning should be organized around a central theme.

Listed below are some progressive experiments:

- **University of Chicago Laboratory School** (1896–1904) was managed by Alice Dewey, wife of John Dewey. Students were actively engaged in projects and worked in groups. The Lab School of Chicago is still in existence today and continues to be innovative.
- **The Gary Plan** (1908–1915; Gary, Indiana) attempted to reorganize the school building more efficiently. The school building was divided into spaces allocated for specific use, such as classrooms, playground, shops, laboratories, etc. Schools were organized so that every space was in constant use.
- **The Dalton Plan** (1919; Dalton, Massachusetts) divided the curriculum into units that were contracted by students in a specified period of time.
- **The Winnetka Plan** (1919; Winnetka, Illinois) separated the curriculum into subjects and used the Dalton technique. It also employed the use of cooperative social activities as advocated by John Dewey.

could not take place in the abstract. He wrote that students needed to connect the objects of a lesson with the ideas behind them. From this notion Dewey developed his idea of "learning by doing." Rather than learning each aspect of the operation of a grocery store such as buying, selling, and making change, Dewey argued that students should learn the entire operation of the facility by working in a simulated (or play) grocery store. By actually running the store, the connections between each of the elements of its operation would become clearer and learning could take place (Dewey, 1899).

For Dewey then, the abstract, subject orientation of teaching, so common in schools at that time, had caused students to lose their sense of wholeness and interconnectedness with society (Dewey, 1916).

As a result, he argued that the primary role of the school should be to help reacquaint students with the fundamental interdependency of society. For Dewey, no man was an island, despite America's ongoing love affair with "rugged individualism." As a result, he favored an "open classroom" environment where students could work in groups, learn to cooperate with one another, and grapple with real social problems in the context of classroom activities. In their famous Lab School, established by John and his wife Alice Chipman Dewey at the University of Chicago, many of these ideas were successfully implemented (Dewey, 1916).

CURRICULAR INNOVATIONS OF THE 1960S AND BEYOND

The Deweys' emphasis on innovative, socially responsible group instruction, linked to rigorous scientific evaluation, became the basis of the progressive education movement of the 1920s and 1930s. In turn, many of these progressive forms of instruction provided the basis of curricular innovations of later years, from the 1960s to the present. Of these, inquiry-based instruction, individual contracting, preschool education, multi-age grouping, differential staffing, flexible scheduling, team teaching the open classroom, whole language and magnet schools are the most well known. Each of these innovations, moreover, owes an intellectual debt to the progressives (Dewey, 1916).

Whole Language

Whole language teaching emphasizes reading through an integration of language arts skills with a special emphasis on literature. Whole language rejects the use of phonics as the primary method of learning to read. Even relatively new instructional programs such as *whole language* are rooted in the ideas of the social progressives, especially John Dewey. The developers of whole language argued that (following Dewey) reading should not be an abstract process but a holistic one that consists of the text, the reader, and the social context of the student. Moreover, since reading, spelling, handwriting, etc., were learned in the same way children develop oral language; these subjects should be taught as a whole and not fragmented into isolated subject areas.

THE RECENT STRUGGLE TO CONTROL
CURRICULUM AND INSTRUCTION

As teachers embraced innovations such as the basal reader, the open classroom, and programs like whole language, they paid an enormous *social* and *political* price. Whole language, as we have seen, integrates all the language skills in the process of learning to read and write and emphasizes the expression of ideas rather than the correct spelling of words. To individuals outside the classroom, this technique seemed remote and abstract and suggested to parents that teachers were "dumbing down" the material. Similarly, the simplified language of the basal readers appeared remedial and the apparent lack of structure in the open classroom often irritated them.

On the other hand, parents of the 1800s were often inspired by the spectacle of their young children competing in a spelling bee, reading a piece of classical literature, or reciting a famous speech by one of the founding fathers. Moreover, parents routinely observed their child's progress during year-end examinations. This *validated* the educational experience for them.

With the emergence of the graded school however, direct parental observation and evaluation gradually became more limited. Other than the annual open house or the occasional school play, parents had few formal opportunities to see what actually was happening in the classroom.

During the late 1970s, a broad-based educational backlash had begun. As the cost of education rose, due in part to the extension of services and programs to disadvantaged children, and as standardized test scores continued to fall, due in part to the larger and more diverse groups of students actually taking those standardized tests, some Americans demanded changes in education. For example, a number of conservatives rejected the more innovative progressive-based educational programs that had been initiated during the 1960s. They claimed that these programs lacked rigor and academic credibility and were seen as damaging our competitive position in the emerging global economy. Of course, Americans were the most productive in the world during this period—and continue to be so today—but the sluggish economy of the late 1970s seemed to validate their criticisms (Spring, 1990).

Others argued that the solution to our "educational crisis" was greater student accountability through "competency based" instructional programs rooted in the behaviorist psychology of B. F. Skinner and Edward Thorndike. Still others rejected the basal reader and instructional methods such as whole language and demanded and in some cases actually *legislated* phonics, and memorization as the primary method of reading instruction. Some schools even resurrected "Old Guff," requiring the McGuffey Readers be used as the basis of reading instruction.

By the early 1980s, the educational backlash reached a crescendo with the publication of *A Nation at Risk* (1983; see chapter 2). This controversial document warned the American people that "for the first time in the history of our country, the educational skills of one generation will not surpass, will not equal, will not even approach those of their parents" (National Commission on Excellence in Education, 1983).

The language of this report alarmed many Americans and added further momentum to the educational backlash. By the end of the decade, many conservative political leaders were calling for wide-ranging reforms in education such as "privatization" of public education where for-profit companies would be engaged as education providers.

This micromanagement of the curriculum by local communities and state legislators has also become a persistent reality in recent years. State legislators often mandate that schools include politically popular subjects in the curriculum. These have included drug education and abstinence education programs instituted throughout the country. And of course, pressure to ban certain books from school libraries and from use in the classroom has long been a reality in our schools. Classics like William Shakespeare's *Romeo and Juliet*, Mark Twain's *Huckleberry Finn*, Nathaniel Hawthorne's *The Scarlet Letter,* as well as a host of more contemporary works like J. D. Salinger's *The Catcher in the Rye*, and all of Judy Blume's books, have been banned in some primary and secondary school libraries throughout the nation. Other schools simply remove the "dirty words" or controversial material from these and many other books and leave them on the shelf.

These forms of censorship, of course, have been challenged over the years by vigorous action of professional educational organizations as well as informed exchange within the field of education itself. Throughout this exchange, the secondary (and primary) curriculum has been reshaped and reformed by professional educators. Sometimes these reforms have been implemented in response to critics of the curriculum and sometimes they were made in anticipation of that criticism. For the most part, however, these changes were grounded in educational research and not the whims of the politicians.

Journaling Activity

Go to the American Library Association Web site listed below and make a list of the 10 most frequently challenged books. Why do you think that these books are challenged? What is your position on censorship in schools?

http://www.ala.org/ala/oif/bannedbooksweek/bbwlinks/100mostfrequently.htm

The work of teachers in the classroom is complex and difficult. Nevertheless, our profession has never been so prepared, so well educated, and as talented as it is today. Despite the external and internal pressures on the schools, teachers have endured in the past, and clearly we will teach the children well as we forge into the 21st century.

SUMMARY

The link between European educational forms and American education was the Reformation of the 1500s and 1600s. It was this religious tumult that directly led to the settlement of the Puritan colony of Massachusetts Bay and the American education revolution that followed.

Colonial Education

The Puritans settled the Massachusetts Bay Colony in the early 1600 and launched the first comprehensive system of universal primary education in America. Since Puritan leaders felt strongly that the ability to read the Bible would help thwart the delusions of Satan, they passed a series of educational laws including the colony's first compulsory education law in 1647—the Old Deluder Law. So powerful was this educational model that it spread west as New Englanders migrated to New York and the upper Midwest in the next two centuries and became the basis of the common school movement of the nineteenth century. In addition to the New England model of education the middle colonies experimented with a variety of private schools and academies that centered on religious and moral education. In the South, tutors were employed to teach the children of plantation owners while a handful of charity schools provided some education for the poor. Slaves on the other hand were often forbidden to receive an education.

The Common School Movement

From the beginning of our nation's history, the founding fathers understood that American children needed a common set of cultural and social experiences in order to appreciate the concepts of nationhood and civic responsibility. Earlier educational experiments during the colonial period were simply too uneven and too narrowly centered on religious training. While it would take over a generation to realize the educational dreams of these and other reformers, the common school movement took root and began to grow in the first half of the 1800s. Common school teachers embraced a curriculum that would nurture a passionate patriotism among their young charges and promote the values of the new market economy—especially hard work, competition, and achievement. It was during this time that the examination emerged as an important instrument of evaluation.

Problems in the Common School

But while the common school sought to encourage patriotism and develop the values of the marketplace among diverse Americans, its curriculum was rooted in the values and culture of Protestantism. This would eventually cause problems for the common school. European immigrants, for example, often rejected the protestant values of temperance and prohibition that had become an important component of the public school curriculum. For these new Americans, this moral focus conflicted with their cultural beliefs. Moreover, since virtually all instruction at the primary and secondary level was given in English, many immigrants suffered. German-, Polish-, Russian-, and Italian-speaking immigrants, for example, resented English-only instruction that often branded their children as deficient and even ignorant because they had difficulty speaking English. This problem persists today with some new Asian and Hispanic immigrants.

While the cultural conflict between the dominant Protestant population and other Christian and non-Christian people would continue to rage in the common schools throughout the 1800s, the question of race would ultimately have a deeper and more lasting impact on public education in this country. African American slaves, of course, typically were not afforded educational opportunities. In fact, some states passed laws prohibiting them from receiving an education. Following emancipation however things did change—especially with the creation of the Freedman's Bureau Schools established throughout the South. But initial excitement soon waned and a form of segregated schools was established in most southern states. The famous Supreme Court decision *Plessy v. Ferguson (1896)* capped this legalized segregation until *Brown v. Board of Education (1954)* opened the doors for integration of all American public schools.

European and American Educational Reform

While problems would continue to plague the common school and its curriculum, new ideas would begin to energize American education and transform it into a modern system of instruction. This transition would begin in Europe and gradually make its way to the United States. The most import influences on American education during this period can be found in the writings of John Locke, Jean Jacque Rousseau, and Johann Pestalozzi.

By the late 1800s and early 1900s, teachers began to improve instruction by introducing innovations into the classroom that were based on scientific, educational research. Among the most important of these were Herbart's lesson plan; Kilpatrick's "project method;" Thorndike's educational measurement, and Dewey's enormous contributions of the "laboratory school" and concepts of "learning by doing." Each of these powerful figures in their own way contributed to a virtual revolution in teaching.

Implementing Reforms in the Schools

The collective influence of these and other educators clearly can be seen in reading instruction, especially with the development of basal readers in the early 1920s. These readers incorporated Pestalozzi and Herbart's ideas of distinctive developmental levels through the use of a controlled vocabulary. They used Kilpatrick's idea of drawing on the interests and experiences of students by providing familiar settings for the readers. They drew on Herbart's idea of the lesson plan in terms of the presentation and review of materials. They used Pestalozzi's concept of "objects" in the form of vivid illustrations of everyday life. They borrowed the concept of measuring the progress of student comprehension from Thorndike and they drew on Herbart's concepts of sequencing reading materials. The basal readers were the first to be based on scientific educational research.

As the basal reader gradually made its way into the classrooms of America beginning in the 1920s, socially progressive educators were also introducing other innovative reforms. In turn, many of the progressive forms of instruction that emerged from that movement provided the basis of curricular innovations of later years, from the 1960s to the present. Of these, inquiry based instruction, individual contracting, preschool education, multi-age grouping, differential staffing, flexible scheduling, team teaching, the open classroom and whole language instruction are the most well known. Each of these innovations, moreover, owes an intellectual debt to the progressives.

Reform and Reaction in Contemporary Education

As teachers embraced innovations such as the basal reader, the open classroom and programs like whole language they paid an enormous *social* and *political* price. Since parents had few opportunities to see what actually was happening in the classroom other than the annual open house or the occasional school play, they often were puzzled, perhaps even annoyed, by what they saw. The simplified language of the basal readers appeared remedial and the apparent lack of structure in the open classroom often irritated them. More recently, the emphasis on writing and expression in whole language—where spelling words correctly is *less important* than the expression of ideas—seemed remote, abstract, and suggested a "dumbing down" of material. At the same time some rejected the more innovative progressive-based educational programs that had been initiated during the 1960s. They claimed that these programs lacked rigor and academic credibility and might damage our competitive position in the emerging global economy. By the early 1980s, the educational backlash reached a crescendo with the publication of *A Nation at Risk* (1983). The language of this report alarmed many Americans and added further momentum to the educational backlash.

Despite these criticisms however it is clear that teachers have never been so prepared, so well educated, or as talented as they are today. Despite the unending criticisms teachers have endured in the past and clearly will teach the children well as we forge into the 21st century.

DISCUSSION QUESTIONS

1. What is the significance of the "Old Deluder Law" for American education? Discuss.
2. What was the Common School? Who supported its development? Why was it important?

3. Why was there so much conflict regarding the curriculum of the common school? Discuss the basis of this conflict. Has it ever been resolved?
4. Discuss the educational opportunities of African American children before the Civil War and during Reconstruction. What role does the *Plessy v. Ferguson (1896)* play?
5. Briefly discuss the important European educational reformers of the 1800s. What role did they play in the development of Progressive education?
6. What was the "Lab School?" Discuss the role of John Dewey and Alice Dewey in the establishment of the Lab School.
7. Discuss some of the great Progressive educators. Briefly describe their contributions to education today.
8. Discuss the conservative backlash against progressive education.

Chapter 7

America's Diverse Society

Today some Americans still believe that our nation was once ethnically and racially homogeneous and that our multicultural society is a recent development. Others see the traditional subjugation of immigrants and people of color as part of our national heritage. Most educated Americans recognize that xenophobic ideas and discrimination are dangerous. As an American teacher you have a responsibility to correctly inform students about the true nature of our heterogeneous society. It is up to you to provide them with a true image of our society and the multicultural history which created it.

The distinctive ethnic settlements of colonial America, the major immigration of Europeans, the northern migration of African Americans, and the immigration of Asians and Hispanics have contributed to our present multicultural society. Ethnic, religious, and racial diversity has been the rule and not the exception in America. Yet, throughout American history, each religious and ethnic group faced discrimination as they have attempted to assimilate into society. As teachers we need to understand the nature and reasons for this discrimination in the past and recognize how those patterns persist today so we can demonstrate inclusive attitudes to our students. By embracing religious, ethnic, and diversity in general, in our classrooms, we can create a more supportive and nurturing environment in which all our students can learn.

ETHNIC AND RELIGIOUS DIVERSITY IN COLONIAL AMERICA

During the 1600s and early 1700s the colonies of New England, Massachusetts, Rhode Island, Connecticut, and Vermont were settled by staunch Puritans (Calvinists) from England, remaining relatively homogenous. While this region would gradually become more diverse later in the colonial period, in the middle colonies of New York, New Jersey, and Pennsylvania, distinct ethnic communities were a prominent feature of early settlement.

Middle Colonies

Throughout much of its settlement history, New York enjoyed a rich diversity of ethnic people and religious groups. During the early 1600s, for example, New York (called New Amsterdam before the British seized the colony from Holland) was an amalgam of ethnic people. As one contemporary observer noted, at least 18 different languages were spoken in and near New York City. The Dutch established a large settlement in the central region of the city that eventually extended north into the Hudson River Valley. On Long Island, English settlers dominated, but scattered throughout the colony were Norwegians, Danes, Jews, Irish, Scots Irish, and Germans (Axtell, 1985; Elliot, 2006).

The religious diversity among the ethnic groups of New York was even more striking. As a result of the open immigration policies of the Dutch in the 1600s, many religiously oppressed groups such as the French-speaking Walloons (Protestant exiles from the lower Netherlands), French Huguenots, Baptists, Quakers, Presbyterians, Lutherans, and Mennonites made there way to the colony. During the 1700s the colony became even more diverse with the arrival of French Calvinists, French Lutherans, Sabbatarians, Anti-Sabbatarians, Anabaptists, Independents, and even Dunkers. Each of these groups found a measure of religious freedom in New York State (Ellis, Frost, Syrett, & Carman, 1957).

New Jersey was originally part of the colony of New York and it too had a rich ethnic and religious heritage, though not as diverse as New York or Pennsylvania. During the 1600s, Quakers settled the western part of the colony with Dutch and Swedish settlers in the east. Then, as migration from New York and New England began in the 1700s, thousands of Scottish, Scots Irish, Germans, and displaced New Englanders flooded into the colony (Axtell, 1985).

The most diverse of all the middle colonies, however, was Pennsylvania. Since William Penn founded it in the early 1600s, Pennsylvania had become a refuge for people who had been persecuted for their religious beliefs. Penn had originally envisioned the colony as a haven for Quakers (Friends) which was established on the principle of religious freedom guaranteed by the "Great Law," enacted by the colonial Assembly in the 1680s. Thousands of colonial "dissenters" from Connecticut and other parts of New England settled in Pennsylvania's rich Wyoming Valley. Similarly, many Europeans, who had been persecuted because of their religious beliefs or who had been displaced because of economic change, also sought asylum in Pennsylvania. In addition, thousands of Scotch-Irish and Germans who had also suffered religious persecution migrated to Pennsylvania and settled in the foothills of the Appalachians. By the time of the American Revolution, it was estimated that at least 30 different German religious groups were living in Lancaster County, Pennsylvania alone (Bronner, 1962; Schwartz, 1987).

Southern Colonies

Like the middle colonies, the South had a rich mixture of ethnic people. From Virginia to South Carolina, English and Welsh Anglicans had settled and dominated throughout much of the colonial period. There also were numerous pockets of other ethnic groups throughout these colonies. In the southern piedmont and coastal plain of North Carolina, for example, there were large settlements of Scots Highlanders and Scotch-Irish who had migrated to the colony during the 1700s. There also were numerous isolated settlements of German and Swiss farmers in the foothills of the Carolinas extending south through Georgia. In the coastal communities around Baltimore, Roman Catholics who had escaped the ravages of religious wars in the 1600s settled there.

While more than 100,000 Germans and 250,000 Scots-Irish came to America during this period, by far the largest immigrant group was African slaves who were brought here in bondage. Dutch traders transported the first slaves to Jamestown in 1619 and their importation continued through the beginning of the 1800s. Prior to the American Revolution it was estimated that more than 300,000 slaves had been brought to this country (Gomez, 2005, 2006).

Slaves came from many ethnic and tribal groups in Africa but most were from Angola, the Gold Coast, the Bight of Biafra, and Senegambia in West Africa. Some slaves were transported to the Caribbean to labor in large sugar cane plantations. Others were brought to the American colonies and worked on both rice and later cotton plantations. By the eve of the American Revolution, the colonies reflected a rich mixture of ethnic people from all over Europe and Africa (Gomez, 2005, 2006; Simmons, 1976).

EDUCATION DURING THE COLONIAL PERIOD

The rich ethnic and religious mixture of the colonies was reflected in their schools. In New England, schools were established in the early 1600s to promote Bible reading and Calvinist religious beliefs. Although not all children attended, these schools provided an early example of public education for the nation. In the middle colonies the ethnic and religious diversity of the region was reflected in a wide range of schools, each centering on religion and moral education and each serving the communities in which they were established. Finally in the South, private schools and in-home tutoring for wealthy planter children was the norm. Black slaves and poor white children, however, had few educational opportunities.

MIGRATION IN THE 19TH CENTURY

As the new nation developed, the number of immigrants from abroad grew steadily. During the first decades of the 19th century, thousands of immigrants arrived in the new United States, continuing the general settlement pattern established during the colonial period. Beginning from the 1830s through to the 1880s, the number of new arrivals increased dramatically to more than 9 million people (U.S. Bureau of the Census, 1961).

The Old Migration

The immigrants of this period (1830–1861) hailed from countries all over the world, including nearly a quarter million from China. The majority, however, came from northern and western Europe. These included families from Great Britain, Scandinavia, Ireland, and Germany. They settled primarily in northern cities along the Atlantic coast where factory and laboring jobs were plentiful, but hundreds of thousands of Germans (and others) pushed further west and settled in the areas that would soon become the Midwestern states of Indiana, Illinois, and Wisconsin (U.S. Bureau of the Census, 1961).

Immigrants came to the United States for a variety of reasons, but generally to escape poverty, oppression, and religious intolerance in their native lands. Over 1.8 million Irish immigrants fled their homeland as the potato famine swept across the land. During this very difficult period more than 1 million Irish farmers died of starvation. At the same time, hundreds of thousands of British immigrants left England because of lack of employment, and over a million Germans left their homeland because of religious intolerance (U.S. Bureau of the Census. 1961).

EDUCATION BEFORE THE CIVIL WAR

As we have seen, the common school gradually emerged in the United States during the first half of the 1800s. Although many saw these institutions as providing a solution to the basic education needs of all young Americans, the curriculum of the common school was rooted in Protestantism. While this approach worked in homogeneous white Protestant communities, as our society became more diverse, its parochial nature was exposed. Some immigrants, such as Germans, did not speak English, and felt excluded in English-speaking schools. As a solution, many immigrants established their own schools that were taught in their native language. Others, such as the Irish, found the common school curriculum offensive to their religious beliefs, objecting to the use of the King James Bible and Protestant prayers as the basis of moral lessons. As a result, by the end of the 1800s many Catholics established their own parochial schools (see chapter 6.).

The New Wave of Immigration

Following the American Civil War (1861–1865), the face of immigration slowly began to change and from the 1880s to the onset of World War I settlers from southern and eastern Europe made there way to this country. While Irish, English, and Germans would continue to move to the United States during this period, these more recent immigrants were Italians, Hungarians, Poles, Russians, and Jews. The number of immigrants to the United States during this period was unparalleled in American history. Between 1880 and the onset of World War I, nearly 35 million arrived in this country. These new Americans brought their diverse cultures and provided much of the labor that energized the American economy (U.S. Bureau of the Census, 1961).

Despite their enormous contributions to American life, by the end of World War I, there was a growing resentment against immigrants. Their numbers alarmed Americans and because of the faltering economy of the early 1920s, they were seen as taking jobs from "real" Americans. In 1921, and again in 1924, Congress passed immigration quota laws; then in 1927, it passed the National Origins Act, limiting the number of European immigrants to 150,000 per year. With the exception of the Chinese Exclusion Act of 1882, this was the first major immigrant restriction legislation at the national level.

One of unintended consequences of these quotas was a dramatic change in the nature of immigration and migration. Because fewer European immigrants were coming to America, the door of opportunity opened slightly for African Americans, Mexicans, and Puerto Ricans. These new migrants would eventually transform northern cities into the multicultural centers that they are today.

EDUCATION AFTER THE CIVIL WAR

As the nation became more ethnically and religiously diverse, educators attempted to assimilate new immigrants and promote the idea of America as the cultural melting pot. Schools taught patriotic values designed to develop good citizens. In order to produce efficient workers, they emphasized hard work, promptness, and persistence. Many immigrants received a basic education that enabled them to read, write, and perform simple math. This knowledge allowed them to obtain jobs and helped them adapt to their new world. However, the struggle to maintain the language and values of their homeland while they assimilated to their new nation would continue. Sensitive teachers throughout this period understood this dilemma and often reached out to immigrant children to help them learn. Today, as a new generation of immigrants grapple with similar problems, American teachers try to create classrooms where all children can learn. We must continue this important tradition.

AFRICAN AMERICANS MOVE NORTH

When the United States entered the war in 1917, over 4 million American men were sent to Europe to fight. This situation led to a severe shortage of workers and American manufacturers began to recruit African-Americans through factory labor agents and advertisements in newspapers (Henri, 1975).

Links to the Past: Living with Jim Crow

Many African Americans who lived in the South moved to the North in the 1920s. They were striving to find a better life. Many were encouraged by the black newspaper, the *Chicago Defender*, and wrote letters such as the ones below inquiring about work and living conditions:

Troy, Ala, Oct. 17, 1916

Dear Sirs: I am enclosing a clipping of a lynching again which speaks for itself. I do wish there could be sufficient pressure brought about to have federal investigations of such work. I wrote you a few days ago if you could furnish me with the addresses of some firms or co-operations that needed common labor. So many of our people are starving . . . quite a number here would go anywhere to better their conditions. If you can do any thing for us write me as early as possible.

Bryan, Tex., Sept. 13, 1917

Dear Sir: I am writing you as I would like to no if you no of any R.R. Co. and MFG. that are in need for colored labors. I want to bring a bunch of race men out of the south we want work some where north will come if we can git passe any whear across the Mason & Dickson. Please let me hear from you at once if you can git passes for 10 or 12 men. Send at once. (Meltzer, 1967, p. 4)

Reflection

What were the concerns of many African American people during this period? Why did they want to come to the North? How would a lynching affect you, your family, and your community?

THE GREAT MIGRATION

During what historians call the period of Jim Crow (1877–1920), many African Americans wanted to leave behind the hostile attitudes of the South and were determined to start new lives in the North. By 1920, over 300,000 blacks had moved to Chicago's South Side with thousands of others moving to Midwestern cities such as Cleveland and Detroit. New York's Harlem also became a major destination for blacks, especially during the 1920s, with over 87,000 settling in that one neighborhood alone (Henri, 1975).

A steady migration of African Americans would continue throughout the 1920s. During the years of the Great Depression in the 1930s, the numbers of blacks moving North slowed but their migration increased dramatically once again during World War II, the 1950s and through the 1960s. The early 1900s is known as the Great Migration when over a half million African Americans permanently left the South for the North (Henri, 1975; Sernett, 1997). In recent years, however, there has been a significant "return migration" with thousands of African Americans returning south to a much more tolerant and open southern society.

Links to the Past: Discrimination and Segregation

During the period of Jim Crow, state laws effectively segregated public accommodations and transportation facilities. This not only humiliated black people but made it difficult for them to make a living. The following account of travel to Texas illustrates this problem.

When William Pickens traveled to Texas to visit friends, he encountered humiliation and degradation. When he arrived at the train station in El Paso, his friends were not there to meet him. So William had to walk through the nice, well-equipped station to a "hole in the wall" for Negroes. Mexicans, Native Americans, and Chinese were allowed to use the nice section of the station along with white people. Just the blacks were segregated into the dreary room.

On his way back home, he was not allowed to use the sleeping car for the twenty-four hour trip. Even though he had paid for a sleeper, he had to sit-up in the "Jim Crow car" which was actually the back of the smoking car, separated by a partition. Smoke filled this section of the car. For an additional fee, he received a pillow. The next morning he went to the dining car early for breakfast, before the white people were awake. The porters left him waiting while they decided what to do with him. Finally, he was seated in the back of the dining car where the porters ate. They pulled the curtain across the car, so that if whites entered the car, they would not see him. (Meltzer, 1967, p. 5)

Reflection

Describe some of the more subtle ways that African Americans were discriminated against during this period. How do you think William Pickens felt during his journey? How would you feel under similar circumstances?

Journaling Activity

What does the term de facto segregation mean? Compare and contrast it with the term de jure segregation. Are public schools in your community segregated? Describe what type of segregation that exists in some communities today. Record your responses in your journal.

EDUCATION OF AFRICAN AMERICANS BEFORE INTEGRATION

One of the key reasons that African Americans left the South during this period was a lack of educational opportunities for their children. Due to official policies of segregation, black children were forbidden by law to attend white schools and as a result were either forced into poorly equipped black schools or excluded altogether. As a result, illiteracy among black children during this period was nearly 50%. Opportunities for education in the North were much better during this period but there were problems nevertheless. After a half century struggle for civil rights, monumental Supreme Court decisions—including Brown v. Board of Education (1954)—and aggressive legislation during the 1960s—including the Civil Rights Act of 1964—African American children now have access to a first-rate education. By developing policies of inclusion and modeling accepting behavior for our students though, we create democratic classrooms where all children regardless of skin color, learn (Anderson, 1988; Williams, 2005).

MEXICAN SETTLEMENT AND IMMIGRATION

Mexicans, like some African Americans, were able to take advantage of the changes in immigration law during the 1920s and migrate north for jobs. Like African Americans, Mexicans have also had a long history of settlement in the United States. For centuries, Mexican people lived in the old southwest and in southern California. Their rich heritage is found everywhere in the West. In fact, prior to the War of 1846, Mexico controlled much of what is now the western part of the United States. The Treaty of Guadalupe Hidalgo (1848), which ended the Mexican War, provided that the United States take possession of over one million square miles of land and assume political control over the region.

Mexican Migration in the 1920s

During the 1920s, many Mexican people took advantage of America's new immigration policies and came to this country for jobs and a new life. By the end of the 1920s, they comprised one of the nation's largest immigrant groups with nearly 500,000 residents. In Los Angeles alone, Mexican immigrants represented about a fifth of the entire population (U.S. Bureau of the Census, 1961).

Reflection
Why did the level of Mexican immigration increase during the 1920s?

Education of Mexican Immigrants

During this period, many Mexican children attended school around the schedule of agricultural work. In the off season, some attended classes if they remained in this country but many returned to their homeland with their families. Well meaning teachers understood these problems and often tried to help these children catch-up by working with them individually, in small groups, or having another student or resident of the community who was fluent in Spanish tutor them. Unfortunately, there were few official bilingual programs available to these children. Rather, the policy of "submersion"—English only instruction—was common at the time.

PUERTO RICAN MIGRATION

In addition to America's growing Mexican population, in the West, were thousands of Puerto Ricans who immigrated to this country during the first decades of the 20th century. Puerto Rico had become a U.S. possession following the Spanish American War in 1898 and then in 1918 Congress passed the Jones Act which gave Puerto Rican people United States citizenship. As the United States entered World War I, the government recruited more than 10,000 Puerto Rican laborers to work in the war-related industries. In addition, as the harvesting of Puerto Rico's principal crop, sugar cane, became more mechanized during this period, nearly 40% of the poor agricultural laborers on that island moved to the United States. One important destination was New York City's East Harlem (Coto-Thorner, 1967; Cruz, 1998; Fernandez, 1996).

Links to the Past: Puerto Rican Immigrants

During the 1920s, a steady stream of Puerto Rican immigrants arrived in New York. The mechanization of Puerto Rico's sugarcane crop pushed almost half of the people out of their native land. They were seeking work elsewhere and many settled in New York City. The migration continued, on and off through the 1960s, when New York City actually had more Puerto Ricans than San Juan. The Puerto Rican neighborhood or El Barrio had groceries, stores, restaurants, and churches that were designed to serve the Latin community. As one resident noted: "This is our neighborhood, El Barrio.It's said that we Latins run things here." El Barrio created a little bit of home for these immigrants living in a foreign land. (Coto-Thorner, 1967)

HARD TIMES AND HISPANIC IMMIGRANTS

As hard economic times descended on the country during the 1930s, the number of Mexican and Puerto Rican immigrant populations declined sharply. Jobs were no longer plentiful and the few that did exist often were reserved for white Americans. A familiar pattern of prejudice, typical during periods of economic slowdown, had emerged. In California, thousands of Mexican farm workers were deported. In fact, more than a quarter of a million were forcibly returned during the dark years of the Depression (Acuna, 1988).

Reflection

Why was El Barrio so important to Puerto Rican immigrants? Compare El Barrio with other ethnic neighborhoods with which you may be familiar.

EDUCATION OF HISPANIC AMERICANS

Today, many schools have developed effective language programs that help Spanish-speaking children learn. These include bilingual education where children are taught in both English and Spanish during their first years in school and then gradually are introduced to English-only instruction. Other programs include structured immersion where Spanish-speaking children receive English-only instruction from a bilingual teacher who encourages them to speak English. Finally, English as a Second Language programs (ESL) have emerged in recent years. Here teachers instruct students in Spanish in a few subjects while making a transition to English instruction. These programs have dramatically helped Hispanic children succeed in the classroom, remain in school, and assimilate to the broader culture.

EARLY ASIAN MIGRATION

In addition to the immigrants from southern and eastern Europe, African Americans from the South, as well as Mexicans, and Puerto Ricans, hundreds of thousands of Chinese and Japanese migrated to the United States and Hawaii during this period. Chinese migration to the United States actually began in the early 1850s when news of California's gold rush spread across the Pacific. Lured to what was called the "Land of Golden Mountains," thousands of immigrants from southern China made their way to this country. By the time the Chinese Exclusion Act of 1882 was enacted, over a quarter of a million Chinese had settled in the West. As a result of this federal legislation Chinese immigration virtually ceased for over 60 years (U.S. Bureau of the Census, 1961).

As Chinese immigration slowed however, Japanese people began to settle in both Hawaii and California. Although early on there had been a number of small Japanese settlements in both of these locations, it wasn't until the 1890s that their numbers increased significantly. Between 1890 and 1900, for example, the number of Japanese in California grew tenfold from about 2,000 settlers to over 24,000. During this same period, the number of Japanese immigrants in Hawaii grew by over 50,000 from about 6,000 to over 60,000. The Japanese in California had a much more difficult time politically, socially, and economically than those who settled in Hawaii. But despite these problems, they continued to immigrate to the Golden State with their numbers reaching nearly 140,000 just prior to WWII (Takaki, 1993).

JAPANESE IN RELOCATION CAMPS

During World War II, discrimination towards the Japanese immigrants became even more evident. The Japanese attack on Pearl Harbor on December 7, 1941 not only brought the United States into World War II, it also made life for foreign-born Japanese Americans (Issei) and American-born Japanese Americans (Nisei) unbearable. Energized by the tragic events in Hawaii, politicians through the states (especially West Coast states) demanded a solution to the "Japanese Problem." Eventually they convinced President Franklin Roosevelt that this was a serious issue and on February 19, 1942 he reluctantly signed Executive Order 9066 to move "dangerous persons" (notably Japanese) to "relocation camps." By August of that year, more than 110,000 Japanese (64% of whom were American citizens) were forced from their homes and placed in remote camps located in California, Arizona, Colorado, Wyoming, Utah, and Arkansas (Wegyln, 1996). In 1944, the Supreme Court decision Endo v. United States declared the camps unconstitutional and soon they were closed.

Reflection
Why were Japanese Americans sent to camps during WWII? Did they present a danger to national security? Do you think something like this could happen again? Why?

Japanese Postwar Migration

Many Japanese did not return to their former homes. Thousands chose to establish communities in Midwestern cities, like Chicago, Cleveland, and Minneapolis. For example, over 10,000 Japanese settled in Chicago in the immediate postwar period. Others made their way to the East Coast and established communities in New York City and New Jersey (Brooks, 2000).

Today Japanese are respected members of our society and play an important role in on our political, cultural, and social life. The acceptance of Japanese culture and our embrace of their food testify to the inclusion of Japanese in the United States.

Links to the Past: Japanese Internment

During World War II, under Executive Order 9066, 110,000 Japanese-Americans (64% of whom were U.S. citizens) were placed in Detention Camps. The following are descriptions by some Japanese residents of the camps.

"I was separated from my husband: he went to the Santa Fe, New Mexico, camp. All of our letters were censored: all our letters were cut in parts and all that. So we were not sure what messages were getting through..." While Kazue was detained in another camp with her children and mother and father-in-law, her mother-in-law became quite ill and died. Her husband was not allowed to come back for the funeral for his own mother. Kazue's son was old enough to realize what was going on and asked his mother many times "why?" Like many other Japanese, Kazue had no explanation for what was happening to them. (Tateishi, 1999, pp. 125–126)

THE CHANGING FACE OF IMMIGRATION

The 1960s brought many changes to this nation, including a new policy on immigration embodied in the Immigration Act of 1965. By shifting our immigration quotas from those based on an individual's nation of origin (established during the 1920s) to ones based on economic need or ideology, this law changed the face of migration. Gone were the millions of Europeans and African Americans from the rural South searching and struggling for opportunities in the north. Now Asian and Hispanic (Spanish-speaking) people formed the centerpiece of America's new immigrant population.

In the early 1960s relatively few immigrants came from countries in Asia, Mexico, and other Latin American and Caribbean nations. But by the early 1970s nearly 40% of all immigrants were Asian and about half came from countries south of our border. In addition to Mexicans, Puerto Ricans, and Cubans other Hispanic immigrants from El Salvador, Guatemala, Nicaragua, and Honduras were making their way to this country. Today, Hispanic and Asian people represent the largest immigrant groups in this country (U.S. Bureau of Census, 2000).

THE ASIAN IMMIGRATION: A TALE OF TWO CULTURES

By the early 1980s, the number of Asian immigrants to the United States had increased dramatically. Thousands of Samoans, Koreans, Taiwanese, Filipinos, Cambodians, and Vietnamese people joined Japanese and Chinese Americans and settled in southern California and other parts of the nation.

South Asians

Typically, south Asians, Indians, and Filipinos as well as Chinese and Koreans were middle class when they arrived in this country and as a result, their assimilation has been much smoother than other groups. Their enrollment in primary, secondary, and postsecondary educational institutions is among the highest in the country and they also have higher levels of business ownership than most immigrants. Maintaining their old world culture was important to them, as was assimilating to the norms of the new world. Like the Japanese before them, these immigrants embraced a set of middle class values that not only allowed them to participate fully in the American economy but helped their children to achieve in school. Young Japanese, Asians, Indians, Filipinos, Chinese, and Koreans were encouraged to learn English and embrace the powerful material culture of America. This "will to assimilate" has helped many "new Asians" do well in school and adjust to life in the United States (Portes & Rumbaut, 1996).

Southeastern Asians

On the other hand, the experiences of Southeastern Asians such as Cambodians and Vietnamese have been different. Like millions of immigrants before them, these agricultural-based people lack the skills necessary to compete in U.S. cities for jobs and as refugees, many suffer a kind of psychic trauma because of their exile from repressive and war-torn nations. As a result of these experiences, many of these immigrants have been preoccupied with coming to terms with their personal history and as such have often preferred to settle in ethnic communities, not mainstream America. While this has provided them with a refuge from the unfamiliar American society, it has also slowed both their assimilation into society and their achievement in school. As American teachers we must reach out to any immigrant in this situation to understand their cultures, styles of learning, and tap into their persistence and determination so they can succeed. In this way, we can help them to achieve in school, assimilate into our society, and adapt to their new world (Portes & Rumbaut, 1996).

CUBANS

In the late 1950s and early 1960s, Hispanic immigrants from Mexico and Puerto Rico, were joined by thousands of Cuban refugees. Following the Cuban socialist revolution in 1959, many supporters of the former dictator, Fulgencio Batista, as well as a host of business owners and professionals who feared the new government under Fidel Castro, left the island and settled in the South Miami area, now known as Little Havana. Between 1959 and 1962, over 150,000 Cubans migrated to this country. Moreover, since race and economic success were tied together on the island, this first wave of migrants typically were wealthier than those who came later and the vast majority of them (90%) were white. Cubans, of course, were not unique in this regard. Research has demonstrated that white or light-skinned immigrants (irrespective of race or ethnicity) typically have greater economic success in this country than darker-skinned immigrants (Rothstein, 1995).

Immigration to this country slowed in the next few years as relations between the United States and Cuba became strained and flights between the two countries were prohibited. However, when Lyndon Johnson signed a "memorandum of understanding" with Cuba in late 1965, flights resumed and immigration grew dramatically, reaching over 257,000 by 1972 when the airlift program was again suspended. Since then, immigration from the island has slowed considerably except for thousands of Cubans who were released by Castro in the early 1980s (Rogg, 1974).

Education of Cuban Americans

Cuban immigrants who left the island in the late 1950s and early 1960s were middle class, wealthier, and well educated. From the very first, middle class Cubans in the south Miami area established their own private elementary and secondary schools under the auspices of the Roman Catholic Church and they encouraged their children to attend regularly. Many were concerned with the social upheaval in public schools during the 1960s and most were determined to maintain their culture and language in the United States. Moreover, in recent years, members of the community have established many private, secular schools. Classes in these schools are taught in Spanish and the curriculum places special emphasis on their vision of Cuban history, especially its repudiation of Castro and the Revolution of 1959 (Rogg, 1974).

The refugee experiences of postrevolutionary Cuban immigrants have created a unique community, quite different from the general immigrant populations of this country and certainly distinct from the Cuban population on the island. Partly because of this uniqueness however, Cuban Americans are better educated than other immigrant groups. For example, the majority of Cuban Americans over the age of 25 have graduated from high school, one in six have a college degree, with 39% of native born Cuban Americans graduating from college (Aguirre, 1976; Perez, 2001).

THE IMMIGRATION ACT OF 1965

In 1965, the United States opened the doors of immigration to people whose labor and skills were needed in this country. The Immigration Act passed that year abandoned the immigration quota system that it had employed since the 1920s. By the late 1970s and early 1980s, the effect of this new immigration policy was being felt throughout this country with increasing numbers of Hispanic and Asian immigrants. Along with their important skills and labor they also brought their rich diversity of culture (Portes & Rumbaut, 1996).

THE IMMIGRATION AND CONTROL AND REFORM ACT

However, as the United States economy slowed in the early 1980s, it appeared, once again, that all was not well. In 1983, Attorney General William French Smith alarmed the American people by declaring that we had "lost control of our boarders." With the image of millions of illegal immigrants from the south flooding the country with cheap labor and taking jobs away from Americans, Congress passed the Immigration Reform and Control Act of 1986 and amended it 4 years later in 1990. The debate over illegal immigration is far from over.

ILLEGAL IMMIGRATION

While thousands of legal immigrants live and work in the United States today, we do have a problem with illegal immigration. Some blame the immigrants themselves while others focus on the business community. Clearly the higher incomes in the United States as compared to Mexico and other Latin American countries act as a powerful magnet for immigration—both legal and illegal—to the United States. In addition, businesses sometimes ignore immigration laws and hire illegal immigrants because they can pay them much less than American citizens and control them with threats of exposure and deportation.

Reflection
What are the two related issues that encourage illegal immigration to the United States? How can we solve the problem of illegal immigration to the United States? What can you do as a teacher?

Strategies for Teaching Students from Diverse Cultures

There a number of strategies that you can use to teach culturally diverse students in your classroom. These include some of the following ideas:

- Focus on verbal interactions
- Select activities that encourage students to respond verbally, such as group discussions, skits, role playing, oral reading, and games.
- Use small groups activities and cooperative learning
- Have students work in small groups and use cooperative learning.
- Encourage divergent thinking
- Have students brainstorm, and use problem-solving techniques to solve issues.
- Use active learning
- Employ activities that require active involvement of students such as interactive bulletin boards, games, hand motions, clapping, etc.
- Employ activities that focus on experiences
- Include activities in your lessons that children can relate to such as when teaching a unit on fractions, have your students bake a cake (from scratch). By measuring ingredients, students can obtain a real application of the use of fractions.
- Encourage your students
- Give positive feedback to your students. Be encouraging; for example, say "good job" or "nice work."
- Celebrate holidays of ethnic, racial, and religious groups represented in your class
- Include holidays, food, music, and art from the cultures in your classroom.
- Include literature from diverse cultures
- Select stories and poems from cultures represented in your classroom. Read these selections aloud and discuss them and make these books available to your students. (Salend, 2005)

Children of illegal immigrants face the same problems as others that have come to this country over the last 200 years. These include language and assimilation difficulties into the broader culture. In addition, however, they face the fear of being deported because of their illegal status. This directly affects the education of their children in two ways. First, there is the political upheaval surrounding illegal immigration. Since illegal immigrants typically do not pay property taxes, many local residents resent their children attending school. Secondly, because many illegal immigrants are terrified—afraid of being discovered and deported—they do not register their children in school.

Teachers and administrators can work through local churches, neighborhood groups, and Hispanic businesses, such as groceries and restaurants, to encourage parents to enroll their children in school. We may need to waive the usual paperwork and assure parents that we are not part of the Immigration and Naturalization Service. Then, once children are enrolled, we must reach out to them. Give them a welcoming greeting in Spanish, smile and demonstrate your acceptance. By encouraging their attendance in school and modeling accepting behavior, children of illegal immigrants will have a better chance to succeed in the classroom and assimilate into American society. Additionally, your other students will learn how to act appropriately in a multicultural society from your example.

While the political debate over immigration and illegal immigration continues to rage in this country, it is up to American teachers to embrace their students and create democratic classrooms where all students can learn. It is up to you!

SUMMARY

Ethnic Diversity in Colonial America

America has always been a multicultural nation. From the colonies of southern New England, New York, and Pennsylvania to the shores of Virginia, the Carolinas and Georgia, distinctive ethnic communities were a prominent feature of early settlement. This rich diversity provided a basis upon which our multicultural nation was born.

The Early Face of Migration

As the small cluster of colonies grew into a new nation, during the 1800s immigrants from all over the world brought their skills and energy to help make our country great. There were the Irish, Germans, and later Italians, Poles, Russians, and Jews from Europe. And from Asia came the Chinese and Japanese settlers. During the 1920s, however, Americans had become less tolerant of immigrants and as a result Congress passed the first immigrant restriction legislation in history. Ironically however, these restrictions "opened the door" for African Americans and Mexicans who were able to move to northern cities and to the West Coast for jobs and education for their children. Their reception, however, was often mixed and a new era of racial and ethnic hatred swept the nation.

The Changing Face of Migration

By the 1960s Americans began to rethink their attitudes toward immigration and Congress passed the Immigration Act of 1965. This important piece of legislation reversed the earlier restrictions imposed during the 1920s and set the stage for a dramatic growth in immigration since the 1980s. However, this new immigration was different. Gone were the boatloads of European immigrants and trainloads of African Americans. Now Asian and Hispanic people had become the centerpiece of the new immigration. These new settlers were joined by thousands of Native Americans who left their Indian reservations to join our multicultural society. The changing face of immigration provides both challenges as well as great opportunities for American teachers. By embracing the new multicultural curriculum we can help transform America into a more open and tolerate society.

DISCUSSION QUESTIONS

1. Why is it important for teachers to recognize the ethnic and racial diversity of America from the colonial era to the present? What are the dangers of ignoring this reality in teaching practice?
2. Discuss the impact of national immigrant restriction during the 1920s on the ethnic diversity of the classroom?
3. Discuss the importance of the Immigration Act of 1965 in creating today's multicultural schools. How did this change in policy effect the ethnic composition of the classroom?
4. Have you seen changes in Americans' attitudes toward immigrants in the last few years? Discuss some instructional strategies that will help to overcome this growing discrimination.

Reshaping Our World through Teaching

Chapter 8

School Curriculum

We now turn our attention to the cornerstone of your teaching experience, the curriculum. But what do we mean by the curriculum? There are many definitions of curriculum, including all the courses offered in a school, the school's "course of study," or the actual learning content of the school.

While each of these definitions helps us understand the meaning of curriculum, we will focus on its three general components: the formal curriculum, the unintended curriculum, and extracurricular activities.

The formal curriculum (also called the explicit curriculum) typically consists of:

- What students are taught
- The selection of subject matter
- The topics included
- The depth of coverage for each topic
- The textbooks that detail this knowledge
- The curriculum guides that lay-out the topics in a systematic way

As we will see, however, the formal curriculum gradually has expanded over time to include more subjects such as economics, technology, and even drug and sex education.

The unintended curriculum, (also referred to as the implicit curriculum) consists of the messages sent to our students about what is valuable. For example, the omission of topics in the curriculum suggests that certain information is not important. A literature text that excludes the contributions of ethnic minorities, African Americans, or women, for example, indirectly tells students that individuals in these groups have not written works that are important. Since the 1960s, educators have become more aware of these implicit messages and we have attempted to make our curriculum more inclusive.

The final component of the curriculum consists of the extracurricular activities in which students are involved. These include school band, athletics, and dramatics. We will discuss each of these aspects of the curriculum and its impact on learning in more detail below.

THE STRUGGLE FOR CONTROL OF THE CURRICULUM

The struggle for the control of the curriculum in American schools has persisted for over 200 years. Politicians, businessmen, and religious leaders throughout history have consistently demanded that teachers conform to their direction as to the courses that are taught and sometimes how those courses are taught.

Curriculum Professional Organizations

The Association for Supervision and Curriculum Development (ASCD) is a professional organization for the study and promotion of curriculum. "We believe that schools should focus on developing students who are academically proficient, physically and emotionally healthy, respectful, responsible, and caring." Following are some of their recent accomplishments:

- Launched a new mission and strategic plan
- Called for a new focus on the whole child
- Embarked on new advocacy initiatives
- Begun building a worldwide community
- Sharpened our focus on school improvement
- Broken new ground in learning and teaching
- Engaged new leaders, members, and constituents
- Extended a helping hand via the ASCD community
- Achieved honors for print and electronic media
- Debuted e-membership and other innovations

Source: Retrieved June 14, 2007, from http://www.ascd.org

During the colonial period, for example, Puritan ministers felt that the primary purpose of education was to teach children how to read the Bible. As a result, the Bible and prayers formed the basis of the curriculum. By the 19th century, local political leaders felt that the curriculum should reflect the prevailing Protestant culture of the nation as well as patriotism and hard work. As a result, those values took center stage in the schools of America. Then, a generation ago, business and political leaders turned to the schools to address social problems such as drugs and alcohol abuse, premarital pregnancy, and sexually transmitted diseases. And today, the curriculum has become "exam driven," mandated by the NCLB and high stakes, multiple choice testing. Since science and math has become a priority among politicians and economic leaders, focusing the curriculum on these subjects and testing students achievement in these areas has begun to define the curriculum itself. Clearly, teachers, administrators, and the community have struggled to address changing visions of the curriculum.

CURRICULUM DURING THE COLONIAL PERIOD: NEW ENGLAND PRIMER

During America's colonial period, the reading of religious material formed the centerpiece of the curriculum and the hornbook was the instructional device that was used to teach reading, writing, and spelling. The hornbook consisted of a paddle-shaped piece of wood inscribed with the letters of the alphabet and the Lord's Prayer that was covered with a transparent sheet of cow's horn. Typically the hornbook showed both manuscript and cursive letters that students would copy to learn to write. The Lord's Prayer on the hornbook served as reading material and students would memorize the spelling of the words and use them to practice their handwriting (Blackwell Museum of History of Education, 1999).

Later, these religious readings were collected in the *New England Primer.* The Primer was introduced in the late 1670s and by 1700 it had become the standard catechism-

---

Hornbooks

Hornbooks typically listed the alphabet, the Lord's Prayer and multiplication tables. They were usually made of wood; however, other materials were sometimes used such as ivory or iron. Some innovative teachers made gingerbread hornbooks and children were rewarded by eating a letter that they had learned.

Source: Blackwell Museum of History of Education, 1999, retrieved June 14, 2007, from www.cedu.niu.edu/blackwell/books.html (Blackwell Museum of History of Education, 1999)

---

reader of the region. The catechism was a book of religious instructions written for children and was usually organized in a question and answer format. For example, the *New England Primer* asked, "Who made you," and then answered, "God made me." The *Primer* was reprinted over the years under different titles, such as *The American Primer* and *The Columbian Primer*. This little volume was so popular that by the end of the 1800s it had sold over 3 million copies (Ford, 1962).

The *New England Primers* consisted of several basic elements: The alphabet, "Easie Syllables for Children," and words of increasing difficulty; then a picture alphabet with accompanying rhymes; and finally, selections to memorize that included the Lord's Prayer." During each stage of the learning process, students memorized stories, verses, and religious/moral selections and then recited those materials verbatim to the teacher. This remained the standard method of reading instruction from the colonial period well into the 1800s (Ford, 1962).

Arithmetic was not included in the primer, with the exception of Roman numerals and numbers for the stated purpose of "the ready finding of any Chapter, Psalm, and Verse in the Bible" (Ford, 1962). In fact, early on there were few textbooks for arithmetic so teachers often used a handwritten "sum book" that they made themselves during their own studies. Students then created their own "sum books" by copying their teacher's

---

Example of the Easie Syllables for Children from the *New England Primer*

ab	eb	ib	ob	ub
ac	ec	ic	oc	uc
ad	ed	id	od	ud
af	ef	if	of	uf
ag	eg	ig	og	ug
ak	ek	ik	ok	uk
al	el	il	ol	ul
am	em	im	om	um
an	en	in	on	un
ap	ep	ip	op	up
ar	er	ir	or	ur
as	es	is	os	us
at	et	it	ot	ut
ax	ex	ix	ox	ux

Source: Ford, 1962

An Example of a Problem from the "Old Pike" Arithmetic Book

A student was considered a master of math, if he could apply the Rule of Three that follows: "The Rule of Three teaches by having three numbers given, to find a fourth that shall have the same proportion to the third, as the second to the first." (Ford, 1962, p. 304)

---

work. "Ciphering" was emphasized with a focus on addition, with subtraction, multiplication, and division included to a lesser degree. By the 1780s, several arithmetic books had emerged, such as one by Nicholas Pike referred to as "Old Pike." The contents of this book may seem bewildering to us today, as we see items like "barter" and "The Proportions and Tonnage of Noah's Ark." Nevertheless, this sort of approach was typical (Ford, 1962).

Handwriting (penmanship) and spelling also were considered valuable skills during this period. Penmanship was mastered by copying the teacher's handwriting. However, paper was generally of poor quality and was rare. As a result, students used the front, back, and the margins of the paper. The goal, in any case, was to have a clear, legible "hand." This was not an easy task to master due to the poor quality paper and the thick, clotting ink.

Spelling initially began by copying the letters of the alphabet and then the sounds of letters. Next, students memorized the spelling of words in their *Primers*. This provided the basis of reading. Spelling moreover was a valued skill. Competitive spelling bees were common throughout this period and the achievements of the great spellers were a source of community pride.

THE COMMON SCHOOL

While reading, spelling, ciphering, and memorizing religious material would continue to be a central component of both the curriculum and instruction for years to come, the democratic and market revolutions that swept across America in the late 1700s and early 1800s fundamentally altered the schools and curriculum of the new nation.

As we have seen, when the American Revolution transformed the 13 independent colonies into the United States of America, many statesmen recognized that the diverse colonial educational experiments focusing exclusively on religion were no longer appropriate. What we needed was an educational system that would instill in young children the important values of patriotism and nationalism. Moreover, education was no longer seen as a luxury for the wealthy. Our democracy demanded that education be within the reach of all Americans, both rich and poor (Parkerson & Parkerson, 2001).

The market revolution of the early 1800s changed our economy from one of self-sufficiency and barter to one based on the exchange of cash for goods and services. This transformation provided many Americans their first taste of the new consumer culture. In addition, it restructured their social roles and provided them with an exciting vision of what the new nation could become. Together, the American Revolution and the market revolution fundamentally changed our attitudes toward education and provided support for the emerging common school (public school).

During the early 1800s, the common school gradually emerged, first in the northeast and then throughout much of the nation. Soon, small one-room schoolhouses dotted the countryside. The goal for these humble dwellings was simple: to teach children "reading, 'riting, and 'rithmetic"—referred to as the three Rs. In some communities students brought their own book from home to use as reading material. Often, these books were Bibles or prayer books. As a result, classrooms continued to reinforce religious values through daily prayer and readings from the Bible, and children were instructed in a set of Protestant values that were acceptable to most Americans.

Soon, however, new standardized readers began to emerge. One of the earliest of these was the "Blue-Backed Speller." (This was the nickname of this small book with a blue cover.) Its formal title was *The American Spelling Book* by Noah Webster. Like its predecessor, the *New England Primer*, the Blue-Backed Speller was used to teach basic reading, spelling, and writing. However, it also stressed pronunciation, the meaning of words, and had less religious emphasis. For example, the text included a section of secular (nonreligious) fables that conveyed moral values.

The McGuffey Reader

The publication of the first McGuffey *Reader* in 1837, however, represented a major revolution in curricular development. While these readers continued to include some religious content (about one in four lessons made some reference to God or the Bible), patriotism was also an important component of these early readers.

In more advanced readers, McGuffey included selections about the founding fathers such as John Adams and George Washington. The rousing tales of their accomplishments and inherent values—such as Washington's truthfulness to his father in the famous cherry tree story—became an essential component of common school curriculum (Parkerson & Parkerson, 1998).

Moreover, since formal speaking continued to be an important skill in early America, teachers often included this subject in their reading instruction. For example, lessons on how to bow formally to the audience and teacher before and following the recitation were a common part of the reading curriculum. As one common school student noted, the primary objective of reciting memorized materials was to display the appropriate classical gestures, "read fast, mind the stops and marks and speak up loud" (Burton, 1852).

In addition to reading, mathematics was becoming more important in the emerging market economy. Young people needed to learn how to count money, make change, tell time, and perform simple arithmetic functions such as addition, subtraction, division, and multiplication. To help children learn basic arithmetic, a number of math textbooks

---

Selections from McGuffey's *Eclectic First Reader*

Lessons/Title
- I. *The New Book*
- II & III. No Titles (short selections about boys, animals, school)
- IV. *The Wild Ox*
- V. *The Cat and the Dog*
- VI. *The Boy and Dog*
- VII. *The Bear*
- VIII. *Time to Get Up*
- IX. *The Poor Old Man* (includes God)
- X. *The Sun is Up* (includes God)
- XI. *Boys at Play* (includes God and the Bible; McGuffey, 1836/1982)

Selections from McGuffey's *Fifth Eclectic Reader*

Title	Author
Respect the Sabbath Rewarded	(none listed)
The Town Pump	Nathaniel Hawthorne
An Old-Fashioned Girl	Louisa M. Alcott
The Village Blacksmith	Henry Wadsworth Longfellow
Supposed Speech of John Adams	Daniel Webster
William Tell	Sheridan Knowles
Hamlet	William Shakespeare

Source: McGuffey, 1879/1962

---

emerged during this period. One of the earliest of these was Warren Colburn's *Intellectual Arithmetic* (1821). This text included word problems and a number of problems to be solved mentally. Nathan Daboll's the *Schoolmaster's Assistant* (1832), on the other hand, called upon students to divide shares of brandy among soldiers. Others such as *Franklin Arithmetic* (1832) had a "moral purpose" and included the following problems that were considered more appropriate for young children: how many letters in the word John? How many hands have a boy and a clock?; take the E from the word HOPE and how many letters would be left?; and what would it be then?; Judas, one of the twelve apostles, hung himself; how many were there left? Whatever its form, by the middle of the 1800s students were routinely receiving basic arithmetic education in the common schools (Johnson, 1963).

Handwriting also was considered an important part of the curriculum because hand-written material was the primary form of communication. Penmanship was mastered by copying letters in a "copybook" using a quill pen and ink. The copybooks were made of coarse paper folded and hand stitched with a heavy covering sometimes made of wallpaper. In fact, a teacher's ability to repair quill pens was considered a valuable skill, though ink was problematic because it often clotted. By the 1830s slates were also being used in the classroom. These slates (and later pencils made of slate) were easier to write with and less expensive than the paper and quill pen. The recommended method was to use the slate for teaching young children to write and when they had become sufficiently skilled, they would switch to paper and pen. Later, the teacher would stand in the front of the classroom and use larger slates for instruction. These "blackboards" were becoming a reality by mid-19th century (Johnson, 1963).

Links to the Past: Early Writing Technique

An innovative approach was used by the Lancaster Schools of the early 1800s. Teachers, assisted by student mentors, taught young children to write with their fingers tracing letters in sand contained in small boxes. (Kaestle, 1973)

THE GRADED SCHOOL

By the end of the 1800s, in response to growing population of American cities and the need to educate more children, the one-room schoolhouse gradually gave way to the graded school. Here, students were grouped according to age level, assigned to separate rooms with their own teacher, and were taught subjects appropriate for their age. The basic three Rs continued to be the curricular focus in lower grades, but other subjects such as geography and history were included in the upper grades.

Basal Readers

Paralleling this change was the emergence of the basal reader. Like the McGuffey *Readers* before them, these books were arranged in increasing difficulty; however, their reading selections were distinctly more secular in nature. By the late 1800s, the student population was not exclusively Protestant, as in the colonial period and early national era, and included children with Catholic and Jewish backgrounds (Parkerson & Parkerson, 2001).

As we have seen, the "Dick and Jane" series had become the most popular basal reader by the mid-1900s. These readers centered on stories about an idealized American family: the children—Dick, Jane, and Baby Sally—and their Mother and Father. They lived in a little white house in a small town. Father worked and mother stayed home and took care of the family (Gray & Monroe, 1956).

While the "Dick and Jane" series remained popular for generations of children, by the 1970s these books were criticized for having racial and gender bias and for being out of touch with American society. In response to these criticisms, the series was revised to portray characters of racial and ethnic diversity: women went to work, men sometimes helped at home, and the families were not always White. This set the tone for the more culturally diverse reading curriculum beginning in the 1970s and was reflected in many subject areas (Parkerson & Parkerson, 2001).

Mathematics

During this same period, math became an even more important part of the curriculum. Addition, subtraction, multiplication, and division were emphasized for children in first through third grades. First-grade students, and sometimes kindergarten, were instructed in single-digit calculations and by second and third grades they were taught how to perform these functions using two, three, and later four digits. Rote learning (memorization), however, continued to be the primary teaching method. Memorizing your multiplication tables, for example, continued to be a "rite of passage" for second- and third-grade children. Students also performed math exercises on worksheets to practice and master their basic arithmetic skills. In addition, however, word problems were included in most students' math textbooks. Finally, students in the upper grades were introduced to fractions and decimals and in high school they learned algebra, geometry, and sometimes precalculus. Later, vocational math skills were incorporated into the high school curriculum. These included bookkeeping and accounting.

Penmanship

Since handwriting was an essential skill throughout much of this period, penmanship was often taught as a separate subject in early grades. The Palmer Method of handwriting emerged during the late 1800s (1894) and was used until the 1960s. This writing method used a style of cursive writing that involved specific arm and shoulder movements. In fact, left-handed children were often forced to switch to their right hand for writing because of the standardized method of teaching! Early exercises in the "copybook" required that students practice making series of connected circles and lines.

Beginning in the 1960s, however, penmanship instruction gradually began to change to the D'Nealian style. In this approach children first learned manuscript writing (printing) and then made the transition to cursive writing. This technique gained popularity because children can learn manuscript writing more easily and thus can express themselves in writing sooner. The transition to cursive in the D'Nealian method involved the addition of connecting strokes to printed letters (retrieved June 16, 2007, from http://www.dnealian.com/lessons.htm).

Spelling

Through most of the 20th century, spelling also was taught as a separate subject. Typically, the pattern for learning spelling words for the week was:

- Monday: Students would take a pre-test to see what words they need to study.
- Tuesday: Students would practice writing all the spelling words in the list four or five times.
- Wednesday: Students would write the definitions for each spelling word.
- Thursday: Students would write a sentence for each word.
- Friday: Students would take the weekly test over the assigned 20 words.

The spelling book listed the words for each week. Early on there was no pattern for the selection of spelling words, but by the 1950s and 1960 the words typically were drawn from a frequently used word list, such as Frye's high frequency words. This was a list of 100 of the most frequently used words in print, beginning with single letter words such as "I" and "a," then single syllable words such as "in," "to," and "be," followed by three- and four-letter words, and then two- and three-syllable words (Frye, 1999).

THE CONTEMPORARY CURRICULUM

The curriculum of the American school has changed considerably over the last several decades. It has become more comprehensive in terms of subject matter, and both students and teachers have become more accountable. The curriculum, moreover, has become more rigorous academically while it has expanded vocational and technical training, as well as foreign language education. In addition, the curriculum has begun to more accurately reflect the growing cultural diversity of American society with more diverse offerings in social studies and literature. Finally, Americans continue to turn to the schools to address major social problems and to socialize young people with beliefs, values, and morals.

Reading Today

Our reading curriculum today bears some resemblance to the past, though there are some important differences. We continue to use basal readers, although their content has become more comprehensive and culturally diverse. Story selections represent characters from various racial and ethnic backgrounds and women are sometimes portrayed as working in professions and other occupations. Similarly, different literary genres, such as poetry, biography, and fantasy are also included in contemporary basal readers and literature texts.

Methods of reading instruction have also changed. Today these include phonics, direct vocabulary instruction, and comprehension. Generally, young children read silently and then aloud in small groups or to the whole classroom. The teacher provides instruction in phonics skills, vocabulary words, and discusses comprehension questions after reading. Students work independently to complete workbook pages or worksheets that provide them with an opportunity to practice these skills.

There are some reading programs that are exclusively phonics-based such as the Open Court series. Using this popular series students learn phonics through drill, memorization, and games. Students then blend or "sound out" words in order to recognize them. The problem here, of course, is that the simple recognition of words is the primary goal—with meaning and comprehension of those words deferred until later. While the "phonics only" approach to reading can be useful, we do not recommend it because its fragmented approach hinders students' comprehension and enjoyment of literature. Nevertheless, some states such as California and North Carolina have mandated the use of phonics as the basis of reading instruction. As a new teacher you must understand these mandates and respond accordingly (Open Court Resources, n.d., retrieved June 15, 2007, from http://www.opencourtresources.com).

Whole Language is a more comprehensive approach to teaching reading. Here, phonics is not emphasized; instead, children learn to read by "encounters" with language. Students bring their own experiences to the reading material and comprehension is the primary goal. Typically, this approach is used in the primary grades (Clearninghouse on Reading, English, and Communication, retrieved July 16, 2007, from http://www.indiana.edu/~reading).

Today elementary school teachers typically use a basal reader that includes some elements of both phonics and whole language. In the middle grades, a basal reader might include phonics skills, some Whole Language elements, and an increased emphasis on different literary genres. In high school, literature books include selections that require higher level reading skills, increased vocabulary, literal as well as figurative and interpretative comprehension, selections written by authors from varying racial and ethnic backgrounds as well as women. These books also include varying literary genres and time periods from ancient to contemporary. Typically you will also encounter English textbooks that focus on grammar, punctuation, capitalization, parts of speech, and diagramming.

Characteristics of Whole Language

Whole Language advocates contend that students learn best by using language through reading, writing, listening, and speaking. Whole Language has the following characteristics:

- It is a learner-centered curriculum
- Teachers provide opportunities for students to read, write, listen, and speak
- Learning proceeds from whole to part
- Collaborative peer activities promote communication skills
- Literature plays a crucial role in the curriculum
- Students are encouraged to write
- Phonics is taught in the context of reading (Goodman, 1986)

Mathematics Today

The mathematics curriculum has also become more complex in recent years. Students in kindergarten through second grade continue to use manipulatives such as Cuisenaire rods and colored disks or "Popsicle" sticks for counting and grouping objects. More advanced mathematical concepts, such as fractions and place value, have been introduced in the primary grades. These concepts then are developed in more depth each year. This approach is referred to as the *spiral curriculum*. Each year the text covers many of the same topics, but in increasing detail. Students continue to complete exercises to master basic skills but texts also include more word problems and problem solving tasks (Bruner, 1996).

At the high school level, students are exposed to more advanced mathematics courses, such as algebra, geometry, trigonometry, and precalculus. Some of these are listed as Advanced Placement (AP) courses and can be taken by students for college credit.

Spelling and Penmanship Today

Spelling and penmanship instruction has also expanded in recent years. Spelling books now focus on high frequency words (as mentioned above) and some language patterns, such as rhyming, vowel sounds, or consonant blends. Also vocabulary and language arts skills are included in the spelling curriculum.

Penmanship is now entirely based on the D'Nealian method. However, some teachers still prefer the Palmer Method for children who have difficulty with fine motor skills, and those with certain learning disabilities and physical impairments. The quality of paper, pens, and pencils has improved dramatically over the years and as a result these instruments are no longer an impediment to handwriting. Interestingly enough, because of changes in the way we communicate today, there is little emphasis placed on penmanship after the third grade. Penmanship now shares lesson time with the computer skills and keyboarding. Once again, as technology changes so does the curriculum and methods of instruction.

THE EXPANSION OF THE CONTEMPORARY CURRICULUM

In the last several decades the curriculum of the American school has expanded considerably beyond its core of reading, social studies, mathematics, spelling, and penmanship. A part of that expansion has been the emergence of a more rigorous and academically challenging kindergarten, vocational/technical training, the inclusion of more foreign languages, a greater cultural diversity of literature, the use of schools as an agent of

---

Wisdom of Teachers: Worksheets

For decades students have used consumable workbooks or worksheets. Students would write their answers in the book and tear-out the pages for the teacher to grade. However, as the cost of replacing these workbook continued to rise, students were required to copy problems onto paper in order to save money so that the workbooks could be reused from year to year. As a teacher, you should be aware of the fact that copying problems from the book to paper is a difficult task for students with learning disabilities. You could make copies of the exercises or reduce the number of problems for learning disability students so they are not overwhelmed by the task.

Reading Readiness Skills Include the Following:

- Recognition of letters
- Distinction between upper and lower case letters
- Knowledge of consonant sounds
- Knowledge of vowel sounds

---

social improvement, the strengthening of character and moral education and an increased emphasis on accountability and standards.

Kindergarten and Emergent Literacy

Today the primary purpose of the kindergarten is not just to simply establish "readiness for learning" and develop social skills. Many children now possess these skills when they enter kindergarten and as a result, basic academic learning such as reading, writing, spelling, and even mathematics often are introduced in kindergarten. However, it is important to remember that not all children will be prepared for learning. Consequently, you must also be equipped to cover readiness skills as well as academic work when appropriate (Polk County Public Schools, 2007).

More recently, educational researchers have developed the concept of *emergent literacy*. Rather than simply mastering a set of discrete skills in order to learn to read and write, emergent literacy considers all the phases of literacy experienced during the child's development. These phases are based on a child's background with print and reading and include the following:

Reflection

How did your lesson help children learn? What could you do to improve your lesson?

See Accountability and Standards section below for more information on INTASC standards. Also see Ann Adams Bullock's and Parmalee Hawk's (2000) *Developing a Teaching Portfolio* (2nd ed.).

Portfolio Activity: Interstate New Teacher Assessment and Support Consortium (INTASC)

INTASC Standard #2: Student Development

The teacher can provide learning that supports the student's individual development. Demonstrate that you understand how children learn and develop and provide learning opportunities.

Create a lesson plan based on the concept of emergent literacy. Use the idea of story sense for your lesson and include an activity for students to demonstrate sequencing of events.

Sample evidence: The following are examples of evidence that would support your knowledge and skills related to this standard:

- Lesson plan
- Strategies used to teach the concept
- Students use of sequencing, such as flow charts, drawings, role playing

- Functions of print—Developing an awareness of the uses of print, such as signs and logos
- Purpose of print—The ability to convey information or a message
- Story sense—Understanding the concept of a story as a sequence of events
- Through these experiences with print, children develop important concepts that are beneficial in learning to read and write (Dickinson & Tabors, 1991).

Vocational Training

In addition to the expanded academic importance of kindergarten and the development of emergent literacy has been the growth of vocational training. While the school curriculum in the early 20th century focused almost exclusively on college preparation, today it includes both vocational and technical training. Many middle grade schools offer keyboarding and business computer technology and in high school, students may enroll in courses such as Fundamentals of Technology, Communication Systems, and Principles of Technology. For students interested in trade and industrial programs, course selections include electrical trades, metals manufacturing and welding, masonry, and automotive service technology. For those interested in the growing health care industry the curriculum includes allied health sciences, biotechnology, and advanced health sciences.

Foreign Languages

As a result of the growing globalization of the economy, the school curriculum has also responded with the inclusion of more foreign languages. In the 1800s, Greek and Latin were the primary foreign languages taught in high schools. Now, courses in Japanese, German, French, and Spanish are routinely offered. Russian gained popularity during the Cold War but today many students have become interested in studying Arabic due to the war in Iraq and political unrest in the Middle East.

Cultural Diversity of the Curriculum

As our society has become more culturally diverse, the school curriculum also has responded. School systems throughout the country now include the study of diverse cultures. The typical social studies curriculum, for example, includes units on South America and Europe in the sixth grade, Africa, Asia, and Australia in the seventh grade, state history in Grade 8, world history in the ninth grade, and United States History in the 11th grade. African, American Studies and Native American Studies and others are also offered as electives and can be taken in Grade 12. (See North Carolina Department of Public Instruction, Program of Study, as an example: http://www.dpi.state.nc.us, reteieved June 20, 2007.)

Foreign Languages listed in Middle Grades/Junior High Curriculum for the State of Indiana				
French	German	Spanish	Latin	
Japanese	Chinese	Russian	Arabic	Korean

Source: Retrieved June 18, 2007, from
http://www.doe.state.in.us/publications/res_middleschool.html

American Literature has also expanded to reflect our multicultural society. For example, in a survey of the Top 25 books teachers of "English I" have selected for their students, women authored eight books. These include *To Kill a Mockingbird* by Harper Lee, *Anthem* by Ayn Rand, and *Mythology* by Edith Hamilton. Three of the women authors selected were African American: Lorraine Hansbury author of *Raisin in the Sun*; Maya Angelou, poet laureate who wrote *I Know Why the Caged Bird Sings*; and Doris Sanders, author of *Clover*. Also chosen was one Chinese American woman, Adeline Yen Mah, author of *Falling Leaves: Memoir of an Unwanted Chinese Daughter*. Walter Dean Myers (author of *Fallen Angles*) was the lone African American male author on the list. This contrasts sharply with the 1800s, when literary works by racially and culturally diverse authors were rare and only a few women such as Louisa May Alcott were included in literature courses.

Social Improvement

Another important component of the expanding curriculum is the area of social improvement. And yet, as we have seen, there is a long tradition of turning to the schools to help cure the perceived ills of society. During the temperance movement of the late 1800s and early 1900s, for example, antidrinking lessons were routinely included in the curriculum. McGuffey's *Eclectic First Reader* contained the reading of "The Whiskey Boy"—the story of a young boy named John whose father was a "drunkard." Young John also drank whiskey and got tipsy everyday. McGuffey then warned young readers that John died in the poor house at the age of 8 (McGuffey, 1836/1982, pp. 141–143).

DARE

Today we continue to teach students the "acceptable" morals and values of society. Since illegal drug use and alcohol abuse is perceived as a major social problem, a number of curricular programs have been initiated. One such program is Drug Assistance Resistance Education (DARE). Typically, the DARE program begins in the fifth grade and is taught by a police officer. The primary purpose of DARE is for students to say "no" to drugs. DARE officers provide a workbook and use role-playing to give students the confidence to say no and to resist peer pressure. Students also sign a pledge not to take drugs, alcohol, or smoke. At the end of the classes, students "graduate" from DARE and the officer distributes buttons, bumper stickers, pens, pencils, and other paraphernalia to motivate students (DARE, 1995).

The DARE program is offered in all 50 states and most school districts and it is very popular. However, some educators have criticized the program because it lacks measurable results in terms of reducing illicit drug use among other criticisms.

Sex Education

Similarly, the problem of premarital sex, the spread of sexually transmitted diseases (STDs), and the physical changes that occur during puberty have led to the inclusion of sex education in the school curriculum beginning in the 1960s. And yet, there has been a great deal of controversy in recent years over both the content and the approach of these programs. For example, approximately one quarter of the school districts do not include any information regarding birth control in their "sex education" classes. Rather, they focus exclusively on abstinence as the only option outside marriage. In "abstinence only" classes, the discussion of contraception is either prohibited or it is limited to a discussion of its "ineffectiveness."

Many educators however, feel that the "abstinence only" approach is unrealistic and does not address ways to prevent unwanted pregnancy and sexually transmitted diseases, such as AIDS. More comprehensive sex education classes include, the biology of human sexuality, methods of birth control (in addition to abstinence), the prevention of STDs, as well as frank discussions of accepting responsibility and acting in a mature manner regarding one's sexual behavior (Kaiser Family Foundation, 2005).

Character and Moral Education

As Americans increasingly turn to the schools as an access point to deal with the problems of society, there also has been pressure to include character or moral education in the curriculum. As we have seen in chapter 2, character education has been very popular in schools over the years. The authoritarian approach to character education focuses on teaching (and memorization) of "desirable" traits such as courtesy, respect, and patriotism. Some states allow school districts to design their own character education programs within State Department of Education guidelines. Cumberland County Public School District in North Carolina, for example, has established a program with the following character traits: courage, self-discipline, perseverance, integrity, respect, responsibility, kindness, and good judgment (retrieved June 15, 2007, from www.ncpublicschools.org/nccep/cumberland/schools.html).

Despite the ongoing popularity of character education, democratic educators argue that in our complex world students also must be equipped with the intellectual tools to solve the ambiguous moral and ethical issues we face. Students should be encouraged to research and reflect on specific issues and draw their own conclusions regarding whether something is morally right or wrong. Policy issues of war and peace and scientific dilemmas such as global warming require careful reasoning and debate rather than simply memorizing lists of platitudes, however well intentioned.

Accountability and Standards

Central to the expansion of the contemporary curriculum has been an increased emphasis on accountability and standards. As we have seen, most preservice teachers are now required to successfully pass the Praxis I and II exams for state licensure. In addition, the Interstate New Teacher Assessment and Support Consortium (INTASC) has developed

---

Ways to Include Character Education

The following are some ideas for including character education in schools.

- Hang pictures of heroes and heroines in classrooms
- Feature a virtue of the month
- Discuss in stories and history: "What is the right thing to do?"
- Involve your class in a charitable project
- Discuss issues of character regularly (good deeds, etc.)
- Have your class perform a service to your school (plant a garden, beautify the hall, etc.)

Source: Retrieved June 15, 2007, from
www.ncpublicschools.org/nccep/cumberland/schools.html

a number of standards that are used to assess beginning teachers. Briefly these INTASC standards include:

- Content Pedagogy—The teacher can make the subject matter meaningful.
- Student Development—The teacher can provide learning that supports the student's individual development.
- Diverse Learners—The teacher can provide opportunities for diverse learners.
- Multiple Instruction Strategies—The teacher uses a variety of instructional strategies.
- Motivation and Management—The teacher uses a variety of motivational and classroom management techniques.
- Communication—The teacher fosters active and collaborative learning in the classroom.
- Planning—The teacher develops an effective instructional plan to help all children learn.
- Assessment—The teacher uses formal and informal assessment strategies.
- Reflective Practice—The teacher uses reflection and journaling to improve instruction.
- School and Community Involvement—The teacher establishes relationships with colleagues, parents, and the community in general.

These standards have been developed from years of educational research on instruction and represent good teaching practices. We encourage you to review them and include them in your teaching. Also, in your portfolio, show evidence and reflect upon how specific standards have been met in your field experiences and student teaching. Clearly, accountability and standards have become a driving force in the development of the curriculum. By incorporating these standards in your teaching, you will help to improve our profession and help all children learn (Council of Chief State School Officers, retrieved June 19, 2007, from http://www.ccsso.org).

STRUCTURE AND ORGANIZATION OF THE CURRICULUM TODAY

Despite the important changes in the curriculum over time, there is little consensus concerning its structure or organization. Years of debate have yielded a variety of curricular options or approaches that may appear a bit daunting on the surface.

Perhaps the most useful way to understand the structure of the curriculum is to conceptualize it as a continuum with subject/teacher-centered (authoritarian) organization on one end and learner-centered (democratic) organization on the other. (See chapter 2 for an in-depth discussion of the authoritarian and democratic approaches to teaching.)

As we have seen, the *subject/teacher-centered* organization is the most traditional form of the curriculum, with each subject taught separately (the authoritarian approach). In the elementary grades for example, spelling, writing, reading, language arts, and math are all taught as individual subjects. In high school, General Math, Algebra, Composition, Literature, and American History are taught as independent subjects. The content is laid-out in a highly structured, sequential method and students are presented with the precise information that will appear on the test. This approach is sometimes referred to as the teacher-centered curriculum. All knowledge comes from the textbook and is imparted to the students by the teacher. Students are expected to master facts and concepts. Teachers lecture, conduct discussions, hold question-and-answer sessions, and then test students over content mastery.

Critics of this approach (usually from the democratic school) contend that each subject is taught in a fragmented, isolated fashion and that there is no attempt to integrate subject

Curriculum Organization Continuum

Learner-Centered   Integrated   Fused   Subject-Centered

matter. For example, after a period devoted to American History, literature follows as the next subject. But typically, there is no attempt to relate American literature to the historical period in which the story takes place. Drawing connections between the two subjects, of course, enriches the learning experience for students. Also, critics argue that in the subject-centered curriculum there is no provision for student exploration or experimentation, which makes learning more meaningful.

The *fused curriculum*, on the other hand, is a less structured approach that attempts to blend related subjects. For example, spelling, reading, writing, and English might be combined into Language Arts. Geography and history would be blended into Social Studies. In the primary grades, the morning might be spent on Language Arts, and for those in the middle grades or in high school a Social Studies course would consist of geography, history, economics, and government.

The *integrated curriculum* goes a step farther. It attempts to unite all the subjects under one theme or topic. For example, in a primary grade unit on the children's folk story "The Little Red Hen," social studies would be included by learning about the farm. Science would be included through a focus on growing plants, while math would be introduced with a discussion of measurements used in baking bread. Finally, a health component would have the children focus on eating healthfully. Regardless of format, all subjects would relate to the story as the focus of the unit. For upper grades and high school, a social issue such as the environment could be used as the organizational theme. Here, students would read literature about the environment, such as the classic *Silent Spring* by Rachel Carson. As a related social studies component students would focus on geographical regions, weather, and pollution problems. As a result of this comprehensive lesson, students' problem-solving and critical thinking skills would be developed.

Teacher- vs. Learner-Centered Instruction

Teacher-Centered	Learner-Centered
Focus is on instructor	Focus is on both students and instructor
Focus is on language forms and structures (what the instructor knows about the language)	Focus is on language use in typical situations (how students will use the language)
Instructor talks; students listen	Instructor models; students interact with instructor and one another
Students work alone	Students work in pairs, in groups, or alone depending on the purpose of the activity
Instructor monitors and corrects every student utterance	Students talk without constant instructor monitoring; instructor provides feedback/correction when questions arise
Instructor answers students' questions about language	Students answer each other's questions, using instructor as an information resource
Instructor chooses topics	Students have some choice of topics
Instructor evaluates student learning	Students evaluate their own learning; instructor also evaluates
Classroom is quiet	Classroom is often noisy and busy

Source: http://www.nclrc.org/essentials/goalsmethods/learncentpop.html, retrieved June 23, 2007.

Portfolio Activity: INTASC

INTASC Standard #1: Content Pedagogy

The teacher can create meaningful learning experiences.

Develop a unit plan with a series of lesson plans that focus on a topic or theme such as the "Exploration of Space." Connect different subject areas to the central theme or topic.

Sample Evidence: The following are examples of evidence that would support your knowledge and skills related to this standard:

- Detailed outline of the unit plan
- 4 to 5 lesson plans that relate different subjects (literature, social studies, science) to the central theme
- Correlate your lessons with the state curriculum
- Include related field trips or guest lecturers

Reflection

How could you include other subject areas in your unit plan? What other types of activities could you include to make learning more meaningful for your students?

On the far end of the curriculum continuum is the *learner-centered approach* (the democratic approach). Here, the curriculum is often fused or integrated with the emphasis on the needs and interests of the students. Using this approach the goal is to teach students to be self-motivated and to develop a desire to learn because of their interest.

With the learner centered approach, writing exercises include, but are not limited to keeping a journal and self-reflection. The teacher guides and facilitates learning rather than simply delivering facts. Whole language, mentioned earlier, is an example of this approach. Here, the teacher allows students the freedom to determine the direction of learning. Sometimes, in the upper grades and high school teachers may have students design a "plan of study" for their project and develop a contract describing the outcome—a paper, or a PowerPoint presentation, play, etc., along with a timeline for completion of the project (Lee & Garrett, 2005). Whatever method is used, however, the learner-centered approach focuses on the needs and interests of the students with teachers providing general structure and guidance.

Reflection

Describe how you could include more verbal interaction between you and your students in your lesson.

The learner-centered approach is not without its critics. Some educators (especially those of the authoritarian school) see it as "piecemeal" and lacking rigor. Others argue that extracurricular courses such as band, newspaper, and career courses have no place in the curriculum. And yet, these courses are not just "fun," but educational as well, as anyone who has been in the school band would testify. Students learn a great deal about their extracurricular activity in addition to developing important life-long skills. Certainly the 1-credit per year is justified.

Learner-Centered Curriculum (The Democratic Approach)

The following list contains some of the characteristics of the learner-centered curriculum.

- Focus on learners and their needs
- Emphasis on promoting overall growth of learners
- Stresses student's understanding
- Develops communication and social skills
- Emphasis on cooperative learning
- Students and teachers are involved in selection and organization of subject matter and materials
- Emphasis on problem solving

Reflection

Think about the ways elective course have added to your personal development. Record your ideas in your journal.

Clearly, the subject-centered/learner-centered curriculum debate is far from over. Those on the more conservative subject-centered side typically argue that our educational problems, both real and imagined, can only be solved with the "back to basics," one-size-fits-all core curriculum. Most educators, however, reject this radical approach and favor a more learner-centered curricular focus that builds on student interests guided by established curricular principles and innovative teaching.

CURRICULUM TRACKS

While the controversy over its structure and organization is ongoing, the curriculum in schools continues to evolve. Today, schools usually embrace a 3-track curriculum. And although they may be referred to differently, these tracks typically include:

Portfolio Activity: INTASC

INTASC Standard #6: Communication

The teacher fosters active and collaborative learning in the classroom.

Design a lesson plan that uses effective verbal communication and the use of technology as an instructional strategy.

Sample Evidence: The following are examples of evidence that would support your knowledge and skills related to this standard:

- Lesson plan based on verbal and written communication
- Include the use of technology such as a PowerPoint presentation
- Use a video to introduce your lesson

Elective Courses

The following points support the inclusion of electives in the high school course of study:

- Provides students opportunities for exploring different areas of interest
  - Music, theater, art, physical education
- Some courses may lead to future hobbies
  - Tennis, painting
- May enrich students lives
  - Playing the guitar, golf
- May serve as an introduction to a career
  - Computers, journalism
- Enhances students enjoyment of school
  - Bowling, drawing, jazz band

- Academic or college oreparation
- Career preparation
- Occupational preparation

In the early 20th century, when only a small proportion of young people attended high school, the curriculum focused on the classics (the academic track) to prepare students for college. As the number of students attending high school increased, other curriculum tracks such as career preparation and occupational preparation were developed. Career preparation guides students into skilled careers that may require further training. Occupational preparation, on the other hand, often incorporates job training or internship components to assist students in securing occupations following graduation.

More recently, the community or technical college has emerged to provide more advanced vocational and technical training for students who do not wish to attend a 4-year college. In response, some high schools have developed a fourth curriculum track for students who plan to attend technical colleges. This Community College preparation track—sometimes called technical preparation—was designed for students who are interested in specialized, technical fields.

Types of Curriculum

In addition to the 3 curricular tracks mentioned above there are three distinct curriculum types, discussed briefly at the beginning of this chapter. While curricular tracks prepare students for a particular field and essentially define their course of study, curricular types function as an integral part of school life. These curricular types include:

- Explicit
- Implicit
- Extracurricular

The explicit curriculum (or formal curriculum) consists of the subject offerings and requirements, syllabi and textbooks, teacher instruction and tests. The implicit curriculum (or hidden curriculum) consists of unintended learning that results from what is omitted from the formal curriculum. Course offerings at the school send students a message about what is important. Courses in African American History and Women's Studies, for example, inform students that the contributions of African Americans and women are important. The omission of various racial and ethnic groups and women from subjects and topics within courses, on the other hand, telegraphs the message that they are unimportant.

The third curriculum type consists of extracurricular activities, such as athletics, drama, debate, computers, and math club. Educators have demonstrated that these activities raise students' self-esteem, improve race relations, enhance aspirations, and improve grades generally. Additionally, extracurricular activities offer constructive, supervised activities for students outside the regular school day. They also supply social interaction with peers, teachers, and coaches as well as introduce students to interests, hobbies, and sports that students may continue throughout their lives. Extracurricular activities may also stimulate career opportunities through clubs such as Future Teachers of America, Math Club, and Computer Club (Holland & Andre, 1987).

The curriculum of the school is complex and controversial. It has evolved over the years in response to America's changing population, politics, and economy. It has sought to provide a basic education, a moral structure for the nation, a sense of nationalism, and a means of social improvement. In short, the school curriculum represents both what we teach and what we do not. As American teachers, we need to be mindful of this. By molding the existing curriculum to our own classrooms we can change the world—one student at a time.

SUMMARY

The Curriculum of the School

The curriculum of the school centers on three general components: the formal curriculum, the unintended curriculum, and extracurricular activities.

The formal curriculum typically consists of what students are taught, the selection of subject matter, the topics included, the depth of coverage for each topic the textbooks that detail this knowledge and the curriculum guides that lay out the topics in a systematic way.

The unintended curriculum of the school, on the other hand, consists of the messages sent to our students about what is valuable. For example, the omission of topics in the curriculum suggests that certain information is not important.

The final component of the curriculum consists of the extracurricular activities in which students are involved.

The Debate Over the Curriculum

The curriculum content and organization has been a political and social issue since the beginning of our nation's history. Over time, education has become more secular in nature in order to accommodate the diverse religious beliefs in this country. During the 19th century, for example, the curriculum shifted from the use of the Bible to teach reading to the *McGuffey Readers,* which were more secular in nature. The *McGuffey Readers,* with their emphases on love of God and Country, as well as being a good person, were the forerunners of the more contemporary basal readers that are more secular and reflect our culturally diverse society. The basal readers, in that regard, are representative of our curriculum today.

Subject-Centered and Learner-Centered Curriculum

The organization of the curriculum today can be represented by a continuum—ranging from subject-centered to learner-centered. The subject-centered curriculum is the traditional organization seen in schools and the curriculum and the accompanying textbook form the basis for the subject-centered curriculum. The learner-centered curriculum, on the other hand, places the student and his or her interests and needs at the center of learning. The curriculum tracks are designed to serve the purpose of learning: academic, business, or trade.

The Expansion of the Curriculum

In the last several decades the curriculum of the American school has expanded considerably beyond its core of reading, mathematics, spelling, and penmanship. A part of that expansion has been the emergence of a more rigorous and academically challenging kindergarten, vocational/technical training, the inclusion of more foreign languages, a greater cultural diversity of literature and social studies, the use of schools as an agent of social improvement, the strengthening of character and moral education, and an increased emphasis on accountability and standards.

DISCUSSION QUESTIONS

1. Describe the characteristics of the McGuffey *Reader*. Which of these characteristics are present in contemporary basal readers?
2. Name the curriculums that comprise school life? What is the importance of each and how does it affect the student?
3. What is the significance of curriculum tracks? Do tracks help students specialize and prepare for a particular future or do they limit students' choices?

Chapter 9

Instruction and Discipline

You have nearly made it! We now enter the classroom and turn to the centerpiece of teaching: instruction and discipline. While the curriculum discussed in chapter 8 represents the course of study of the school, instruction is the delivery of the curriculum content in the classroom. Teachers implement instruction either by explaining to students exactly what they need to know (authoritarian/subject-centered approach), or by guiding student's learning through inquiry or discovery (democratic/learner-centered approach).

In the more traditional subject-centered curriculum, the teacher directly teaches the content from the established curriculum. The approved textbook is the basis for the course content and the primary goal is student mastery of the content and the memorization facts. This subject-centered authoritarian approach is typical of the national and state accountability plans such as the NCLB.

With the learner-centered democratic approach, on the other hand, the teacher guides students through learning experiences and helps them bring meaning to the subjects being studied. Developing student enjoyment, motivation, and interest are important goals of this approach. Moreover, research has demonstrated that students in democratic classrooms typically do well on end-of-grade exams.

While all teachers are different, good teachers vary their methods of delivery and recognize that children learn in different ways. Some learn best *visually*, so reading, maps, charts, diagrams are effective for them. Others learn auditorily, through teacher lectures, discussion, recordings, and videos. Still others learn best tactually, and teachers might use demonstrations, experiments, and small group work where students "learn by doing." Clearly, the "one-size-fits-all" instructional approach is less effective than other methods. By using a variety of instructional approaches, teachers can provide an environment where all students can learn.

Following our discussion of instruction, we turn to discipline as it impacts learning in the classroom. As we shall see, disciplinary methods have changed dramatically over time. In the past, students often were whipped or beaten for bad behavior, but over time other methods such as the use of rewards and penalties have become more common. Today many teachers have embraced the democratic classroom where students have a voice in the selection of classroom rules and consequences for infractions. Other teachers employ student mediators to help deal with anger and conflict in the classroom. Still others use preventive discipline. Each of these disciplinary techniques will be discussed later in this chapter.

INSTRUCTION

The Role of the Teacher in Learner-Centered and Subject-Centered Curriculums

Subject-Centered	*Learner-Centered*
1. Teacher follows the text	1. Teacher serves as a book and curriculum guide
2. Teacher uses direct instruction	2. Teacher encourages student learning
3. Tests used to measure learning	3. Uses multiple indicators of learning
4. Encourages convergent thinking	4. Promotes divergent thinking
5. Subject-matter and instructional materials determine the course of learning	5. Needs and interests of students help determine the curriculum

---

FACTORS THAT EFFECT STUDENT ACHIEVEMENT

While learning is a complex process, educational researchers have demonstrated that there are four important factors that effect student achievement.

- Sociological
- Psychological
- Physiological
- Educational

Each of these factors will help to explain why some students do well in school, while others do not.

Sociological Factors

The sociological factors that affect a student's success or failure in school are often related to the home and community environments. These include the ethnicity and race of the family as well as the socioeconomic and educational background of the parents. Each of these factors can effect a student's achievement. However, what parents do to encourage and nurture the child's interest in learning has a more important effect. For instance, there are many examples of children who grew up in public housing or a depressed rural community and later graduated from college and became successful. Behind each of these success stories, however, is a nurturing family or family member. An important part of the teacher's role, therefore, is to encourage parents or caregivers to help their children learn.

Another important sociological aspect of learning is the language spoken in the home. Some parents are not fluent in English and their numbers are growing as Hispanic immigrants increase. Helping students who are not fluent in English is a challenge for the classroom teacher (see chapter 7.) As a result, many schools have established programs to help both students and their teachers. There are two basic approaches to the instruction of children who are not fluent in English: bilingual education, where children are taught

---

How Parents Can Help Their Children

Following are ways the classroom teacher can share with parents to enable them to help their children:

- Have reading materials present in the home
    - Use the school or public library
    - Purchase inexpensive books at yard sales, flea markets, library book sales, or the "bargain table" at local book stores
- Be a good role model by reading yourself
- Begin reading to children while they are babies
- Allow children to select their own books
- Read together with your children
- With older children, read the same book and discuss it with them
- Express interest in your children's learning
- Be involved with the school
    - Be a room volunteer, join the PTA, be a school "booster"
- Limit the amount of time children spend watching television
- Monitor the television programs that children watch
- Play games as a family
- Enjoy sports and outdoor activities together
- Involve children in daily household activities (grocery shopping, planning a family calendar, preparing meals, cleaning-up, caring for family pets)
- Take advantage of free (or inexpensive) facilities nearby (zoo, museums, nature centers)

Source: Retrieved February 25, 2008, from http://www.nea.org/parents/index.html

---

in both English and their native language and then gradually phased into the English speaking classroom; and English as a Second Language (ESL), where students receive instruction in a few subjects conducted in their native tongue, while learning English.

Psychological Factors

The psychological factors associated with student achievement include learning disabilities such as dyslexia, dyscalculia, dysgraphia, attention deficit disorder (ADD), and attention deficit hyperactivity disorder (ADHD). In fact, educational researchers have estimated that as many as 15% of students today may have a learning disorder (Learning Disabilities Online, 2008, retrieved July 20, 2007, from http://www.ldonline.org/ldbasics).

Sadly, what this means that in a typical classroom, you may have 3 to 5 students with a learning problem. If the learning disorder has not been diagnosed, you should be aware of warning signs such as difficulty in completing work, a short attention span, or reversal of letters when writing. During the first few years of school you should try to recognize these potential problems, obtain testing, and begin early intervention. If the learning disability is not detected early, the student can fall further and further behind academically.

If you notice several or more of these warning signs, first consult your principal and then school specialty staff like the learning disability teacher or school psychologist for

---

Ways to Help Students Who Are Not Fluent in English

- Learn conversational phrases in the child's first language
- Teach your students conversational phrases
- Use a bilingual aid or parent volunteer
- Work and plan lessons with the English as a Second Language Teacher for your school
- Use older students who speak the child's first language to serve as tutors
- Group students who speak the same primary language together to help each other
  - Use these groups for brief periods of time—you do not want to isolate them from the rest of the class
- Obtain books written in the child's native language and books written in two languages (e.g., Spanish on one page and English on the opposite page)
- Place signs on objects in the classroom in both English and the child's native language
- Encourage the students to share their culture with the class (e.g., literature, art, music, photographs, or food)
- Communicate with parents with the ESL teacher or the bilingual aid present
- Greet the parents in their native language

Source: Reed & Railsback, 2003, retrieved July 25, 2007, from http://www.nwrel.org/request/2003may/resources.html

---

an initial confirmation. Next, contact the parents and follow the school procedures for formal psychological testing of the student. Then arrange with your principal a staffing with the specialty staff members to create an Individual Education Program (IEP). In addition to the plan, some practical classroom tips are offered In the ADD/ADHD Focus Box below.

Signals of a Learning Disorder

As teachers we need to be aware of signals that a student may have a learning disorder.

- A student who seems bright, but does not do well in school
- Short attention span
- Easily distracted
- Unable to focus for more than a few minutes
- Difficulty understanding or following directions
- Trouble remembering what was just said
- Confusion with right and left, "on" and "no," "b" and "d," and numbers such as "25" and "52"
- Frequently loses or misplaces items
- Difficulty understanding concepts of time (i.e., yesterday, tomorrow, etc.)

Source: Failure in math, reading, or all schoolwork (Learning Disabilities Online, 2008, retrieved July 20, 2007, from http://www.ldonline.org/ldbasics)

Tips for Working with ADD and ADHD Students

You will find the following ideas helpful in working with all of your students.

- Have established rules and be consistent
- Have established consequences for violating the rules
- Keep yourself under control
    - Speak in a quiet and slow voice
    - Think about what you are saying
    - Do not speak or take any action when you are angry
- Remove the child from the classroom
    - Deal with the situation when you are calm
- Recognize and respond to positive behavior
- Avoid constantly saying "no" and "don't"
- Separate the child from the behavior
    - Example: "I don't like running in the hall"
- Have an established schedule and routine
- Demonstrate new tasks several times
- Give the student one task at a time
- Provide tasks that can be completed in a relatively short period of time
- Avoid noise and objects and activity in the classroom that will distract him or her

Journaling Activity

Go to the Web site below and record additional tips for working with ADD and ADHD students in your journal: http://www.ldonline.org/ldbasics

Physiological Factors

There are also a number of physiological factors that may effect a student's achievement. Various vision, hearing, speech impairments and certain health problems may impede a student's ability to learn. For example, a student who is near-sighted (myopic) may have difficulty seeing the blackboard. Eyeglasses may correct this problem, but you may also want to seat the student closer to the blackboard. Students with more severe disabilities are now placed in the classroom, through a procedure known as mainstreaming. As a result, you may have a student who is partially blind or even legally blind. In this situation, a teacher who is specially trained to work with visually impaired students will work closely with you. He or she will help you obtain special adaptive devices such as large print books or instructional materials in Braille. Your responsibility is to teach the student and the special teacher's responsibility is to help you arrange your classroom to accommodate the blind student and orient the student to the classroom and the school building.

Journaling Activity

Go to the http://www.as.wvu.edu/~scidis/vision.html (retrieved July 25, 2007) Web site for more ideas on how to help students with vision impairment. Record helpful ideas in your journal.

In addition to vision problems, some students may have undiagnosed hearing impairments when they begin school. Teachers in the primary grades should be aware of this

---

Visual Impairments: Indicators and Solutions

Visual Impairments—these range from myopia to blindness.
Indicators
- Squinting
- Getting too close to reading material
- Rubbing the eyes
- Frequent headaches

Solutions
- Refer the student to the school nurse for a vision test
- If the nurse concurs, contact the parent to arrange for an appointment with the optometrist
- Obtain large print books
- Move the student near the board
- For more serious vision problems, such as blindness or partial blindness, work closely and plan assignments with the specialist in vision impairments that is assigned to your school district

---

situation and take appropriate action if they suspect a hearing problem. General inattention, not responding to their name, or tilting their head toward the speaker are all symptoms of hearing difficulties. Typically, severe hearing problems are already diagnosed by the time the child enters school. In this case, you will need to work and plan closely with the speech teacher or audiologist and the special education teacher to provide the student with the education they deserve.

Auditory Impairments: Indicators and Solutions

Indicators
- The student ignores verbal instructions
- Does not respond when you call his or her name
- Ignores teacher's directions
- Tilts one ear toward the speaker
- The speaker has to repeat himself

Solutions
- Have the school nurse conduct a hearing test
- If the nurse agrees, contact the parents to arrange for a doctor's appointment
- Place the student near the teacher's desk
- Speak facing the student so he or she can see you
- Work with the speech teacher in your school district
- For more severe hearing impairments you may need to arrange for a tutor who uses sign language

For more information on working with students with hearing impairments go to Web site http://www.as.wvu.edu/~scidis/hearing.html (retrieved July 25, 2007).

Physical Impairments and Illnesses

Indicators
- Frequent falls
- Always tired
- Moody and cries easily
- Misses school frequently

Solutions
- Consult the school nurse or special education teacher
- Contact the parent if suggested by the specialty staff
- Alternate the pace of school activities (e.g., after gym class plan some quiet activity such as story time, or a film)
- Arrange a place where the student can rest, such as a cot in the nurses office
- Arrange for homework when the child is ill and e-mail assignments to the child

With severe impairments and illnesses, plan and implement lessons and the physical environment of the classroom with specialty staff.

For more ideas on working with students with physical impairments and illnesses go to Web site: http://education.qld.gov.au/curriculum/learning/students/disabilities/resources/information (retrieved July 26, 2007).

In addition, some students may have physical handicaps or other health problems. Again, while severe cases are likely to have been diagnosed before the student begins school, you should be aware of indicators of other problems, some of which may develop later.

Students with impairments such as cerebral palsy may also be placed in mainstream classrooms, except in severe cases. In this instance, you will work closely with the special education teacher and a specialty teacher who is trained to deal with mobility problems; the school nurse and other appropriate staff depending on the nature of the physical problem so that the student receives a proper education.

Regardless of the impairment, you will need to work with related specialists on the school staff such as the speech teacher, special education teacher, school nurse or school psychologist to develop an IEP to help the child learn and function in the classroom.

Educational Factors

As teachers, we do not have a great deal of direct control over the sociological, physiological, and psychological factors associated with learning. But we can adjust our instructional approach, provide effective interventions, and we can act appropriately to deal with the problems of our students.

In terms of educational factors, however, we have much more control. Through careful planning and effective organizing we can dramatically improve the learning and achievement of all of our students.

Although subject–centered, "whole class instruction" traditionally has been the most common method of teaching in the classroom, teachers today often employ student–centered small group work such as cooperative learning. Here, students are assigned to small, heterogeneous groups to work collaboratively on a project. These groups may be

---

Example of a Cooperative Learning Project

The teacher arranges students in small groups of varying abilities. Then each group is given the task of creating ways to recycle used paper in the classroom. Simply taking the paper to the recycling center is not an option. The paper must be used in some manner within the classroom. This example also uses discovery learning that will be discussed later in the text.

Cooperative Learning

The University of Minnesota has a Cooperative Learning Center and sponsors a Web site with helpful information on the topic. See http://www.clcrc.com (retrieved May 5, 2007). Authors David W. Johnson and Roger T. Johnson supervise the center. Go online and examine this important teaching approach.

---

composed of high and low achieving students; students with disabilities and those with none; Blacks, Whites, and additional minorities; or girls and boys. Rather than competing with each other, members of the group work as a team and share information to complete a common goal or project. Moreover, in this situation, students use divergent thinking: that is, they creatively explore ideas and solutions from different sources.

Cooperative learning, also referred to as *collaborative learning,* is a good example of the learner-centered curriculum mentioned earlier. Researchers have found that cooperative learning benefits all students, both the high and low achievers and stimulates interest and motivation (Johnson & Johnson, 1989, 1991; Slavin, 1988).

Discovery learning is yet another learner-centered approach. Here students work either individually or in groups to find patterns. Some science and math programs use this method. For example, when the teacher introduces the multiplication tables, she asks students if they can identify a pattern in the 2s table. Researchers have demonstrated that if students find the patterns themselves, they are more likely to remember it than if the teacher simply tells them the answer.

Portfolio Activity: Interstate New Teacher Assessment and Support Consortium (INTASC)

INTASC Standard #4: Multiple Instruction Strategies

The teacher uses a variety of instructional strategies.

Create a plan for grouping students with varying abilities, assign students a project requiring problem solving and describe your role (guide, coach, etc.)

Sample Evidence: The following are examples of evidence that would support your knowledge and skills related to this standard:

- Explain your grouping strategy
- Describe the problem-solving topic and project assigned to your students
- Discuss your role in the activity

Reflection

Describe the interactions of students in their groups. Was your grouping strategy successful? Do your students need to develop some skills to work in groups?

LEARNING THEORIES

While sociological, psychological, physiological, and educational factors all play a role in student achievement, there are also a number of theories that describe how students learn and explain why students learn in different ways. Two of the most enduring learning theories are the Learning Modalities and Learning Domains discussed below.

Learning Modalities

As we have seen, students learn in different ways and as a teacher you should try to utilize a variety of instructional methods that will accommodate these different learning styles. In so doing, you will begin to recognize how each of your students learns best. To give you a head start, here are four different learning modalities through which students learn:

- Visual
- Auditory
- Kinesthetic
- Tactile

Most students process information visually. These students learn best by actually seeing written words or images. To assist this type of learner, the teacher should consistently write terms and assignments on the board and use charts, maps, and other visual aids. You should encourage these students to carefully take and review their notes.

Other students process information auditorily. These students profit from teacher lectures, discussions, read alouds, and by using recording devices. Typically, they have well developed language skills and can benefit from group work.

Other students learn best in the kinesthetic and tactile modes. These students need to handle and manipulate objects and be physically involved in the learning process. They "learn by doing." Unfortunately, these students may have more difficulties in school because most instruction is through the visual and auditory modes especially in the upper grades and high school.

In kindergarten or preschool, teachers can help these children learn the letters of the alphabet by gluing beans or macaroni in the shape of the letter on construction paper. Then encourage students to trace the letter with their fingers as they articulate its sound. Manipulating plastic or magnetic letters of the alphabet will also help tactile learners as will the use of Cuisenaire rods or Popsicle sticks for counting, adding, and subtracting. In later grades, experiments, skits, and the construction of mobiles and dioramas may be helpful learning techniques as well.

Learning Domains

While learning modalities help us understand the ways in which students process information, educational researchers have also identified a number of learning domains that provide insight into how students learn. There are three learning domains:

Strategies for Helping All Students Learn

The following methods will facilitate learning for students operating in each of the learning modalities:

Visual learners
- Provide written instructions
- Write terms, vocabulary, etc.on the board
- Have students take notes
- Use maps, charts, graphs,videos, transparencies

Auditory Learners
- Provide verbal instructions
- Use videos
- Allow students to use tape recorders
- Set up listening stations with stories or lessons

Kinesthetic or Tactile Learners
- Use demonstrations
- Conduct laboratory experiments
- Construct: murals, mobiles, dioramas
- Use manipulatives for math (Cuisenaire Rods, abacus, Popsicle sticks, etc.)

Note: The use of skits, plays, role playing, or reenactments may be helpful for all of these learners.

Source: Learning Modalities, Center for Teaching Learning
and Faculty Development, Ferris State University
(http://www.ferris.edu/htmls/academics/center/teaching-and-learning-tips)

- Cognitive
- Affective
- Psychomotor

The *cognitive domain* operates in the traditional area of learning and concerns memory, recognition, intelligence, and the development of academic skills. Educators often see these "cognitive skills" as a hierarchy ranging from memorization of facts, analysis, and evaluation to judgments (Bloom, 1956).

The *affective domain,* on the other hand, centers on learning as a reflection of student motivation, interests, attitudes, and values. Here, we are referring to a student's interest in receiving and valuing information. Generally, students do well in subjects in which they are interested. Clearly, if you are good at something you tend to enjoy it, and if you enjoy something, you are usually good at it (DeBono, 1985; Krathwohl, Bloom, & Masia, 1964; Nuhfer, 2005).

Related to the affective domain is ones *locus of control*. This concept centers on a student's sense of responsibility for his or her behavior and performance. If a student attributes performance to be determined by external factors, he or she is said to have an *external* locus of control. For example, if a student receives a low grade on an exam, he or she may say the test was too hard or the teacher did not cover the material. In this case, the student tends to blame someone or something else for his or her failure. If, on the other hand, the student takes responsibility for his or her behavior, the student has an *internal* locus of control. Given the same situation of receiving a low grade, the student would say, "I didn't go back over my calculations," or "I should have gone to bed earlier the night before the test" (McCombs, 1991; Rotter, 1966).

Finally, the *psychomotor domain* involves objectives associated with the development of muscular and motor skills. This area involves skills such as hand–eye coordination including writing, staying between the lines while coloring, as well as dancing and playing sports. Broad objectives that are part of this domain include: perceptual abilities, coordination, agility, and expressive movement. For example, while studying a unit on the Pilgrims, you as a teacher would organize a Thanksgiving Day play or skit. Students would make costumes and reenact the first Thanksgiving with songs, dance, and food (Harrow, 1972).

INSTRUCTIONAL ENVIRONMENT

Up to this point we have examined a number learning modalities that help us understand how students process information and several learning domains that identify how students actually learn. We now turn to the instructional environment, those broad factors associated with the learning process.

While the instructional environment is complex, educational researchers have identified four central components of learning in the classroom.

- Teachers
- Learners
- Subject matter
- Learning milieu

The central component of this model is the *teacher* and includes his or her approach to instruction, how nurturing he or she is with students, as well as his or her personality, attitudes, behaviors, interests, values, and prejudices. The *learner* component consists of students' personalities, attitudes, values, and behavior and how students interact with each other. The *subject matter* deals with the curriculum content, instructional materials, and the methods of instruction and evaluation. The *learning milieu* is the physical and social environment of the classroom that is determined by the interaction of the teacher and students (Schwab, 1973; Schwab & Schwartz, 1984).

Schwab's Curriculum Commonplaces

Schwab (1973) suggested four realms of learning in the classroom:

- Teachers—attitudes, interests, values, and personality
- Learners—attitudes, interests, values, and personality
- Subject matter—content, instruction, and materials
- Milieu—social environment of the classroom and the interaction of the students and teacher

Teachers

Good teachers understand that students process information differently and are cognizant of the various student learning styles. These teachers then create a "family" environment where the students and teachers support each other and work together for a common goal of success (Purkey & Novak, 1996).

Extending this "family" metaphor, educational researchers have proposed six characteristics of what is sometimes called the facilitative teacher. These factors include being:

- Attentive
- Genuine
- Understanding
- Respectful
- Knowledgeable
- Communicative

Taken together, these characteristics describe the facilitative teacher as one who helps students effectively develop "personal growth and achievement." Being *attentive* refers to the teacher carefully listening and understanding to determine what students are thinking and feeling. Being *genuine* involves expressing a real interest and concern for students. *Understanding* is having empathy for each student and their points of view. Being *respectful* means that the teacher recognizes each student is important and helps each to develop self-esteem. Of course, teachers must be *knowledgeable* of their subject matter and impart their love of knowledge to students. Finally, being *communicative* means having good interpersonal skills and being sensitive to the feelings of students. Teachers must choose their words carefully so they do not offend their students. Clearly, good teachers are facilitative teachers who are learner-centered and create democratic classrooms (Wittmer & Myrick, 1989).

Teacher Dispositions/Attitudes

Beyond the teacher's qualifications and competencies are a number of important teacher dispositions or attitudes. These dispositions can dramatically effect your interaction with students. Positive teacher dispositions include:

- Caring
- Nurturing
- Having a "heart"
- Being idealistic
- Interest
- Enthusiasm
- Openness to new ideas
- Sharing
- Attentive
- Genuine
- Understanding
- Respectful (Larson & Keiper, 2007; Purkey & Novak, 1996; Wittmer & Myrick, 1989)

Reflection

In your journal, describe the dispositions that you possess. How could you develop other positive dispositions?

Learners

An essential part of the democratic classroom environment is developing a sense of self-concept among students. In this context, educational researchers have developed the idea of "invitational education" that focuses on five principles:

- All students are able, valuable, and responsible
- Education should be a collaborative, cooperative activity
- The process of education is the product in the making
- Students possess untapped potential
- This potential can best be realized by inviting development (Purkey & Novak, 1996, p. 3)

Invitational education is based on the importance of self-concept and a democratic classroom environment. The first principle centers on the belief that all students can learn, are valuable, and that they must take responsibility for their own learning. The second principle is based on the idea that to make learning meaningful, teachers and students must use cooperative/collaborative-learning activities. Here, the teacher and students work together. The third indicates that while learning outcomes are important, the process of learning is also critical. Just as arriving at the destination is only one part of a vacation, the journey is also important and if students are interested and motivated while learning, they are more likely to remember the material and do well on the exam. The fourth principle involves "untapped potential" and is related to the "worth" of the student and the belief that all people have talents. The fifth and final principle states that the teacher's role is to provide opportunities and an open environment to help the students discover their own strengths and talents.

Inviting Communication

"Inviting" Verbal Comments
- Let's do it together.
- I like that idea!
- Thanks very much!
- That's okay.
- Welcome!
- You can do it.

"Disinviting" Verbal Comments
- Use your head.
- Sit down and shut-up.
- Don't be so stupid.
- What's your excuse this time?
- Forget it. (Purkey & Novak, 1996, p. 194)

Multiple Intelligences

The idea that all students have "untapped potential" and that the teacher should guide the student to discover their talents relates to the concept of "multiple intelligences." Educational research has shown that intelligence is not just a single attribute, but may actually consist of as many as eight different dimensions. For example, we all know people that may not have been good students, but possess great interpersonal communication skills. Some talented musicians may have difficulty with math. These are examples of multiple intelligences. Given the diversity of intelligences, the purpose of schooling must be to expose students to different subjects and extracurricular activities to develop one or more of their intelligences (Gardner, 1983, 1995).

The eight dimensions of "multiple intelligences include:

- Linguistic
- Logical–mathematical
- Musical
- Spatial
- Kinesthetic
- Interpersonal
- Intrapersonal
- Naturalist

Linguistic intelligence includes having well developed verbal skills, vocabulary and grammar usage. These students may be good writers. *Logical–mathematical* intelligence involves the ability to understand logical reasoning and perform calculations. These students typically perform well in math and science. *Musical* intelligence consists of identifying melody, pitch, and tone. These students are musically inclined and may enjoy performing in the school chorus or band. *Spatial* intelligence is the ability to orient one's visual perception. This type of student may be artistic or inclined toward design. *Kinesthetic* intelligence involves agility and physical coordination. Here, the student may be athletic or have an interest in dancing. *Interpersonal* intelligence is the ability to relate to others. These students tend to be social and work well with people. *Intrapersonal* intelligence involves being in touch with one's own feelings. These students may be thoughtful, sensitive, and introspective which may be reflected in writing, music, or art. And finally, the last dimension, *naturalist* intelligence is the tendency to observe, ponder, and seek patterns or laws in nature. These students may be adept in scientific subjects such as biology, chemistry, or physics.

In order to tap into these multiple intelligences, the teacher needs to provide students with a variety of experiences and opportunities including cooperative/collaborative activities, music, art, and sports.

As American teachers we should remember that the focus of education today is almost exclusively linguistic and logical–mathematical. The emphasis on high stakes testing promoted through programs such as the NCLB has emphasized these two dimensions and

---

Continued Research on Multiple Intelligences

Howard Gardner is continuing his research on the dimensions of multiple intelligences. He is investigating what could become a ninth dimension—existential intelligence. This involves the ability to consider philosophical questions about existence, life, and death. (Gardner, 1999)

Emotional Intelligence: Another Measure of Intelligence

Daniel Goleman has proposed another measure of intelligence: Emotional intelligence (EI). This is an indicator of the individual's ability to defer gratification. His research suggests that this is evident in a child by age 4. In his study, children who waited to eat a marshmallow (so they would get another as a reward) tended to be better students, have more friends, and be better adjusted by the time they were in high school.

Goleman describes five components of emotional intelligence:

- Knowing your emotions
- Managing your emotions
- Motivation and focus
- Empathy
- Relationships (Goleman, 1996, pp. 49–50)

---

tends to neglect other important dimensions of intelligence. We must be aware of this problem and when possible, expose students to other forms of learning in the classroom so that all children can learn.

Subject Matter

While the teacher and learner represent the first two components of the learning environment, we now turn to the curricular materials that are actually delivered in the classroom—the subject matter.

As we have seen, there are two distinct forms of delivery of these materials: the subject-centered and the learner-centered. In the subject-centered approach, the curriculum is often driven by the content of the EOG examination or other high stakes examination developed by Educational Testing Service (ETS) or other test providers.

For example, since the NCLB has dictated a primary curricular emphasis on reading and math, those subjects provide the core of the curriculum. Other subjects such as social studies, art, and music receive less instructional time.

The curriculum materials in the subject-centered approach are usually textbooks and tend to focus on the specific factual information and computational skills that will help students prepare for these exams. The delivery of the subject matter typically is direct instruction with the teacher telling students what they must know for the test. Finally, students are evaluated on the basis of how well they perform on these tests. The test itself is often the exclusive measure of students learning.

In the learner-centered approach, both students and teachers have some input into the subject matter and curricular materials. A variety of both traditional and nontraditional instructional materials are used. The subject matter, moreover, is based, in part, on the students' needs and interests while the instructional method is one that actively involves students in the learning process. In addition to whole class instruction, students work cooperatively in groups or independently. Finally, the evaluation of student learning is based on a number of indicators in addition to traditional examinations. These might include projects, PowerPoint presentation, dioramas, skits, and journals.

The subject-centered approach is a kind of "one-size-fits-all" model of learning and evaluation. It tends to ignore both the diversity of learning styles and multiple intelligences and employs a one-dimensional evaluation of students. The learner-centered approach, on the other hand, tends to embrace the diversity of learners and intelligences by engaging and evaluating students in a variety of ways.

The Learning Milieu

The final component of the instructional environment is "the learning milieu"—the physical and social environment of the classroom. Once again, in the subject-centered/authoritarian model of education, the milieu is a structured environment, regimented in terms of time, task, and physical setting. Typically, authoritarian classrooms are arranged in classic rows and columns with the teacher a permanent fixture in the front of the class with passive, quiet, and attentive students in their assigned seats. The classroom is quiet; in fact, silence is a virtue in the subject-centered classroom, and learning proceeds in an orderly, structured fashion.

The learner-centered/democratic classroom, on the other hand, is less structured in terms of the organization of the school day, the selection and delivery of the subject matter, and even the physical setting of the classroom itself. Rather than the teacher permanently installed in the front of the class behind the teacher's desk, he or she may be more mobile, interacting with groups and individuals, depending on the project at hand. If possible, desks are arranged (and often rearranged) depending on the nature of subject. In some class periods, whole class discussion and presentations require standard arrangements of desks while in cooperative and collaborative work smaller groups break from the classic rows and columns. These classrooms may be noisy from time to time; a fact that sometimes irritates and annoys more traditional teachers and administrators. Keeping the roar to a minimum and closing the door may help in these situations.

Also remember some of the facilitative teacher characteristics discussed above. As an American teacher, you should strive to be attentive, genuine, understanding, respectful, knowledgeable, and communicative. By understanding these important characteristics of good teaching, and by creating a democratic environment where students see themselves as active participants of the education process rather than passive clients of education, you will create an inviting "family oriented" classroom where all students can learn and be successful (Purkey & Novak, 1996).

Inviting vs. Disinviting Physical Environments

"Inviting" Classrooms
- Living plants and flowers
- Big, soft pillows
- Rocking chairs
- Area rugs
- Attractive, colorful bulletin boards
- Positively worded signs (e.g., walk in the halls)

"Disinviting" Classrooms
- Artificial plants and flowers
- Dingy colors
- Clutter, dirt, and overflowing trash cans
- Faded bulletin boards (Purkey & Novak, 1996, p. 196)

Journaling Activity

The Classroom as Family
Think about the classroom as family metaphor. How is the class like a family? List characteristics that both the family and the class should have in common.

INSTRUCTIONAL METHODS

Thus far we have considered the factors that effect achievement, how students process information differently (learning modalities), how students learn (learning domains) and the instruction environment including teachers, learners, subject matter, and learning milieu. We now turn to the actual delivery of instruction (instructional methods) and conclude this section with a discussion of testing and evaluation.

As progressive educators in the late 1800s strived to improve the quality of instruction in the classroom, Johann Herbart, noted German philosopher, introduced the "lesson plan" as a general template of the process of teaching. Herbart's 5-step plan proposed that the organization of the curriculum, planning, and structured teaching were important for the students' learning and helped teachers conceptualize the overall delivery of instruction (Herbart, 1904).

The Effective Teaching Model

While Herbart's lesson plan provided the basis of instructional planning for over a century, other models have also been introduced. One of these contemporary lesson plans, called the Effective Teaching Model, is based on direct instruction and learning outcomes research (Hunter, 1994). This model is sometimes referred to as the "7-step lesson plan." While some dislike this model because it reduces teaching to "steps" and appears to organize instruction as a rigid system, we can benefit from its organized sequence of instructional elements. Moreover, this model can be adapted to a variety of instructional styles, especially the learner-centered approach to education.

The Effective Teaching Model consists of:

1. Anticipatory set
2. Instructional objective
3. Instructional input
4. Learner outcome
5. Checks for learner understanding

Herbartian Teaching Method

The Herbartian teaching method, the first lesson plan format, consists of the following five steps:

- Preparation—readiness for the student to learn
- Presentation—teaching the new material or lesson
- Association—bringing together the new ideas with previously learned knowledge
- Generalization—combining ideas
- Application—using the information

---

6. Guided practice
7. Independent practice

The first element, the *anticipatory set*, has to do with introductory remarks and initial enthusiasm of the teacher when introducing a new lesson. By presenting material as an exciting challenge, students are able to focus on the topic and establish interest and motivation. *Instructional objectives* are determined by the teacher and should be formulated as behavioral objectives. Behavioral objectives can be summarized by three questions: What do you want your students to learn; how should they demonstrate that they learned it; and, how well did they actually learn the material?

Instructional input refers to the core of the lesson and may consist of: an explanation, a lecture, a demonstration, or a discussion of a film, chart or map, etc. Again, by using a variety of instructional techniques, we can help all children to learn, irrespective of their learning styles. Next, you will, as the teacher, model or demonstrate *learner outcomes*. Here you will talk through the process as you demonstrate the task. Then, you *check for understanding* by questioning students, using individual or group responses, or checking written work. When you feel the students are ready, you will then provide *guided practice*. At this point, you will carefully monitor the students to ensure they are on the "right track." You can do this by circulating and helping individual students as needed. It

---

Behavioral Objectives

A behavioral objective consists of three components:
- What—a general description of what you want your students to learn.
- How—how you want your students to demonstrate that they have learned the objective.
  - Remember what we have learned about learning modalities—do not rely exclusively on paper-and-pencil techniques, use different methods to evaluate your students: discussion, demonstration, skits, murals, group projects, instructional games, etc.
- How well—specify a performance or satisfactory criterion level for your students.
  - This is an "acceptable level" of student performance determined by you based on the student's knowledge of the topic and their abilities.
  - This is important because it guides your pacing for the next lesson. For example, you would be: ready to go on if most students met the criterion; move faster if all or most exceeded the criterion; or reteach the lesson, if most students did not meet the criterion. When you reteach the lesson, include strategies for students who operate in different learning modalities (that is, visual, auditory, and kinesthetic). Also if you are "moving on" with your class, remember to give individual help to those students who have not yet mastered the skill.

Example of a Behavioral Objective
- What—students will be able to identify compound words.
- How—given teacher prepared cards with small words, students will be able to construct compound words.
- How well—the student will be able to match word cards to form five compound words.

is important that students do not reinforce errors when working independently. Finally, during *independent practice*, the student works without your assistance or supervision. The goal of course is for the student to be able to work independently without difficulty. Independent practice typically is aligned with the objectives in terms of what students will have learned, how they will demonstrate it, and how well they should perform. The evaluation of the student's independent practice will then guide you through the pacing and content of the next lesson.

Reflection

How can you provide for students who learn through the kinesthetic mode? How would you accommodate students who are not fluent in English?

Many teacher education programs use the Effective Teacher Lesson Plan as the model for their students to follow. Sometimes an additional point—*reflection*—is incorporated into the design. Here you complete the reflection component after the lesson has been taught. You reflect on how the lesson went: what specifically went well, what did not go well? What could you have done to improve the lesson? By reflecting on the lesson, incorporating comments in your teaching journal and using these insights as the basis for revision, instruction improves.

There are many different lesson plan formats used by teacher education programs as well as school systems. However, all have similar points that may be arranged or combined in different ways. Once you have used one or two of these plans, adjusting to another lesson plan should be relatively easy. Think about the "Big Picture": Objectives; instruction; materials; and student learning.

THE BENEFICIAL USE OF TIME

Part of being a good teacher involves the beneficial use of time in the classroom. Despite all your planning and structuring of the classroom environment with your lesson plan, it is easy for minutes to drift away during the school day. Every teacher laments that there is not enough time, but proper time management can maximize the amount of time allocated for learning (Berliner, 1979; Fisher & Berliner, 1985).

Portfolio Activity: INTASC

INTASC Standard #7: Planning

The teacher develops an effective instructional plan to help all children learn.

Design three or four lesson plans that would be part of a larger unit plan. Include objectives and ways to adapt instruction for learner needs.

Sample Evidence: The following are examples of evidence that would support your knowledge and skills related to this standard:

- Lesson plans that includes options for reteaching and grouping for remedial instruction
- Behavioral objectives with criterion levels to guide your pacing through the lessons
- Activities that are adapted for students with different learning styles

---

Portfolio Activity: INTASC

INTASC Standard #9: Reflective Practice

The teacher uses reflection (e.g., journaling) to improve instruction.

Read an article related to your teaching field in a professional journal, summarize the article, and record how you could adapt the ideas to your teaching.

Sample Evidence: The following are examples of evidence that would support your knowledge and skills related to this standard:

- Summarize the article in 1–2 pages
- Write some teaching strategies and ideas you obtained from the article

---

Good teachers develop strategies to deal with these situations that result in lost instructional time. First of all, you should be well prepared in order to maximize the use of time in the classroom. Arrive at school early, review the lessons for the day, and assemble instructional materials and handouts. Also try to devise efficient strategies to distribute materials, opening the school day, and closing the classroom at the end of the school day. Be creative in your use of time. Allocate noninstructional time (e.g., free periods, lunch breaks, etc.) for record-keeping tasks such as taking attendance, collecting lunch money, grading papers, and recording grades. In this way you can improve both your productivity and teaching.

Journaling Activity

Strategies for Efficient Use of Classroom Time

Working individually or in small groups, brainstorm some ways you could improve your use of time in your classroom. See box below.

- Transitional Time
- Instructional Time
- Postinstructional Time

Share your strategies with others in the class and record these ideas in your journal.

TESTING AND EVALUATION

Our final consideration of the instructional process is testing and evaluation, that is, determining how well have your students have learned. While paper and pencil tests have been used as the primary method of evaluating students for many years, other forms of evaluation are important as well.

Teacher-made tests that are closely aligned to the material covered in the classroom are excellent indicators of student learning. However, to compare your students' achievement with other classes, schools and states, standardized tests (commercially prepared and graded exams) are useful. The major types of these exams are:

Norm-referenced
Criterion-referenced

Teacher Use of Instructional Time

Some scholars have suggested that there are many periods during the day when time is wasted in the classroom. These have been referred to as "time leaks" that can occur during the following periods:

- **Transitional Time**
  This is the time when you are moving from one lesson or activity to another: e.g., ending math class and starting the social studies lesson; getting ready for gym class; going to and returning from the cafeteria for lunch; the beginning of day activities (students arriving, putting their coats and belongings away, finding their seats); and the end of day activities.
- **Instructional Time**
  This involves inappropriate pacing through the material. In other words, the task is too hard or too easy. Poor directions or instructions also erode instructional time. Inefficient preparation and distribution of materials interrupt the learning process. And of course, external interruptions such as an announcement over the intercom, an unexpected visitor, or fire drills.
- **Postinstructional Time**
  This involves the independent practice time. Perhaps students are overpracticing, working on skills they have already mastered, or allowing too much time for students to complete work, e.g., requiring students to write out the questions in their social studies book as well as the answers.

Norm-referenced exams compare students with others in the same grade or age-level. Scores on this type of exam may be reported in a number of ways including percentiles such as: "Heather is in the 90th percentile in reading." This can be interpreted as: Heather scored higher in reading than 90% of other fourth graders in the United States.

Criterion-referenced exams, on the other hand, have an established acceptable level of performance (criterion score), sometimes called a "cut-score." Students must meet or exceed that set score. For example, individual states have established criterion scores for each of the Praxis Exams. If the prospective teacher does not reach the criteria, he or she will not receive teacher certification. The student must retake the exam until the criterion score is met.

Norm-Referenced vs. Criterion-Referenced Tests

Norm-Referenced

- Compare individual students to others who took the national exam
  - Example: Comparison of others in the same grade or age-group
- Results reported in percentiles

Criterion-Referenced

- A preset score (criterion) must be met or exceeded for passing
  - Generally used as a condition for a decision (i.e., high school graduation, teacher certification, etc.)
- If the test-taker scores below the criterion score, he or she must retake the exam

End-of-grade exams are another example of criterion-referenced exams. Schools typically begin administering these exams several months before the end of the school year. This allows time for the students to retake and pass the exams. And as we have seen, the NCLB Act mandates that students must pass these end-of-grade exams in order to proceed to the next grade of school.

Rather than relying on one test score, however, teachers usually evaluate student learning and achievement with a number of indicators that rely on different learning modalities. These may include grades on exams, homework, participation in discussions, grades on papers, presentations, projects, etc.

Recently, portfolios have been used for the evaluation of teachers. As we have seen, during your teacher preparation program, you will begin teacher professional portfolios that are used for hiring and promotion by school districts. Also, the National Board Teacher Certification requires teachers to develop an extensive portfolio that is an important component of the national board certification process. Portfolios are also used as a central component of the Praxis III.

Reflection

Look over your assessment strategy below. Does it favor students who have certain learning styles? If so, how could you revise your assessment plan?

DISCIPLINE AND CLASSROOM MANAGEMENT

Our discussion of instruction has focused on the organization, delivery, and evaluation of student learning. But in order for that instruction to be effective, teachers must also maintain discipline in the classroom.

Over time there has been fierce debate regarding the discipline of children between educators who favor either the authoritarian or the democratic approaches to behavior management. While this debate continues to the present day, the general shift from physical punishment (sometimes favored by authoritarian educators) to psychological correction (often favored by democratic educators) has been a clear trend since the colonial period.

During the 1600s through the early 1800s, corporal or physical punishment was common in most American schools. During the mid-1800s, however, methods of discipline began to change and some teachers began to use a combination of rewards for good behavior and academic achievement, and humiliation for misbehavior and poor achieve-

---

Portfolio Activity: INTASC

INTASC Standard #8: Assessment

The teacher uses formal and informal assessment strategies.

Devise a strategy to assess your students in a specific subject area. Include both formal and informal assessment. Remember to include multiple measures that reflect different learning styles and intelligences.

Sample Evidence: The following are examples of evidence that would support your knowledge and skills related to this standard:

- List assessments and classify by type
- Include a teacher made test (created by you)
- List activities or projects you could use in the assessment

ment. Then, beginning in the early 1900s, less severe disciplinary methods emerged. These included the social efficiency approach, behavior conditioning techniques, and the progressive/humanistic approach.

CORPORAL PUNISHMENT

Traditional attitudes toward children were rooted in the Biblical interpretation of inheriting original sin. As a result, children were born "stained" with sin and discipline needed to be severe to purge the influence of the devil. In the colonial era schools, discipline was extremely harsh and the use of whipping posts is evidence of the level of brutality. Punishment was usually administered before the class to serve as an example to the other students. Moreover, severe punishment was administered for what we might consider slight offenses, such as not learning the lesson, being tardy, talking in class, not finishing a lesson, or not paying attention (Parkerson & Parkerson, 2001).

REWARDS AND PSYCHOLOGICAL PUNISHMENT

Gradually, during the 1800s, methods of discipline began to change. This was the result of the changing perceptions of children promoted by a number of philosophers and educational reformers and the emerging market economy.

During the 1700s, philosophers such as John Locke and Jean-Jacques Rousseau fostered the changing perception of children. Locke introduced his ideas on psychological discipline consisting of praise and encouragement for correct behavior and humiliation for misbehavior. He considered children to be innocent and malleable, rather than being "stained by original sin." He therefore rejected corporal punishment (Locke, 1705/1968, p. 211).

Rousseau also perceived children as being inherently good, but argued that it was society that corrupted them. As a result, Rousseau also advocated psychological discipline, rather than corporal punishment (Rousseau, 1974).

These "new" ideas concerning child rearing gradually were embraced by middle class American families and paralleled other changes in society at the time. American women, for example were having fewer children and investing more "quality" time in their development. And by the mid-1800s, numerous "advice books" and advice columns in newspapers and magazines were encouraging middle class Americans to avoid corporal punishment in favor of psychological discipline that emphasized rewards and humane punishment.

Educational reformers also embraced these new ideas of discipline in the classroom. The famous educator Joseph Lancaster, father of the so-called monitorial system of education, for example, often rewarded his high achieving and well behaved students with books, medals, and specially engraved coins while he routinely used the "dunce cap" to punish students that misbehaved. Lancaster, however, rarely beat his students. These techniques helped him educate large numbers of children, to the extent that classes had 250 students or more, while he kept them both motivated and on-task.

Educational professors who trained teachers popularized the ideas of *psychological discipline*. They stressed the importance of *motivation,* the *desire to learn,* and the value of encouraging good behavior and achievement through *praise*. Clearly, a sea change in disciplinary techniques was at hand by the mid-1800s (Hewett, 1884; Northend, 1853; Parkerson & Parkerson, 2001).

In addition to this fundamental shift in attitudes among philosophers and educational reformers, the emerging market society made a shift from trading and bartering to a cash-based economy. This new economy also fostered new attitudes toward discipline.

Joseph Lancaster's Methods of Discipline

Lancaster provided rewards (little toys, books, medals, etc.) for academic achievement and good behavior. For misbehavior such as tardiness, talking, or not completing lessons, Lancaster used the psychological methods of humiliation. Students might wear a small log around their neck, or a paper crown on their head (perhaps a dunce cap), and boys who came to school with dirty hands suffered the embarrassment of being washed by a girl in front of the class. (Kaestle, 1973)

As a result of this change, a person's status was no longer ascribed simply by inheritance, but also by one's individual achievement.

Middle-class Americans soon recognized that education for their children was crucial to enable them to succeed in the new economy. Moreover, students had to be *motivated* to do well and simply forcing them to "go through the motions" in school was discovered to not be in their best interest. This motivational concept also helped to transform discipline. *Encouragement and rewards* for achievement was found to be superior to, and more successful than, brutal punishment and fear of that punishment. Finally, the relationship between teachers and students began to change as well. Rather than the teacher demanding absolute deference, and enforcing that deference with the whip, an environment of mutual respect between teachers and students became more common.

SOCIAL EFFICIENCY MOVEMENT

The new methods of discipline continued to gain popularity as we moved from the rural one-room schools of the 1800s to urban "graded" schools and high schools and the early 1900s. But while the routine use of the whip became less common during this period, and student–teacher relations generally improved, the growing size of classrooms called for new approaches to discipline. Among these was the *social efficiency movement*. This approach was characterized by standardized classrooms with wooden desks and chairs bolted to the floor and arranged in rows, facing the blackboard and teacher's desk. In addition, there was a new emphasis on student regimentation to control large classes of 40 or more students. This organizational arrangement endured during most of the 20th century.

William Bagley first suggested the social efficiency movement in his work, *Classroom Management*. He argued that the main purpose of school was to develop habits for good workers in the new industrial society including being prompt, not missing work, following instructions, and working hard. Strict discipline and regimentation were deemed necessary (Bagley, 1925).

Dismissal of a Teacher because She "Don't Lick them at all"

Young Mary Augusta Roper was educated in the new psychological methods of discipline in her teacher education program at the Hampton Institute during the mid-1800s. Her first teaching position was in Mill Point, Michigan. She taught her school using the disciplinary methods in which she was trained. Miss Roper "never used the rod unless a scholar refused to obey." Parents, however, did not like her new methods and demanded her dismissal for the reason that she "don't lick them at all." (Kaufman, 1984, p. 163; see also Parkerson & Parkerson, 2001)

He suggested that children move through the halls in line, quietly, and in lockstep. To avoid class disruptions and promote efficiency, children had scheduled restroom breaks, sometimes called "toilet recess."

Well into the 1970s, "toilet recess" continued to be a common practice. Indeed, some schools still use this practice today. This may be in part due to the physical structure of the school buildings—typically in schools there are long halls with large central restrooms for girls and boys, as well as drinking fountains located in each hall. Many newer elementary schools today have an adjoining restroom for each classroom. Most high schools still have several large central restrooms. The monitoring of restrooms continues to be a problem for teachers. Teachers have tried many strategies to control behavior in restrooms, including the use of individual restroom passes, student monitors, and even listening at the door.

Students were required to sit up straight at their desks, with hands folded and their feet flat on the floor. Teachers sometimes would call their students to "attention" with a clap or other signal, such as a bell. Although this method of discipline encouraged students to remain silent and obedient, critics argued that these students were not necessarily engaged in the learning process.

Extending this structure even further was a method called "squads for discipline" developed by E. W. Elmore along the line of military units. Each squad consisted of a row that had a nickname such as "bluebirds." The head of each row was the leader who kept his squad in control. The misbehavior of one student in the group resulted in the punishment of the entire squad. Here, peer pressure was used to control the behavior of students (Elmore, 1923).

This classroom management approach was part of the "social efficiency" or "scientific management" movement and was especially popular with administrators. Many educators, on the other hand, were not comfortable with its rigid structure, arguing that it smothered students. Remnants of the social efficiency movement are evident in some schools today.

BEHAVIORISM

During the early to mid-1900s, behavioral psychology developed from the work of John Watson and others. As we have seen in chapter 2, Watson had argued that all human behavior was a response to external conditioning and, as a result, could be molded. By the mid-1900s, B. F. Skinner popularized these ideas and developed the concept of reinforcement and rewards based on his stimulus–response research. He advocated that teachers establish classroom discipline through *positive reinforcement and reward*. Misbehavior,

---

Walden Two

B. F. Skinner wrote a novel called *Walden Two*, that attempted to demonstrate how his ideas on behavioral psychology should be implemented in schools. In his fictional community, children were happy, peaceful, and well-behaved. He claimed that all problems in schools could be eliminated if teachers would strictly adhere to his behavioral conditioning techniques. He was very critical of teachers and the "excessiveness" of students. (Perhaps this was a conservative reaction against the liberal youth movement of the 1960s and early 1970s.) His book, however, was very influential. (Skinner, 1974)

he argued, should be ignored (if possible) so that the student is not given attention for their misbehavior and inadvertently rewarded for it.

Skinner was influential in establishing the field of *behavioral psychology* and today so-called "neo-Skinnerians" have continued to develop disciplinary techniques that are used in schools today. One such approach is *Positive Classroom Discipline*, developed by Fredrick Jones in the late 1980s. His method encouraged teachers to control their students by using nonverbal methods such as eye contact, facial expressions, hand gestures, and physical proximity (Jones, 1987; Skinner, 1951, 1971).

Assertive discipline was another behavioral approach that was developed by Marlene and Lee Canter. This model suggested that teachers "take charge," clearly lay out a discipline plan, and establish a system of rewards and punishments. While the punishment component of their model differed from Skinner—who did not favor punishment—these sorts of behavioral modification techniques are common in classrooms today with the use of certificates, stars, and smiley faces as rewards for good behavior and achievement (Canter & Canter, 1976, 1993).

PROGRESSIVE/HUMANISTIC APPROACHES

Despite the popularity of social efficiency and behavioral modification approaches to student discipline, many educators rejected them. They contended that "keeping order" in the classroom did not mean that learning was taking place. Furthermore, they argued that these authoritarian approaches squelched students and diminished their motivation.

These ideas are rooted in the work of Pestalozzi and Rousseau (see chapter 6). As we have seen, these important educators argued that one way of maintaining discipline was to keep students engaged in activities in which they were interested. Pestalozzi also developed a child-centered approach to education that emphasized the interests and needs of students and promoted love and understanding as the basic theme of teaching (Parkerson & Parkerson, 2001).

Corporal Punishment

As a teacher you need to know what your state and school system advocate in terms of punishment. If you are allowed to paddle students, make sure you follow the guidelines. And before you undertake the task, ask yourself some important questions:

- Have you exhausted all other methods to control the student's behavior?
- Is there anything else you might try? Consult your school psychologist, counselor, social worker, and special education teacher.
- Is physical punishment (violence) the message you want to send to the student concerning how to handle problems?
- Has this student been punished physically at home? Probably so, and apparently this approach has not been successful. Indeed it may have made the child worse.
- What will the effect be on the student and others in the class?

Corporal punishment should be avoided. If it is used, it should be as a last resort and only in extreme circumstances.

Francis Parker embraced these new ideas in the late 1800s when he implemented this method in his Massachusetts school. His approach, called the *Quincy Method,* focused on the child and used innovative instructional techniques such as grouping students, and encouraging teachers and students to work together cooperatively (Parker, 1883).

A few years later, John and Alice Dewey adapted these ideas and put them into practice at their University of Chicago Laboratory School. They employed an activity-based approach to learning based on cooperation rather than competition. The Deweys and their progressive colleagues felt that if students were kept actively engaged in learning something socially useful, in a cooperative setting, discipline would not be a problem. In addition to gaining academic knowledge, they contended, students would also develop important social skills (Dewey & Dewey, 1915).

Other progressive schools that emerged during this period developed students who were highly motivated, had higher self-esteem, and displayed fewer discipline problems. This democratic approach to both instruction and discipline in the schools was a dramatic shift from the authoritarian approach that focused on regimen, structure, and discipline.

Today, many neoprogressives argue that democratic classrooms and the use of positive reinforcement can best maintain discipline. For example, Alfie Kohn has shown that the use of praise is more effective, in the long run, than rewards and prizes (as advocated in assertive discipline). He also argued that we need to develop classrooms that are democratic environments where students assume responsibility for themselves. In so doing they develop an active "proprietary interest" in their classroom and their behavior improves significantly (Kohn, 1996).

These progressive ideas continued to operate in democratic classrooms across the nation. In the early 1970s, Rudolf Dreikurs formulated his ideas of democratic discipline that became very popular. Dreikurs felt that the classroom should be one of mutual respect where the group, rather than the teacher alone, established classroom rules. When students were given input into the rules and the consequences for violating the rules, they tended to take more responsibility for their own behavior. Additionally, this situation engages students in the democratic process that is so beneficial (Dreikurs & Cassel, 1972).

Other neoprogressive reformers advocated activity-based learning to prevent misbehavior. The movement and pacing of activities as well as the transition from one activity to

---

Kohn's Problem-Solving Techniques for a Democratic Classroom

- Establish a positive relationship with your students.
- Help students develop behavioral skills.
- Diagnose why a problem occurred.
- Look for underlying problems and causes.
- Expand student's role in decision making.
- Encourage children to develop solutions.
- Help the student understand their misbehavior and how they might correct the situation (i.e., clean up, repair, etc.).
- Have class or group meetings to develop problem solving strategies.
- Follow up on student problem-solving strategies.
- When other measures do not work, a punishment should be given, such as a time-out, but the teacher should express a genuine concern for the child, regret about the action, and confidence that this will solve the problem. (Kohn, 1996)

the next was crucial in keeping students "on track." Teachers also needed to be aware of everything that was going on in the classroom, what Jacob Kounin called "with-it-ness" and "overlapping." Here teachers should be able to deal with several groups or individuals at the same time, perhaps similar to the idea of multitasking today (Kounin, 1971).

Other neoprogressive reformers such as Hiam Ginott argued that *communication* was crucial in maintaining student discipline. They also argued that the teacher should demonstrate self-discipline and self-control to set an example for students. Moreover, instead of labeling students (such as dummies), blaming them for misbehavior, or attacking them with "you" messages, such as "Johnny—you never pay attention," the teacher should instead say, "Johnny, I would like you to listen quietly." This message is more effective as it tells the student what behavior is expected. These researchers also contended that *self-esteem* plays an important role in classroom discipline and that students with low self-esteem are more likely to cause problems in the classroom (Ginott, 1965 1971).

CORRECTIVE DISCIPLINE IN THE DEMOCRATIC CLASSROOM

Progressive educators such as Parker and the Deweys, as well as neoprogressives such as Dreikurs, Kounin, and Ginott, each favored preventative disciplinary methods rather than corrective methods for misbehavior. But even in the best managed, democratic classrooms, discipline problems are possible. To deal with this situation, a number of democratically based disciplinary techniques have been developed. One of the most successful is William Glasser's *Reality Therapy*, an approach that focuses on the modification of one's own behavior. He argued that schools should be a pleasant place, that teachers should treat students with respect and that teachers and students should participate together in a democratic environment. Then, if a student misbehaves, the teacher can implement steps to help the student modify his or her behavior.

First, the teacher must assist the child in identifying the misbehavior. The student must acknowledge that the behavior is incorrect and understand why it is incorrect. For

---

The Role of Student Mediators

Students who serve as mediators for their peers should be able to do the following:

- Serve as role models for other students.
- Be alert to potential problems or conflicts between students.
- Follow specific procedures in conflict resolution:
  - Only one person talks at a time.
  - Listen to both sides, or all involved.
  - Find out what behavior needs to be stopped.
  - Ask the student to stop the behavior.
  - Have both students apologize and shake hands.
  - Check back with the students to see if the problem has been resolved or if the teacher needs to take over.
  - Refer unresolved problems to the teacher.
- Refrain from passing judgment.
- Don't act like a "policeman." (Calhoon, 1988, pp. 92–93; Roderick, 1988, pp. 86–91)

Portfolio Activity: INTASC

INTASC Standard #5: Motivation and Management

The teacher uses a variety of motivational and classroom management techniques.

Select a classroom management technique that you feel would work best for you as a teacher. Describe how you would implement the classroom management system.

Sample Evidence: The following are examples of evidence that would support your knowledge and skills related to this standard:

- Write a page describing the classroom management system
- Describe how you would introduce your students to the management system
- Discuss ways to implement and handle the classroom management plan

---

Reflection

How could you modify your plan, if it does not work well? Remember to take your students' needs and interests into consideration.

---

example, it's not enough for the student to passively admit that he or she has "been bad." The teacher should then guide the student to develop a plan to correct the problem. The student must take responsibility for developing the plan with the teacher making some suggestions. The student should write down the plan of action and commit to it. The teacher then guides the student to adhere to the plan. Although this may appear to be a cumbersome and difficult process (it might seem easier simply to discipline the student and make him or her remain silent), this technique has proven to be remarkably effective (Glasser, 1965, 1969).

During the 1970s and 1980s, the use of *conflict resolution* or *mediation programs* also emerged in schools. Recently, these programs have resurfaced as useful solutions to discipline problems. These programs employ communication, cooperation, and problem-solving skills. Students are taught to be mediators for their peers and help them resolve minor problems. Two students are assigned to work out a problem with their peers and students are responsible for themselves and their classmates (Calhoon, 1988; Roderick, 1988).

Today, we see more and more democratic/humanistic discipline methods used in the classroom, though the remnants of the authoritarian, social efficiency approach and the use of humiliation remain. It is important to remember, that the use of public humiliation as a disciplinary measure may be counterproductive in the sense that the student may become sullen, resentful, and have lower self-esteem, resulting in more behavioral problems. Humiliation of students should be avoided at all costs. Good teachers are kind and fair to their students and treat them with respect.

AN INVITATION TO TEACHING

With the help of this book and your professors during your education, you will have a good understanding of our noble profession and what it takes to become a good teacher. You have taken the first step in an exciting journey into the classrooms of the nation. We welcome you as the newest generation of American teachers.

SUMMARY

Instruction and Discipline

Instruction

While the curriculum represents the course of study of the school, instruction is the delivery of the curriculum content and works in concert with the curriculum and the textbooks. Teachers implement instruction either by explaining to students exactly what they need to know (authoritarian/subject–centered approach), or by guiding student's learning through inquiry or discovery (democratic/learner–centered approach).

Learning is a complex process, but educational researchers have demonstrated that there are four important factors that effect student achievement. These include psychological, sociological, physiological, and educational factors. Each of these factors will help to explain why some students do well in school, while others do not. Teachers must be alert to each of these factors and employ steps to help students learn.

Students learn in different ways so teachers need to be aware of various learning modalities. Some students receive information auditorily, some visually, while others process information kinesthetically or tactilely. While most teachers incorporate auditory and visual methods in their teaching methods, the kinesthetic or tactile learner is often neglected. To accommodate all of their students, teachers should include "hands-on" learning in their classrooms.

Learning modalities help us understand the ways in which students' process information. In addition, there are a number of learning domains that provide insight into how students learn. The three learning domains are the cognitive, the affective, and the psychomotor.

Although the instructional environment is complex, there are four central components of learning in the classroom. These include the teacher, the learner, the subject matter, and the learning milieu. By understanding each of these components and how they interact, we can create a positive learning environment where all students to learn.

Discipline and Student Management

Classroom discipline has also changed dramatically over time. Rather than employing harsh physical punishment, such as whippings and beatings, teachers have shifted from authoritarian methods of discipline to more democratic methods.

In the democratic classroom, teachers use motivation, rewards, and positive reinforcement to encourage good behavior. Here, students have an active role in the process, as they create their own classroom rules and define consequences for misbehavior.

Mediation is a more recent technique used to deal with student conflicts. In this case, students learn communication skills, cooperation, and problem-solving skills.

Finally, educational research has demonstrated that teachers should never use humiliation to discipline their students, since this approach is counterproductive and fosters poor self-concept and negative attitudes.

DISCUSSION QUESTIONS

1. What instructional methods were used in the common school? Describe the problems the teacher must have encountered teaching children of different ages and various abilities. Do some of these challenges exist for the teacher today?
2. Discuss invitational schooling. How would you create an inviting classroom?
3. What are the advantages of the democratic classroom in terms of the effect on student discipline?

Section 5

The Noble Profession

Chapter 10

The Organization and Funding of Schools

While the organization of public schools has changed considerably over the last 200 years, one thing remains constant. Throughout our long educational history, teachers have been the center of all school organizations. It is the teacher and her schools that are the heart of education.

SCHOOL ORGANIZATION TODAY

There are a number of ways to understand the organizational structure of schools. Most models, as they are called, are hierarchical (top-down) and as such they present a misleading message about the nature of education today.

Typically these schemes picture the state legislature, school board, and other administrative structure as layers "above" the local school. In this way, teachers are depicted at the bottom, often placed "below" the school custodian and secretary.

Hierarchical Model of School Administration

School Board

Superintendent

Assistant Superintendent---- Curriculum
Coordinators

School A   School B   School C   School D   School E

Principal----Site-Based Council

Secretary------
--------Assistant Principal
Custodians----

Teacher   Teacher   Teacher   Teacher   Teacher   Teacher
&   &
Team Leader   Dept. Head

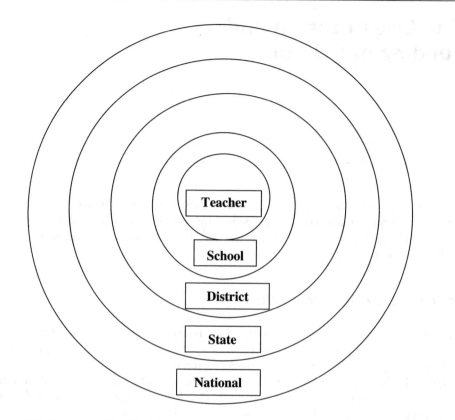

Figure 10.1 Concentric Ring Model

While there is nothing inherently wrong with the top down model, we prefer a representation that demonstrates the central role of the teacher in the organization scheme. As such, we have chosen a concentric ring model to illustrate school organizations today. This concentric ring model will not change the administrative relationships of the public school but it may help to symbolically restate the importance of teachers in the structure of modern education.

Stated very simply, there are five basic components or "rings" of educational administration. Reading from the outer ring, they are:

- The Federal Government Administration
- The State Administration
- The Local School District Administration
- The Local School Administration
- The Teacher

In addition to understanding the various concentric rings of administration, American teachers should also be aware of the kinds of relationships between individuals within the educational system. Generally speaking, there are two types of professional relationships in education: line and staff. Line relationships represent the direct authority of one individual to another such as the principal's relationship to you or the superintendent's relationship to the principal. While your principal does not have arbitrary power over you as a professional, he or she is your "boss" and has the formal power to supervise and evaluate you. Staff relationships, on the other hand, are less formal and have no supervi-

Links to the Past: Local Community Involvement in Public Schools

Delos Hackley, a commercial farmer from Batavia, New York, was a school trustee in his local community and he took an active role in the affairs of the public school. Throughout the spring and summer of 1862, he voluntarily gave his time and energy to rebuild the old schoolhouse.

In the spring of 1862, Delos recorded in his diary that "the old schoolhouse burned down." Over the next 8 months he helped to repair the school. About a week after the fire, he noted that he "went up to the Welches (swamp) to engage some poles for rafters for the old schoolhouse." Two days later he and "John went up to the Welches swamp and cut rafters for the schoolhouse. The following day he "drew home a load of rafters." Delos then prepared his fields by fertilizing, rolling the ground and eventually sewing peas, barley and corn. However, in mid June he managed to squeeze in some more time to work on the schoolhouse. On June 16 he "drew timber to the schoolhouse" and later in the day he returned home and "hoed corn." Several weeks later on June 30, he "commenced on the schoolhouse." Delos also worked the following Saturday and two days of the next week on the schoolhouse. At this point the building was suitable for the next term and his work ceased until the fall. (Parkerson & Parkerson, 1998, p. 82)

sory or evaluation component. Your department chair, team leader, or mentor each have a staff relationship to you. You certainly will respect their "authority," but they do not have administrative power over you. Keep these sorts of administrative relationships in mind as we begin our journey into the complex world of educational administration and organization.

THE FEDERAL GOVERNMENT ADMINISTRATION

While a number of countries throughout the world have centralized, national systems of public education, the United States does not. Because of our decentralized form of government, individual states traditionally have maintained a great deal of power and autonomy. Moreover, under the provisions of the 10th Amendment to the U.S. Constitution, all powers not specifically granted to the federal government are assumed to be powers of the states. As a result, when public schools emerged in this country during the 1800s, they naturally (although very gradually) came under the authority of the states.

Throughout much of the 1800s, however, public schools were controlled by local communities and funded exclusively through local property taxes. Local residents shared responsibility for the construction and maintenance of the schoolhouse (as Delos Hackley did in the 1860s), as well as the boarding of teachers. Their organization was simple, with elected school officials, sometimes called trustees, responsible for the hiring, firing, and annually "examining" of both children and teachers.

As the educational needs of the nation increased, however, control of public schools was gradually assumed by the state, with shared responsibility for funding through state tax revenues and local property taxes. With state money, however, came the call for greater accountability; and in the late 1800s, schools adopted the corporate model of organization. With this hierarchical system, state departments of public instruction and superintendents defined policy and directed the curriculum of the schools. Local superintendents carried out these directives and delegated authority to school principals who, in

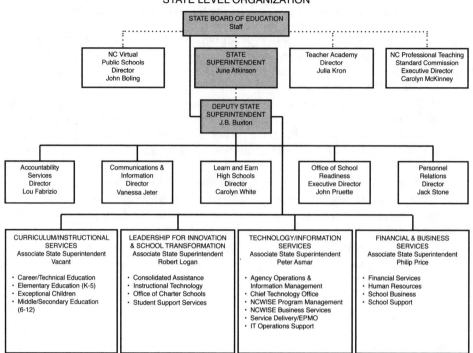

Figure 10.2 State Level Organization. Retrieved July 20, 2007, from North Carolina Public Schools: http://www.ncpublicschools.org/about_dpi

turn, supervised and evaluated schoolteachers. Local boards of education would continue their involvement in the schools by monitoring the actions of states; however, their power gradually became more indirect (Parkerson & Parkerson, 2001).

Reflection

In the last half century, the federal government has grown in size and function. It now has more influence in our live than ever before. Should the federal government increase its involvement in education? Should there be national credentialing standards? Should we have a national curriculum? Discuss both sides of these issues.

While the state-controlled, corporate, bureaucratic model remains powerful, in recent years, it has been subjected to a great deal of criticism. For example, inequities in funding between rich and poor regions of states, as well as between suburban and urban communities, have caused serious problems and tended to reinforce poverty. Moreover, the recent perception of failure in the public schools has led many Americans to question the foundation of the state school organization.

Because of these and other problems, a host of new solutions such as privatization and educational vouchers have been proposed. Moreover, as the federal government increased funding of public education, it also began to demand greater accountability of schools. As a result of these political, social, and economic changes, some control of schools has very gradually begun to shift to the national level.

Department of Defense (DOD) Schools

The Department of Defense provides schools for military bases both abroad and in the United States. The requirements for obtaining a teaching position in these schools include a degree in the field of education you wish to teach, successful completion of the Praxis exams, and a teaching certificate. For example, Ft. Bragg in Fayetteville, North Carolina, has a number of elementary and middle schools on base. At the high school level, children of the military attend the Cumberland County Schools. To find out more information regarding these teaching positions contact http://www.militaryconnection.com and register.

This "control," however, is more indirect and virtual, at least for now! For example, since the beginning of our nation's history the content of the curriculum has been defined by local communities and states. Recently however, national academic standards such as the No Child Left Behind Act have begun to redirect the curriculum. Similarly, credentialing standards defined by national organizations such as NCATE, Carnegie, and the Holmes Group now play an important role in the professional lives of teachers.

States and local communities, of course, will continue to direct school policy, but their roles have gradually begun to change from direct control to advocacy. The 300-year shift from local to state to national control appears to be an emerging reality.

Direct Federal Control

The federal government, of course, does have direct control of public education in a number of areas. For example, schools in the nation's capitol, Washington D.C., are directly funded and administered by the U.S. Congress. Similarly, the children of National Park employees; children in U.S. "outlying possessions" such as the Marshall Islands; children on Indian reservations, and children of military personnel all attend schools that are either directly or indirectly controlled by the federal government. In addition, the Department of Defense maintains the Military Academy at West Point, New York; the Naval Academy at Annapolis, Maryland; the Coast Guard Academy at New London, Connecticut; and the Air Force Academy at Colorado Springs, Colorado.

Links to the Past: The Call for the Establishment of a National Bureau of Education

At a meeting of the National Association of State and City School Superintendents in 1866, three educators, E. E. White (Ohio), Newton Bateman (Illinois), and J. S. Adams (Vermont), called for the establishment of a national bureau of education. In their important statement (which led to the establishment of the Department of Education the following year), these educators argued that such an institution would "impart to the cause of education a dignity and importance which would surely widen its influence and enhance its success."

The document concluded by saying: "Universal education, next to universal liberty is a matter of deep national concern.It is an imperative necessity of the American Republic that the common school be planted on every square mile of its peopled territory. The creation of a bureau of education by Congress would be a practical recognition of this great truth." (Cohen, 1974a, pp. 1290–1291)

In addition, the federal government has traditionally maintained a policy of funding, advocacy, and research for public education. Throughout its existence, the U.S. Department of Education has maintained this tradition.

U.S. Department of Education

Much of the virtual and real power of the federal government in the area of education today is expressed through the U.S. Department of Education. This cabinet level federal agency was established relatively recently in 1979, under President Jimmy Carter, but it has existed in one form or another for well over 135 years.

In 1867, the first Department of Education was established by an act of Congress. The Department assisted with the important work of the Freedman's Bureau schools during Reconstruction following the Civil War. As we have seen, these schools brought education to former slave children as well as poor whites and represented the first system of public schooling in many parts of the South. In addition, the Department of Education was charged with the responsibility of "collecting such statistics and facts as shall show the condition and progress of education" in the United States (U.S. Bureau of Education, 1895).

The following year, however, the Department of Education was "downgraded" to the status of an "Office" within the Department of Interior. For the next 70 years the Office of Education worked in obscurity and dutifully compiled statistics and issued official educational reports to Congress.

Then in 1939, the Office was reassigned to the Federal Security Agency, a New Deal–Great Depression program that later (1953) was renamed the Department of Health, Education and Welfare. The Office of Education remained here until 1979 when it achieved cabinet level status.

Funding, Advocacy, and Research

Throughout its short life, the U.S. Department of Education has continued its tradition of funding, advocacy, and research rather than direct control. In fact, one of the most important roles of the federal involvement in public education is in the area of categorical financial aid. As Congress perceives problems within society, it sets aside money to deal directly with them. Funds are earmarked for specific purposes such as bilingual education, vocational education, disabilities education, and programs such as antidrug education and Head Start.

In addition to funding, officials within the federal government often advocate educational policies and programs. Sometimes these programs are promoted through the

---

Regional Resource and Federal Centers

The Regional Resource and Federal Centers (RRFC) Network is made up of the six Regional Resource Centers for Special Education (RRC) and the Federal Resource Center (FRC).

The six RRCs and the FRC are funded by the federal Office of Special Education Programs (OSEP) to assist state education agencies in the systematic improvement of education programs, practices, and policies that affect children and youth with disabilities. These centers offer consultation, information services, technical assistance, training, and product development.

Source: RRFC Network, retrieved July 15, 2007, from http://www.rrfcnetwork.org

---

Regional Education Laboratories

There are 10 regional education laboratories that conduct research and provide support to schools in their region. Each region has specialty areas; for example, the Midwest region focuses on math and science.

Source: Institute of Education Sciences, 1996

---

authority of the Secretary of the Department of Education. Secretaries William W. Bennett and Lamar Alexander, for example, used their positions to advocate school choice, privatization, and voucher plans for the nation's public schools (U.S. Senate, 1985).

Similarly, the President of the United States has used his power to influence educational policy. For example, the influential report *Nation at Risk*, discussed earlier, was written under the direction of an educational committee created by former President Ronald Reagan. A decade later, President Bill Clinton proposed mandatory national reading examinations in Grade 4 and mathematics tests in Grade 8. And, of course, the current national educational agenda, No Child Left Behind, emerged under the presidency of George W. Bush (National Commission for Excellence in Education, 1983).

Regional Resource Centers and Educational Laboratories

In addition to the funding of specific educational programs through categorical aid and advocating educational policies, the federal government also plays an important role in educational research. As part of the Elementary and Secondary Education Act of 1965, passed during the Great Society Programs of Lyndon Johnson, a series of Regional Resource Centers and Educational Laboratories were established. Today there are six regional centers that serve states throughout the nation.

The federal government has also established 10 Regional Educational Laboratories that inform educators of cutting edge research through seminars, workshops, and conferences. In addition to disseminating research findings, each lab has a specific research agenda and conducts it own educational research and curriculum development. For example, the Southeast Region focuses on early childhood education; the Midwest Region focuses on math and science; and the West Region addresses assessment and accountability.

National Centers, Clearinghouses, and Regional Assistance Centers

The federal government also maintains a number of Centers, Clearinghouses, and Regional Assistance Centers. These diverse organizations conduct educational research, disseminate research findings, and provide technical assistance. There are 15 Comprehensive Regional Assistance Centers that provide training and technical assistance to improve teaching and learning. For example, the Eisenhower Regional Mathematics and Science Education Consortia disseminate instructional materials and provide a network for math and science education. The National Clearinghouse for Comprehensive School Reform, on the other hand, provides a virtual "literature library" for educators and assists in planning and implementing reform programs in the schools. Finally, the Equity Assistance Center helps schools achieve equity goals in areas of race, gender, and national origin, while the National Clearinghouse for English Language Acquisition and Language Instruction Educational Programs disseminates information to schools on effective English language instruction.

National Foundations and Organizations

In addition to the direct and indirect role of the federal government in the area of education, there are a number of nongovernmental national foundations and programs that provide funding and services to schools and educators throughout the country. Others provide external evaluation of teacher education programs.

Philanthropic Foundations

Some of the largest philanthropic foundations in the country are the W. K. Kellogg Foundation, the Ford Foundation, the Carnegie Corporation, the Lilley Endowment, and the Rockefeller Foundation. Each of these endowments (as they are called) provides funding and support for educational initiatives. For example, the Carnegie and Rockefeller foundations both support the National Commission on Teaching and America's Future. This group works to reform and nurture teaching in America. Similarly, the Carnegie Corporation supports the work of the National Board for Professional Teaching Standards. As we will see in chapter 13, this organization promotes teaching excellence and provides a career ladder for teachers (Nielsen, 1972).

Despite the important work of these and other philanthropic foundations, however, conservatives in this country consistently have criticized them. In 1978, for example, William Simon, President of the Olin Corporation, challenged the work of these foundations

Interstate New Teacher Assessment and Support Consortium (INTASC)

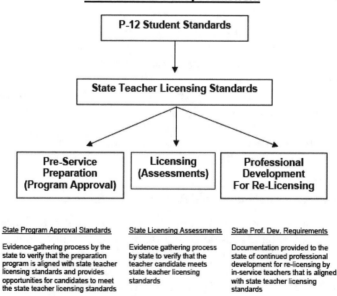

°INTASC/CCSSO

Figure10.3 State Teacher Policy Framework. The above model represents The Interstate New Teacher Assessment and Support Consortium (INTASC's) recommendation for teacher preparation and licensing for each state.

    The INTASC State Teacher Policy Framework diagram was developed by the Council of Chief State School Officers and member states. Copies may be downloaded from the Council's Web site at http://www.ccsso.org/content/pdfs/StateTeacherPolicy-Framework.pdf.

as having a liberal bias. He called upon conservative corporate leaders to create what he called a "counterintelligencia" to fight against this alleged bias (Simon, 1978).

As a result of this reaction, a number of conservative agencies have been created in recent years. These include the Heritage Foundation, The American Enterprise Institute, The Hudson Institute, The Manhattan Institute, The Olin Foundation, and the John Locke Society—to name just a few. These groups support programs of school choice, charter schools, and the privatization of schools (Spring, 2000).

National Evaluation Organizations

While national philanthropic foundations have played a major role in funding educational programs and influencing educational policy, other national organizations have emerged over the years to evaluate schools and teacher education programs. The Interstate New Teacher Assessment and Support Consortium (INTASC), for example, was created in 1987 to improve the quality of teachers. The 10 INTASC principles published in 1993 describe what new teachers should know and be able to do when they first enter the classroom. (See http://www.ccsso.org/content/pdfs/corestrd.pdf, retrieved February 25, 2008). In addition, the National Council of Assessment of Teacher Education (NCATE) plays a major role in assessing the quality of teacher education programs throughout the country. NCATE has developed rigorous standards for departments, schools, and colleges of education, and requires annual assessments as well as periodic "on site" evaluations of teacher education programs. For more information see http://www.ncate.org.

THE STATE ADMINISTRATION

While the federal government, national philanthropic foundations, and assessment organizations represent the outer ring of our educational administrative model; the state is the next ring of administration.

State Governors, Legislatures, and the Courts

As we noted above, states gradually assumed control of public schooling from local communities during the late 1800s. They often modeled their organization on the successful corporate business structure that was emerging at that time.

Typically, state constitutions provided governors, legislatures, and courts with the power to define public school policy. Today, state legislatures shape general school policy through statues (laws) and they often proscribe the duties of other educational units in the state such as the state board of education.

The governor's role as the state's chief executive officer is to monitor the actions of the legislature and he or she often has veto power over legislation. The governor can also use the enormous political power of that office to direct educational policy. For example, the governor might create specific commissions to reform education or simply use a "bully pulpit" to encourage new legislation or new policy. The bully pulpit is another name for appearing on television and radio to promote a particular idea or plan.

Finally, state courts act as a check to balance the actions of the legislative and executive branches of state government. State courts often rule on the constitutionality of a particular school law or policy. Just as the U.S. Supreme Court declared state school segregation laws illegal in its famous Brown v. Board of Education decision of 1954, state courts routinely grapple with the constitutionality of other school laws.

And yet, despite the "checks and balances" built into the system, legislators, governors, and even judges are often influenced by lobbyists, agencies, groups and individuals who influence policy according to their needs. "Lobbyists" include taxpayers groups, civil rights groups, labor unions, teachers' unions, manufacturing associations, local chambers of commerce, religious groups, and political parties.

State Boards of Education

As a result of these powerful lobbyists, state legislators often seek the advice and counsel of State Boards of Education. These bodies were created to provide advisory and regulatory functions regarding education. State Boards of Education often study the educational needs of the state and make recommendations to the governor and the legislature. They also work in tandem with educational commissions. These commissions might be formed to study the issue of school violence or how to increase test scores among students, or they might study district reorganization or even statewide textbook adoption. State Boards of Education also have a regulatory function. Often they define standards for teacher credentialing and licensure and oversee the collection of educational statistics.

Members of the State Board of Education are usually appointed by the governor and confirmed by the legislature. In some states, however, they are elected directly by the people. While most serve without pay, board members have enormous power to shape educational policy.

The State Superintendent

While State Boards of Education give advice and help to regulate state educational policies, the chief executive officer of the state is the superintendent. Though not a member of the State Board, the superintendent works directly with the board on matters of educational policy. However, while the board might advise and provide standards for regulation of the schools in the state, the superintendent is in charge of carrying out these educational policies. As they say, the "buck stops here." The superintendent is the ultimate arbiter of educational policy and his decisions are final.

And yet, like members of the State Board of Education, the position of the superintendent can be partisan (subject to political influence). Of the 50 state superintendents, over half are appointed by the State Board of Education, nearly 40% are appointed directly by the governor, and only about 10% are elected directly by the people. Given the political

---

Duties of the State Board of Education

Members of the State Board of Education are elected or appointed by the governor. The Board's responsibilities typically include the following:

- Regulate school curriculum
- Make school attendance policy
- Establish teacher licensure requirements
- Implement policy mandated by the state legislature
- Make policy recommendations to the state legislature
- Monitor teacher education programs
- Evaluate school test data

nature of educational policy, the independence of political appointees must be called to question.

State Department of Education

Whether the superintendent is appointed or elected, his executive arm is the State Department of Education, sometimes called the State Department of Public Instruction. It is this agency that carries out the educational policy of the state.

State Departments of Education typically regulate the certification requirements of teachers, maintain school bus schedules, and administer special programs for the state. They also advise the superintendent, collect educational data, and develop plans for the organization of the agency itself. Finally, they engage in public relations and program-support activities that relate to public education.

THE SCHOOL DISTRICT

As we move further toward the center of our organization, the next administrative ring represents the local school district. Local districts typically operate at the municipal (city), township, or county level, depending on the size of the community. In fact, many rural school districts throughout the country have only one or two schools with fewer than 100 students, while a number of large cities have hundreds of schools under their jurisdiction attending to the educational needs of thousands of students. Similarly, some school districts are organized as elementary schools only, some with high schools only, while others are more comprehensive with the full range of schools including elementary, middle, and high schools.

Journaling Activity

Research the organizational structure of your county or district school system. One way to find this information is to conduct an online search. In your journal describe the organizational structure. Are there associate or assistant superintendents assigned to specific tasks such as personnel, public relations, or curriculum? Are there coordinators of specific subjects such as technology, math, or reading? Is there a professional support staff listed here? For example, is there a learning disabilities specialist or school psychologist listed?

What does this structure tell you about your school system?

State Department of Education Responsibilities

(In some states it is referred to as the State Department of Instruction.)
The responsibilities of this department include the following:

- Implement and monitor statewide testing programs
- Review teachers' credentials and issue teaching licenses
- Establish curriculum guidelines and standards
- Conduct training sessions for teachers and administrators
- Approve teacher education programs and teacher specialty areas
- Approve new charter schools
- Implement new initiatives such as the NCLB

Although the size and structure of school districts differ significantly, they have similar organizations and functions.

Local Boards of Education

The local school district is governed or administered by the local school board. Local boards are given a legal mandate to govern the schools through state laws that often specify election procedures, term lengths, and responsibilities. The vast majority of local boards—over 90%—are elected directly by the people of the district, usually in special nonpartisan elections. Although local school boards are regulated by the state, they have enormous power in a number of areas:

- Funding
- Maintenance
- Property and construction
- Materials and supplies
- Curriculum and programs
- Hiring of teachers
- Admission and regulation of students

Given their enormous responsibilities, local boards of education often delegate authority to others but they have ultimate jurisdiction over these matters. For example, while local principals or superintendents conduct much of the recruiting, interviewing, and negotiations with teacher candidates, local boards are responsible for the actual hiring of teachers.

Local boards also have a great deal of discretionary power. For example, they can decide whether to continue or discontinue athletic programs, initiate drug testing in the

---

School Dress Codes

Many schools have adopted dress codes as a proposed solution to disciplinary problems. The following is an example of the dress code for elementary schools from Houston County Schools, Georgia.
All clothing is to be worn appropriately: a shirt designed to be tucked in the trousers or skirt should be worn with the shirttail tucked in; and belts should be buckled.
    The following are some rules for dress and apparel:

- Outer clothing which resembles loungewear, pajamas, or underwear is prohibited.
- See-through clothing is prohibited.
- Proper underclothing which insures modesty is required.
- Shoes/sandals must be worn at all times. Cleated shoes are prohibited inside the building.
- Clothing which has holes cut or torn that may expose the seat or parts of the body is prohibited.
- Halter tops, backless blouses, strapless blouses and dresses, sleeveless T-shirts, bike shorts and short-shorts are prohibited.
- Students may not wear hats, caps, combs, or picks, etc., inside the building. (Houston County Schools, n.d.)http://www.hcbe.net/dresscode.html)

schools, provide bonus incentives to attract teachers to their district, and as we have seen above, define dress codes for the schools.

Reflection

What do you think about dress codes? Do you think they should be imposed upon both students and teachers? Why?

The Local Superintendent

One of the most important powers of the local school board is the appointment of the local superintendent. While some states, especially in the Southeast, elect local superintendents, most are appointed directly by the board.

The local superintendent, in a position similar to that of the state superintendent, is the chief executive officer of education within the local community. His or her job is to provide leadership and is often the spokesperson for the local board. As a chief executive, the superintendent attends to the day-to-day operations of the school district, oversees the school budget, and deals with controversial issues involving school law and policy such as redistricting, periodically reassigning students in the district to achieve racial balance.

Depending on the size of the local school district, local superintendents may maintain an extensive staff including a number of assistant superintendents who attend to such administrative functions such as business affairs, personnel, curriculum, and instruction and special programs. Working with each of these assistant superintendents are other staff members. For example, the assistant superintendent of schools assigned to curriculum and instruction might have his or her own staff including a team of supervisors, library and media specialists, research consultants, evaluation experts, and staff development officers. These individuals work directly with the schools and provide direction, information, and assistance to teachers in the development of a curriculum for the schools.

Reflection

Do you notice some areas that seem to be missing in the school organizational box below? Why do you think Driver Education is listed in the organizational chart? Under what division would art, music, and physical education be placed? How about testing and athletics? Extra curricular activities?

School District Organization—Beaufort County Schools, Washington, North Carolina

Board of Education

Superintendent

| Human Resources | Child Nutrition | Curriculum |
| Driver Education | Finance | Plant Operation |

| Student Services | Transportation | Technology |

Adapted from the Beaufort County Schools Web site, retrieved February 25, 2008: http://www.beaufort.k12.nc.us/administration.htm

---

Once again, it is important to remember that the structure and complexity of these administrative units depends on the size and nature of the local school districts they serve. Some larger districts have superintendent staff organizations whose size rival those of large corporations while others districts are quite modest in size and function.

LOCAL SCHOOL ADMINISTRATION

Near the center of the school administrative structure is the local school itself. While the state and the school district administration have important regulatory and advisory roles in the operation of schools, it is in the local schools that the day-to-day business of education actually takes place. Moreover, as a new teacher, it is the school administration that you will work with directly.

The Principal

The chief administrator of the local school, of course, is the principal. It is his or her job to provide leadership for the school and assume final authority in its day-to-day operations. Typically, the principal is directly responsible to the local school district superintendent although in larger systems he or she may report to an assistant superintendent.

The principal has numerous responsibilities. These include the administration of:

- Staff personnel
- Business office
- Buildings and grounds
- Teachers and students
- Community relationships

Principals are responsible for the hiring and firing of all staff within the school including the custodian, groundskeepers, secretaries, and administrative assistants. Management of the school's business office is also the responsibility of the principal. He or she prepares the budget, pays the bills, and allocates funds for various programs within the school. The principal is also responsible for the maintenance of the school building and grounds and works directly with the custodian and groundskeeper (if appropriate) to keep the school clean, safe, and beautiful.

The central role of the principal, however, is his or her relationship with teachers and students. The principal is responsible for the selection, supervision and evaluation of teachers. He or she acts as a liaison between teachers and parents in case of disputes or conflicts, and is responsible to bring together appropriate staff members to deal with student learning problems or discipline. In addition, principals often play a leadership role in curriculum development and work directly with teachers to improve learning among all children.

Finally, principals are the direct link between the school and the community and are instrumental in developing relationships with parents, businesses, and advocacy groups. In recent years, teachers and parents have begun to assume greater responsibility in the selection of the curriculum, the establishment of school policies, codes, and the general operation of the school. As a result, principals may now establish teaching teams and teacher–parent advocacy committees, hold hearings on new policies, such as disciplinary codes or redistricting, and generally expand communications between the community and the school itself. This is no easy task.

Principal's Responsibilities

The administrative organization of a school varies according to the size and the level of the school. Larger schools, as well as high schools and middle schools, are more likely to have assistant principals. Below are some of the duties of the school principal:

- Selects teachers for his or her school. The interview with the principal will determine whether you will work in his of her school.
- Evaluates teachers.
- Handles and allocates funds from the school budget.
- Coordinates special support staff services (i.e., school counselors, school psychologists, social workers, nurses, etc.) for teachers and students.
- Maintains the school facilities and grounds and coordinates the maintenance staff.
- Coordinates curriculum and instruction in the school.
- Handles scheduling of classes, teachers, and room assignments.
- Supervises office staff.
- Acts as the chief disciplinarian.
- Schedules special events such as athletic games, open houses, parent conferences, and holiday concerts.
- Serves as a mediator between teachers and parents in case of conflict.
- Serves as a liaison between the school and the PTA.
- Coordinates and schedules testing. (adpated from Sebring & Bryk, 2000, pp. 440–443)

The Assistant Principal

In smaller schools, the principal may attend to each of these varied functions as well as a host of others. In larger schools, however, an assistant principal, sometimes referred to as a vice principal, often lends a hand. Larger elementary schools and most middle, and high schools will have at least one, and sometimes as many as five or six, assistant principals.

These administrators are often assigned specific functions within the school such as discipline or teacher evaluation. Sometimes they are referred to as "directors" such as the director of athletics. Whatever their official designation, these administrators function to facilitate communication between the administration and teachers, students, parents, and the community.

School Support Staff

Working directly with the principal and assistant principal are a number of school employees known as the support staff. These individuals "keep things running" and are essential for the smooth operation of the school. While the size and nature of support staffs differ according to the school and its mission, there are some similarities. Among the support staff members that you may work with at your school include the following:

- School secretary
- Custodians
- Cafeteria workers

Duties of the Assistant Principal

In large elementary, middle, or high schools, the assistant principal may:

- Schedule classes and classrooms
- Order supplies and textbooks
- Arrange the cafeteria schedule
- Handle discipline
- Schedule the use of special school facilities such as the gym, athletic fields, computer labs, or library
- Coordinate school testing and assessment
- Maintain and follow-up on student attendance
- Budget school funds

School Secretary

At the heart of the support staff is the school secretary. He or she is on the front lines of the administrative office and often seems to know where everything is and what everyone is doing. The secretary is the central source of information about the school. School secretaries greet visitors and guests to the school; they inform parents that their child is sick; they can help you locate a student's file; or remind you of staff meetings. It is important for new teachers to develop a good relationship with the school secretary because his or her knowledge of procedures and protocol is essential for your transition into the classroom.

Custodians

Custodians are also vital. They keep the school clean and safe and can be called upon in all sorts of emergencies. Custodians may help you rearrange your classroom, build a bookcase, move furniture, help you locate supplies, clean up a mess, or simply change a light bulb. The custodian may have been employed at your school for years and can help you understand school traditions, the background of controversies and have a good sense of what is happening at the school. They are a valuable resource.

Cafeteria Workers

Finally, in larger schools, cafeteria workers are an essential part of the support staff. They plan and prepare the meals, maintain the kitchen and cafeteria facilities, and often have a keen sense of the activities of children outside the classroom. They often can informally identify bullies, students who are in trouble emotionally, and those who have been isolated from their peer groups. Not only do they play a critical role in nurturing your students through healthful meal planning, they can also bring out the best in both students and teachers.

Academic Administrators: Team Leaders and Department Heads

In addition to the formal administrators within the school (principal, assistant principal, etc.) are a number of "academic administrators." These less formal administrators are full-time teachers but act in the capacity of leadership within a grade level or subject area. They are usually senior members of the teaching faculty and can be appointed by the principal, elected by their peers, or simply volunteer their services. These individuals have a staff relationship to you as a teacher.

Wisdom of Teachers: School Maintenance Personnel

It was Jill Ripley's first full day of school as a beginning teacher. All of the buses had arrived and she was starting to teach math. Suddenly, one of her students wretched and threw up all over his desk, chair, and floor. What should she do? Her college coursework had not prepared her for this! Ms. Ripley hustled the students to the bathroom and she wrote a hasty note asking for clean up help! As the sight and smell wafted through the classroom, other students started gagging. She opened the windows and took her class outdoors for an unscheduled recess. When she returned with her class 10 minutes later, the custodian was completing the clean up. She thanked him and apologized for asking his help with such a disgusting tasked. He responded that this was part of his job and he gave her a small bag of chemically treated "sawdust" to be used for such events. This material would not only cover the offense but diffuse the odor as well. The custodian was a lifesaver. (NBTS, 2002)

In elementary schools, they might assume the role of a team leader for a grade level (or grade levels) while at the middle school or high school, they may be referred to as department heads. These academic administrators often help coordinate the activities, curriculum, and policies of teachers in particular subject areas such as mathematics, social studies, or English. In smaller schools they might head-up a co-curricula area such as art and music or math and science. Once again, their functions and organization depend on the size and nature of your school.

Journaling Activity

Research the administrative structure of a nearby elementary or high school or select a school that you have attended. You may find this information by conducting an online search for the county or district school system and then from the website select the particular school you wish to examine.

In your journal describe how the school administration is organized. For example: is there an assistant principal? Are there several assistant principals for specific tasks such as discipline? Are there department chairs or coordinators? Describe the professional support staff listed such as counselors, special education professionals, social workers, etc.

Wisdom of Teachers: School Cafeteria Worker

Ms. Ripley recalled that when the school cafeteria purchased a bread and roll machine, she complimented the cafeteria workers for their delicious rolls. (School cafeteria workers typically receive many complaints and very few compliments.) Ms. Ripley's class was scheduled for a late lunchtime and frequently they were out of rolls by the time her class arrived in the cafeteria. But the workers remembered Ms. Ripley and would set aside a roll or two and give it to her when she entered the cafeteria line. Ms. Ripley was delighted to be guaranteed her favorite food—freshly baked rolls. Each day she looked forward to the congeniality of the cafeteria staff who talked and joked with her. (NBTS, 2002)

Whatever the organizational scheme, however, these team leaders and department heads play an important role in the organization and function of the school. They are the critical link between teachers and the administration. They typically preside over regularly scheduled teacher meetings where issues of curriculum and policy are discussed in detail. At these meetings you will learn a great deal about your school and how it functions. Team leaders and department heads can also be informal mentors for new teachers, providing you with direction, advice, and encouragement.

THE FUNDING OF SCHOOLS

American public schools are funded with tax revenues from federal, state, and local governments. These revenues are then distributed by governmental agencies to local school districts. And yet while this financial scheme may appear to be simple and fair, it is neither. Let's examine the financing of public education in this country by looking at each source of revenue and how those revenues are distributed.

FEDERAL AID

As we have seen, the federal government has traditionally played a minor role in the administration of schools. You will recall that the U.S. Constitution's 10th Amendment provided that all powers not specifically granted to the federal government were assumed to be powers of the state. As a result, the federal government's role in the administration and funding of public schools has been limited.

And yet, it is worth noting that prior to the adoption of the Constitution (1787) and the passage of the first 10 amendments to the Constitution in 1792 (The Bill of Rights) the federal government actively supported public education in this country. Through the provisions of the Northwest Ordinance of 1785 the federal government, organized under the Articles of Confederation, awarded territories in the Western part of the North America a portion of land to be used for public education. When these territories became states, they were able to sell this land to new settlers and use the revenues they received from those sales to fund public education. In fact, as a result of this one, far reaching provision, local communities throughout the country were able to establish and support public schools (Parkerson & Parkerson, 2001).

With the adoption of the 10th Amendment to the U.S. Constitution, however, the role of the federal government became less concrete and more symbolic. As we have seen, the federal government deferred to the states and local communities in the area of education and intervened only occasionally through legislation, judicial decisions, advocacy, and categorical aid.

Federal aid to education, however, continues to be controversial. Opponents of federal involvement in education argue that it is unconstitutional, noting the provisions set forth in the 10th Amendment. They argue further that education should remain a local enterprise, free from the control and direction of a powerful central authority. Those who favor a greater role for the federal government, on the other hand, note that the most important function of government as outlined in the Preamble to the Constitution is to "promote the general welfare" of the people and that there is no better way to achieve that goal than by supporting public education. They argue further that a progressive income tax, rather than property taxes at the local level, is the best way to provide funding for schools and assure that all children benefit equally from that funding.

The 10th Amendment to the U.S. Constitution

The powers not delegated to the United States by the Constitution; nor prohibited by the States, are reserved to the States respectively, or to the people.

Reflection

What effect has the 10th Amendment to the U.S. Constitution had on public schooling? What role does the federal government play in education?

While the controversy over the role of the federal government in education will certainly not be settled soon, as teachers we should be aware of the debate and try to understand both sides of the argument. It should also be noted, however, that whatever their position on this issue, states and local school districts are usually quite anxious to receive their fair share of federal funding which amounts to about 18 billion dollars annually! Given the tight budgets of local school districts, these extra funds can often make a big difference for a number of critical educational programs.

And yet there are "strings attached" to the disbursement of these funds. States and local school districts are held accountable for their use of this money. Sometimes they must conform to federal mandates and, of course, they must demonstrate that they have used the funds for the specific purpose for which they were intended. It is this accountability that is sometimes resented by school administrators.

Reflection

Do you agree with their position? Why is this group opposed to the use of federal funds for public schools?

Red Tape or Accountability?

The National Center for Home Education is highly critical of federal involvement in education. Read the following statement from their Web site and respond to it:

Although statistics show that only seven to eight percent of an average school's budget is subsidized by the feds, local districts complain about overwhelming paperwork and red tape required to receive these skimpy funds. A 1991 survey of Ohio school districts found that each district was required to fill out an average of 330 forms—157 were from the state and 173 from the federal government. Responsible for only seven to eight percent of the budget, the federal government causes 55 percent of the red tape. (Retrieved July 28, 2007, from http://www.homeschoolfoundation.org)

STATE FUNDING OF SCHOOLS

While federal funding of public education has traditionally been limited, states have maintained much of its administrative leadership and financial support. As we have seen, states gradually assumed control of schools from local school districts in the late 1800s and since then have provided administrative oversight and a steady source of revenue.

State Tax Revenue

States typically rely on sales taxes and income taxes to help fund their schools but they also use revenues from a host of other sources including licensing taxes, such as motor vehicle, hunting, boating, fishing, etc., and miscellaneous taxes, such as inheritance, gifts, mineral extraction, etc. In addition, states have experimented with lotteries as an additional source of funding for schools.

Income and Sales Tax

Income taxes are "progressive" because they are graduated according to ones ability to pay. In other words, those with higher incomes pay more tax. Sales taxes, on the other hand, are "regressive" in that the poor must pay a larger proportion of their income on the sales tax of food or clothing than do the rich. Nevertheless, when state governments are in financial trouble, they often resort to an increase in sales taxes since these are much easier to get through state legislatures.

Lotteries

In recent years, states have seen lotteries as a new source of revenue. In 1964, New Hampshire created a state lottery to supplement their tax revenues and to support public education. The success of this system was immediate and it allowed New Hampshire to eliminate its state income tax. This in turn attracted new businesses to the state that created new jobs and stimulated economic growth. Other states soon jumped on the bandwagon and today most states throughout the nation have established lotteries.

Lotteries clearly have increased the revenues of states. In fact, they have generated billions of dollars. But while these revenues were often intended to supplement public education, during periods of economic slowdown, some states expropriate money from the lottery fund to use for other projects. In fact, a few states provide no lottery money for education.

Thus while lotteries have the potential to significantly improve public education, they must be carefully monitored and safeguarded for educational use only. Otherwise, lottery funds are destined to become just another revenue stream for the general state budget.

LOCAL TAX REVENUES

While states have a number of methods of raising revenues for schools, local communities must rely exclusively on property taxes.

Property Tax

Property taxes have been the primary source of funding for schools for many years. Property tax includes both real estate tax including taxes on land and buildings on that land such as homes, commercial structures, and factories. Personal property taxes include taxes on personal items such as automobiles and furniture in homes, inventories of commercial establishments, machinery in factories, and livestock on farms.

Property taxes are a stable source of income because they are generally fixed and cannot easily be moved in order to avoid taxation. On the other hand, property taxes are often assessed unevenly. In some communities, tax assessors are locally elected officials who have little or no training in real estate taxation or appraisal. This can lead to unfair assessments. On the other hand, some communities hire professionals to make these assessments. In either case however, assessors are often pressured to keep their assessments low in order to keep the tax rates low.

Artificially low tax bases, of course, can dramatically effect the funding of public schools in the community. Low tax assessments may make those communities more attractive to some businesses looking for lower taxes, while rural farming communities with low property assessments will satisfy local farmers. In each case, however, low tax assessments negatively impact the local schools. In other words, while property taxes are a stable source of tax revenue for schools, they can be problematic.

Rich and Poor Communities

However, even if communities were required by state law to standardize their tax assessment schemes, there would still be a major problem with property taxes as the basis of school revenue. That problem, simply stated, is that some communities are much wealthier than others. Even if tax rates in poor communities were at their maximum level, revenues would still be dramatically lower than more developed, richer communities. These differences can be seen clearly between richer and poorer states. Per pupil expenditures in

---

San Antonio Independent School District v. Rodriguez
(1973) Supreme Court of the United States

When Demetrio Rodriguez sent his children to Edgewood Elementary School in the late 1960s, he was appalled. The school lacked books, it was not air conditioned, and the upper two floors had been condemned by the city of San Antonio! Moreover, only about half of the teachers were certified. Just a short drive from Edgewood, however, was Alamo Heights School. This facility, centered in a more affluent community, was air conditioned, had adequate learning material for its students, and all the teachers were certified.

Demetrio's questions was simple. Why? Why should his children be forced to attend a public school that literally was falling down around them while more affluent public school students had a well-equipped modern facility with experienced teachers?

Demetrio sued the city of San Antonio under the Equal Protection Clause of the U.S. Constitution. His class action suit was upheld by the United States District Court for the Western District of Texas in 1968, but the Supreme Court overturned the decision in its landmark San Antonio School District v. Rodriguez (1973). The effect of this decision was dramatic. Although the court noted that the system of financing public schools had "obvious imperfections," it argued that it was up to the states to correct those imperfections.

Source: Retrieved, February 25, 2008, from http://hrcr.law.columbia.edu/safrica/equality/
san_antonio_rodriguez.html

Mississippi and Idaho, for example, are about one half that of New York or New Jersey (Yudof, Kip, & Levine, 1992).

Similar differences can be seen between counties within states. Urbanized counties typically have much greater revenue than rural communities. As a result, these rural communities have less money to spend on teacher salaries, computers, after-school programs, or even organized sports.

Although this may seem unfair, the Supreme Court argued in the landmark San Antonio v Rodriguez decision that while the system of state school financing had "obvious imperfections," it was the state's responsibility to remedy those problems. This remains one of the central complications of the current system of financing education (Coons, Clune, & Sugarman, 1970).

Reflection
Was Demitrio Rodriguez justified in suing San Antonio? What do you think about the court's decision? Should there be some form of equity funding for poorer schools? Why?

NO CHILD LEFT BEHIND

In January 2001, the No Child Left Behind Act became national law. While this law is ambitious and sets goals for schools today, funding problems between rich and poor school districts, discussed above, have now become critical (U.S. Department of Education, 2002).

Reflection
Will testing improve students learning? Why is it more difficult for students with learning disabilities and limited English proficiency to take a standardized test? What do they mean by "proven ways of teaching children to read?" Do you think the NCLB will improve education in the United States? Why?

In their efforts to recruit "qualified" teachers, school districts throughout the country have used supplements of all sorts to lure educators. As we have seen previously, everything from salary bonuses to free computers have become relatively commonplace in this new, competitive "teachers race" environment.

Reflection and Journaling Activity
What do you think could be done to recruit and retain good teachers? Why is this a problem in poorer schools? What could they do to overcome this problem? Brainstorm with several of your classmates. Record your ideas in your journal.

While new teachers certainly will benefit from these supplements and bonuses, many children will not. Poorer school districts, by definition, have lower property tax bases and are therefore unable to compete for "qualified" teachers. The sad result is that poorer districts are able to hire only inexperienced new teachers or lateral entry teachers with little or no formal teacher education. And while inexperienced teachers can bring optimism, enthusiasm, and creativity to the classroom, children in poorer districts often have the greatest need for experienced educators.

In addition to recruitment of new teachers, recent educational research has demonstrated that teacher retention is also a related problem. As teachers in city schools gain experience in the classroom they often seek a transfer to suburban school districts where

Four Pillars of NCLB

The No Child Left Behind law proposes stronger accountability for results, more freedom for states and communities, proven education methods, and more choices for parents.

Stronger Accountability for Results

Under No Child Left Behind, states are working to close the achievement gap and make sure all students, including those who are disadvantaged, achieve academic proficiency. Annual state and school district report cards inform parents and communities about state and school progress. Schools that do not make progress must provide supplemental services, such as free tutoring or after-school assistance; take corrective actions; and, if still not making adequate yearly progress after 5 years, make dramatic changes to the way the school is run.

More Freedom for States and Communities

Under No Child Left Behind, states and school districts have unprecedented flexibility in how they use federal education funds. For example, it is possible for most school districts to transfer up to 50% of the federal formula grant funds they receive under the Improving Teacher Quality State Grants, Educational Technology, Innovative Programs, and Safe and Drug-Free Schools programs to any one of these programs, or to their Title I program, without separate approval. This allows districts to use funds for their particular needs, such as hiring new teachers, increasing teacher pay, and improving teacher training and professional development.

Proven Education Methods

No Child Left Behind puts emphasis on determining which educational programs and practices have been proven effective through rigorous scientific research. Federal funding is targeted to support these programs and teaching methods that work to improve student learning and achievement. In reading, for example, No Child Left Behind supports scientifically based instruction programs in the early grades under the Reading First program and in preschool under the Early Reading First program.

More Choices for Parents

Parents of children in low-performing schools have new options under No Child Left Behind. In schools that do not meet state standards for at least 2 consecutive years, parents may transfer their children to a better-performing public school, including a public charter school, within their district. The district must provide transportation, using Title I funds if necessary. Students from low-income families in schools that fail to meet state standards for at least 3 years are eligible to receive supplemental educational services, including tutoring, after-school services, and summer school. Also, students who attend a persistently dangerous school or are the victim of a violent crime while in their school have the option to attend a safe school within their district (U.S. Department of Education, 2002).

their incomes will be greater and "schools are perceived to be better—higher achieving and lower proportions of low income and minority students" This creates a kind of revolving door teacher crisis in city schools and negatively impacts the children in these communities (DeStefano & Foley, 2003, p. 44).

There are a number of solutions to this problem. These include targeting financial support for teacher recruitment in lower achieving, poorer schools; providing alternatives to seniority for moving up the pay scale, and providing pay scales that are both differentiated by field of qualification and are incentive based. These solutions require coordination and above all financial support from the state and federal government. Without that coordination and support, the competitive teacher environment will continue and students from poorer districts will suffer.

THE FUTURE OF EDUCATIONAL FINANCE

As we have seen, the current system of financing public schools is troubling. Over the last three decades—since the famous San Antonio v Rodriguez case of 1973—the courts have grappled with public school finance and often have found it unfair. In fact, Supreme Court Justice Potter Stewart once remarked that the system was both chaotic and unjust (Yudof, Kip, & Levin, 1992).

School Finance Equity Reforms

While the Rodriguez decision was a major setback for a more equitable system of funding of public schools in Texas, the Serrano v. Priest (1971) decision set the stage for a fundamental overhaul of this system. In the Serrano decision, the California Supreme Court declared that the state's system of school finance was unconstitutional; arguing that the dramatic differences in funding based on the property tax system had created major inequities among students. Since education was seen as a constitutional right in California, the system of school finance had violated equal protection of that right.

Taking their lead from the Serrano decision, a number of states throughout the country began to overhaul their school finance systems to make them more equitable. Two kinds of reforms resulted. Some states embraced a fundamental redistribution of educational funds, sometimes nicknamed by detractors as a Share our Wealth or Robin Hood System. Here, some money is redirected from richer to poorer school districts.

Links to the Past: Proposition 13—Taxpayers' Revolt in California

The Serrano decision forced California and other states to reconsider its educational funding scheme and promised to transform the way schools were financed.

But while many Californians saw the Serrano decision as a major victory for equity reform, others in the state resented it. They felt it was unfair that money from their community would be diverted to poorer school districts.

The result was a groundswell movement sometimes known as a "taxpayers revolt" that was determined to lower property taxes throughout the state. This led to the passage of California Proposition 13, which dramatically lowered the property taxes in the state but also damaged California public schools.

Reflection

Was the taxpayers revolt in California justified? Did Proposition 13 solve the problem of equity funding in the state? Who benefited from this legislation? Who did not?

One of the most successful of these programs was implemented in Kentucky. In 1989, the Kentucky Supreme Court ruled that the state's system of financing schools violated the state's constitution because it did not provide equal educational opportunities for each person in the state (Rose v. The Council for Better Education Inc., 1989). The state legislature responded with the creation of the Kentucky Education Reform Act of 1990 (KERA) that has since become the model of equity throughout the country. (For information on KERA, see: http://www.wku.edu/library/kera/orgs.htm)

As you might expect, these sorts of programs have consistently been challenged by wealthier school districts. Nevertheless, other states have initiated guaranteed tax base or equity programs. Here, state funds are used to supplement the budgets of poorer school districts.

School Finance Adequacy Reform

While some states have struggled mightily with equity reforms over the years, others have moved cautiously toward so-called adequacy reform. The most common of these "reforms" provides a minimum or "foundation level" of funding for each student in the state. Far from redistributing funds from one district to another, the foundation level system recognizes a basic level of services for students in the state. Unfortunately, these levels are typically determined by an ad hoc committee of political appointees and are based on lower bound estimates of student expenditures. As a result, funding levels are often well below the minimum expenses for education today.

A good example of this sort of funding reform can be seen in the New Jersey Supreme Court case of *Abbott v. Burke* (1971). In Abbott, the court recognized that schools in some districts, notably, Camden, New Jersey, were in appalling condition and that students in these districts were not becoming "productive members of society." Something needed to be done. The court mandated that the state spend significantly more money on these 28 failing school districts, known as "Abbott districts."

And yet, this was not the end of the story. The New Jersey State Legislature opposed the Abbott decision and used a variety of delaying tactics to avoid further funding of these schools. Eventually there was a showdown between the Supreme Court and the state legislature and the court shut down all the schools in the state. The legislature backed down and eventually provided tens of millions of dollars for Camden schools (See Education Law Center, http://www.edlawcenter.org/ELCPublic/AbbottvBurke/AboutAbbott.htm, retrieved February 25, 2008, for additional information on this important decision.)

In New York, years of bitter struggle led to a classic adequacy decision of the New York Supreme Court—Campaign for Fiscal Equality v. New York (1995). Rejecting the concept of equal funding for all New York state students, the court ruled that a minimal foundation of services and resources was all that was necessary to address issues of equity in education (Keller, 2000).

New Directions in School Financing

While many school districts have grappled with the funding of public schools, often taking either an equity or adequacy approach, Michigan has recently presented us with a third alternative. This funding compromise involved a shift away from the traditional

---

Abbott v. Burke Decision

The following points were designed to clarify the *Abbott v. Burke* decision.

1. The New Jersey Constitution requires that every child receive a "thorough and efficient" education. For students in poorer urban (Abbott or Special Needs) districts, the Supreme Court defines this education as one that will prepare them to compete effectively in the economy and become active citizens in their communities.
2. The Supreme Court requires that every Abbott school—elementary, middle, and high schools—provide an education that has two program components: Rigorous standards-based education programs and supplemental programs.
3. Schools and districts are responsible for planning and budgeting these programs.
4. School-based management teams (SMTs) under Abbott are driven by the program needs of the school's students.
5. Existing SMTs must make all necessary changes to ensure compliance with the district's new SMT policy and to carry out their new responsibilities under Abbott.
6. The process of school-based planning under Abbott involves eight critical steps. Each SMT must: Assess the students' academic, social, and health needs; plan a rigorous standards-based education program in all the subject areas; plan all required supplemental programs; evaluate current standards-based education and supplemental programs and determine whether each program should be continued, improved, or eliminated; prepare a budget for the total school-based plan; identify and total all currently available funding; determine whether funding is sufficient; and prepare budget.
7. Schools and districts jointly share the responsibility for school-based management.
8. School-based program plans and budgets must be driven by the academic, social and health needs of students.

Abbott opinions are written and distributed by Education Law Center (http://www.edlawcenter.org) on specific issues pertaining to *Abbott v. Burke*. This opinion is part of ELC's ongoing effort to assure effective and full implementation of the remedies ordered by the Supreme Court.

---

reliance on property taxes to fund schools toward the broader use of state income taxes for schools. After years of debate over the failure of the traditional property tax approach to school finance in the state, the people of Michigan voted overwhelming in 1994 to raise the state sales tax by 50% from 4 cents to 6 cents per dollar.

The idea was simple. By raising the sales tax and using state revenues as a source of school funding, property taxes could be reduced and the age-old problem of inequities caused by rich and poor school districts could be addressed.

Educational researchers who investigated this new approach found that the plan was a success. Property taxes for schools dropped significantly by 50% and poor school districts actually received a 30% increase in funding under the new plan while rich districts experienced only a slight decline in funding. Moreover, it appears that the funding gap between rich and poor districts will narrow significantly in the future (Prince, 1997).

Reflection
Since sales taxes are regressive, who benefits and who does not with the Michigan plan?

"Bake Sales" and Bond Issues for Public School

While the Michigan plan of shifting the tax burden from property taxes to a state sales tax is promising (though flawed), other states and districts have moved toward more controversial forms of school funding. Some school districts have turned to advertising as a source of revenue; others have resorted to bake sales. Numerous school districts now sell advertisements on their school buses as a new source of income. Other schools have sought corporate sponsorship for endangered programs such as art, music, and sports.

Still other schools have embraced the idea of student fees for busing, parking, computer equipment, yearbooks, and participation in athletics. And yes, some have had bake sales to support specific educational programs or have sold musical CDs from the school band to buy new uniforms.

While external sources of revenue in the form of fees or special fundraisers is not a new idea for the public schools, the degree to which many schools are forced to rely on these schemes in recent years has alarmed many educators. Once again, poorer school districts are vulnerable. Historically, under-funded by less than equal property tax finance, these schools are placed in a situation where they must rely on external sources of revenue simply to operate. This represents a troubling trend in public education.

Finally, many communities borrow money for education by issuing bonds. Bonds are certificates of debt that guarantee payment by a specific date. Before a community can issue a bond, however, it must be approved by the electorate in a referendum or during a general election. Money generated from bonds allows a community to build new schools or to repair aging ones.

HOMESCHOOLING AND VOUCHERS

While bake sales, advertising, and issuing bonds have been used successfully over the years to supplement the funding of public schools throughout the country; a more fundamental change involves homeschooling and school vouchers. American teachers must understand the ramifications of these important developments.

While the controversy over homeschooling has only recently come to the attention of the American people, the idea of school choice actually is not new. In fact, private education was the norm in this and other countries until the 1800s when the "greatest experiment of man," public schooling, first became a reality. And of course, the tradition of choosing to send your child to a private school rather than a public school continues to be alive and well in the United States.

Today, however, there is a new wrinkle in this debate. In the last 30 years, since the famous *Gideon v. Wainwright* (1963) Supreme Court decision declared that mandatory prayer in public schools was unconstitutional, many conservative groups including large numbers of Protestant fundamentalists have argued that public schools have turned their backs on Christian values. As a result, many of these fundamentalists have argued for homeschooling where those values can freely be taught.

Journaling Activity
Go to http://www.homeschools.org Web site and examine the homeschooling curriculum. What are your impressions of this curriculum? Do you think this curriculum would reflect a multicultural perspective?

Others have embraced vouchers. Here, state or federal money would be allocated to each family to use as they wished for the education of their children. If the family wanted to send their child to a private school, they could use those funds to do so. Moreover, under some plans, parents would receive tuition tax credits to help them afford more expensive institutions.

During the last two decades, a number of these voucher plans have been implemented. For example, in 1990, Milwaukee, Wisconsin adopted a voucher plan that was vigorously supported by then governor Tommy Thompson. It should be noted that the superintendent of Milwaukee schools, Robert Peterkin, opposed the plan, arguing that it drained needed resources from the public school budget. In 1998, the Supreme Court entered into the controversy by arguing that the plan was secular and as a result, voucher funds could not be used for religious schools.

Journaling Activity

The use of school vouchers is very controversial. As we have seen, reformers and educators have lined up on either side of this issue. What do you think? Are vouchers a good idea or do they divert scarce funds from public schools? Discuss both sides of this important issue.

Despite the bitter political infighting and controversy, it appears that the vast majority of the American people support the traditional public school system. Ernest Boyer's study of vouchers, *School Choice*, demonstrated that only 2% of American families have participated in voucher programs and that 70% of parents with school-age children preferred public schools for their children. Moreover, these parents were opposed to private school choice plans by a margin of 2 to 1 (Boyer, 1992).

"McSCHOOLS?"

If homeschooling and school choice/voucher plans represent a new chapter in the ongoing debate over the school finance, the "privatization of public schools" represents an important footnote in that chapter. As we have seen, school voucher plans typically provide public funds, or tuition credits, to be used for private education. They also provide funds so that students can choose to attend public schools outside of their districts.

Privatization plans are different because they essentially turn over the public schools to a private company. These "for profit" school businesses, sometimes called "McSchools" by their critics, then receive funding from the state and district and keep the profits they

Florida Supreme Court Rejects School Vouchers

The Florida Supreme Court rejected the school voucher program by a 5–2 ruling. The court cited that it violated the state's constitution that requires a "uniform, efficient, safe, secure and high quality system of free public schools." It also ruled that vouchers divert money from the public schools to private schools that are exempt from many of the laws that apply to public schools such as teacher certification and student assessment. (NEA, 2006)

make. This of course transfers money—designated for public schools—to private institutions and thereby reduces revenues for public education.

Reflection and Journaling

What do you think about the privatization of schools? Are there advantages? What are the disadvantages? Do you think that privatization is a threat to the public school? Record your answers in your journal.

In the early 1990s, two conservative governors, William Weld of Massachusetts and Buddy Roemer of Colorado, supported legislation in their respective states to allow school districts to award contracts to private educational companies. Within a few years, other states followed suit. One of the most aggressive of these new companies was the Edison Corporation.

The Edison Corporation used modern marketing techniques to promote their for-profit schools and literally "wined and dined" school superintendents and school board members in lavish sales promotion "seminars." They also promised school representatives additional resources from private foundations, such as the Fisher Family Foundation, which gave over $25 million to a number of school districts in California, for those districts that signed-on with Edison. These "seminars" were quite successful. By 2000, Edison boasted that it was operating over 50 for-profit schools throughout the country with an enrollment of more than 23,000 students (Walsh, 1998).

SAVAGE INEQUALITIES

But as we settle into the 21st century, the problems of school finance continue to trouble us as educators. The basic problem is what Jonathan Kozol (1992) has called savage inequalities. These inequalities are caused, in great measure, by the traditional property tax funding of schools. Wealthy districts often supplement their annual operations budgets with local funds and as a result are able to maintain better school facilities, attract more experienced teachers with higher salaries, and offer students more equipment such as computers, Internet access, and software.

Poorer districts, on the other hand, are often unable to maintain older school facilities, have little money to supplement the incomes of their teachers, and must make due with fewer computers and other amenities. And since poorer school districts often have a greater proportion of poorer students with special needs than their richer district neighbors, the savage inequalities not only persist but are getting worse (Kozol, 1992).

Given this basic problem, states and districts have embraced a variety of solutions. State supplements to poorer districts, lotteries earmarked for schools, choice and voucher plans and even for-profit schools have become more commonplace in the last 20 years. Nevertheless, these savage inequalities persist.

As we continue to experiment with a variety of funding options and as state courts and legislatures grapple with these problems, it is becoming clear that inequalities in educational facilities and opportunity will persist until we embrace some form of universal equity finance reform. Whether we have the political will to embrace such reform, however, continues to be the central issue in the financing of public education today.

SUMMARY

There are four basic levels of public school administration today: the federal government, the state, the local school district, and the local school. At the heart of this administrative organization, however, are teachers and their students.

Federal Government Administration

Early in our nation's history, the federal government supported the development of public education with enormous land grants to the states. But with the ratification of the U.S. Constitution and the 10thAmendment, its role became limited. More recently, however, the federal government has increased its involvement in education especially in the areas of student and teacher accountability—often tied to "categorical" financial aid for specific educational programs.

State Control of Public Education

However, while the federal government's involvement in education continues to grow, the central administrative control of school is at the state level. Through the power of governors, legislatures, and courts, states maintain their control of schools. Their power is administered through State Boards of Education and a State Superintendent whose staff attends to the operations, services development, and public support of education.

The Local School District

The next level of administrative organization is the local school district. School districts typically have a local board of education. These boards hire a local superintendent who in turn attends to the day-to-day operations, budget, and policies of the schools in the district.

The Local School

At the center of the local school's administration is the school principal. His or her responsibilities include the hiring and firing of school personnel, the business management of the school, the overall maintenance of the school and grounds, the evaluation of teachers, and the maintenance of community relations.

Financing Public Education

Directly paralleling the administration of public education is the funding of schools. The federal government continues its categorical funding of specific programs that range from Head Start to Antidrug Programs. And yet, the federal government provides only about 7% of all funds for public education. The remaining 93% of the total education budget comes from the states and local communities.

State and local Funding of Schools

States use a variety of tax revenues to support public education today. These include income tax, sales tax and, in more recent years, state lotteries. But while states have a variety of sources of tax revenues with which to support public education, local school districts have only one source: property taxes.

Rich and Poor Schools

The central financial problem facing schools today is our failure to achieve equality of educational opportunity for all our students. Because property taxes are at the heart of all school funding, poor school districts have less revenue to maintain school properties, purchase school supplies, or hire experienced teachers. Rich districts, on the other hand, typically have more revenues for each of these purposes. While educational reformers have embraced a number of solutions to this problem including state educational lotteries, charter schools, and even for-profit schools, the problems of unequal educational opportunity continue.

DISCUSSION QUESTIONS

1. Discuss the changing role of the federal government in the administration and funding of public education. Should it have a greater role today? What are the potential problems and possibilities with the involvement of the federal government in education?
2. How do your state and local governments share administrative responsibilities of the schools?
3. Discuss the duties of the local school principal and staff.
4. How do states raise revenues to support public education? How do local districts raise revenues?
5. Discuss the problem of rich and poor schools. Why is it a problem at all? How have states and districts dealt with this issue?
6. Discuss the pros and cons of for-profit schools in this country.
7. What can be done to solve the problem of equality of education? Are there examples of how the problem has been addressed successfully?

Chapter 11

Rights, Responsibilities, and the Law

When an important educational historian traced the history of public education in America nearly a century ago, he remarked that local control of schools in the early republic was a "dog in the manger." While this statement may seem a bit puzzling to us today, he may have been right. We sometimes forget that local majorities, that dog in the manger, often have a darker side. Over the years, they have imposed religious beliefs and prejudices on the public schools; segregated schools on the basis of gender, ethnicity, and race, and sometimes have acted irresponsibly in hiring and firing of teachers and school employees. The struggle to protect the rights of students and teachers from that "dog in the manger" has been a central theme in the legal history of public education in America.

Guaranteeing the constitutional provision of separation of church and state under the 1st Amendment, for example, has been an ongoing struggle. Throughout the 1800s and early 1900s individual states and local communities often promoted a kind of "pan Protestant" religious education in their public schools. This compulsory religious education appealed to some white, Protestant Americans who lived in these communities, but it alienated broad segments of our growing immigrant population. This resulted in years of social conflict. Only through the vigorous action of the courts has the question of separation of church and state been resolved, at least for the time being!

Local majorities also excluded individuals from public schools because of gender, race, language and disability. In the 1800s, for example, women often were denied access to education and when they were allowed into the classroom, they were typically segregated from young men. This policy gradually began to change as women fought for and won greater educational opportunities. But many local schools persisted with this form of segregation.

Links to the Past: "Bible Riots"

As the common school developed during the 19th century, it reflected a pan-Protestant curriculum. The Protestant Bible and Protestant prayers were used in public schools. As Roman Catholics (from Ireland and Germany) entered this country during the 1800s, they objected to the Protestant values inherent in the public school curriculum. In predominantly Catholic areas in Philadelphia, schools adopted the Roman Catholic Bible for instruction. Protestants were outraged and there were a series of "Bible Riots" that left 13 people dead and Catholic Churches burned to the ground. Similar struggles took place in other large cities, such as New York City. Eventually, Catholics formed their own separate school system(Higham, 1988; Kaestle, 1983)

Segregation on the basis of race, of course, has had a more pernicious history. For example, the federal government ignored its responsibilities to African Americans in the civil right cases of 1883, and again with the dark capstone of segregation, Plessy v. Ferguson in 1896, where states throughout the nation were legally permitted to have separate, but (not) equal educational facilities for black children. Only through a long civil rights struggle and the intervention of the federal government, a half a century later with the landmark *Brown v. Board of Education* (1954) decision, were black children gradually allowed to attend previously all-white schools. Since then, the courts have slowly turned their attention to the discrimination and exclusion of other ethnic and language "minorities" as well as people with disabilities. Their rulings have provided a measure of open access to public schooling in this country. And yet the struggle continues.

While we have made progress in some areas, as late as the mid-1970s, students had virtually no legal rights within the school. Despite the fact that students were U.S. citizens, they routinely were denied due process as guaranteed under the 14th amendment to the Constitution. As a result, they were not able to challenge suspensions, detentions, or other disciplinary rulings of school administrators. With the Supreme Court decision *Goss v. Lopez* (1975) however, students gained the right to tell their side of the story in an open hearing and challenge these kinds of arbitrary disciplinary rulings.

Of course, "student rights" such as due process are controversial and sometimes are resented by administrators and school board members. As teachers, however, we should remember that other student rights such as access to segregated public school were also "resented" by some school boards and administrators who desired to "act unilaterally, unhampered by rules." Over the years, however, we have learned that these "rules" are essential in an open, democratic society.

Teachers have also had to struggle to achieve basic rights. In fact, for over 200 years teachers have been forced to challenge school officials through the courts. As we will see in chapter 12, during the early 1800s teachers had few legal rights and could be fired arbitrarily. Young Augusta Hubble, for example, was dismissed from her teaching position because of "tongues of slander"—unsubstantiated rumors about her riding in a buggy with a young man.

Goss Decision

The prospect of imposing elaborate hearing requirements in every suspension case is viewed with great concern and many school authorities may well prefer the untrammeled power to act unilaterally, unhampered by rules about notice and hearing. But it would be a strange disciplinary system in an educational institution if no communication was sought by the disciplinarian with the student in an effort to inform him of his defalcation and to let him tell his side of the story

Source: http://www.departments.bucknell.edu, retrieved July 2, 2007

Journaling Activity

Teachers today have much more freedom regarding their personal lifestyle and habits than in the past. Unmarried teachers may now live with a member of the opposite sex. However, in more conservative communities, teachers may still have difficulty with their school board regarding these lifestyles.

Do you think a teacher's personal lifestyle in regard to living arrangements, alcohol, or drug consumption should have any effect on the hiring or firing of teachers? Why or why not? Are there any personal lifestyle issues that you consider justifiable grounds for dismissal? Record your responses in your journal.

We will also see in the next chapter that women teachers, until quite recently, were not allowed to marry and often were required to adhere to elaborate dress codes—such as wearing dresses that were no shorter than three inches from the ground—in order to maintain their employment. Even the basic right to negotiate a fair salary with school boards continues to be controversial. Additionally, over half the states across the country have declared labor stoppages illegal.

The world of school law is complex, baffling and sometimes a bit overwhelming for both new and experienced teachers. You may find that some of your colleagues and certainly many of your administrators are sometimes infuriated with the direction of school law today. Rather than seeing school law as a long series of regulations and restrictions arbitrarily imposed on you and your school, we will examine its historical context and discern its sometimes overlooked progressive nature. By understanding that the legal history of American education has often been a monumental struggle to overcome the darker side of local majorities and to limit their power, you will be better able to appreciate the direction of school law.

Certainly we can understand the frustration that some administrators and school board members have with particular school regulations and laws. Nevertheless, these "rules and regulations" represent a positive good for our society and our schools. They are not just "another hoop to jump through." Providing equal access to schools, eliminating segregation based on color or gender, protecting teachers and students from sexual harassment, and providing basic legal rights such as due process and freedom of speech, is worth any potential inconvenience and is at the heart of the democratic educational experience.

But before we get too far ahead of ourselves, let's examine the primary issues in educational law that effect both students and teachers.

STUDENTS' RIGHTS AND RESPONSIBILITIES

As an American teacher you will be expected to understand the basic rules of your school and district as well as the basic rights (and responsibilities) of your students. And while this may appear to be a difficult task, it is not. Generally speaking, there are two areas that we will consider:

- The right to an education
- Individual rights

THE RIGHT TO AN EDUCATION

One of the fundamental rights enjoyed by Americans is the right to a primary and secondary education. Unlike many other countries throughout the world, we have made a strong commitment to our children by guaranteeing them a basic education. But this right has not come easily.

First of all, the "right" to education was not specifically guaranteed in the U.S. Constitution. In fact, education was not mentioned in this important document. And yet, as we have seen in chapter 10, the federal government did play an important role in encouraging the spread of public education in this country through its important land grant program under the Northwest Ordinance of 1787. Moreover, education was enthusiastically supported by a number of powerful national political leaders such as Benjamin Franklin and Thomas Jefferson.

The actual implementation of public education in this country, however, was up to local communities and states. Gradually, the seed of the common school, one accessible to all American children, was planted. By the 1830s and 1840s, common schools had been established throughout the country and by the eve of the American Civil War in 1861, many young people in this country were attending some school.

And yet, despite the remarkable success of the common school movement, it was flawed. Although the situation varied by state and community, many schools were segregated directly on the basis of gender and race and indirectly on the basis of national origin, language, religion, and physical condition. Let's examine each of these in detail.

Segregation Based on Gender

Women were typically excluded from most early schools in the country. Conventional "wisdom" of this era suggested that only men should receive an education and this idea was difficult to overcome. In the famous "public schools" of New England, for example, young women were not allowed to attend school until the end of the 1700s. In Boston, women were not allowed in public schools until 1789 and then only on a rotating basis with boys. This situation continued until 1828, when young women finally were allowed to attend schools with young men.

But even as women were gaining access to schools during the early 1800s in private academies and elementary common schools, some teachers refused to provide them a thorough and rigorous education. When Susan B. Anthony recalled her early school years, she noted that when she and her sisters enrolled in a common school in upstate New York, the schoolmaster refused to instruct them in long division. His reasoning was simple and typical of the period. Long division was an unnecessary skill for women who would be better served by learning how to cook, sew, and clean the house (Clifford, 1989; Parkerson & Parkerson, 2001).

Despite these long held conservative beliefs, women gradually challenged the status quo and demanded access to schools throughout the nation. In the late 1700s and early 1800s, at least six private "Female Academies" were established. One of the most important of these was the Young Ladies Academy of Philadelphia in 1787. This institution provided women with instruction in reading, writing, arithmetic, English grammar, composition, rhetoric, and geography, and demonstrated that women were as capable as men in dealing with a rigorous curriculum (Parkerson & Parkerson, 2001).

Then in the early 1800s, Emma Willard's Troy Female Seminary (1821) and Mary Lyons' Mt. Holyoke Female Seminary (1837) were established. The Troy seminary provided women with a strong academic curriculum and was also the first institution

---

Links to the Past: The Young Ladies Academy of Philadelphia

The Young Ladies Academy of Philadelphia, founded in 1787, soon became a well respected academic institution that drew students from across the country. The academy was one of the first to offer more advanced learning such as arithmetic, composition, and geography for young women. The academic progress of the young "ladies" was monitored by a board of "gentlemen visitors." They examined the students and awarded prizes for achievement. (Lerner, 1977, p. 209; Woody, 1929)

---

in the country to train women teachers for the common schools. In fact, by the 1860s, the Troy Female Seminary had trained over 600 teachers for schools throughout the country.

At Mt. Holyoke, Mary Lyons introduced written compositions and lectures as the basis of instruction and she encouraged her graduates to become scientists, college teachers, and to "go where no one else will go and do what no one else will do."

Graduates of these and other important institutions transformed attitudes toward the education of women and by the end of the 1800s; women generally had equal access to schools throughout the country. Yet, there was a long way to go. While women were allowed to attend primary and some of the new high schools of this era, sex discrimination persisted in most institutions of higher learning.

There were a number of private women colleges established in the late 1800s and early 1900s, and a few progressive colleges such as Oberlin in Ohio allowed women and African Americans into the classroom, but it was rare. Things did change, however, with the suffrage movement and the passage of the 18th Amendment to the Constitution that guaranteed women the right to vote. Through the 1930s, 1940s, and 1950s, women gradually made their way into colleges and universities throughout the country. By the 1960s, women were no longer an unusual sight on college campuses and today there are more women enrolled in American colleges and universities than men (Willingham & Cole, 1997).

These changes have come about gradually as a result of the hard work of women students, teachers, and administrators. And yet even as the numbers of women in school increased, there was still a great deal of gender discrimination in this country. At the beginning of this century, women still made up only about a fifth of all the nation's doctors and lawyers and represented less than 10% of its engineers. Moreover the "wage gap" between women and men, although improving gradually, is still unacceptable. Women

---

Links to the Past: Schools for Young Women

Emma Willard established her school for girls in Troy, New York, in 1821. Girls from around the country enrolled and studied math, English, science, history, foreign language, and literature (http://www.emmawillard.org/about/history/index.php).

Mary Lyon founded Mt. Holyoke College, a seminary for young women in the fall of 1837 in South Hadley, Massachusetts. It was one of the first colleges for women, although it was called a "seminary" because at the time, many people objected to women attending college. She used the same curriculum and textbooks that were required in men's colleges. (http://www.mtholyoke.edu/marylyon)

Title IX of the Higher Education Act (1972)

No person in the United States shall, on the basis of sex, be excluded from participation in, be denied benefits of, or be subjected to discrimination under any education program or activity receiving federal assistance.

Source: Retrieved February 26, 2008, from
http://www.dol.gov/oasam/regs/statutes/titleix.htm

---

earn only about 70% as much as men even when we take into consideration factors such as experience, education, and ability (AAUW, 1992; U.S. Bureau of Census, 2005).

During the early 1970s, the federal government recognized some of these problems and intervened to ensure equal access to education. In its landmark legislation, often called Title IX of the Educational Amendments (or simply Title IX), Congress moved to eliminate gender discrimination in schools.

Reflection

Why is Title IX legislation important? Does it directly or indirectly discriminate against men? Why was it necessary to pass such legislation in the first place?

The effect of Title IX legislation has been dramatic. In sports, for example, women were now allowed to fully participate in high school athletics. In 1970, on the eve of Title IX legislation, there were only about 295,000 women involved in organized sports. Today, as a result of this legislation, over 2.7 million women freely participate in a variety of varsity and intramural sport activities. While women continue to be underrepresented and underfunded, women have come a long way in a generation (White, 1999).

In other academic areas, however, problems continue. Young women are often subjected to subtle forms of discrimination in the classroom. For example, many teachers "call on boys" more often than girls, especially in areas of math or science. Moreover, women are clearly underrepresented in educational materials and textbooks, especially history and social studies. This can reinforce feelings of low self-esteem among women.

Increasing Girls' Self-Esteem

Generally young children have high self-esteem, but by the teen years, approximately half of boys feel good about themselves but only 29% of the girls feel good about themselves. Poor self-esteem can lead to dropping out of school, premarital pregnancy, alcohol and drug abuse, and depression. As teachers we can do a great deal to improve the self-esteem of girls:

- Begin a mentoring program
- Reward girls for academic and athletic performance
- Deemphasize the importance of physical attractiveness
- Select activities that value student individuality
- Encourage both genders to work together
- Call on girls to respond to questions as often as boys
- Give girls time to respond
- Ask questions that require an opinion or problem-solving skills

---

For example, researchers have demonstrated that while primary school girls often are equal to or ahead of young boys in measures of both academic achievement and self-esteem, by high school they have fallen behind boys in both areas. By then, women have collectively experienced a 31% decline in measures of self-esteem! This translates into significantly lower standardized test scores, an average of 50 points on the SAT (Sadker & Sadker, 1995).

Reflection

Look over the points in the box above. Do you think these strategies would benefit both girls and boys? Do you think that the self-esteem of students might vary by race or ethnicity? Think about some additional things you could do in your classroom to improve the self-esteem of all your students.

Title IX legislation has had a far-reaching effect on the lives of women today. Prior to 1972, for example, young women students who were either married or who became pregnant could be legally barred from attending school. The logic of this policy was that a married woman had responsibilities that made it virtually impossible for her to do well in school and that a pregnant woman was a distraction to other students. While many school officials still have these concerns, Title IX legislation makes it illegal for them to bar these women from the classroom.

As a result of Title IX, school officials have become more sensitive to the needs of both married and pregnant women. Some schools offer after-school programs that allow women to work during the day and complete their studies at night. Other schools offer family counseling that helps young women adjust to childrearing.

Finally, Title IX has made sex discrimination and sexual harassment illegal. This general provision allows female students, teachers, and school staff members to challenge school policies that may be discriminatory. The Department of Education's Office of Civil Rights enforces this provision of Title IX legislation. Moreover, the Supreme Court ruled in its 1992 case *Franklin v. Guinneth County Schools* that an individual who has been a victim of sexual discrimination can sue the school district for monetary damages.

Unfortunately, the increasingly conservative Supreme Court has recently made it more difficult for women and others to challenge discrimination in the workplace. In *Ledbetter v. Goodyear* (2007), the court ruled that challenges to pay discrimination based on "race, sex, religion or national origin" must be filed within 180 days of the initial act of discrimination. If not, they will not be allowed. As Justice Ruth Bader Ginsberg noted in her dissenting view, "the court majority does not comprehend or is indifferent to the insidious way in which women can be victims of pay discrimination" (Sherman, 2007).

Title IX also prohibits sexual harassment of all students irrespective of grade level, as sometimes even elementary students are sexually harassed. This provision includes harassment by teachers and by other students. And the victim may be male or female.

Title IX: Pregnant Students may Continue Schooling

Title IX (1972) protects young pregnant women from being excluded from public school. Some school systems establish special facilities, such as Lady Pitts High School in Milwaukee. The school accommodates 165 pregnant or parenting teenage girls. The school also includes a daycare center for the student's babies.

Source: Retrieved July 5, 2007, from
http://www.rethinkingschools.org/archive/17_04/teen174. shtml

---

Behavior that Might be Considered Sexual Harassment

Although some suggest that sexual harassment is difficult to define, generally both students and teachers should conduct themselves in a manner that does not offend members of the opposite sex. Sexual harassment can be either verbal or nonverbal. Teachers should model positive behavior to set good examples for their students. Following are some guidelines to help teachers avoid sexual harassment.

Verbal Comments
- Always refer to your students by name, never call a student "honey," "sweetheart," or "girl."
- Never make sexual comments or innuendos.
- Do not discuss sexual topics (unless you are a health teacher teaching a unit on human reproduction).
- Avoid making comments about a student's appearance or clothing.
- Do not make derogatory statements about any of your students or other teachers.
- Do not tell "dirty jokes"—not even in the teachers' lounge.
- Never joke about one's "sex life."

Nonverbal Behavior
- Do not wear revealing clothing to school.
- Do not touch, hug, pat, or rub one of your students, unless you are teaching primary grade children (K–2).
- Never display sexual literature or cartoons, or ones that contain sexual innuendo.
- Do not block a student's path, or intentionally "bump" them.
- Do not ogle a student or another teacher.

Source: Source: Retrieved July 9, 2007, from http://www.educationminnesota.org

---

Sexual harassment includes groping, sexual teasing, making sexual comments or innuendos, telling sexual jokes, snapping bra straps, inappropriate touching, using inappropriate language when addressing another person, or any form of physical abuse. Today, the Department of Education, Office of Civil Rights, will enforce complaints of sexual harassment. As American teachers however, we must set a standard in our classrooms that prohibits any form of sexual harassment. By modeling behavior that is professional and respectful we can gradually overcome this offensive behavior both inside and outside of school.

Journaling Activity
Develop more ways that teachers can provide positive models that avoid sexual harassment. Search your other education books and the Internet. List other guidelines in your journal.

In short, we have made some important progress in areas of gender equity but we still have a long way to go. Teachers must carefully monitor their interactions with students to avoid subtle forms of discrimination. By recognizing that sometimes this bias is unintentional, we can model behaviors that will improve gender equity and eliminate discrimination. Once again, it's up to you as an American teacher.

Handicapped and HIV-Infected Students

While women's educational rights were guaranteed by Title IX legislation, the rights of handicapped students were protected under P.L. 94–142 in 1975. This act was strengthened in 1992 with the passage of the Individuals with Disabilities Education Act (IDEA). This law required that all children with disabilities have the right to a free public education. The courts, moreover, have ruled that HIV-infected students are also protected under P.L. 94–142.

In addition to protecting the rights of handicapped students to education, IDEA also established the Office of Special Education Programs at the federal level. This agency makes certain that these special children receive a free public education.

Segregation Based on Race

In the last generation, legislatures and the courts have addressed issues of gender equity as well as the rights of handicapped students. Racism in both its overt and subtle forms, however, remains a central problem for schools throughout America.

From the beginning of our nation's history, the vast majority of African Americans were slaves. As such they had no legal rights and other than the good will of a slave owner or the occasional charity school, slave children had no access to formal education.

In fact, from the early 1800s to the passage of the 13th Amendment to the Constitution in 1865, many Southern states passed laws that made education of slaves illegal. North Carolina, for example, prohibited teaching slaves to read or write and imposed a penalty of $100 fine, the equivalent of $1000 today, or imprisonment for a White person who dared to challenge the law. A free black who was caught teaching slaves to read could receive 20 to 39 lashes while a slave could receive "39 lashes on his or her bare back." Similar laws were passed in Virginia, Mississippi, Louisiana, Alabama, and South Carolina (Cohen, 1974d, p. 1622).

Journaling Activity

Have we broken the "cycle of poverty" among African Americans? How have integrated schools improved schooling for African American students? Record your responses in your journal.

Race: An American Dilemma

In 1944, Gunnar Myrdal, a social economist, wrote *An American dilemma*. In it he introduced the concept of the "cycle of poverty" among blacks. He demonstrated that the cycle was a consequence of racial discrimination that resulted in segregated and poorer schools for blacks. Blacks were then limited to lower paying jobs and poorer living conditions. Their children were also restricted to poor quality schools and lower paying jobs. Thus the cycle of poverty persisted. Myrdal wrote that:

> The American Negro problem is a problem in the heart of America. It is there that the interracial tension has its focus. It is there that the decisive struggle goes on. . . . [A]t the bottom our problem is the moral dilemma of the American— the conflict between his moral valuations . . . [and] group prejudice against particular persons or types of people. (Myrdal, 1944, p. 1)

Links to the Past: Prudence Crandall

In spite of the efforts of Northern abolitionists, racial prejudice existed in the North as well as the South. As in the South, some communities and states had laws that prohibited educating blacks, and other communities resorted to mob violence. In 1831, Prudence Crandall began her own private school for girls in Canterbury, Connecticut. Shortly after she opened, she admitted a young black girl. The community was outraged. Prudence was threatened by her neighbors and the white parents withdrew their daughters from her school. Prudence was forced to close her school, but she was resilient. A few years later, she opened a school for "girls of color." The situation reached a climax when her enrollment reached 15. She was threatened with violence and was in danger of the community closing her school. Connecticut soon passed a "Black law" which made it illegal to establish or teach in any school for the education of blacks. Prudence refused to close her school; she was arrested and thrown in jail. When she was released, she found that her house had been burned to the ground! Poor Prudence! She abandoned her dream and left town. (Fuller, 1971)

Reflection

Why do you think Prudence defied the "Black law?" What would you have done if you were in her situation?

In the North, there were educational opportunities for free blacks, though they were limited. A few communities allowed integrated schools but most were segregated on the basis of race. Some religious groups such as the Quakers supported the education of blacks by establishing schools in their churches. The most successful of these was the African Free School that provided an education for hundreds of African American children during the early 1800s (Morgan, 1995).

The turning point for the education of African American children, however, came with the Freedman's Bureau schools established at the end of the American Civil War.

When slavery ended in 1865, Freedman's Bureau schools were established all over the South and brought what Booker T. Washington called a "veritable fever" for education to that region. By 1869, there were over 9,000 teachers instructing in Freedman's schools, providing hundreds of thousands of black children and many adults with their first chance for a formal education.

And yet, despite the great success of the Freedmen's Bureau schools, the experiment was short lived. Many Southerners resented these schools as a symbol of the "northern oppression." As a result, many Bureau schools were burned and a number of teachers were tarred and feathered or beaten by angry mobs. By 1870, federal funding for these schools was withdrawn and local communities abandoned them.

Reflection

Many brave teachers and students had to suffer intimidation and violence. What do you think were the motivations of the teachers in the Freedmen's Bureau schools? Why did so many blacks of all ages endure such suffering and fear to attend school? Would you be so brave? Record your responses in your journal.

Links to the Past: Freedmen's Bureau Schools

Miss Sarah Jane Foster left her home in Maine in 1865 under the guidance of the American Missionary Association to teach in the Freedmen's Bureau School in Martinsburg, West Virginia. She taught in a one-room school 4 hours a day and conducted an evening writing class for working adult blacks. The day school had children of all ages as well as several adults. Regarding her first days of teaching, she wrote:

> There were but sixteen out to day, but we hear of many more who want to come and the evening school will doubtless be fuller. (p. 33)

> Of the night scholars thirty-six are over twenty years old, one being sixty-two . . . One evening is set apart for instruction in writing, . . . I [also] make efforts to teach that reading and spelling are only the beginnings of a good education, and get all who can to take up Arithmetic and Geography. (p. 34)

Sarah Jane was housed with a family who lived in a log cabin in which you could see daylight between the logs. No doubt, it was drafty, cold, and leaked when it rained. Sarah Jane was a real American hero!

Sarah Jane's next teaching assignment was in Charleston, South Carolina in 1867.

She wrote:

> I lodge in the house of Father Haynes, the colored proprietor of the farm. He and his wife are excellent people. I have no white neighbors at all." After she had opened her school a few months, she recorded: "I have sixty two day scholars now, and twenty-eight at night. A class of seven who began the alphabet [a little over a month ago] now read well in three lettered words." (p. 179)

Sarah Jane was pleased with the progress of her Black pupils, both young and old. (Reilly, 1990)

Thus while some progress in the area of education was made during the period, the great experiment was stalled. Then between the late 1870s and the first decade of the 1900s, the condition of African American education deteriorated significantly in the South. This period, known as "Jim Crow," was punctuated by growing racism, lynching, and violence against black people. The capstone of this difficult period was the Supreme Court ruling of *Plessy v. Ferguson* (1896).

Reflection

How did the "separate but equal" ruling affect the lives of African Americans? Describe the effect on school attendance, railroad road travel, eating in restaurants, staying in hotels, the use of public restrooms and drinking fountains.

Links to the Past: Burning of Black Schools and other Violence

After the Civil War, as the Freedmen's Bureau attempted to establish schools to educate the recently freed blacks, they met sometimes violent opposition from whites. The following are several recorded incidents of such violence in the Freedmen's Bureau Records:

> March 11th, 1866—Two white men burnt the colored church at Centreville, Queen Anne's County, Md. because a colored school was held in it.

> March 17th, 1866—The Asst. Comr. D.C. reports the opposition to educating the colored people in Maryland is widespread and bitter. Teachers have been stoned, meetings were held and resolutions passed to drive them out. School houses have been burned. Colored churches too have been destroyed to prevent schools being held in them.

Some whites prevented the establishment of Freedmen's Schools in their communities, as shown in the example below:

> September 22nd, 1865—Col. John Eaton, Asst. Comr. Reports the opposition of Judge Wylie and his family to the opening of colored schools in their neighborhood. . . . Even before its opening Mr. & Mrs. Wylie protested in person at the Bureau against it, Mrs. Wylie suggesting that if her influence was not sufficient to prevent it more protest would be invoked and the Judge . . . made conditional threats of indictment and assured Col. E. that "a storm would wake up around his head the like of which her had never known" and the Judge made efforts to get neighbors arrayed in opposition to the location of colored schools there. (Freedmen's Bureau, 1865–1869)

Links to the Past: *Plessy v. Ferguson* (1896)

In the early 1890s, Homer Plessy was arrested in Louisiana because he sat in the "white only" railroad car. He refused to sit in the separate "black" designated car. This violated the Jim Crow Laws in existence at that time regarding segregation in the South. Plessy sued, contending that the Jim Crow Laws violated the 14th Amendment of "equal protection under the law."

In 1896, the Supreme Court issued its landmark decision in the case of *Plessy v. Ferguson*. It ruled that Homer Plessy's rights under the 14th Amendment had not been violated. The Court ruled that the 14th Amendment said that blacks had the right to equal facilities, not the same facilities. In this case, the Supreme Court gave legitimacy to the "separate but equal" doctrine that existed for the next half century.

Source: Cornell University Law School, retrieved February 25, 2008, from
http://www.law.cornell.edu/supct/html/historics/USSC_CR_0163_0537_ZS.html

Briefly, the Plessy decision ruled that separate but equal transportation facilities were legal in this nation. By extension, the Plessy decision gave federal approval to the practice of segregation in all public facilities including schools. This decision, in short, was the beginning of the modern era of school segregation in this country. In many ways it also marked this nation's darkest moment in race relations.

In the face of these difficult times, African Americans and some liberal whites banded together to challenge this and other decisions of the courts and fight the growing racism in this country. Within a decade they had formed the National Urban League and the National Association for the Advancement of Colored People. For the next 50 years, these two groups, as well as a host of others, challenged the legal basis of segregation in this country.

By the early 1950s, their hard work began to pay off. Because of consistent pressure on the courts for more than a half century, the Supreme Court finally ruled in their favor. In its landmark *Brown v. Board of Education* (1954) decision, the court argued that the "separate but equal" doctrine of Plessy was inherently wrong. The Brown decision affirmed that segregation in public facilities was illegal and ordered that it be remedied "with all deliberate speed."

De jure and De facto Segregation

The Brown decision was a catalyst that initiated the transformation of American education by focusing on *de jure* segregation—segregation due to law. And yet, in the years following the Brown decision, there was little progress toward desegregation of schools. As a result, both the Supreme Court and the Congress acted to facilitate the Brown decision. The court challenged a number of school systems throughout the country, arguing that they had stalled the process of desegregation.

Eventually Congress passed its landmark Civil Rights Law of 1964. Title IV of this legislation gave the federal government the legal power to sue school districts that had either ignored or were slow to implement the Brown decision. Title VI of this important

---

Links to the Past: Brown v. Board of Education (1954)

Brown v. Board of Education (1954) was a landmark Supreme Court decision that overturned the *Plessy v. Ferguson* (1896) "separate but equal" doctrine. The Brown decision declared that "separate" was by its very nature unequal and it called for the desegregation of all public facilities including schools.

The case in brief:

Seven-year-old Linda Brown, a black girl, had to walk 5 miles to attend the black school in Topeka, Kansas, during the 1950s. Just across the railroad track from her home was a white school, but because Linda was black she could not attend. Her father garnered the aid of the NAACP to help and they charged that the segregation of the school system violated the 14th Amendment. The state claimed that the Plessy decision had settled this issue, but the Supreme Court overturned the decision in favor of the Browns. This ruling initiated the integration of public schools in the United States.

Source: Cornell University Law School, Retrieved February 25, 2008, from http://supreme.justia.com/us/420/308/case.html

---

Links to the Past: School Integration Brings Violence

In some communities, violence erupted when the courts ordered the desegregation of public schools.

Schools in Little Rock, Arkansas also delayed integration for several years and then they implemented a 3-stage plan for the school year 1957–58: first to integrate the high school, next the junior high school, and then the elementary school. Nine black students volunteered to attend the all-white Central High School. Whites filed an injunction to delay the integration plan, but a federal judge overruled it. A number of anti-integration groups formed including, the Mothers League of Little Rock Central High School. The Governor, Orval Faubus, ordered the Arkansas National Guard to surround the school and keep black students from entering the high school. President Eisenhower called the 101st Airborne to patrol the school and escort the black students. Each black student was assigned a guard to protect them. Still, many black students endured insults and humiliation and feared for their lives. Some were beaten up or had flaming paper wads thrown at them. Poor Melba Pattillo had lighted sticks of dynamite thrown at her, she was stabbed, and had acid thrown in her eyes. Finally, out of frustration, Minnijean Brown dumped her lunch tray on the heads of two boys who were taunting her unmercifully. She was suspended from school for 6 days. Two months later, she was expelled from school for calling a girl who was tormenting her "white trash." Eventually, eight of the nine original black students completed the school year.

Source: School Integration in the United States, 1998, retrieved February 25, from http://www.watson.org/~lisa/blackhistory/school-integration

---

law denied federal funds to those communities that discriminated on the basis of race, color, or national origin.

Journaling Activity

Despite the Brown decision of 1954 and the Civil Rights Act of 1964, many communities throughout the country—such as Prince George County in Maryland and Prince Edward County in Virginia—fought against desegregation in their communities. What do you think of this sort of activity? Has your community had a similar history? Record your thoughts in your journal.

In order to deal with the problem of *de facto* segregation—segregation due to patterns of residence—the court ordered that some communities must bus students. In its landmark Charlotte–Mecklenburg busing decision of 1971, (*North Carolina State Board of Education v. Swann*) the U. S. Supreme Court ruled that it was appropriate for school districts to bus students to achieve racial desegregation. This ruling began a controversial process that eventually would affect school districts all over the nation. Later the court would approve racial quotas and the pairing of black and white schools, the so-called Finger Plan, to achieve racial balance.

The Conservative Reaction to Desegregation

By the late 1970s and early 1980s, U.S. schools were beginning to achieve some racial balance for the first time in American history. But the social and political cost of this

---

Links to the Past: Resistance to Court Ordered Integration of Schools

Many communities resisted integrating public schools. Some quietly ignored the ruling, and others tried to get around the law.

Prince Edward County, Virginia, for example, closed all their public schools in 1959 to avoid integration.

Prince George County, Maryland on the other hand, operated two separate school systems: one for white children and one for black children. After the Brown Decision, the county delayed taking any action for several years, then in 1955–56, they adopted the "freedom of choice desegregation plan." Under this plan, students attended the same school as before, but parents could request a transfer to another school. The procedure to transfer, however, was difficult. Parents had to request the form, complete it as directed, and submit it within a narrow deadline. Procedures and deadlines were not openly publicized. Transfer requests that were not submitted on time or not thoroughly completed were rejected. After 1964, the Supreme Court made it clear that Prince George schools must desegregate immediately. In 1971, the school system was found to be "noncompliant" with the HEW (Health, Education, and Welfare) Guidelines and federal funds were threatened to be cut off. Judge Frank Kaufman ordered the system to come up with a plan that utilized busing to achieve integration. When the day came to implement the busing plan, 15,000 people rallied to protest the plan. Mothers made cardboard tombstones that read "Here Lies Democracy, Freedom and Justice, 1776–1973," and some parents kept their children home. By 1974, the school system reluctantly had implemented a desegregation plan.

Source: Retrieved Feb. 25, 2008, from http://www.watson.org/~lisa/blackhistory/school-integration

---

victory was high. Many Americans resented the aggressive involvement of the federal government in what they saw as a local matter. Others took exception to their children being bused to black schools or African Americans being bused to white schools.

Second-Generation Segregation

As a result, school districts searched for ways to appease parents in their communities. Some schools promised improved instruction in desegregated schools through programs of tracking and ability grouping. Black and Hispanic students, however, were often placed into one academic track while whites were placed into another. This policy created rigid racial boundaries within schools that were difficult to transcend. These policies are generally referred to as second-generation segregation.

Of course, all second-generation segregation is not intentional. But some is. Professor Joel Spring in his influential *American Education* (2000) notes a case in Selma, Alabama, where Norward Roussell, the first African American superintendent was fired because he wanted to increase the presence of minorities in "upper ability tracks" of a high school from 3% to 10%. Dr. Roussell found that 90% of all white students had been placed into college preparatory tracks while only 3% of African Americans had similar placement. Spring notes that ". . . the obvious purpose of the tracking system was to segregate white from African American students." As a footnote to the firing of Dr. Roussell, a boycott by African American students led to his rehiring but white parents in the district threatened to remove their children and send them to private schools (Spring, 2000, p. 121).

Links to the Past: *Swann v. Charlotte–Mecklenburg* **and the Finger Plan**

In 1971 the Supreme Court ordered busing as a remedy for the segregated Char-lotte–Mecklenburg School System. The court supported federal Judge McMillan's decision that North Carolina's "freedom of choice" plan had not achieved a deseg-regated school system. McMillan appointed a consultant, John Finger, to develop a desegregation plan. It consisted of the following:

- Adjusting student assignments so all schools had the same proportion of black and white students.
- Preventing schools from having all black or mostly black student population.
- Using nontraditional measures for student assignments, such as pairing students from black and white neighborhoods.
- Limiting student transfers.
- Maintain approximately the same ratio of black and white teachers in each school.
- Have competent black and white teachers.

The Supreme Court ruling mandated busing as the strategy to achieve these guidelines for desegregation. (Dowling-Sendor, 2002)

Resegregation

While second-generation segregation continues to be a problem in American schools, it also appears that the courts have retreated from their previous positions of promoting desegregation and affirmative action. For example, in its 1991, *Board of Education of Oklahoma City Public Schools v. Dowell* decision, the court ruled that federal supervision of desegregation was intended only as a temporary measure. Supporters of desegregation feared that this might have signaled the beginning of the end of court-ordered busing. Then, in *Freeman v. Pitts* (1992), the court ruled that busing was not necessary to remedy racial imbalances caused by recent demographic changes. This ruling was particularly troubling because of the dramatic rise of Hispanic and other minority students who had recently migrated to this country. In fact, educational research has demonstrated that segregation of these ethnic and language minority students has become more pronounced in recent years. One researcher has shown that the percentage of Latino students in this country who are attending "*de facto* minority schools" has doubled from about 40% to about 80% in one generation (Fears, 2001).

Affirmative Action

While the controversy surrounding busing has directly impacted elementary and second-ary students throughout the country, policies of affirmative action regarding admission to colleges, universities, and professional schools like law schools, medical schools, etc., indirectly affect all students and our American society as well. During the 1960s and 1970s, there was a favorable climate for affirmative action created by the Civil Rights Law of 1964 and President Johnson's Executive Order 11246 of 1965 which developed the policy of affirmative action among federal employees. These and other measures essentially argued that in order to correct past injustices against racial and other minori-ties, it was acceptable for institutions of higher learning to expand the pool of qualified minority *candidates* in order to increase diversity.

Affirmative Action

There has always been affirmative action in higher education—but for many years it operated to exclude, rather than include, women and people of color. Consider one example: There is little doubt that George W. Bush's grades were lower than those of hundreds of students who were rejected by Yale University the same year Bush was welcomed there.

Yes, George W. Bush was a beneficiary of one kind of affirmative action—the kind that favored the sons of overwhelmingly white and well-to-do Yale graduates. Yet there was no White House denunciation of the "extra points" universities, including Michigan, give to children of donors or alums—only a condemnation of efforts to offset those preferences (which go mostly to white students) by also considering race and ethnic background. (Gandy, 2003, p. 1)

Reflection

What do you think about the above statement by Kim Gandy, President of the National Organization of Women (NOW)? Do you think some wealthy white students may have received preferential treatment? Is that fair to poorer and minority students? Record your responses in your journal.

In 1978, however, things began to change. Allan Bakke sued the University of California, alleging that they had discriminated against him when he was not admitted to the University of California Davis Medical School. The Bakke decision brought the concept of "reverse discrimination" into the public eye. The Supreme Court ruled in its *Regents of University of California v. Allan Bakke* (1978) that he had been discriminated against because of "racial quotas." However, they also declared that while quotas were unconstitutional, affirmative action clearly was within the law.

Since the Bakke decision, there have been hundreds of suits alleging "reverse discrimination." In the landmark case *Hopwood v. State of Texas*, 1996, the court eliminated what are known as racial "set asides" for law school admissions. Five years later, the court dealt another blow to affirmative action in *Johnson v. Board of Regents of the University of Georgia* (2001). In this case, the court ruled that the University's policy of awarding "points" to non-white applicants was unconstitutional.

Journaling Activity

What is your position on "reverse discrimination?" Are you aware of it? If so, record an example and comment on it in your journal. If not, reflect on this idea.

However, more recently in *Grutter v. Bollinger* (2003), the court ruled that the University of Michigan's Law School's admission policy was an acceptable method of achieving a diverse student body. In a related decision, *Gratz v. Bollinger* (2003), it decided that the point formula used by the University of Michigan to determine undergraduate admissions was too narrow and therefore unconstitutional.

While these rulings appear to be mixed, most legal experts see them as a major victory for affirmative action because race can be used as a factor in admissions. Race-point formulas, such as those used by the University of Georgia, the University of Michigan,

---

"Reverse Discrimination": Bakke Case

Regents of the University of California v. Bakke case was decided in 1978 by the U.S. Supreme Court. The court held in a closely divided decision that race could be one of the factors considered in choosing a diverse student body in university admissions decisions. The court also held, however, that the use of quotas in such affirmative action programs was not permissible; thus the University of California, Davis, medical school had, by maintaining a 16% minority quota, discriminated against Allan Bakke (1940–), a white applicant. The legal implications of the decision were clouded by the Court's division. Bakke had twice been rejected by the medical school, even though he had a higher grade point average than a number of minority candidates who were admitted. As a result of the decision, Bakke was admitted to the medical school and graduated in 1992.

Source: Columbia University Encyclopedia Online, retrieved February 25, 2008, from http://www.law.umkc.edu/faculty/projects/ftrials/conlaw/bakke.html

---

What is "Reverse Discrimination?"

Several Supreme Court cases such as Bakke have involved charges of "reverse discrimination"—that is charged "unfair treatment" for whites. The charges claim that minorities received special treatment and that it is wrong to give blacks preference, thus treating whites unfairly. However, according to historian Stanley Fish, "the adverb 'unfairly' suggests two or more equal parties . . . but blacks have not simply been treated unfairly; they have been subjected to decades of slavery, and then to decades of second-class citizenship. . . the word 'unfair' is hardly an adequate description of their experience." Those in favor of affirmative action would argue that a policy of "fairness" cannot overcome years of mistreatment and exclusion. Blacks and other minority groups must be provided opportunities in order to achieve equality. (Fish, 1993, p. 1)

---

and many other schools throughout the country will have to be replaced with a more individualized approach.

INDIVIDUAL RIGHTS

The right to education for women, handicapped, African Americans, and other minority groups has been a monumental social, political, and legal struggle that has taken over 2 centuries to achieve. And yet, other basic student rights such as access to personal school records, due process, protection from unlawful search and seizure, freedom of the press, and protection from sexual harassment have only recently become an issue. In fact, in the last generation, society has accepted that students have certain rights which must be protected. This is different from the traditional way students were treated, which was primarily *in loco parentis,* where schools, not the Constitution, determined the rights of the student. As a result we have begun to address these issues.

Affirmative Action Decisions: *Grutter v. Bollinger* (2003)

In its landmark Supreme Court decision, *Grutter v. Bollinger* (2003); the court ruled that the University of Michigan's Law School admissions policy that considered race as one of a number of factors for admission was constitutional. Justice Sandra Day O'Connor issued the opinion of the majority stating: "[T]he law school has a compelling interest in a diverse student body . . . [it] is at the heart of the law school's proper institutional mission. . . . [L]aw schools cannot be effective in isolation from the individuals and institutions with which the law interacts."

Source: Cornell University Law School, Supreme Court Decisions, retrieved July 20, 2007, from http://www.law.cornell.edu/supct/html/02-241.ZS.html

Journaling Activity
Begin a list of students', teachers', and schools' rights in your journal. Add to this list during the semester.

Reflection
Do some of the students' rights interfere with the teachers' ability to teach?

The Right to Sue

What may have been the turning point in the struggle for the legal rights of students came in 1975, in the landmark *Wood v. Strickland* decision of the Supreme Court. Two 10-grade girls (Peggy and Virginia) from Mena Public High School in Arkansas "spiked" a punch, with two bottles of malt liquor, intended for a home economics meeting attended by parents and students. For this action, the school board suspended them for the remainder of the school semester—about 3 months.

The girls challenged this action in court arguing that their civil rights, due process, had been violated since neither they nor their parents were allowed to attend the suspension hearing. A lower court ruled that the students had been punished unfairly. However, the school board claimed they had "qualified immunity" because they were unaware that they had violated these students' basic constitutional rights.

The Supreme Court heard this case and ruled that ignorance of "settled indisputable law" on the part of a school official did not protect him or her from being sued. In response to this decision, a federal judge in Arkansas ruled that students had the right to sue individual school board members, though not the school board as a body. (Retrieved February 25, 2008, from http://supreme.justia.com/us/420/308/case.html)

Reflection

Wood v. Strickland: The "Spiked Punch" Case of 1975

What do you think about the girls spiking the punch? Do you think the 3-month suspension was justified? If you were a member of the school board what action would you have recommended?

Students' Rights v. *In Loco Parentis*

Students' rights have become an important issue in recent years. Below are some of the rights students are guaranteed by the U.S. Constitution and recent court rulings:

- Children have the right to a free public education.
    - Parents do not have to pay real estate taxes, or be citizens, or legal aliens for their children to be eligible for a free public education.
    - Homeless children have a right to education.
    - Students with disabilities are entitled to an "appropriate" education.
    - Students cannot be prohibited from attending school because of pregnancy or marriage.
- Students have the right to due process.
    - Students have a right to a hearing in cases involving suspension or expulsion.
    - Students or their parents have the right to sue individual school board members for the violation of their "due process." (They cannot, however, sue the school district or the school board as a whole.)
- Students have the right to Freedom of Speech.
    - Students' speech or behavior, however, cannot be aggressive or provide a disruption in the school.
    - Students, moreover, cannot make sexual remarks or innuendos, because this is disruptive to the school environment and may be considered sexual harassment.

Rights of Schools (*in loco parentis*)
- Schools can establish dress codes.
- Schools may administer corporal punishment, depending on state law and school district policy.
- Schools have the right to conduct drug testing for athletes and students participating in extracurricular activities.
- Schools have the right to search lockers, desks, and cars parked in school parking lots.
- Schools can suspend dangerous students for a maximum of 10 days.

Access to Student Records

What began as a prank by two Arkansas 10th graders would eventually alert educators throughout the country to the constitutional rights of students. The *Wood v. Strickland* (1975) decision along with a handful of other rulings during this period would revolutionize the legal relationship between students and school officials. While the right to sue school board members was the cornerstone in this changing relationship, access to personal records also was critical.

Prior to the early 1970s, neither students nor their parents/guardians were allowed to examine their personal school records. Administrators routinely held *incognito* all records including test scores, grades, comments by teachers, disciplinary actions, health, and attendance. This tradition made it difficult for students and their parents to challenge decisions made by the school on matters of promotion or discipline and essentially deprived students of their basic right to know.

Buckley Amendment

During the early 1970s, however, there were numerous court challenges to this tradition and eventually the U.S. Congress intervened, passing landmark legislation, P.L. 93–380. This law, commonly known as the Buckley Amendment, was important both substantively and symbolically. It allowed students and parents to examine their own personal school records in order to understand the decisions of school officials and it symbolically changed the basis of teacher student relationships from *in loco parentis*, or in place of parents, to individual students' rights.

While this important legislation is now over 30 years old, many administrators and teachers, and most students and parents, are unaware of its existence. Nevertheless, the Buckley Amendment is one of the important cornerstones of student rights today. It has a number of provisions but in essence it gives parents and legal guardians access to all educational records that a school district keeps on their child. In addition, students over the age of 16 years also have the right to access these records.

Due Process

Related to the right of students to sue and having access their personal records is their right of "due process" under the 14th Amendment to the Constitution. This important Amendment guarantees that states will not "deny to any person within its jurisdiction the equal protection of the laws." In other words, all individuals including students who are accused of a crime must be afforded full protection under the law. Generally speaking, the courts have made an important distinction between procedural and substantive due process. Procedural due process assures that the rules of law (the procedures) are followed, while substantive due process deals with an individual who is deprived of his or her basic constitutional rights such as personal liberty, property, or privacy. (Fischer, Schimmel, & Kelly, 1999)

Buckley Amendment: Students' Rights

In 1974, P.L. 93–380 went into effect (it was amended in 1976 in order to clarify its intent by P.L. 93–568). The law required that schools receiving federal funds comply with "privacy rights" for students. Schools are required to:

- Allow parents access to their child's school records
- Establish a policy regarding parents viewing school records
- Inform parents of their rights under the Buckley Amendment
- Acquire written parental approval before releasing individual student records to others (except appropriate school personnel, such as teachers, counselors, special education teachers, etc.)

It is important to remember as teachers that parents have the right to see written comments that you might add to a student's records. Also, be sensitive to the fact that whatever you place in a student's records will remain there throughout their lives.

Goss v. Lopez

In *Goss v. Lopez* (1975), The Supreme Court argued simply that "students have property and liberty interests that give them due process rights where they are suspended from schools."

Source: University of Missouri, retrieved February 25, 2008, from http://www.law.umkc. edu/faculty/projects/ftrials/firstamendment/hazelwood.html

---

Procedural Due Process

As we have seen students have the right to "tell their side of the story" in disciplinary matters. Like other U.S. citizens, students must be informed of what offenses they have been accused and the evidence that will be used against them.

In the early 1970s, a number of students sued the Columbus, Ohio, school system claiming that they had been suspended from Central High School without a hearing. The students alleged that their rights of due process under the 14th Amendment had been violated. Dwight Lopez, then a student at the school, was suspended for causing a disturbance in the lunchroom. His case became the focus of the Supreme Court decision *Goss v. Lopez* (1975) that upheld his right to a hearing.

Substantive Due Process: Freedom of Speech

Issues of procedural due process are typically associated with students' rights to a hearing in cases of discipline. Substantive due process issues, on the other hand, are usually associated with cases of student free speech.

Prior to the late 1960s, students had few rights associated with free speech. As with other matters, school administrators were seen as acting in place of parents (*in loco parentis*). The war in Vietnam, however, was an issue about which many students felt strongly and some spoke out against the conflict both in and outside of school. In December 1965, John and Mary Beth Tinker and Christopher Eckhardt from Des Moines, Iowa, wore black armbands to school to protest the war. The principals of their schools were angered by such a protest and suspended the students. In turn, the students sued the school board, arguing that they had deprived of their 1st Amendment rights of free speech.

The district court dismissed their case but in its landmark decision *Tinker v. Des Moines* (1969), the Supreme Court ruled against the school board and upheld the right of free speech of students and teachers. Justice Fortas, writing for the majority noted: "The armbands did not cause a disturbance and are closely akin to pure speech deserving comprehensive protection." He noted further that "teachers and students do not shed constitutional rights at the schoolhouse gate" (University of North Texas, n.d.).

But the question of "free speech" is not that simple. Nearly 15 years later, on April 26, 1983, Matthew Fraser, a student at Bethel High School in Washington State gave a speech at a school assembly. During the speech he used an "elaborate graphic and explicit sexual metaphor" to describe another student's qualifications for school office. While there was no "obscenity" used in the speech, he was suspended for 3 days and not allowed to give a commencement speech. Matthew sued the school board, claiming that they had violated his 1st Amendment right of free speech. The court of appeals ruled in his favor, but in 1986 in its *Bethel School District v. Fraser* the Supreme Court argued that his speech was

Matthew Fraser's Speech

The following is the text of the speech that the Supreme Court Justices considered "obscene, vulgar, and offensively lewd." Matthew Fraser gave this speech to the student body of his high school in support of a student government candidate.

I know a man who is firm—he's firm in his pants, he's firm in his shirt, his character is firm—but most . . . of all, his belief in you, the students of Bethel, is firm.

Jeff Kuhlman is a man who takes his point and pounds it in. If necessary, he'll take an issue and nail it to the wall. He doesn't attack things in spurts—he drives hard, pushing and pushing until finally—he succeeds.

Jeff is a man who will go to the very end—even the climax, for each and every one of you.

So vote for Jeff for A.S.B. vice-president—he'll never come between you and the best our high school can be.

Source: Retrieved February 25, 2008, from http://www.law.umkc.edu/faculty/projects/ftrials/firstamendment/hazelwood.html

not related to a political position and therefore had no 1st Amendment protection. Since Matthew's speech contained "vulgar" language, the court ruled that the school district was within its rights to suspend him (http://www.law.umkc.edu).

Reflection

Matthew's speech was said to have contained sexual innuendo that resulted in boisterous behavior from the students gathered in the assembly. Do you think this speech is offensive? Did the school administration overreact?

Do you think there are other ways the school might have dealt with this situation? What could the sponsor of the student government association have done to prevent this?

While the Supreme Court ruled that it was an appropriate action to suspend Matthew because of the "vulgarity" in his school speech, in other rulings the court has protected such forms of speech when expressed outside school or when they were not part of the school curriculum. In 1970, for example, two Illinois students published an "underground" newspaper (*Grass High*) from their home that was both "vulgar" and critical of the school they attended. The two students were suspended. While a lower court and a federal court upheld the decision, it was overturned in appeal. The court ruled that the students had not disrupted the school with their publication and that they had the right of free expression to publish a newspaper at home.

Publications that use school facilities or those that are part of the school curriculum, such as a school newspaper, are subject to greater scrutiny. In its important *Hazelwood School District v. Kuhlmeir* (1988), the Supreme Court ruled that school officials could regulate supervised learning experiences such as those that are part of the curriculum (www.law.umkc.edu/faculty/projects/ftrials/firstamendment/hazelwood.html)

Wisdom of Master Teachers: Balancing Student's Freedom of Speech

Jill Ripley recalled her experience as editor of the school newspaper when she was a junior in high school. She was a good student, interested in writing, and was very excited about her journalism class. She also was thrilled with the opportunity to be the editor of the *Rileyan*, the school newspaper. She quickly became disillusioned as her teacher who was the sponsor of the newspaper edited her editorials with a very heavy hand. One mildly controversial editorial that Jill wrote was replaced by an article on "Good Manners" with her name on it! Jill was very embarrassed, she sounded like a nerd! (NBPTS Survey, 2002)

Reflection

If you were the sponsor of the school newspaper, how would you handle this type of situation? Think of some creative ways in which you might guide your students. Remember, do not crush your student's enthusiasm.

Search and Seizure

While access to personal school records and the right of due process in cases of disciplinary matters have been clarified by legislation and the courts, protection from illegal "search and seizure" is more complex and less clear. While certain kinds of searches—especially strip searches—have generally been declared illegal, others searches can legally be conducted by school administrators.

In the mid-1970s, two students, Cassandra and Onieka, from Graham Elementary School were accused of stealing $4.50. The girls were brought to the restroom and allegedly were ordered to take off their clothes, including their shoes and socks, to check for the missing money. Both of the girls pulled down their underpants though the teacher claimed she told them only to "check their clothes for the money." Nevertheless, the girls sued the school district for unlawful search and seizure arguing that they had been illegally "striped searched."

The lower court ruled in *Bellnier v. Lund* (1977) that strip searches "are inherently among the most intrusive of all searches" and declared them illegal. The decision noted: "strip searches are probably only permissible in the school setting . . . where there is a threat of imminent serious harm." The Supreme Court upheld this decision in *New Jersey v. T.L.O.* (1985) (http://www.law.emory.edu).

Yet, the courts have generally allowed other kinds of student searches. Even though the 4th Amendment to the Constitution protects individuals from "unlawful search and seizure," students do not have those rights. In fact, the courts have reasoned that since discipline in schools is so important, 4th Amendment rights can be abridged.

School officials must have a good reason to search a student and must suspect that they have broken a school rule or a law. For example, they may search a student's locker or car parked on the school campus without a warrant to look for drugs or weapons. And yet, the courts have placed a "higher standard" on personal searches. Only when "reasonable suspicion" exists that a student is in possession of something harmful such as a knife or a handgun, or that he or she is engaged in drug dealing, can a personal search be made. Once again however, strip searches are not legal.

Students' Opinions on School Locker Searches

Students were asked to respond to the statement, "Random locker searches at schools are necessary for the safety and well being of students."

- 23% strongly agreed
- 51% agreed
- 35% disagreed
- Remainder uncertain

The survey found that there was *no* correlation between the race of students and levels of safety concerns in the schools.

This survey was conducted by the American Bar Association Division for Public Education, in February and March of 2000 of approximately 800 high school students, who participated in a week-long civic education program sponsored by the Washington, D.C.-based Close Up Foundation.

Source: Retrieved July 12, 2007,
http://www.abanet.org/publiced/lawday/studsurvey2000.html

Drug Testing

One of the most controversial forms of "search and seizure" of students is in the area of drug testing. In the last two decades—since the onset of America's War on Drugs—the issue of drug testing has spread from the workplace to the school campus. Not only have school officials routinely searched student's lockers and cars parked on campus for drugs, but drug testing has become commonplace for athletes, and more recently, students involved in extracurricular activities.

During the 1980s, school officials in Vernonia, Oregon, decided to deal aggressively with what they saw as a growing drug problem among students, especially their athletes. During that period there were an increasing number of disciplinary problems among students that school administrators attributed to the use of drugs. In 1989, the school district initiated the Student Athlete Drug Policy. Students who wished to participate in sports were required to sign a consent form to the drug testing and parents had to give their written consent. Student athletes were tested at the beginning of the season and then, once a week, individuals were selected at random and tested.

Reflection

What is your opinion regarding "suspicionless" drug testing? Were you surprised by the research findings regarding lower drug use among athletes and students involved in extra curricular activities? Does this seem to justify the expense (generally $20–$40 per sample) and disruption to the school routine? Record your responses in your journal.

In 1991, James Acton, a seventh grader from the district, signed up to play football but he and his parents refused to sign the drug consent forms. As a result, James was not allowed to join the team and his parents filed suit against the school's policy. The case went all the way to the Supreme Court and in *Vernonia v. Acton* (1995), it ruled that the school's policy was constitutional. Since the school acts as a "guardian and tutor of children entrusted to its care," it had the right to randomly test student athletes for drugs.

**Findings Regarding Drug Use among Athletes and
Students involved in Extra Curricular Activities**

Research has shown that athletes and students participating in extra curricular activities are not more likely to use drugs, in fact:

- Students' participation in athletics or extracurricular activities serves as a "protective factor" that reduces the likelihood of using drugs, alcohol, or tobacco.
- For Grades 9 and lower, they have the lowest involvement with drugs.
- For Grades 10–12, they are more likely to use alcohol during weekend parties, but are less likely to use drugs such as marijuana, cocaine, and "speed."
- High school athletes are more likely to use steroids, although steroids are not detected by the type of urine tests generally used.
- "Coke," "speed," or barbiturates are not detected several days after their use by a urine test. Only marijuana and tobacco are likely to be detected by a random urine test. (Indiana Prevention Resource Center, 2008)

Source: Retrieved February 25, 2008, from http://www.drugs.indiana.edu/

Reflection
Do you think the purpose of the testing outweighs the possible effect on school morale? Discuss your opinion with your classmates.

As a result of *Vernonia v. Acton* (1995) decision, other school districts across the nation began drug testing of their student athletes. In 1998, the school board of Tecumseh, Oklahoma, expanded its drug-testing program to include all students involved in extracurricular activities. Students were required to be tested at the beginning of each school year and then randomly thereafter.

Lindsay and Lacy Earls and their parents, however, challenged this policy. Lindsay was a member of the school's choir, color guard, and the academic team while Lacy was an officer in the Future Farmers of America (FFA). Both sisters tested negatively several times but they and their parents resented the intrusion into their privacy and claimed that drug testing was a violation of their rights under the 4th Amendment to the Constitution (unreasonable search and seizure). They also claimed that there was little evidence of a drug problem among students in Tecumseh, nor was there a safety issue as was claimed by the school district.

Reflection
In districts that have had no positive tests, do you think the program is cost effective? Do the benefits outweigh the costs? (It costs approximately $20–$40 per test.)

This case eventually made its way to the Supreme Court in 2002. In its *Board of Education v Earls*, the court ruled that drug testing of students in extracurricular activities was not an unreasonable search under the 4th Amendment. Writing for the majority, Justice Clarence Thomas, referring the Vernonia decision of 1995, noted that public schools have "custodial and tutelary responsibility for children" and as a result, school officials have a constitutional right to test students for drugs. Moreover, on the question of whether there was a drug problem in the district, Thomas wrote "it would make little sense to require a school district to wait for a substantial portion of its students to begin

The Effect of "Suspicionless" Drug Testing on Students and Teachers Morale

Opponents of suspicionless drug testing argue that it can have a detrimental impact on school morale. Following are some of the possible effects:

- Students as well as teachers may resent the testing program
- The implication of the policy is that students cannot be trusted
- The collection of urine samples is disruptive to the school environment
- The use of a monitor for the collection is an invasion of personal privacy
- Some students may avoid participating in athletics or extracurricular activities in order to avoid having someone monitor their urine sample collection
- Since urine samples must be refrigerated until testing, teacher morale will be effected if they are stored in the staff refrigerators along with teachers' lunches, bottled water, and soft drinks.

Source: Retrieved February 25, 2008, from http://www.drugs.indiana.edu/

Drug Testing: School Board Survey

In an Illinois School Board survey conducted in 2000, only 8% (41) of the school districts used random drug testing. Ninety-two percent of the districts responding did not conduct drug testing and had no plans to implement a drug testing program. Of those 8% of the school districts in the state of Illinois that use random drug testing, following are some of the survey results.
Groups that were tested for drug use:
- 75% tested athletes
- 46% tested students in extracurricular activities
- 17% tested marching band members
- 7% tested student drivers

Summary: Most districts test athletes and students in extracurricular activities.
Percentage of the student body tested:
- 34% of the districts tested less than 10% of the students
- 14% of the districts tested between 10%–15% of the students
- 20% tested between 25–50% of the students
- 7% tested more than 50% of the students

Summary: Almost half of the districts tested less than 25% of the students.
Number of "positive" drug tests since testing began (generally 1–5 years):
- 61% of the districts had less than five "positive" tests
- 7% of the districts had between 5–10 positive tests
- 4% had between 10–15 positives
- 2% or less had 15–50 positives

Summary: The majority of the districts had five or fewer "positive" drug tests.
   In other words, among the districts that have drug testing programs for athletes and students in extracurricular activities, very few students have tested "positive" for drug use (Pierson & Rittenmeyer, 2001).

using drugs before it was allowed to institute a drug testing program designed to deter drug use." This suggested that a *potential* drug problem in the school was reason enough to begin a drug-testing policy (www.Whitehouse Drug Policy.gov).

Reflection
Do you think that the school district's safety issue was valid? Why? What do you think of the Earls decision? Has drug testing gone too far?

Corporal Punishment

Corporal punishment or physical punishment is still legal in 23 states. Once the preferred form of discipline in the classroom, most educators today reject paddling, punching, or whipping students. Nevertheless, the Children's Defense Fund has estimated that today a student is physically punished every 10 seconds (Fischer et al., 1999).

Reflection
Go to Web site http://www.stophitting.com/disatschool/statesBanning.php and see if your state has banned physical punishment of students. What are your impressions of this form of punishment? If legal would you use it in your classroom?

Perhaps ironically, the same Supreme Court that helped to secure basic constitutional rights for students has also declared that corporal punishment was not a violation of the 8th Amendment to the Constitution, cruel and unusual punishment. In its landmark *Ingraham v. Wright* (1977) the court ruled that school officials may choose to adopt a policy either to use corporal punishment or not. As an American teacher, however, we recommend that you be familiar with the specific rules of your state, district, and school that regulate the use of corporal punishment on students. As a rule of thumb—avoid it!

Journaling Activity
What kinds of punishment do teachers administer today? Look in some of your education texts, or conduct an online search and obtain 10 nonviolent strategies for dealing with student infractions of classroom rules. Record your ideas in your journal.

Justice Ruth Ginsburg's dissenting opinion on *Board of Education v. Earls* (2002)

Responding to the argument that drug testing was necessary because of school safety in extracurricular activities such as Future Homemakers of America, Future Farmers of America and Marching Band, Justice Ginsburg wrote:

> Notwithstanding nightmarish images of out-of-control flatware, livestock run amok, and colliding tubas disturbing the peace and quiet of Tecumseh, the great majority of students the school district seeks to test in truth are engaged in activities that are not safety sensitive to an unusual degree. (*Education Week*, 1982)

Corporal Punishment in U.S. Public Schools

In the 2002–2003 school year, 301,016 school children in the United States were subjected to physical punishment. This is a significant drop of 12%, continuing a steady trend from the early 1980s. Corporal punishment is now illegal in 28 states and the District of Columbia. (U.S. Department of Education, Office of Civil Rights)

THE RIGHTS OF TEACHERS

Many of the legal issues we have discussed in the context of students such as basic civil rights, protection from sexual harassment, due process, and freedom of speech also apply to teachers. And yet, there are a number of legal matters that apply specifically to teachers. These include academic freedom, personal lifestyle, the right to collective bargaining, and legal liability.

Sexual Harassment and Gender Equality for Teachers

As mentioned before, Title IX legislation has served to protect students from discrimination and sexual harassment. This same legislation also protects teachers. In the late 1970s, for example, a number of teachers from North Haven, Connecticut, sued their school board, claiming sexual harassment by a school administrator. The Supreme Court heard this case *North Haven Board of Education v. Bell* (1982) and decided in their favor. In this landmark ruling, the court argued that Title IX legislation applies to both students and teachers.

Links to the Past: Corporal Punishment

The use of corporal or physical punishment was the primary form of discipline used in schools through the 1700s and early 1800s. Whippings, frequently severe, were routine. Following are several accounts of the severe punishments administered by teachers.

John Dean Caton, who later became a Justice of the Supreme Court, decided to settle things with an unruly student who challenged his authority. He "cut several birch whips about five feet long" on the way to school. He then called the student forward, and "applied the birch about ten blows as hard as [I] could lay it on." Then he "struck him over the head and face." He sensed that the student still did not feel remorse for his behavior, so he "took a fresh whip and laid on perhaps fifteen lashes with [my] best effort. The cotton from [the student's] shirt sleeves actually flew across the school house in bits" (Finkelstein, 1989, p. 155).

Some teachers devised other forms of physical punishment for students who didn't learn their lessons, or didn't pay attention. Miss Mehitabel Holt administered some of the following punishments: Children who whispered during class were locked in a "windowless closet." Those who fidgeted in their seats were "tied to her chair-post for an hour." Miss Holt frequently twisted ears and snapped her "thimbled finger" on the head of children for slight infractions. (Burton, 1852, p. 25)

Reflection

Why was *North Haven v. Bell* an important decision? How has this ruling affected the lives of women teachers?

Similarly, Title IX guarantees that pregnant students as well as teachers cannot be denied access to the classroom. As we have seen, pregnant students were routinely dismissed from schools prior to Title IX legislation in 1972. But many school districts also required that pregnant teachers take maternity leave. In 1974, the Supreme Court ruled in *Cleveland Board of Education v. LaFleur* that mandatory maternity leaves were a violation of the rights of teachers under Title IX.

Other areas of gender equity have dealt with questions of a fair salary. As we have seen, women consistently are paid less than men even when we take into account their education, ability, backgrounds, and time on the job! In the late 1970s, a female coach by the name of Mary Burkey sued her school system, arguing that she was paid one half that of her male counterparts. The Supreme Court ruled in *Burkey v. Marshall County Board of Education* (1981) that this pay policy violated the Civil Rights Act of 1964 and therefore was unconstitutional. While the gap in wages between women and men continues in the private sector, it is much smaller within the teaching profession (www.hklaw.com).

Due Process

In the area of due process (procedural and substantive), both students and teachers have benefited from rulings of the court. Since the *Goss v. Lopez* (1975) decision, students have had the right of due process. Similarly, teachers have these basic constitutional rights as well. In the area of procedural due process, for example, teachers may not be refused a teaching certificate or license if qualified. While the courts have argued generally that licensure is a not simply a right bestowed on individuals who are prepared to teach, a license cannot be revoked without due process. Similarly, teachers have a right to tell their side of the story in all matters of employment at an appropriate hearing. We cannot simply be "fired on the spot."

Finally, in the area of substantive due process both students and teachers enjoy limited free speech in and out of school. The courts allow a great deal of free expression for students, though their rights are limited in the context of school-sponsored events such as student newspapers, school assemblies, or plays. Teachers also have achieved a measure of free speech.

Title IX: Teachers are Protected Against Sexual Discrimination

The Supreme Court delivered another important decision regarding teachers' rights in the *North Haven Board of Education v. Bell* (1982) case. Two cases involving sexual discrimination were combined: Elaine Dove, a tenured teacher in North Haven who took a year maternity leave and then was not retired; and Linda Potz, a guidance counselor in the Trumbull school district who accused the district of discrimination because of job assignments, working conditions, and the failure to renew her contract. The Supreme Court ruled that Title IX of the Education Amendments applied to teachers as well as students. Furthermore, the Department of Education can cut off funds to school districts that discriminate against female employees. (*Education Week*, 1982)

Gender Differences in Salaries

The Equal Pay Act (1982) was enacted as an amendment to the Fair Labor Standards Act of 1938, to provide a remedy for sex discrimination in wages. The Equal Pay Act prohibits employers from determining wages based on gender and requires employees to receive equal pay for equal work. In determining what constitutes equal work, courts have required that the plaintiff prove that the jobs are "substantially equal." When establishing that the jobs are "substantially equal," the plaintiff's burden is limited to comparing the two jobs and not the two individuals that hold those jobs. (Strick, 2001)

Source: Retrieved July 26, 2007, from http://vls.law.vill.edu/publications/ womenslawforum/Comments/Spring%202001/stanleyvusc.htm

In 1964, Marvin Pickering, a teacher in Will County, Illinois, wrote a letter to the editor of his local newspaper criticizing his school board's allocation of money. Too much money, he argued, was going to athletics and not enough to academics. The letter angered members of the school board. They called him before their body and claimed that his letter had caused a disruption in the community and was "detrimental to the efficient operation and administration of the schools of the district." The board then fired Pickering.

Journaling Activity
Marvin Pickering was very brave to express his freedom of speech. Do you think teachers have the right to criticize the school board or administration? Are there issues you feel strongly about to express your feelings publicly? Would you risk your job? Record your responses in your journal.

Pickering appealed this decision through the courts, and the Supreme Court eventually reviewed his case in 1968. In their landmark decision, *Pickering v. Board of Education*, the court ruled that the school board had violated Pickering's rights under the 1st and 14th Amendments to the Constitution. In other words, unless you have made irresponsible, reckless, or false statements, a school board cannot fire you because it does not like what you have written or said about them (http://www.freedomforum.org/templates/document.asp).

Pickering Case Ruling

Writing for the majority on *Pickering v. Board of Education*, the renowned Supreme Court Justice William O. Douglas noted: "Absent proof of false statements knowingly or recklessly made by him (Pickering), a teacher's exercise of his right to speak on issues of public importance may not furnish the basis for his dismissal from public employment."

Marvin Pickering—Update

Marvin Pickering was reinstated in September 1969 and worked as a teacher at Lockport Township High School until his retirement in 1997. His 1st Amendment battle was a milestone for teachers and all workers.

Marvin Pickering's Letter that Cost Him His Teaching Job

Following are some excerpts from Marvin Pickering's letter to the editor which was published in *The Lockport Herald* regarding the school board's "mishandling" of funds.

- He charged that "the two new high schools have deviated [far] from the original promises by the Board of Education."
- "That's the kind of totalitarianism teachers live in at the high school, and your children go to school in."
- "To sod football fields on borrowed money and then not be able to pay teachers' salaries is getting the cart before the horse."
- "They have been spending [$200,000 a year] on varsity sports while neglecting the wants of teachers."
- "The Board of Education is trying to push tax-supported athletics down our throats. . ."

Marvin Pickering's closing statement was "I must sign this letter as a citizen, tax-payer and voter, not as a teacher, since that freedom has been taken from the teachers by the administration."

Source: Freedom Forum, retrieved July 27, 2007, from http://www.freedomforum.org/templates/document.asp

LEGAL ISSUES SPECIFIC TO TEACHERS

In addition to basic constitutional rights enjoyed by both students and teachers, there are a number of legal matters that are the concern of teachers alone. As we have seen, these include collective bargaining, academic freedom, religion in the school, personal lifestyle, and legal liability.

Collective Bargaining

The areas of collective bargaining and labor rights have a long history among teachers. As we have seen, teachers traditionally have had few employment rights and could be fired because of a perceived infraction of a rule or for virtually any other reason, such as riding in a carriage with a man or not using corporal punishment on their students. Over the years, teachers have attempted to organize to protect their labor rights, but since we are "public servants" and not part of the private sector of the economy, our rights in this area are limited.

Reflection
What do you think about this important debate?

In hundreds of legal actions over the last century, the courts have ruled on teachers' labor rights. We do have the right to join organizations such as the NEA and the AFT and we can use "collective bargaining" to achieve a fair wage. On the other hand, our right to a labor stoppage or strike is legal only in 11 states. In fact, about half of the states in the country prohibit teacher strikes by law.

Teachers' Right to Strike: The Debate

The right of teachers to strike is a highly debated issue, both in the courts and with the general public. Below is a summary of some of the arguments presented in a pro and con format.

Pro
- Teachers have the right, under the 14th Amendment, to engage in union activities.
- Teachers have the right to collective bargaining.
- If teachers do not have the right to strike, unions cannot effectively represent their members.
- Unions can negotiate issues such as: allocation of money, academic freedom, class size, planning time, released time for lunch, insurance benefits, and teaching supplies.
- Unions can enforce the hiring qualified, licensed teachers.
- Unions can seek special support services for students (i.e., school counselors, special education teachers, speech therapists, school social workers, etc.).

Pro comments are from Oscar Weil, who taught in high school and the community college for 9 years. He is currently legislative director for the Illinois Federation of Teachers (Bergren & Weil, 1977).

Con
- The right to strike for teachers cannot be allowed because it would then be extended to all public employees.
- Collective bargaining applies to the private sector, not to the public sector.
- Public employee collective bargaining is inconsistent with the concept of tenure for teachers.
- "Collective bargaining tends to be destructive of governmental sovereignty." The government must be sovereign.
- The citizen is not involved in decisions that effect his taxes.
- Collective bargaining creates stress between employer–employee relationships.

Con comments are from Orville Bergren, who is President of the Illinois Manufacturer's Association (Bergren & Weil, 1977).

In its landmark decision on this issue, *Hortonville Joint School District v. Hortonville Education Association* (1976), the Supreme Court ruled that striking teachers in Wisconsin could be fired by their school board. The court noted that their dismissal was not a violation of due process under the 14th Amendment because in Wisconsin it was illegal for teachers to strike. (http://www.departments.bucknell.edu)

Reflection
Teacher strikes are considered a last resort. What other alternatives do teachers have when the board of education refuses to reach an agreement through collective bargaining?

States that Permit Teachers "the Right to Strike"

Many states prohibit public employees from striking. Although both the NEA and the AFT consider striking a last resort, they argue that it may be justifiable in some situations.

Below are some of the states that permit strikes as part of their statutes regarding collective bargaining:

- Alaska
- California
- Colorado
- Hawaii
- Illinois
- Louisiana
- Minnesota
- Montana
- North Dakota
- Oregon
- Pennsylvania

Although Minnesota allows teacher strikes, it is interesting to note that from 1983–2002 there were only 15 school districts that resorted to strikes. (Department of Public Education, Minnesota, n.d.).

Source: Retrieved July 27, 2007, from http://www.educationminnesota.org

---

Reflection

Do you see any patterns among those states that permit teacher strikes? Do you see any reasons why these states permit strikes?

Yet, as in so many other areas of the law, what is illegal and what is prosecuted are two different things. Yes, strikes are illegal in a number of states and if you go out on strike you may be fired, but communities often "look the other way" and will not prosecute striking teachers. On the other hand, while we clearly have the legal right to join teachers' unions such as the AFT, some school boards will use every extralegal ploy and excuse not to renew your contract if you join. Then it's up to you to sue them for damages to get your job back. And that can be a very difficult process. As a rule of thumb, be aware of the legal and extralegal labor restrictions that may exist in the community in which you teach.

Journaling Activity

As we have read, teacher strikes are illegal in some states. Check the status of your state. Do teachers have the right to strike? Conduct a search on the Internet. It is important to know your rights as a teacher.

**Landmark Supreme Court Decision: *Hortonville School
District v. Hortonville Education Association* (1976)**

This ruling stated that teachers could be fired for striking, if strikes by public employees are in violation of state law. Therefore, their rights under the Fourteenth Amendment to due process were not violated. The teachers had worked all the previous year without a contractual agreement, this means that among other things, the teachers were receiving no salary increase, additional benefits, or improved working conditions. During the following school year, the board of education still refused to reach a collective bargaining agreement.

Source: Bucknell University, etrived July, 2. 2007, from
http://www.departments.bucknell.edu

ACADEMIC FREEDOM

In addition to our basic employment rights, one of the most important issues facing us as teachers is academic freedom. What can we teach? Can we be fired for teaching about issues that are considered controversial by parents, school officials, or school boards? Can we present a lesson on birth control, HIV/AIDS, or whether a particular war is appropriate or moral? While the Supreme Court has not made a definitive ruling on these issues, there have been numerous state and federal court decisions that have dealt with a teachers' academic freedom.

Generally speaking, these decisions have demonstrated that the classroom is a "marketplace of ideas" and that as long we do not "propagandize" or attempt to indoctrinate our students, we have significant academic freedom. For example, in *Cary v. Board of Education* (1977), the Federal Appellate Court argued that "[teachers] cannot be made to simply read from a script prepared or approved by the [school] board" (http://www.ahcuah.com/lawsuit/federal/hart2.htm).

If the state legislature or school board wishes to limit what we can teach in the classroom, specific guidelines must be provided. For example, in North Carolina (and many other states), state law forbids teachers to discuss birth control, abortion, or prevention of HIV and STDs except with reference to abstinence until marriage. In this case, a discussion of the use of condoms or birth control pills is not allowed (http://www.dpi.state.nc.us).

Wisdom of Teachers

Jan Swanson, a school guidance counselor in a rural K–8 elementary school, was assigned the responsibility of teaching sex education to seventh- and eighth-grade girls. She is restricted by the North Carolina Department of Public Instruction from teaching about birth control, abortion, and the prevention of HIV and sexually transmitted diseases. The emphasis of the state curriculum is "abstinence until marriage." She reported feeling very frustrated when her students ask about condoms or birth control pills, but was prevented by state law from talking about such issues. (NBPTS, 2002)

New York Regents' Prayer

"Almighty God, We acknowledge our dependence on Thee, and we beg Thy blessings upon us, our parents, our teachers and our Country."

Source: OYEZ, retrieved July 22, 2007, from http://www.oyez.org/
cases/1960-1969/1961/1961_468

Reflection

How would you feel if you were in this situation? Can you think of any possible solutions?

In general then, you should be familiar with state and district regulations regarding limitations of academic freedom. Nevertheless, you do have a great deal of freedom regarding what you can teach in the classroom. As long as the material is not "obscene," is relevant to the subject you are responsible to teach, does not disrupt the class, and is not specifically prohibited by state law or school policy, you have the right to teach it in your classroom.

SEPARATION OF CHURCH AND STATE

But what about religion? Can you discuss religious concepts in your classroom? Can you lead a prayer or moment of silence before, during, or after class? Can you promote a particular religion or denigrate another? These and other questions have been the center of a heated debate for many years.

The key Supreme Court case that dealt with the issue of required prayer in public schools was *Engle v. Vitale* (1962). During the 1950s, the Regents of the State of New York developed a "nondenominational prayer" for the schools of the state. Although the prayer was voluntary, many New Yorkers objected to it being used in the public schools.

Parents of ten Long Island, New York, students sued the New York State Board of Regents because they felt that despite the nondenominational nature of this public school prayer it still was a violation of their 1st Amendment rights. The case went to the Supreme Court where its use was declared unconstitutional.

Engle v. Vitale (1962) Decision

Justice Black wrote for the majority:

> By using its public school system to encourage recitation of the Regents' prayer, the state of New York has adopted a practice wholly inconsistent with the establishment clause (of the 1st Amendment). There can be no doubt that New York's program of daily classroom invocation of God's blessings as prescribed in the Regents' prayer is a religious activity.

Source: OYEZ, Retrieved July 22, 2007, from http://www.oyez.org/
cases/1960-1969/1961/1961_468/

CONTROVERSIAL ISSUES: EVOLUTION, MOMENTS OF SILENCE, EXEMPTIONS AND USE OF FACILITIES

While the Supreme Court has ruled on the general issue of separation of church and state as well as prayer in the classroom, there are other important aspects of religion and schools that also have been the subject of controversy. These include the prohibition of teaching evolution, the inclusion of "intelligent design" in the curriculum, allowing moments of silence in the classroom, exempting students from certain secular teachings, and the use of school facilities for religious organizations.

Journaling Activity

Find out what the position of your state is on the evolution/intelligent design debate. Look at state-approved science textbooks and examine the state science curriculum. The state-approved curriculum can be found in bound notebooks in your college or university library. You may also be able to access the state science curriculum via the Internet. Record your findings in your journal.

With regard to the prohibition of teaching evolution in the science curriculum, the court ruled in *Epperson v. State of Arkansas* (1968) that this practice was a violation of the 1st Amendment to the Constitution. Similarly in *Edwards v. Agulard* (1987) the court ruled that states cannot require that schools teach "creationism" as part of the public school curriculum. More recently, the court has ruled that incorporating "intelligent design" into the curriculum is a thinly veiled attempt to teach a form of creationism and therefore is unconstitutional.

CREATIONISM AND INTELLIGENT DESIGN CONTROVERSIES

Creationism

The controversy surrounding the inclusion of creationism in the curriculum is far from over. Some proponents have developed new ways to promote creationism. For example,

Links to the Past: Scopes "Monkey Trial"

In the summer of 1925, 24-year-old John Scopes was on trial for illegally teaching evolution in his high school biology class. Ironically, he was teaching chapters on evolution from the state approved textbook, *Hunter's Civic Biology*. However, the state of Tennessee had recently passed a law banning the teaching of evolution. The trial received national attention and two prominent attorneys participated. William Jennings Bryan, an old guard traditionalist politician, represented the prosecution and Clarence Darrow, a champion of liberal causes, defended young Scopes. After many eloquent, lengthy speeches on both sides, the jury found Scopes guilty and the judge fined him $100. The case was appealed to the Tennessee Supreme Court who reversed the decision on a technicality—contending that the fine should have been set by the jury, rather than by the judge.

Source: Retrieved February 26, 2008 from http://xroads.virginia.edu/~ug97/inherit/1925home.html

in 1999, the Oklahoma State Textbook Committee mandated that publishers of science textbooks include a disclaimer in biology books. The disclaimer states that evolution is "a controversial theory which some scientists present as a scientific explanation for the origin of living things, such as plants and humans." The statement also concludes that evolution is "the unproven belief that random, undirected forces produced a world of living things." Utilizing another tactic, in 1999, the Kansas Board of Education removed evolution from the high schools biology curriculum.

Intelligent Design, Silent Prayer and Exemption

Recently, the school science curriculum has been challenged to include "intelligent design" in addition to evolution. A number of school districts have struggled with the issue of "intelligent design" and whether it has a valid place in the science curriculum. Intelligent design is related to the notion of creationism, that is, the biblical interpretation of the creation of the world and a rejection of evolution. "Intelligent design" is based on the creation of the world by God. Schools that have included "ID" in the science curriculum have created turmoil in the community. The courts have consistently upheld the idea that the public schools should be religiously neutral. The Supreme Court ruled in 1987 that teaching creationism in the public schools is unconstitutional.

The Court also has ruled in *Wallace v. Jaffree* (1985) that a "silent prayer" or a moment of silence led by teachers was unconstitutional. Similarly, the Court ruled in *Lee v. Weisman* (1992) that prayers as an official part of school graduation ceremonies were a violation of the 1st Amendment.

Additionally, students cannot be exempted from certain teaching in the public school based on their religious beliefs. In *Mozert v. Hawkins County Public Schools* (1987), the court ruled that a group of fundamentalist children were not unduly burdened by receiving instruction in a basal reader series used by the school system.

LANDMARK SUPREME COURT DECISION: *MOZERT V. HAWKING COUNTY BOARD OF EDUCATION* (1987)

In 1987, the Supreme Court made another important decision in this case regarding the use of the basal reader in public schools. A group of seven families complained about some of the themes in the Holt Basal Reader that their children were reading in the Hawkins County elementary and middle schools in Tennessee. The text is used to teach "critical reading" which involves higher order thinking skills, evaluation, and making judgments about the reading material. The mother of four children, Vicki Frost, a fundamentalist, claimed that some of the themes violated her religious beliefs, such as what she perceived as mental telepathy, secular humanism, "futuristic supernaturalism," pacifism, magic, and secular views of death. In her testimony, Mrs. Frost cited passages that fell into each category. In a selection about Leonardo da Vinci, he was described as having a creative mind that "came closest to the divine touch." She felt that another selection related to the occult, as it described the imagination as a way of seeing things not discernible through our eyes. Another selection, "A Visit to Mars," that involved transfer and telepathy she charged was presented as "scientific concept." Another parent, Bob Mozert, had some of the same objections but he also objected to biographical material about women for accomplishments outside the home.

The Supreme Court ruled that the readers did not violate their religious beliefs and that the public schools teach fundamental values "essential to a democratic society."

These values "include tolerance of divergent political and religious views" while taking into account "consideration of the sensibilities of others." One remedy, the plaintiffs had proposed, was to "opt-out" of the basal reader and the related assignments. The court determined that this would become disruptive to the public schools and become a burden on classroom teachers to determine what materials and information might be objectionable to parents. Furthermore, other parents might object to other themes for other reasons. This would create a dilemma for the public schools (http://www.soc.umn. edu/~samaha/cases/mozert_v_hawkins_schools.html).

Reflection

What do you think about the objections of these families to stories dealing with magic or the imagination? What do you think about basal readers including biographies about notable women and their accomplishments "outside the home?" Why do basal readers include selections from different genres (i.e. fantasy, poetry, biography, etc.)?

Finally, the court has ruled that student religious clubs and organizations do have the right to use school facilities. In its *Board of Education of the Westside Community Schools v. Mergens* (1990), the court ruled that if one extracurricular student group has the right to use school facilities, then the school cannot restrict the use of those facilities to religious clubs. Similarly in *Lamb's Chapel v. Center Moriches Union Free School District* (1993), the court ruled that churches may use public school property after school and that doing so is not a violation of the 1st Amendment.

PERSONAL LIFE AND LIFESTYLE

As teachers we clearly enjoy both academic freedom and freedom of speech. We also have some freedom regarding our personal life and lifestyle. These freedoms, however, vary according to the state and district where we teach and whether our behavior negatively affects our relationship with our students and colleagues.

For example, the Supreme Court ruled in *Thompson v. Southwest School District* (1980) that a teacher could not be fired because she was living with her boyfriend. They ruled, moreover, that since her action was not disruptive and did not interfere with her effectiveness as a teacher, the school board had violated her rights by firing her.

Journal Activity

Research the "personal lifestyle" rules for your local school system. Record your findings in your journal.

Teachers Rights: Living with your Significant Other

There have been a number of cases involving teachers living with a boy friend or girl friend. One of the most notable was the case of *Thompson v. Southwest School District* (1980). First year teacher, Ms. Thompson, was fired when the board of education became aware of the fact that she was living with her boy friend. She sued, won her case, and was able to keep her job. The court ruled that her living arrangements had not interfered with her teaching responsibilities.

Public School Teachers' Rights Regarding Sexual Orientation

Generally, under the 1st and 14th Amendments, homosexual public school teachers have the right to behave in the same way as heterosexuals, for example, displaying photos of their partner, talking about their weekend, etc. However, like heterosexuals, they do not have the discretion to discuss sex or sexual acts. Being open about one's sexuality depends on whether it is inside or outside the classroom and also varies according to the tolerance of the community and school district.

- Outside the school, teachers have the greatest freedom of speech. In school, the administration can restrict the speech of teachers, if it is perceived to be a disruption to school discipline.
- Gay teachers should be able to be open about their sexual orientation. Intolerance should not be a reason for different treatment by the school administration.
- California State Constitution provides greater freedom of speech for gay and lesbians than the U.S. Constitution. Additionally, the California Supreme Court declared that "public employers could not discriminate against gay employees and that being 'out of the closet' was a protected political activity."
- In California, gay teachers are further protected by the state Labor Code that "prohibits employers from discriminating against an employee or treating them differently because of their sexual orientation."

Source: Retrieved February 26, 2008, from http://www.lambdalegal.org

---

But what if her partner was of the same sex? In this case, a number of states and cities throughout the country have ruled against this sort of discrimination in the workplace, including the classroom. And in communities that do not have specific protective legislation in place, the courts have protected gays and lesbians from being fired because of their lifestyles (Lambda Legal, http://www.lambdalegal.org).

Reflection
California has led the way in establishing rights for gay people. Using the Internet or a book on school law for your state, find out if there are specific legal protections for gay teachers.

Other issues regarding one's lifestyle, such as not attending church are not reasons for dismissal, though dress codes continue to be part of the life of teachers. As with other legal matters, carefully check the specific policies of your school and school district.

Journaling Activity
Are dress code rules necessary? Are there reasons some things are not allowed? Check your local school system and see if they have a dress code. Is the dress code for both students and teachers? Record the dress code in your journal.

Finally, can teachers be fired for breaking the law? It all depends. Receiving a traffic citation should not be a problem but in some states, getting a DWI ticket (driving while intoxicated), or being arrested for smoking marijuana can be used as grounds for dismissal. In other communities it may not. And as you probably would expect, most school districts will not tolerate other crimes such as murder, child molestation, armed robbery,

---

Links to the Past: Teachers' and Students' Rights—Dress Codes

Today, many schools have established dress codes that apply for both students and teachers. Following are some examples from the past and present:
Rules for Female Teachers—Nebraska, 1915:

- You must not wear bright colors.
- You may not under any circumstances dye your hair.
- You must wear at least two petticoats.
- Your dresses may not be shorter than 2 inches above your ankles. (*Nebraska Farmer*, 1999)

Dress Code for Female Students and Teachers—Fayetteville, NC, 2007

- No midriff can be exposed
- Blouses or sweaters must either be tucked-into slacks or skirts, or if worn outside, must cover the waist band of the slacks or skirts by 2–3 inches
- Skirt or dress length can be no shorter than 3 inches above the top of the knee
- No sandals, flip flops, or open-toed shoes
- No clogs or open back shoes
- No tanks, halters, or low-cut tops
- No sleeveless tops or dresses

Dress Code for Male Students and Teachers—Fayetteville, NC, 2007

- No shirts without collars
- No shirts without sleeves
- No sweat shirts or sweat pants.
- Shirts must be tucked-in pants
- No underwear can show
- Pants or slacks must be worn with a belt
- No caps or headwear
- No flip flops or sandals

Source: Retrieved February 26, 2008. from http://www.choice.ccs.k12.nc.us/2008-2009ChoiceGuidePRN.pdf

---

burglary, or having sex with a minor. Conviction of these crimes will not only land you in the jail but will end your career as a teacher. Avoid them!

LEGAL LIABILITY

Most of the legal issues we have discussed thus far have dealt with the advancement of rights of both teachers and students. Sometimes, however, the rights of teachers and students collide. When this happens, there is the possibility of legal liability.

Our society is litigious. In the last generation, Americans have increasingly turned to the courts to seek relief from injustice. And while this has served us well as a nation, sometimes teachers find themselves at the center of the litigation. While the vast majority of teachers will never be caught up in a lawsuit with students, a few of us may. For this reason it is important to understand our legal responsibilities and rights in this area.

Generally speaking, the area of teacher negligence or legal liability involves four distinct areas of the law:

- Misfeasance
- Nonfeasance
- Malfeasance
- Educational Malpractice

Misfeasance is a failure to act in an appropriate manner with a student. An example of misfeasance would be using too much force when breaking up a fight. **Nonfeasance**, on the other hand, is a failure to perform your assigned duty. As an example, you leave your assigned post—for example on recess duty—for a personal reason and then a student is hurt. **Malfeasance** on the other hand is simply breaking the law like smoking marijuana on school grounds or slapping your principal. (Must not do that!) Finally, educational **malpractice** deals with the issue of whether you have provided a student with an adequate education.

The courts have dealt with many of these sorts of cases and generally have ruled that there are two standards to be considered when determining liability in the areas of misfeasance and nonfeasance. The first is whether another teacher with similar training would have acted in the way you did. In the instance of misfeasance, would another teacher have hurt a student when breaking up a similar fight? With nonfeasance, would another teacher have left their post in a similar situation? The second standard deals with whether you could have foreseen an injury. Should you have known you would have hurt the child when breaking up that fight? Was there reason to believe that the student would have been hurt when you briefly left your post during recess break?

As a rule of thumb, we should not leave our posts under any circumstances. If you are ill or have a real emergency, contact your principal and arrange to have someone else to take your position at recess, cafeteria duty, or in your classroom. Don't just slip out hoping that everything will be all right. When you are breaking up a fight or disciplining a

---

Types of Negligence

The following is a description of the types of negligence that could result in legal liability.

1. **Malfeasance**—a teacher does something illegal and results in injury to the student (spanking).
2. **Misfeasance**—the teacher does not perform his/her duties according to an established standard of conduct (safety code violations.
3. **Nonfeasance**—failing to perform a required act (the teacher fails to notify the office of a serious injury).
4. **Contributory and Comparative Negligence**—failure of an injured party to exercise due to care for his own good and welfare.
5. **Act of God**—a child is injured by a lightening bolt. (Fischer et al., 1999)

Teacher Duties and Negligence

The teacher has three basic concerns related to contributory and comparative negligence:

Instruction
- The teacher must provide instructions and procedures to students beforehand.
- The instruction must be documented.
- Students' skills regarding safety should be assessed.

Supervision
- The teacher must supervise students at all times.
- Students who are not conducting themselves in a safe manner should not be allowed to participate.

Maintenance
- All equipment and supplies must be well maintained.
- Inspect and test equipment for safety and repairs made.
- Unsafe equipment that cannot be repaired should be reported to the school administration and removed from student use.

Although these points are especially designed for science and physical education classes, they apply to all teachers. (Health, Mental Health, and Safety Guidelines for Schools)

Source: Retrieved February 26, 2008, from http://www.choice.ccs.k12.nc.us/2008-2009ChoiceGuidePRN.pdf

---

student, do not try to overpower him or her. You may become angry and hurt the child, or you may get hurt yourself. Rather, use your verbal skills and your voice to try to stop a fight or discipline a child. Get the help of another teacher and your principal. After all, that is the principal's job, not yours. Your role in the school is to teach! In chapter 9, we will discuss a number of tried and true methods of disciplining students.

In the area of malfeasance, the law is clearer. Breaking the law or school rules will most likely be grounds for malfeasance. As a teacher you must be a role model for your students and by breaking the law or school rules, you are not providing that model. We all get angry. We all get frustrated. As professionals, however, we must learn to control our anger, our emotions, and our frustrations with students, colleagues, and administrators. If you have an anger management problem, seek professional help. If you are simply "stressed out," try exercise, meditation, relaxation, religion, or a combination of all of these.

Finally, we come to the controversial area of educational malpractice. You and your fellow teachers have struggled mightily with a student all semester, trying to help him learn. He refused to listen, he would not do the work, he never completed his assignments or homework, and he talked incessantly during lessons. You assessed his progress at the end of the semester and despite his poor record, decide to award him a "D" for the class. Other teachers also passed him and he barely graduated from high school. The following year, however, you and your colleagues discover that he and his parents have sued the school district for educational malpractice!

While this example is very unusual, it has happened. Fortunately, the courts have ruled in our favor. Generally speaking, they note that there are many factors that affect learning and that to hold the school solely responsible for a student's failure is inappropriate (Fischer et al., 1973; Menacker & Pascarella, 1983).

SCHOOL LAW: ONE FINAL THOUGHT

The constitutional rights of students and teachers have expanded greatly in the last generation. And yet, despite these dramatic changes, in areas such as student drug testing, corporal punishment, and teachers' labor rights, there has been less progress. One thing we should learn from this is that the school law is not a set of rules that is "carved in stone tablets." Rather, it is an ongoing process that involves students, teachers, school officials, the legislature and the courts.

Over the years, laws have been passed and policies adopted that have negatively affected students and teachers. These include restricting enrollment in school based on race or gender, limiting an individual's right to due process or freedom of speech, or using invasive search and seizure in the name of security. Most of us simply acquiesce to the new rules and regulations while a handful have disputed their constitutionality. Students like Linda Brown, Peggy and Virginia Strickland, Dwight Lopez, John and Mary Beth Tinker, Matthew Fraser, and teachers like Marvin Pickering, Mary Burkey, and hundreds of others could simply have quietly obeyed the imposition of new school rules but rather they had the courage to challenge them. As a result of their actions, they have forever changed the relationship between students, teachers, and school officials.

Some school officials resent many of the landmark rulings we have discussed here. They see these changes as simply more paperwork or more "hoops to jump through," but the actions of these elementary, middle school, and high school students and teachers have strengthened our schools and our democracy.

Change is always difficult. It requires us to rethink our past actions and forces us to confront our future. As American teachers we should welcome this opportunity.

SUMMARY

For all our celebration of local democracy, we sometimes forget that local majorities often have a darker side. Over the years, local communities have imposed their religious beliefs and prejudices on the public schools; they have segregated schools on the basis of gender, ethnicity, and race, and sometimes they have acted irresponsibly in hiring and firing of teachers and school employees. For these reasons the central theme in the legal history of public education in America has been the struggle to protect the rights of students and teachers from the dark side of local majorities.

Student Rights

There are two basic areas of student rights and responsibilities we must consider. The first is their basic right to an education while the second has to do with their individual rights.

One of the fundamental rights enjoyed by Americans is the right to a primary and secondary education. Unlike many other countries throughout the world, we have made a strong commitment to our children by guaranteeing them a basic education.

While the right to education for women and minorities has been a monumental social, political, and legal struggle that has taken over two centuries, students individual rights such as access to personal school records, due process, protection from unlawful search and seizure, freedom of the press, and protection of sexual harassment have only recently become an issue. In fact, in the last generation, society has gradually begun to see students as individuals with fundamental constitutional rights, rather than children under the protection of educators (*in loco parentis*). As a result we have now begun to address these issues.

Rights of Teachers

In addition to basic constitutional rights enjoyed by both students and teachers, there are a number of legal matters that are the concern of teachers alone. These include the right to collective bargaining, academic freedom, religion in the school, personal lifestyle, and legal liability.

Negligence and Legal Liability

The area of teacher negligence or legal liability involves four distinct areas of the law: misfeasance, nonfeasance, malfeasance, and educational malpractice. Misfeasance is a failure to act in an appropriate manner with a student. Nonfeasance is a failure to perform your assigned duty. Malfeasance is simply breaking the law, while educational malpractice means that you have not provided a student with an adequate education. In each of these cases common sense should inform you of your rights and responsibilities as a teacher. With regard to other school policies, be familiar with the rules and stick with them.

DISCUSSION QUESTIONS

1. Discuss some of the positive and negative consequences of local control of public schools. Have local majorities always acted responsibly with regards to the inclusion of students as well as the hiring and firing of teachers and school employees?
2. What are the two basic areas of student rights? Are these rights guaranteed by law?
3. What is Title IX? Discuss its importance. What is P.L. 94-142? Discuss its impact.
4. What is the difference between *de facto and de jure* segregation? What is the difference between racial quotas and affirmative action? Are these policies legal? Discuss.
5. Discuss the concept of *in loco parentis*. In this context, discuss the impact of *Goss v. Lopez* (1975).
6. Discuss the four areas of teacher liability: misfeasance, nonfeasance, malfeasance, and educational malpractice. Give an example of each.

Chapter 12

The Noble Profession

THE PROFESSIONALIZATION OF TEACHING

When you first thought of becoming a teacher you may have looked at the requirements for admission to the teacher education program and found that you needed a number of "professional education" courses such as Educational Psychology, Introduction to Education (Foundations) and Field Experiences. Also, you may have seen references to "the teaching profession" in your teacher education brochure or other materials from your school. But what is a professional and is teaching as a profession?

Typical Requirements for Admission into a Teacher Education Program

The following is an example of admission requirements for Teacher Education. Check the requirements for your college, school, or department of education.

- Submit an application for admission
- Cumulative grade point average of 2.5
- Completion of a minimum of 60 semester hours that include:
  - English 101 and 102
  - History 101 and 102
  - Math 105
  - Science (3 hrs.)
  - Fine Arts (3 hrs.)
  - Speech (3 hrs.)
- Passing scores on Praxis I (PPST or CBT): Reading, Writing, and Math
- Grade of C (2.0) or higher in each course in the major
- Grade of C (2.0) or higher in the professional sequence:
  - Field Experience I and II
  - Introduction to Education
  - Educational Psychology
  - Introduction to Special Education
- Three recommendations from faculty members
- Preadmission interview
- Approval by the Teacher Education Committee (Methodist University, 2006–2007)

WHAT IS A PROFESSIONAL?

Simply stated, a professional is an individual engaged in an occupation that serves society and requires specialized knowledge gained through intensive preparation. In addition, there are four generally accepted features of all professions:

- A specialized body of knowledge
- A rigorous and extended course of study that leads to licensure
- Training that allows individuals to make complex decisions often without the consultation of others
- A set of ethical standards of conduct

A Body of Specialized Knowledge

Given these general characteristics of all professions, let's see how teachers measure up. As to acquiring a body of specialized knowledge, teachers do very well. First of all, we must gain knowledge of our content area whether it is elementary education or a specialty area such as history, math, or literature. Teachers must master general pedagogical knowledge such as techniques to maintain discipline in the classroom or methods of leading a class discussion. We must also develop content knowledge such as the ability to demonstrate difficult concepts to our students such as "sharing" in elementary education, the concept of discrimination in history, or the idea of the least common denominator in math. Finally, teachers must also develop knowledge of the nature of learning, such as understanding that students learn differently and the distinction between cognitive, affective, and physiological development. In short, as a new teacher you will have mastered a body of specialized knowledge in a number of areas by the time you enter the classroom to teach.

A Course of Study That Leads to Licensure

As a new teacher you also will benefit from a balanced curriculum typical of colleges, schools, and departments of education that leads directly to licensure. In addition to a number of general education courses, required for all degrees from universities and colleges, many states require the Praxis I exam as a prerequisite for formal admission to the education program. You will also take specialty courses in your content area and a series of professional courses before graduation. Most programs in education also require you to have a number of education field experiences sometimes called internships, and a semester of student teaching or clinical experience. Here you will gain actual experience teaching lessons, maintaining discipline, and tutoring students in a classroom for the good part of a semester. With this rigorous preparation you will not only receive your Bachelors of Science or Bachelors of Arts degree (B.S. or B.A.) but you will be ready to take the Praxis II exam to be licensed as a teacher in your state.

Journaling Activity

Compare the licensure requirements for your college, school or department of education's teacher education program and compare them with the one's outlined above. Discuss the importance of professional coursework.

Typical Licensure/Professional Courses for Teacher Education Program

The following is an example of licensure area or professional courses required for completion of the Teacher Education Program. Check the requirements for your college, school, or department of education.

- Field Experience III
- Human Growth and Development
- Reading and Writing in the Content Areas (Middle Grades, High School, and K–12 Specialty Areas)
- Elementary Education—Methods (K–6 only)
- Education in the Middle Grades (6–9 only)
- Instructional Technology
- Audio–Visual Education
- Professional Orientation
- Student Teaching

Special Requirements:
- Teaching Methods for Secondary and Special Subjects K–12
- Teaching Foreign Language in the Elementary School (for Foreign Language Majors or Minors)
- Methods of Teaching Learning Disabled (Special Education Majors)
- Adapted Physical Education (Physical Education Majors) (Methodist University, 2006–2007)

The Ability to Make Autonomous Decisions

As far as making autonomous decisions, you will soon become a master. Educational research has demonstrated that the typical elementary school teacher makes over 1,000 decisions in a typical 6-hour day! These decisions range from determining the disciplinary strategy for a group of unruly boys to selecting the proper instructional methods for a student with a learning disability to explaining an evaluation decision to a parent. As a new teacher you will make many autonomous decisions, most of which are of crucial importance to your students. But don't worry. Your coursework and field experiences will prepare you for these classroom decisions (Jackson, 1968).

A Set of Ethical Practices

Finally, the teaching profession embraces a clear set of ethical practices such as those outlined by the NEA (National Education Association) or the AFT (American Federation of Teachers). The NEA's code of ethics, principle 1, section 4, for instance, holds that educators "shall make a reasonable effort to protect the student from conditions harmful to learning or to health and safety." Principle 2, section 7, as another example, states that educators "shall not knowingly make a false or malicious statement about a colleague" (NEA, http://www,NEA.org). Take a moment to read these important documents that clearly outline the ethics of teaching today.

NEA Ethics

NEA: National Education Association

Great Public Schools for Every Child

Code of Ethics of the Education Profession

Principle I

Commitment to the Student

The educator strives to help each student realize his or her potential as a worthy and effective member of society. The educator therefore works to stimulate the spirit of inquiry, the acquisition of knowledge and understanding, and the thoughtful formulation of worthy goals.

In fulfillment of the obligation to the student, the educator—

1. Shall not unreasonably restrain the student from independent action in the pursuit of learning.
2. Shall not unreasonably deny the student's access to varying points of view.
3. Shall not deliberately suppress or distort subject matter relevant to the student's progress.
4. Shall make reasonable effort to protect the student from conditions harmful to learning or to health and safety.
5. Shall not intentionally expose the student to embarrassment or disparagement.
6. Shall not on the basis of race, color, creed, sex, national origin, marital status, political or religious beliefs, family, social or cultural background, or sexual orientation, unfairly—
    a. Exclude any student from participation in any program
    b. Deny benefits to any student
    c. Grant any advantage to any student
7. Shall not use professional relationships with students for private advantage.
8. Shall not disclose information about students obtained in the course of professional service unless disclosure serves a compelling professional purpose or is required by law.

Principle II

Commitment to the Profession

The education profession is vested by the public with a trust and responsibility requiring the highest ideals of professional service.

In the belief that the quality of the services of the education profession directly influences the nation and its citizens, the educator shall exert every effort to raise professional standards, to promote a climate that encourages the exercise of professional judgment, to achieve conditions that attract persons worthy of the trust to careers in education, and to assist in preventing the practice of the profession by unqualified persons.

In fulfillment of the obligation to the profession, the educator—

1. Shall not in an application for a professional position deliberately make a false statement or fail to disclose a material fact related to competency and qualifications.
2. Shall not misrepresent his/her professional qualifications.   *(continued)*

3. Shall not assist any entry into the profession of a person known to be unqualified in respect to character, education, or other relevant attribute.
4. Shall not knowingly make a false statement concerning the qualifications of a candidate for a professional position.
5. Shall not assist a noneducator in the unauthorized practice of teaching.
6. Shall not disclose information about colleagues obtained in the course of professional service unless disclosure serves a compelling professional purpose or is required by law.
7. Shall not knowingly make false or malicious statements about a colleague.
8. Shall not accept any gratuity, gift, or favor that might impair or appear to influence professional decisions or action.

Source: Adopted by the NEA 1975 Representative Assembly, retrieved May 4, 2007, from http://www.nea.org/aboutnea/code.html

THE STRUGGLE FOR RECOGNITION

As we have seen, teaching clearly is a profession given the criteria widely accepted by our society. We have a specialized body of knowledge; a course of study leading to licensure; training to make complex decisions, and a set of ethical standards. Then what is the problem? Why is there any question about the professional nature of teaching? Over the years, some critics of education have questioned whether teaching is actually a profession at all, often arguing that it is "just a job." While we may bristle at this notion, it is important for new teachers to understand these arguments and deal with them intelligently and persistently.

Previously, we found that there has been a great deal of criticism of education over the years. And, of course, some of that criticism has been directed unfairly toward teachers. Some critics of education have asserted, incorrectly, that teachers lack rigorous training—that anyone can teach—that teachers simply follow the dictates of their state, community, and department of public instruction and finally, that teachers lack accountability. Let's examine each of these arguments.

AFT Organization

Mission Statement

The mission of the American Federation of Teachers, AFL–CIO, is to improve the lives of our members and their families, to give voice to their legitimate professional, economic and social aspirations, to strengthen the institutions in which we work, to improve the quality of the services we provide, to bring together all members to assist and support one another and to promote democracy, human rights and freedom in our union, in our nation and throughout the world.

Source: From the Futures II report adopted at the AFT Convention, July 5, 2000. (AFT, 2000)retrieved July 18, 2007, from http://www.aft.org/about/mission.htm

---

Links to the Past: Getting Hired

Obtaining a teaching position in the 19th century frequently depended on who you knew, rather than your qualifications. For example:

> Pretty, young Mary Smith secured a teaching job over a local girl, Polly Patch, because Mary's uncle had recently become a member of the school board. Miss Smith, however, was a good teacher and won the hearts of her young scholars with her sweet and gentle manner. (Burton, 1852)

Reflection

What do you think about how Mary Smith got her first teaching job? How have things changed today?

The "Lack of Rigorous Training" Argument

While some of these points may have been valid in the distant past, today they are not. In addition, we should remember that other professions have experienced similar criticism. A little over a century ago, prior to the establishment of the American Medical Association, for example, virtually anyone could call themselves a doctor and "practice medicine." Typically, a young man interested in medicine would "study with a doctor" for several years, read the classic *Gray's Anatomy,* and then simply declare himself a physician. With the establishment of the AMA, however, this began to change. By the late 1800s, all physicians were required to study formally at an accredited medical school and then pass a licensure exam before they could go into practice.

There is a direct parallel to teaching during America's early history. During this period, teachers often were hired by local school trustees who cared little about formal education. Typically, they were more concerned about the "virtue" of the teacher, his or her ability to discipline unruly children, and perhaps most importantly, a willingness to work for little pay and live with a member of the community during the school year.

With the establishment of the NEA at the end of the 1800s, however, the standards of teaching became more rigorous and over the years, teachers were expected to attend normal schools or teacher institutes before entering the classroom. By the early 1900s, standards for teachers became even more rigorous and teachers were required to attend college and take specialized courses in education before they were allowed to teach.

As society became more complex and the body of our collective knowledge expanded, so did our expectations for teachers. By the 1950s and 1960s, teachers were required to obtain a bachelor's degree in education and pass a National Teachers Exam in order to receive state licensure. Today, prospective teachers must pass a series of rigorous exams such as the Praxis series—established by Educational Testing Service—and earn a bachelor's degree in education before they enter the classroom. Today's American teacher is well educated and rigorously tested in a variety of content and pedagogical areas.

Alternative Licensure Programs

Despite this rigorous training in preparation for licensure, however, state legislators often "ease" requirements for teaching when there is a teacher shortage. In recent years, for example, many school districts across the nation have encouraged alternative licensure programs such as "lateral entry." Here, individuals with bachelor's or advanced degrees in specialty areas, but with no formal training in education, are allowed to enter the classroom with provisional certification. The misplaced notion that one needs only knowledge of their subject area to be a teacher drives these and other alternative licensure programs. Certainly there is more to being a teacher than good intensions and a general knowledge of the subject. A good teacher needs pedagogical training and field experiences to be successful.

The "Lack of Autonomous Decisions" Argument

The second major argument against the idea that teaching is a profession concerns the alleged lack of autonomous decision making among teachers. As we have seen, teachers typically make hundreds of autonomous decisions each day concerning the discipline, instruction, and safety of their students. And yet, over the years, teachers have also been required to conform to the changing dictates and requirements of the local, state, and even national governments.

Once again, an understanding of the historical development of the teaching profession will provide us with some insights into the position we find ourselves today. During the late 1700s and early 1800s, schools were funded and controlled by the local community. Teachers had some autonomy in their small one room school houses, though they were required to teach and discipline children in a way that reflected the established values of that community.

As our society grew more complex during the mid 1800s and as larger schools replaced the "little red school houses" of the early republic, a more standardized curriculum and a more systematic organization of the schools at the municipal or state level became a priority for educational reformers. By the end of the 1800s, the bureaucratic model of organization, borrowed from successful corporations at the time, became the standard of efficient school organization.

But while teachers (mostly female) now had a more standardized curriculum and often a better physical facility in which to teach, their status changed considerably. For example, the new model of school organization often placed the superintendent of schools at the top of the school's administration as a kind of corporate "chief executive officer" (CEO) with principals occupying positions similar to that of corporate middle managers. Teachers were relegated to the ranks of workers under the direction and supervision of an increasingly male administration. (See chapter 10 for an example of the bureaucratic hierarchal model of school organization.)

While most experienced teachers today work independently, the corporate/bureaucratic model of the late 1800s persists. Many quality administrators have recognized this situation and have actively worked to provide an environment that provides autonomy for teachers. And yet, as American teachers we must recognize our position within the educational administration and the limitations of our independent action.

Yet, despite some inflexible administrators and the imposing dictates of zealous state legislators, teachers continue to have a great deal of autonomy inside the classroom. Once the classroom door is closed, it is the relationship between teacher and student that is the heart of the learning experience. State legislators and administrators may evaluate from afar but it is the teacher and his/her lessons that will impact the lives of children.

Teacher Accountability

Perhaps the most persistent argument against the idea that teaching is a profession has to do with accountability. Critics argue, incorrectly, that teachers are not accountable for student learning. They suggest that if a student fails to learn, there are no consequences for that teacher. Some critics actually believe that if a teacher is ineffective, he or she cannot be fired. These are serious charges and reflect a fundamental misunderstanding of the history of teaching and accountability.

First of all, let's set the record straight. *Teachers are accountable and always have been.* As professionals we are accountable to the members of the community we serve, our school districts, our educational administrators, our colleagues in our schools and most importantly, we are accountable to our students.

Teacher Accountability in the 1800s

During America's early history, teachers were directly accountable to the communities in which they taught. Community members carefully monitored their dress, personal lives, and their "effectiveness" as disciplinarians. As we have seen, dress codes were common throughout the 1800s and they continue to be a part of the lives of many teachers today. In fact, it wasn't until the late 1960s and early 1970s that women teachers were allowed to wear "slacks" to school. Until then skirts and blouses and preferably dresses were required of all women classroom teachers. Men were required to wear a shirt and tie and could remove their jackets only when it was oppressively hot.

In addition to strict dress codes, members of the community carefully monitored the personal lives of teachers. Of course, women teachers were required to remain single and celibate. Marriage was strictly forbidden for women teachers. In some states, this provision was still in force as late as the 1940s. Dating was frowned upon and dancing with a member of the opposite sex was tolerated only at community-sponsored events. Even riding in a carriage with a young man was a good excuse for dismissal. And of course, most teachers in the 19th century were required to board with a member of the community during the period of their teaching contract. "Boarding" not only saved the community money, but it also assured that the moral virtue of the teacher was beyond question.

Reflection

Some school districts across the country are reinstating dress codes for both teachers as well as students. What are some of the positive and negative arguments regarding dress codes? What do you think?

Wisdom of Teachers: Dress Codes of the 1970s

Dress codes for women teachers were common as late as the 1970s. The following, drawn from the words of master teacher Jill Ripley illustrates the importance of freedom of dress.

It was the fall of 1973 and the halls in a suburban Indianapolis school district were buzzing. The new contract with the local teacher's union had been signed and one of the critical issues in the settlement was a provision to allow women teachers to wear slacks!

The agreement allowed women to wear "pant suits" with jackets "at least six inches below the derriere."

This was an important issue, especially for kindergarten through second-grade teachers who spent a great deal of time sitting in small chairs, sitting on the floor and bending over small desks while leading games and exercises. Wearing a dress for such activities was awkward, cumbersome and restrictive. (NBPTS, 2002)

Links to the Past: Moral Codes during the 1800s—Riding in a Buggy

Young women teachers in the past were required to adhere to strict moral codes that included not walking or riding alone with a man, unless he was a family member or minister. The following excerpt illustrates the consequences of minor violations of such rules.

> Nineteen-year-old Augusta Hubble had traveled from New York State to Tipton, Iowa to obtain a teaching position. Miss Hubble roomed with the Goodriches who ran an inn near the school house. One day, Mr. Goodrich, her benefactor, suddenly died. From then on, Mrs. Goodrich and her "hired girl" vented their jealousy of young Augusta by spreading false rumors and gossip about her. During her brief stay, Augusta had "accepted invitations a number or times to ride out [with a young man in a horse and buggy] on Saturday afternoons [but] always returned before dark." Soon, stories spread about her moral character and then when she became ill, more rumors spread that she was not really sick, but just getting out of work. She was then visited by "two directors" of the school who terminated her employment. (Kaufman, 1984, p. 158)

Reflection

What did Augusta Hubble do that resulted in her termination? Are there safeguards in place today that protect teachers from "false rumors?" What can you do so that you are not vulnerable?

Finally, teachers were routinely evaluated by members of the school board and by the entire community during the annual examination process. In fact, "examinations" during this period were as much an evaluation of the teacher as they were an indication of the progress of students. Teachers in the 1800s often recorded in their diaries that they had "surprise visits" from a local school board member, the local minister, or a school trustee.

Typically, teachers were evaluated on the basis of how well their students were able to recite a piece of poetry or a reading from the Bible. Additionally, teachers were often questioned as to their methods of discipline.

The National Teachers Exam

This form of local evaluation continued through the 1800s and well into the 1900s. In the mid-1940s however, educators demanded a national assessment instrument that could evaluate teacher candidates. The result of this was the National Teachers Exam (NTE). The NTE was prepared by the Educational Testing Service (ETS) at Princeton, New Jersey, and provided a comprehensive assessment of the academic preparation of teachers. It included three core battery tests that focused on communication skills, general knowledge, and professional knowledge. The exam also provided 27 distinct specialty tests ranging from elementary education to 9–12 mathematics. Gradually, through the 1950s and 1960s, most states adopted this examination as their primary assessment of teachers' academic and professional preparation.

Links to the Past: Teacher Evaluation during the 1800s—"Keep your feet warm!"

Teachers have always been anxious about being evaluated. In the 19th century, the evaluation of both teachers and their students was usually conducted by the superintendent or a school board member. The evaluation was unannounced and included hearing recitations by the students to determine how much they had learned. The following account illustrates how many teachers felt.

Laura was near the completion of her first winter term as a school teacher in the small one room schoolhouse. On this cold wintry day, the wind blew snow through the cracks in the walls. Laura felt sorry for her students because the room was cold, "so she let her students stand by the stove to study". The students had hardly settled into their seats, when there was a knock at the door. It was the superintendent, Mr. Williams. She gave Mr. Williams her chair by the stove. Every student was nervously bent over their work and tried to look studious. Laura was nervous too and her heart beat wildly as she tried to appear calm and steady. She was pleased though that all she students were making an effort to do their best work. Mr. Williams listened to each student recite their lessons.

After a while, one student, Charles raised his hand to ask if he could come near the stove to warm-up. Laura gave him permission, but Martha who was studying from the same book came also without asking permission. When they were warm, they returned to their seats, again without permission. This did not look good; it appeared that Laura lacked discipline in her classroom. After a while, Mr. Williams announced that he must leave. Laura asked if he would like to speak to the class. He stood silently for a moment, then he said: "whatever else you do, *Keep your feet warm.*" Then he smiled, shook Laura's hand and left. (Wilder, 1971, pp. 79–80)

Reflection

On what basis was Laura "evaluated" by Mr. Williams? What are some of the similarities and differences with teachers' evaluations today?

Links to the Past: "He didn't Whip 'em Enough"

Teachers in the 1800s were often hired or fired at the whim of the school board and members of the community. Below is an excerpt from the diary of a 19th century teacher who was fired because he "didn't whip 'em enough":

During his first term as a school teacher, young Lester Ward recorded in his diary on January 5, 1861 that because he "didn't whip his students enough" he was fired from his teaching position. Ward went on to record that Mr. Smith, the school trustee, took him outside his classroom and told him that he was "sick of hearing so many rumors and complaints against the order in the school." Someone had even reported that students were heard laughing during class! (Ward, 1935, p. 26–27)

By the late 1980s, however, there was yet another call to raise standards for teachers. Some state departments of education raised their criterion score on the NTE (the grade necessary to pass). Meanwhile, educational researchers criticized the NTE as an inadequate measure of a teacher's ability to teach.

THE NEW ACCOUNTABILITY: THE PRAXIS EXAMINATIONS

In response to this criticism, ETS developed a new teacher assessment instrument, the Praxis series, and formally introduced it in 1992. The Praxis, billed as the "new generation of teacher assessment," captured the imagination of educational reformers and within a few years it was embraced by states throughout the nation. The exam series has three primary components.

Praxis I

The first, Praxis I, is designed to measure your academic skills and focuses on reading, writing, and mathematics. Typically you will take the Praxis I during your sophomore year. It can be administered as a paper and pencil exam (known as the PPST) or in a computer-based format (known as the CBT). This exam often is used as a criterion to formally enter the teacher education program.

Praxis II

Praxis II, the second in the series, consists of two components. The first, the Principles of Learning and Teaching (PLT), assesses your pedagogical knowledge derived from courses such as Educational Foundations (yes, the material in this book!), Educational Psychology, Human Growth and Development, Classroom Management, and Instructional Design. The exam is arranged by grade level to be taught: K–6, 5–9,7–12, and consists of a series of multiple choice questions as well as a number of "case histories" to which you will provide written responses.

The second component of the Praxis II is the Specialty Exam. This specialty exam measures your knowledge of an area of expertise such as Special Education, K–12 Art, or 9–12 History. This assessment has a traditional, multiple-choice section and a "constructed response" component. In the later section you are given a teaching situation or "problem" to which you will respond, describing an instructional approach and outlining steps necessary to solve the problem. The Praxis II typically is used as a criterion for graduation and/or teacher certification.

Praxis Alert

Praxis I: Pre-Professional Skills Assessments (PPST®) are designed to measure basic skills in reading, writing, and mathematics. The reading, writing, and mathematics assessments are available in two formats: paper-based or computer-based.

The following states require the PPST or CBT for teacher licensure:

Alaska	Maine	Pennsylvania
Connecticut	Maryland	South Carolina
Delaware	Minnesota	Tennessee
District of Columbia	Mississippi	US Virgin Islands
Georgia	Nebraska	Vermont
Guam	Nevada	Virginia
Hawaii	New Hampshire	West Virginia
Indiana	North Carolina	Wisconsin
Kentucky	North Dakota	DODDS*
Louisiana	Ohio	
	Oklahoma	
	Oregon	

* Department of Defense Departments Schools

Praxis I Session Descriptions and Time Periods
- PPST
  - Reading Test, Multiple Choice 1 hour
  - Mathematics Test, Multiple Choice 1 hour
  - Writing Test, Multiple Choice: 30 minutes
    - Essay Writing: 30 minutes
- CBT Each testing session is 2 hours to allow for tutorials on the use of the program, the test, and information for score reporting.
  - Reading Test, Multiple Choice: 75 minutes
  - Mathematics Test, Multiple Choice: 75 minutes
  - Writing Test, Multiple Choice: 45 minutes
    - Essay writing: 30 minutes (Praxis Series, n.d.)

Source: Retrieved May 23, 2007, from http://www.ets.org/praxis/taags

Journaling Activity

Select the state in which you would like to teach. Go online and find out the requirements they have for the Praxis II. Write a short summary of these requirements.

Praxis Alert: Preparing for the Praxis I

- Register for either the PPST or CBT
    - For the PPST you may register online at http://www.teachingandlearning. org.
    - Computer-based testing (CBT) registration is made by appointment at over 300 Prometric test sites throughout the United States. Call 1-800-853-6773, 1-443-751-4859, or call the test center directly.
- Use the computerized tutorial called LearningPlus. It is designed to help you review and learn new skills and practice tests are available. Ask your advisor if you have this software program available on campus. There are also books that contain practice exercises.
- Obtain the Tests "At a Glance" booklet for the Praxis I that are available free of charge at http://www.teachingandlearning.org. These booklets describe the test items and provide sample questions and answers.
- Practice taking the test.
    - Your score is based on the number of questions that you answer correctly, so pace yourself and try to answer every question.
    - There is no penalty for guessing.
    - Watch the allotted time and allow time to go back to questions that you may have skipped.
    - If you do not know the answer, try to eliminate some choices and make an "educated guess" based on the remaining choices.
- Get a good night's sleep and eat a light meal before you go to the testing center. You will not have breaks during a test administration and only a brief break between tests. You will not have time to go out to eat and there may not be food available onsite.
- Bring the following to the testing site:
    - Photo ID that has your name, photo, and signature (for example, a photo driver's license, photo employment ID, photo student ID)
    - Your Social Security Card
    - Test Registration Receipt
    - Institutions that you would like to receive your test scores (you may select three institutions)

Source: Retrieved May 23, 2007, from http://www.ets.org/praxis/taags

Praxis III

The final component of this series is the Praxis III. Actually, the Praxis III is not an exam, but rather an evaluation of your performance in the classroom as a teacher. Educators have long recognized that any assessment of educational progress requires more than a simple multiple-choice exam or even a series of short essays in response to instructional situations as in the Praxis II.

The Praxis III observation, conducted in your classroom, typically takes place by a trained assessor once you have begun your teaching. You will be evaluated on the basis of criteria that represent the four domains of practice. These include:

Praxis Alert: Praxis II, State Requirements

There are several different types of tests in the Praxis II series. States have different requirements regarding the type of test teachers need for licensure.

- Principles of Learning and Teaching Tests (PLT)
- This exam consists of four levels: PLT Pre–K; PLT K–6; PLT 5–9; and PLT 7–12. Each of these tests is 2 hours in length and has 45 multiple choice questions and 6 constructed-response questions. Four categories are measured: organizing content knowledge, creating a learning environment, student learning, and professionalism.
- Teaching Foundations Exam (TFE) is used in California. The test was developed by ETS and California Commission of Teacher Credentialing. There are separate tests for English, Math, Science, Social Studies, and Multiple Subjects.
    - Required in California
- Subject Assessments/Specialty Area Tests are 2 hours in length and depending on the exam may consist of multiple choice questions, and/or written responses. Some states require these tests in certain specialty areas.
- State requirements change frequently. Check the current issue of the Praxis Registration Bulletin for the state in which you wish to teach. You may also go directly to the state regarding their certification requirements.

Source: Retrieved May 23, 2007, from http://www.ets.org/praxis/taags

---

- Organizing Content Knowledge for Student Learning
- Creating an environment for Student Learning
- Teaching for Student Learning
- Teacher Professionalism

How to Apply for Teacher Licensure

States vary in the procedures for teacher licensure, but generally the type of materials you submit are similar. Below is a list of materials:

1. Complete the Form (Application for a State License): This form requests general information, such as name, address, phone, gender, race, social security number, birth date, licensure area.
2. Collect documentation to support your application:
   Transcripts
   Licensure from other states
   University recommendation
   Test scores
   Verification of experience
3. Assemble your application materials in the order listed.
4. Include the processing fee with your application materials. Mail to the address provided.

Assessors evaluate your pedagogical knowledge, your skill and application of that knowledge, your ability to reflect on your teaching, to recognize your strengths and weaknesses, and to learn from your experiences.

The Praxis III classroom assessment is designed to assist in making licensure decisions. After successful completion of your teacher education degree and, depending on your state, the Praxis II, you will be issued a provisional, initial, or probationary license. This license allows you to teach for 1–3 years, again, depending on the state. During this period, you may be assessed under the Praxis III criteria in order to receive your permanent teacher's license.

Although states have been slow in requiring the Praxis III for licensure, it will only be a matter of time before most states adopt it. Certainly by the time you enter the classroom, the Praxis III will be a standard licensure requirement.

Praxis Alert: Praxis III—Evaluation Form

The following is an observation form based on Praxis III standards developed by the Ohio State University. Although your college or university may use different criteria, this form will give you an idea of what to expect.

Student Teaching Observation/Evaluation Form Based on Praxis III

Student Teacher _____ Date of Observation____

Circle the appropriate numeral that corresponds to the student teacher's level of performance. 1 = Unsatisfactory, 2 = Needs Improvement, 3 = Proficient, 4 = Very Good, 5 = Distinguished.

Classroom Environment

A. Creating an Environment of Respect and Rapport   1 2 3 4 5
B. Establishing a Culture for Learning   1 2 3 4 5
C. Managing Classroom Procedures   1 2 3 4 5
D. Managing Student Behavior   1 2 3 4 5
E. Organizing Physical Space   1 2 3 4 5

Instruction

F. Communicating Clearly and Accurately   1 2 3 4 5
G. Engaging Students in Learning   1 2 3 4 5
H. Providing Feedback to Students   1 2 3 4 5
I. Demonstrating Flexibility and Responsiveness   1 2 3 4 5

Comments:

_____

_____

_____

_____

Cooperating Teacher/Student Teacher
University Supervisor (Ohio State University, n.d.)

Source: Student Teaching, College of Education, Ohio State University;
http://www.coe.ohio-state.edu

Take a moment to examine the sample evaluation criteria of the Praxis III devised by Ohio State University. While your assessor may have a slightly different set of criteria, this sample will give you a better idea of what to expect.

Reflection

What does this form tell you about the Praxis III evaluation process?

PROFESSIONAL SUPPORT NETWORKS FOR TEACHERS

While the Praxis exams may seem daunting, standing alone before 25 children each day, participating in regular conferences, interacting with 20 to 30 parents during school "open houses," or even facing the principal with a problem can be a bit intimidating, especially for a new teacher. We understand because we both have been there! As a result of these experiences, teachers sometimes feel isolated from the communities that they serve. However, this should not be the case. One thing that you must always remember is that you are not alone! We have a long, rich heritage and our careers have been built on the struggles and work of millions of teachers in the past. On a more concrete level, you will have a school support network that includes guidance counselors, administrative staff,

---

You Are Not Alone

There are many support staff to help you as a teacher. They can give you advice regarding how to help students with learning disabilities, discipline problems, and physical disabilities. The organizations mentioned below are just a sample.

School Support Staff:
- Nurses
- Counselors
- Secretaries
- Fellow teachers
- School Psychologist
- Speech and Hearing Therapists
- Reading Specialists
- Special Education Teachers
- School Social Workers
- Administrators

Specialty Organizations:
- Council of Exceptional Children
- Association for Curriculum & Supervision Development
- Association for Educational Communications and Technology
- American Council on the Teaching of Foreign Languages

International Organizations:
- Phi Delta Kappan
- Association for Childhood Education International

and of course, other teachers. Beyond that, however, is a vast network of professional organizations at the local, state, regional, and national level that will provide you with professional information, support, consultation, camaraderie, and even job protection.

SCHOOL SUPPORT STAFF

Members of the school support staff will assist you in many ways. They will help you develop individual education plans (IEP) for students with learning disabilities, physical disabilities, and emotional disorders. They can also provide assistance in dealing with children with domestic, personal, and discipline problems.

School Counselor and Nurse

The school counselor can help one of your students cope with a divorce, a death in the family, or substance abuse of a parent or guardian. As we have seen previously, you may become aware of a sudden change in a child's behavior, health, or academic performance. The child may complain of a stomachache or a headache, may cry in class, or seem to lose interest in class work. At this point, you may want to consult the school counselor who can talk privately with the child to determine the cause of the problem.

Similarly, the school nurse might be brought into consultation with the school counselor to help determine if the child has a health problem or if the illness is a result of an emotional crisis. The point is that you are not alone. You can readily call upon the support staff available in your school to help you help students who have problems.

Administrative Staff

Your administrative staff also plays an important role in the educational process. Your principal, for example, can help you determine the support staff that might provide assistance and will help you contact them and set up an informal meeting or a formal "staffing" if necessary. The principal can also assist you in disciplinary matters. As a teacher, you will take care of the vast majority of disciplinary problems in the classroom but occasionally you may need to call upon the help of the principal. In the elementary grades this may not be necessary, but in middle grades and high school, the principal often is the "chief disciplinarian" of the school. Sometimes even the possibility of "going to the principal's office" is enough to deter the misbehavior of the more difficult student.

School Secretary

The school secretary also can be very helpful. For example, she can help you maintain your attendance records, direct you to school supplies that are available, and show you how to order special supplies such as a globe or state map. The school secretary is also an important source of information concerning school policies. She will know the specific rules regarding photocopying, the use of the ditto machine, or special equipment such as overhead projectors, LCD projectors, televisions with VCRs and DVDs, etc. Finally, school secretaries often are the first line of communication with parents relaying their messages to you and in the case of a student's illness, they will contact parents.

Fellow Teachers

But the most important part of your support staff is your fellow teachers. To begin with, some school districts will assign you to a mentor teacher who will provide advice, counsel, and general information during your first years in the classroom. Typically, he or she will help you locate teaching resources in the school, alert you to upcoming meeting and events, help you understand both the informal and formal rules of the school, and provide you with some tips for discipline and classroom management. Mentor teachers are valuable.

Other teachers in the school can be helpful as you begin your career. They can alert you to the learning difficulties and disciplinary problems of particular students, and they may share successful strategies for dealing with these students. They may also provide you with helpful information regarding parents and their participation in their child's education. Much of this information is gained informally through hallway discussions, at lunchtime, before and after meetings and of course, in the teachers' lounge.

Remember, however, the teachers' lounge can also be a discouraging place for young teachers. It is here that you will hear complaints, gossip, and rumors that are often upsetting and may tend to disillusion you. Keep this in mind as you dare to enter the teachers' lounge!

Selected List of Professional Organizations

Teacher Organizations
- National Education Association (NEA): http://www.nea.org
- American Federation of Teachers (AFT): http://www.aft.org
- Phi Delta Kappa (PDK): http://www.pdkintl.org

Child-Centered Organizations
- Association for Childhood Education International (ACEI): http://www.acei.org
- National Association for the Education of Young Children (NAEYC): http://www.naeyc.org
- National Middle School Association (NMSA): http://www.nmsa.org
- Council for Exceptional Children (CEC): http://www.cec.org

Subject-Centered (Specialty) Organizations
- International Reading Association (IRA): http://www.reading.org
- National Council for the Social Studies (NCSS): http://www.ncss.org
- National Council of Teachers of English (NCTE): http://www.ncte.org
- National Council of Teachers of Mathematics (NCTM): http://www.nctm.org
- National Science Teachers Association (NSTA): http://www.nsta.org
- American Council on the Teaching of Foreign Languages (ACTFL): http://www.actfl.org
- American Alliance for Health, Physical Education, Recreation and Dance (AAHPERD): http://www.aahperd.org
- Music Teachers National Association (MTNA): http://www.mtna.org
- National Art Education Association (NAEA): http://www.naea.org

SPECIALTY ORGANIZATIONS

Professional Organizations

In addition to the school support staff, there are many professional organizations that can provide you with information about your profession, research in your area as well as teaching tips from experienced teachers.

Specialty Organizations

Some organizations, such as the Association for the Supervision and Curriculum Development, are concerned with the changes in the curriculum and the role that teachers and administrators have in that development. Others like the Council for Exceptional Children and the American Speech Language Hearing Association focus on issues of interest to both special education teachers as well as those who teach children with hearing or speech impairments.

The Association for Childhood Education International and the International Reading Association provide a forum for elementary and middle grade teachers while a host of other specialty organizations provide professional information and direction for teachers at the secondary level. These include the American Council on the Teaching of Foreign Languages, The American Association of Physics Teachers, and The National Council of Teachers of English. As you select your specialty area later in your professional development, discuss with your professor the kinds of organizations and associations that represent your specific interests.

Journaling Activity

Choose three professional organizations that are related to your teaching interests. Go online and visit each of these Web sites. Briefly describe the kinds of programs they offer.

INTERNATIONAL ORGANIZATIONS

While these organizations were created to support specific specialty areas and disciplines, there are a number of broader-based international professional organizations that serve the entire field of education. Perhaps the best known of these is Phi Delta Kappan International (PDK). Phi Delta Kappan is a kind of "umbrella" organization that publishes a wide array of professional materials including the prestigious *Phi Delta Kappan Journal*, *News, Notes and Quotes* newsletter, as well as hundreds of information booklets on educational topics, research reports, surveys, and instructional materials. In addition, PDK sponsors grants, awards, workshops, educational meetings, and trips. We highly recommend that you explore the range of interesting publications and programs sponsored by PDK and seriously consider membership in the organization. Their Web site, http://www.pdkint.org, is excellent and provides information on becoming a member.

NATIONAL TEACHER ORGANIZATIONS AND UNIONS

In addition to these professional associations are a number of important national teacher organizations and teacher unions that represent your interests. The oldest and largest teacher organization is the National Educational Association (NEA). Organized first as

---

NEA—Student Membership

Student memberships are available through the National Education Association. Membership for a nominal fee provides these benefits:

- Publications
    - *NEA Today*—monthly newspaper
    - *Tomorrow's Teachers*—annual magazine for students
- Current research
- Workshops and conferences
- Leadership training
- Guidance for teaching diverse students
- Opportunities for networking

Source: Retrieved February 27, 2008, from
http://www.nea.org/student-program/membership/index.html

---

the National Teachers Association in 1857, it became the NEA in 1886. Today the NEA boasts a membership of about 2.3 million teachers, administrators, and educational support staff. The NEA also encourages students to join the organization with membership in the student NEA, sometimes called the Student Education Association (SEA).

NEA Initiatives

- Legislative Action Center
- From the online site http://www.nea.org you can read about current pending legislation that effects education. From this site you may also contact legislators via email and express your support for the legislation.
- Publications
    - *NEA Today*
    - *Thought & Action*
    - *Higher Education Advocate*
    - *NEA Almanac of Higher Education*
    - *Tomorrow's Teachers*
    - *This Active Life*
    - *Education Statistics*
- Events
    This section describes upcoming events, such as the national meeting for the NEA, state meetings, etc.
- NEA Read Across America
    This project, sponsored jointly with the International Reading Association (IRA) is celebrated on Dr. Seuss's birthday. Celebrities, teachers, and others are encouraged to read aloud to children on this day.
- Help for Parents
    Through the NEA Web site, http://www.nea.org, parents can get ideas on how they can help their children learn in school.
- Online resource for educators

The Student Education Association (SEA) is an organization that has over 1 million education students in its ranks. Your college or university may have a chapter and membership in it will give you an idea of how the larger NEA operates the kinds of services it provides and its role in your professional development (Parkerson & Parkerson, 2001).

Journaling Activity

Go online to http://www.nea.org and read about educational legislation in Congress. In your journal describe this legislation and NEA's position on it.

While the NEA is *not* a teacher's union, the American Federation of Teachers (AFT) is proud of its status as a labor organization, associated with the AFL–CIO (American Federation of Labor–Congress of Industrial Organization). The AFT was founded in 1916 with John Dewey as the organization's first official member. Although membership in the AFT is smaller than the NEA (slightly less than 1 million), its important role in fighting for higher wages and better working conditions for all teachers is undisputed.

The AFT's connection to organized labor provides it with the political power to successfully demand changes in the schools that benefit teachers and their students. The AFT traditionally has supported its local affiliates in disputes with local boards of education. Following World War II, for example, the AFT supported the first successful teacher strikes in this country. While these strikes were difficult for teachers, students, and parents, they did help secure decent wages for teachers and set the tone for rational collective bargaining between teachers and boards of education.

The AFT continues to act as an outspoken advocate of teacher's rights. It publishes a weekly column in the *New York Times* that is written by its president and addresses controversial issues facing teachers. Clearly, the AFT is a powerful political force in its own right, actively representing the rights of teachers in the larger society. Aligned with the National Education Association on important issues such as national educational policy, accountability, and "high stakes testing" we have a strong advocate of our rights as teachers. You are not alone (Parkerson & Parkerson, 2001).

AFT Initiatives

- Meetings and Conferences
- Legislative Action Center
  Available on the AFT Web site, http://www.aft.org allows you to link to pending legislation that effects education and has links to legislators.
- Publications
  - *Inside the AFT*
  - *American Educator*
  - *Public Service Reporter*
  - *American Teacher*
- The Parent Page
  This is part of the AFT Web site, http://www.aft.org and provides assistance for parents who want to help their children with schoolwork. It also provides links to other helpful sites for parents.
- Web Resources and Local Web Sites
  Available through the AFT web site, http://www.aft.org this provides links to resources that are valuable for educators.
- Teacher Salary Survey
  This provides comparative information regarding teacher salaries.

Go online to http://www.aft.org and examine the education legislation that is currently pending. Briefly describe the AFT's position on this legislation. Compare their position with that of the NEA. What do you think?

PROFESSIONAL STANDARDS FOR TEACHERS

As a new teacher, you will want to demonstrate your ability to teach and also show how you have developed as a professional over the years. As we have seen, in order to be certified as a teacher, you will be required to receive a degree from an accredited teacher education program, pass a series of licensure examinations—often the Praxis series—and meet other state requirements.

Professional Folios and Portfolios

But sometimes neither your grades in college nor your scores on the Praxis exams will reflect the enthusiasm, dedication, and vision you may bring to the classroom. For this reason, professional folios and portfolios have become an important part of the evaluation process. They can be very useful when you are trying to land your first teaching position because they can help demonstrate to principals and superintendents your level of professionalism as well as your commitment to teaching.

But what is a folio and a professional portfolio? Basically, the folio is a collection of all the documents, products, and information that demonstrate your professional development, while the professional portfolio is a specialized selection of folio materials that

---

Portfolio Contents

The following is a suggested list of contents for you professional portfolio. You will probably begin your portfolio during your field experiences or education courses. During your student teaching, however, you will add a significant number of items. By the time you complete your student teaching you should have developed a professional portfolio that you can show to potential employers.

- Philosophy of Education Statement
- Resume
- Photographs of your school, students, classroom, projects, etc.
- Lesson Plans (five or more, and include one that uses technology)
- Sample of student work for each lesson plan
- Reflection on each lesson plan
- Student Teacher Forms: i.e., Student Teacher Responsibility Sheets, Student Time Records
- Evaluations of your teaching performance from your cooperating teacher and college supervisor
- Other activities that you participated in such as faculty meetings, PTA, etc.
- Videotape of a lesson

Source: A Handbook for the Facilitative Teacher Intern: 2006–2007, Department of Education, Methodist University, Fayetteville, NC

will highlight your professional development. You could think of it as a large, carefully organized "scrapbook" that tells the story of your professional development.

The folio, therefore, is an organized collection of your professional teaching materials while the professional portfolio is a much smaller selection of those materials often used when you are seeking employment, promotion or National Board Certification (NBPTS), something we will discuss at the end of this chapter.

Portfolio Activity

Purchase a three-ring binder or other folder for your professional portfolio. Create a table of contents with the above items and tabs to match the example above. (Or use the portfolio format suggested by your professor.) Begin placing your professional activity contents in this folder.

Most colleges and universities today will help you begin your folio development. Your Education Foundations professor (Introduction to Education), for example, may already have required you to write a statement on your personal philosophy of education. And as you develop as a teacher you will want to revise your philosophy statement. It's important to keep these statements and place them in your folio because they illustrate how you have grown during your training. Moreover, as you have noticed, we have included journaling opportunities throughout this book to help you begin this process.

During your methods courses you will begin your folio in earnest. Typically you will develop "lesson plans" and present them to your classmates and professors. Similarly, you may be required to read and summarize contemporary educational research articles and produce other writing assignments such as case studies. All these materials should be included in your folio. Remember, however, the creation and maintenance of your folio is up to you. Don't expect to be reminded that you must update your materials. This is *your* career after all.

Creating Your Folio

How should you begin to create your folio? This is a good question and there are a number of ways to proceed. If you use the computer a great deal and feel comfortable with it, you may want to begin an "electronic portfolio." Here you would simply make copies of your written assignments, article summaries, and essays to be accessed at a later date. Other material might also be scanned and saved as files in your folio directory. Later these files can be retrieved and arranged for presentation in your professional portfolio. Remember, however, that your folio is an ongoing enterprise and you will be adding material later. And of course, make sure that you make several copies of your files to disks, carefully label them, and put them in a safe place! You should also have "hard copies" of all your work, as electronic files have a funny habit of disappearing just when you need them!

On the other hand, if you would rather create a more traditional "hard copy" folio (they typically have four sections) you can begin by purchasing four large accordion files, a large four drawer file cabinet or even four large envelopes and start collecting your material. This certainly is the most common method of folio building and is perfectly acceptable. You may also use this same organizational scheme when you develop your professional portfolio. These four sections are:

- Background and Experiences
- Awards and Recognitions
- Teaching Performance
- Student Outcomes

Background and Experiences

In the Background and Experiences section of the folio you will want to include your professional resume, a statement on your educational philosophy, and evidence of your special skills—such as the ability to speak a foreign language, play a musical instrument, or your expertise in sports etc. In this you should include short descriptions of volunteer work that you may have done in the past, such as Boy Scout or Girl Scout leader or church activities, as well as paid work with children or young people such as a day camp counselor or instructor with a park district. Also include photos of the children that you have worked with, a short description of the kinds of activities that you were involved with, and the professional insights you may have developed during these experiences. For example, this might include a paragraph on how you developed a better understanding of adolescent behavior.

Portfolio Activity

Using the general form suggested in the Web site below, create your own professional resume. For your B.S. degree, simply write "expected" in parenthesis after the date you expect to graduate. Print out your resume and place in your professional portfolio. Remember, revise your resume regularly.

Source: Retrieved February 27, 2008, from http://education.depaul.edu/html/current/
writing_resume.asp.

Awards and Recognition

In the Awards and Recognition section, you should include evidence of awards that you may have received in school, church, sports, clubs, or other organizations. Brainstorming with your parents may help as they might be able to recall things you did in the past that you may have forgotten. Also, you should mention honorary or professional societies to which you may belong such as the National Honor Society, or the Deans, Chancellors, or President's List. If you have a copy of a program with your name on it, include it in your folio. If you have a membership certificate for Kappa Delta Pi (the Education Honorary Society), the Student Education Association, or any other professional organization such as the Student Council for Exceptional Children, include originals or copies of these materials.

Also list any special activities that you were involved with in high school or college such as assisting with a "field day" at a local elementary school. Be sure to mention any leadership positions that you may have held in organizations or clubs such as treasurer of the Student Education Association, or secretary of the Student Government Association. Finally, include any letters thanking you for your help that might serve to document these activities as well as copies of any certificates that you may have received.

Teaching Performance

In the next section of your folio, Teaching Performance, you will include copies of lesson plans, unit plans, and resource files that you have developed in your education courses, especially your methods courses.

Journaling Activity

Go online to http://www.eduplace.com/ss/act/story.htmWeb site —or a Web site of your own choosing—and find an activity that is appropriate for the subject and grade level that you intend to teach. Print out the activity and record the site in your journal.

You will also want to include lesson plans taught in K–12 schools during your field experiences or student teaching (clinical practice). Also include video or audiotapes of your teaching in these schools as well as photographs of your classroom.

Journaling Activity

Check to see if your program has a lesson plan form online. If not, get a paper copy from your education department, school, or college. What are the primary components of the lesson plan? Does it include reflection? Why is the lesson plan an important part of teaching?

Formal evaluations of your teaching performance by your cooperating teacher (the teacher you are assigned to work with during your field experience), as well as your college supervisor (the education faculty member who observes you in the schools during your field experience), also belong in your folio. Include official copies of scores that document successful completion of required exams such as the Praxis I (Reading, Writing, and Math Exams) to provide evidence of your knowledge and communication skills necessary to teach. Finally, mention any special activities or events that you assisted with during your field or clinical experiences, such as helping your teacher with a school play, holiday concert, or providing additional supervision for students on a field trip.

Journaling Activity

Go online to the Web site listed below and examine the student teacher observation form. Compare this form with the one used by your education department, school, or college.

Source: Retrieved February 27, 2008, from http://edwebsfiles.ed.uiuc.edu/ci/oce/documents/StudentTeachingStructuredObsForm_000.pdf.

Student Outcomes

The final section of your folio, Student Outcomes, should provide evidence of your ability to help all students learn. Here you might include students' test scores on a math test after you have taught a lesson. You also can include samples of K–12 student work, such as essays, exams, or projects that were the result of your teaching. For example, if you instructed students on the techniques of expository writing, then include samples of their essays in your portfolio. Also include copies of awards that your K–12 students may have received, such as first place or even honorable mention in a History or Science Fair, or a photo of a winning poster in a contest on fire safety.

Folio development is a long-term enterprise. It begins in your first year of college and will last throughout your career. By creating a structure to collect and assemble your materials early in your career you will not only have a wealth of material to choose from when it is time to produce your professional portfolio, but you will have an enormous resource file to draw from when you enter the classroom. Copies of successful lesson plans from methods classes, field experiences, and student teaching will come in handy if you are searching for an appropriate lesson for your students. Finally, by spending time and energy in the organization of your folio, you will become a more organized person.

LIFELONG LEARNING

As we have seen, professional development is a long-term process. It involves years of formal education, clinical experiences (student teaching), as well as systematic assessment and evaluation of your progress. But professional development is more than that. It involves lifelong learning at the university level, in the classroom, and through the process of self-reflection. As you may already know, some states may require you to complete postgraduate course work in your field of expertise at the university or college level in order to renew your teacher certification. You may also be required to enroll in specialized education workshops and seminars that focus on a specific problem in the schools such as conflict resolution or a new reform that is being instituted in your district such as block scheduling or character education.

These opportunities for formal course work, seminars, and workshops are an important part of your professional development. They help you keep abreast of the newest educational research and technology in your specialty area and help you grow as a professional educator. In addition, however, is the important role of self-observation and reflection through journaling. In recent years, there has been a growing consensus among educators at all levels that reflective journaling is an excellent way to personalize and improve individual learning.

YOUR PROFESSIONAL JOURNAL

Journaling can be as informal as jotting down some ideas or insights you may have gained through an experience, reviewing your notes later—a process called reflecting—and then modifying your course of action as a result. In fact, we often do this sort of informal journaling in our daily lives. For example, you may have kept a diary in the past. Your very personal entries, though they may seem a bit naïve or even silly as you look back on them now, can often help you better understand yourself and your relationships with others. By reflecting on events in light of what you know now, you may be able put your personal life into perspective and understand the pettiness of certain behavior such as excluding someone from your group because of the way they looked.

Your reflective journal can help you understand more fully your professional development. In some ways, class note taking is a form of journaling in that you try to record insights gained through lectures or discussions and later you reread your notes and try to make sense of the many ideas scrawled in your notebook. Reflective journaling is similar to the note taking review process, but it is more personal and individualized.

As part of your teacher education program you may be required to begin a reflective journal. And while the whole process may seem a bit odd at first, we feel strongly that if you stick with it, there will be some great benefits to your overall professional development. Even if your teacher education program does not require that you begin a journal, we urge you to begin this process.

Through all of this however, at least two questions come to mind. First of all, what is a reflective journal? And secondly, how does one begin a reflective journal? These are very good questions.

What is a Journal?

A reflective journal is both the process and the product of recording your experiences and insights gained through an education course, a field experience, a student teacher experience, or in the classroom as a professional educator and then reflecting on those experiences at a later date. Once you have recorded your personal insights in your journal, you should revisit them on a regular basis, reread them, and then reflect on how they might improve your teaching. By doing so you will become a reflective practitioner.

How to Begin Your Journal

Begin your reflective journal by purchasing a spiral notebook at the bookstore, label it as your professional journal, and then tuck it away in your book bag—right next to your date book in which you have recorded all your assignments and appointments! If you like, you could also begin an "electronic journal." In either case, when you feel you have had a professional experience that is worth recording, simply jot it down, or enter it with a date. That's all it takes! It does not have to be fancy. You don't have to worry about grammar or punctuation or even style. This is *your* journal for *your* development and does not necessarily need to be seen by others.

For example, you have encountered a defiant student during one of your field experiences. You document this situation, how you felt, how it started, and how it was resolved. Later you discover that the child comes from a home where the father has died and the mother is now in a position of trying to raise several children by herself. As a result of this discovery and reflection you become more compassionate toward the child. During your student teaching, you have a similar problem. By reflecting on this experience, recorded in your journal, you will recall it in vivid detail and it will help reinforce your earlier insight that by understanding the personal problems and domestic situations of that student you were in a better position to help him learn.

Your Journal as a Personal Learning Tool

You may think that you will surely remember such an important event without recording it in a journal. But you probably will not. You will be amazed as to how many situations you will encounter during your field experiences alone, not to mention your student teaching and professional classroom teaching. Memories fade, you move on, but the journal entry will last and provide you with a permanent record of that important event and the insights you gained from it. In this way, reflective journaling becomes a powerful tool that reinforces learning in a personal and individual way. This is not just a highlighted item in a textbook nor even a point made by your professor in a lecture. This is your personal discovery!

GETTING YOUR FIRST TEACHING POSITION

Early in your student teaching semester you will begin to look for your first teaching position. At this point you will have completed your coursework, taken the Praxis I exam, and successfully completed several field experiences. Before you begin your job search, however, you should prepare your resume and professional portfolio. Although you will continue to develop and update these credentials throughout your teaching career, it is important to have materials available to show prospective employers at this time. Don't worry that it is not "perfect"—just do the best you can.

Job Fairs

During your student teaching semester, if not before, you should attend job fairs offered by your college or other universities in your area. You can find out about these fairs from your director of student teaching and you can consult the job placement service on your campus. Also keep an eye on campus bulletin boards for announcements of these important events.

When you attend a job fair, bring your professional portfolio, 25 copies of your resume, and place all these materials in some form of a brief case. Don't bring your backpack and avoid novelty totes or plastic bags. In short, try to make a good impression. Dress professionally. Women should wear a dress or suit, stockings, and heels. Men should wear a suit or sports coat with dress pants, a collared shirt, and tie and dress shoes. Casual shoes are acceptable but avoid "gym" or sport shoes. And by all means avoid flip-flops.

Representatives from school districts in the area and even other states and regions will occupy tables and have displays with brochures at the fair. Introduce yourself to the representatives at the table and express an interest in their school. Be professional, pleasant, and polite, and try to smile! Even if you've never heard of a particular school system, express interest. Leave your options open. You never know, you may end up teaching in one of these schools. Remember, if these representatives have taken the trouble to come to this job fair, they are serious about recruiting teachers. Sometimes they might even conduct a preliminary interview and occasionally may offer contracts on the spot! Whatever happens at this point, politely ask for an application and brochure, give them a copy of your resume, thank them, and move on.

Networking during Your Student Teaching

In addition to attending job fairs, you will also want to make contacts in your student teaching school. It goes without saying that you should do your best to develop a positive relationship with your cooperating teacher. If you impress her, you have maximized your job prospects. She will evaluate your performance in the classroom and may even be in a position to recommend you for a job in that school or in the district. Remember, you

---

Interviewing Tips

- Relax, but focus on the interview, not your date later that evening.
- Smile and be polite, but don't gush.
- Make eye contact, but do not stare at the interviewer.
- Shake hands firmly, at the beginning and end of the interview.
- Be positive about your student teaching experience and your school, do not criticize or be negative.
- Put a positive "spin" on previous experiences and work relationships.
- Answer all questions in a positive manner.
- Be prepared to discuss your "philosophy of education." Practice your answer and even role play with a fellow student.
- Be prepared to discuss how you handle discipline in the classroom. You might want to say that you try to use "preventative discipline" before things get out of hand.
- Be prepared to discuss a number of current issues in education such as "phonics" in the reading program or how you might use technology for instruction.
- Be ready to "think on your feet." You may be asked a personal question that you were not expecting, such as why you are getting married or if you plan to have a child soon. Don't be offended by such questions.

are a guest in her classroom. Listen to her advice, be punctual, pitch in, and help when something needs to be done—don't wait to be told to do something. Be a self-starter!

In addition to your cooperating teacher, remember to be polite and friendly with other teachers and staff members in your school. They could be your colleagues in a month or two! Also, teachers at your school might know of job openings at another school in the district due to a retiring teacher or one who is getting married and leaving the district. If this should happen, take advantage of this "insider information," and send your resume and a letter to the superintendent of the district explaining your interest in that position. Whenever you submit your resume for a position, you should always follow up with a phone call as you near the completion of your student teaching. By all means though, let others in your school and elsewhere know that you are looking for a teaching position.

As a student teacher, you should also look for opportunities to participate in other school activities. Attend teachers' meetings and take notes. Help prepare for and attend open houses, holiday programs, or sporting events. Volunteer your services as a tutor to hone your teaching skills or participate in PTA fundraising activities such as a Fall Carnival or a Pancake Dinner. In other words, do not run from the school at 3 p.m.! Show your interest in the school and its students and by all means demonstrate that you can be a valuable colleague.

Once you feel comfortable with your student teaching abilities, perhaps after you have successfully given several lessons, invite your principal to observe you in the classroom. But make sure you clear this with your cooperating teacher first. Always go through the normal communication channels, sometimes called the "chain of command" of your school. If you do not, you may offend someone. After the principal has observed you, ask him/her to provide you with a written evaluation that you can include in your portfolio. You might also give him/her a copy of your resume and express an interest in teaching at his/her school. If the principal is pleased with your teaching performance, you may be offered a job beginning in the next school year. Alternatively, the principal may recommend you to another principal who has an opening.

The job search process may seem a bit overwhelming. Try to think of it as an adventure. It is! The more you prepare for this process the, easier it will be. By maintaining an updated resume and portfolio, and by using some of the networking ideas suggested above, your job search will be a successful one. Good luck to you!

NATIONAL BOARD CERTIFICATION—NBPTS

The career path to your first classroom is an exciting one. You begin as an education student, proceed through field experiences and clinical experiences as a student teacher, then you pass a series of licensure exams, graduate, and finally become a certified classroom teacher. But the pinnacle achievement in our profession is National Board Certification.

Journaling Activity

A number of states provide financial assistance to NBPTS candidates (state support). Others provide salary incentives (state supplements) for teachers who receive board certification. Go online to http://www.nbpts.org Web site to see if your state offers financial supplements.

In 1987, the Carnegie Foundation for the Advancement of Teaching established the National Board for Professional Teaching Standards (NBPTS). Its goal was to establish "high and rigorous standards for what teachers should know and be able to do, to certify

---

Career Ladders Defined

In 1984, Tennessee became the first state to establish a statewide career ladder program, and a number of states followed suit by creating similar career ladder or performance pay programs. While each state initiative was designed differently, career ladder programs can generally be placed in one of three categories:

- *Performance-based ladders*: As teachers demonstrate increased competence, they progress to different or more complex levels of work, e.g., novice teacher license to career teacher license, career license to master teacher.
- *Job-enlargement ladders*: These include progression to activities outside of the classroom such as curriculum development, supervising and mentoring new teachers, serving as a professional development trainer, or lead teacher.
- *Professional development ladders*: Advancement is based on obtaining more knowledge or skills through credit, staff development activities, advanced degrees, or National Board certification (National Association of State Boards of Education, http://www.nasbe.org/Educational_Issues/New_Information/Policy_Updates/10_09.html).

For additional information on Career Ladders, see: Milken Family Foundation: at http://www.talentedteachers.org/tap.taf, retrieved February 27, 2008. or http://Consortium for Policy Research in Education (CPRE): http://www.wcer.wisc.edu/cpre.

---

teachers who meet those standards and to advance related educational reforms for the purpose of improving student learning in America" (NBPTS, http://www.nbpts.org).

In 1994, the NBPTS published a booklet entitled *What Teachers Should Know and be Able to Do.* Since then, the plan has gained support from a number of professional teachers' organizations, including the AFT and the NEA. Meanwhile, classroom teachers all over the country have embraced the concept of a "career ladder" within the profession and sought national board certification.

THE CAREER LADDER

The Carnegie career ladder consists of four distinct steps. The first is a licensed teacher preparing for national board certification. The second level is a national board "certified teacher," followed by the "advanced teacher" who has passed further rigorous evaluation, following the 10 year, initial board certification period and finally the "lead teacher" elected by others teachers and is an instructional teacher.

Before you can apply for initial national board certification, you must have completed all degree requirements in education and specialty areas, have been certified by your state's department of instruction, and have at least 3 years of classroom teaching experience. The certification process can take several years to complete and involves portfolio assessment, classroom observations, written evaluations, and a series of interviews with the national board. There are five "core propositions" upon which the overall assessment is based.

- Commitment to students
- Knowledge of their subject matter
- Effective classroom management skills
- Systematic instructional practices
- Direct membership in the learning community

The first proposition, that board certified "teachers are committed to students and their learning," is based on the beliefs that all students can learn; all students should be treated equitably; and that differences in students needs and interests should be considered in the planning and delivery of instruction. Teachers should also be able to motivate their students, help them develop self-esteem and respect for racial and cultural differences in society.

The second proposition is that board certified teachers "know the subjects they teach and how to teach those subjects." Teachers should have a deep understanding of their subject matter and be able to help students develop critical and analytical thinking and problem solving skills. Additionally, teachers should be able to convey the subject matter to their students and apply instructional strategies and materials that are appropriate. Finally, teachers should be able to "create multiple paths" to the subjects they teach, recognizing that not all children learn in the same way.

The third proposition is that board certified teachers are able to manage and "monitor student learning." Teachers must be able to plan, implement, and modify their instruction, make effective use of instructional time, have a range of instructional techniques, and ensure a "disciplined learning environment to promote student interest and learning" (http://nbpts.org/about_us/mission_and_history/the_five_core_propositio). Teachers should also be able to assess student progress and employ multiple measures of student growth.

The fourth proposition is that board certified teachers should "think systematically about their practice and learn from experience." Teachers should be able to use an experimental and problem-solving perspective toward student learning. They should also be able to reflect on their "practice" (teaching) and implement necessary changes to improve their instruction. Finally, teachers should "engage in life-long learning" and encourage the same in their students.

The fifth and final proposition is that national board certified teachers should be members of learning communities, working collaboratively with other professionals and parents to improve both the curriculum and instruction.

Although the language of the National Board Certification may be daunting and its requirements overwhelming, remember that these are the professional standards for teachers at the top of our profession. They challenge American teachers to grow throughout their careers in a lifelong learning environment to become masters of their subject area, committed to their students' learning and effective managers of instruction and curriculum. Welcome to the Noble Profession!

SUMMARY

The Professionalization of Teaching

Given the criteria widely accepted by society, teaching clearly is a profession and teachers are well-trained professionals who make autonomous decisions and embrace a set of ethical standards. And yet, over the years, teachers have had to struggle for professional recognition.

Teacher Accountability

During the 1800s, teachers were directly accountable to the communities they served and were routinely examined by trustees and local board members. By the 1940s, educators embraced its first standardized assessment instrument, the National Teachers Exam. Then in the 1980s, there was a call to "raise the standards" of teachers and the three-part Praxis exam series was adopted as the "new generation of teacher assessment."

Professional Support Networks for Teachers

As teachers we have an extensive professional support network to assist us with our teaching. This network begins with the school support staff of counselors, nurses, secretaries, administrators, and fellow teachers. Beyond the school is a vast network of professional specialty, international and national organizations, and unions that provide us with information, research, and job protection.

Professional Standards for Teachers

In order to demonstrate your ability to teach and secure your first teaching position, we have recommended you begin to develop a professional portfolio and a professional journal. This is your first step in reflective, lifelong learning. By maintaining your professional credentials, attending job fairs, and networking during your student teaching assignment, you will in a strong position to obtain your first teaching position. But the pinnacle of our profession is national board certification NBPTS. These master teachers challenge us to grow throughout our careers to become masters of our subject area, committed to student learning.

DISCUSSION QUESTIONS

1. What are the generally accepted characteristics of a professional? Using these criteria, do you think that teaching is a profession? Why?
2. Discuss the changes in teacher accountability from the mid-1800s to the present day. What is the role of the Praxis exam in the accountability of teachers?
3. Discuss local, state, and national support networks for teachers today.
4. What is a portfolio and why is it important for your professional development?

References

Acuna, R. (1988). *Occupied America: A history of Chicanos* (3rd ed.). New York: Longman.

Adler, M. J. (1982). *The paideia proposal: An educational manifesto*. New York: Macmillan.

Adler, M. J., Fadiman, C., Goetz, P. W. (Eds.). (1990). *Great books of the Western world* (2nd ed.). Chicago: Britannica.

Aguirre, B. (1976). Differential migration of Cuban social races. *Latin American Research Review, 11*, 103–104.

American Association for Employment in Education. (2000). *The job search handbook for educators*. Evanston, IL.: Author.

American Association of University Women. (1992). *How schools shortchange girls*. Annapolis Junction, MD: Author.

American Federation of Teachers. (2004-2005). Annual Survey of Teachers' Salaries.

American School Board Journal. (2002, July). You say: A mixed message on the benefits of Sex Ed. *American School Board Journal, 189*: 7.

Anderson, J. D. (1995). Literacy and education in the African American experience. In V. L. Gadsen and D. A. Wagner (Eds.), *Literacy among African American youth* (pp. 19–37). Cresskill, NJ: Hampton Press.

———. (1988). *The education of Blacks in the South, 1860-1935*. Chapel Hill, NC: University of North Carolina Press.

Axtell, J. (1985). *Invasion within: Cultural origins of North America*. New York: Oxford University Press.

Bagley, W. C. (1925). *Classroom management*. New York: Macmillan.

Barbe, W. (1979). *Teaching through Modality Strengths: Concepts and Practices*. Columbus, Ohio: Zaner-Bloser.

Barr, R. and Parrett, W. (2001). *Hope Fullfilled for At Risk Youth*. Boston: Allyn and Bacon.

Benard, B. (1993). Fostering Resilence in Kids. Educational Leadership, 51 (3), 44-48.

Bender W., and Mc Laughlin P. (1997). Violence in the Classroom. *Intervention in School and Clinic*, 32 (4) 196-198.

Bergren, O., & Weil, O. (1977, April). The Right to Strike? *Illinois Issues*.

Bergren, O. Comments, President of the Illinois Manufacturer's Association.

Berliner, B. A. Helping Homeless Students Keep Up. *Education Digest* Sept. 2002, vol. 68, issue 1, 49-52.

Berliner, D. C. (1979) Tempus educare. In P. L. Peterson & H. J. Walberg (Eds.) *Research on teaching: Concepts, findings, and implications* Berkeley, CA: McCutchan.

Bert, L. (1996). *Infants, Children and Adolescents* 2nd ed. Boston: Allyn and Bacon.

Bestor, A. (1954). *Educational wasteland*. New York: Wiley.

Binder, F. (1970). *Education in the history of Western civilization, selected readings*. New York: Macmillan.

Bloom, B. (Ed.). (1956). *Taxonomy of educational objectives, handbook 1: Cognitive domain*. New York: David McKay.

Boger, J. G. and Olfield, G., eds. (2005). *School Resegregation: Must the South Turn Back?* Chapel Hill, NC: University of North Carolina Press.

Bowen, J. (1972). *A history of Western education. The ancient world: Orient and Mediterranean, 2000 B.C.–A.D. 1054* (Vol. 1). New York: St Martin's Press.

Boyer, E. (1983). *High School*. New York: Harper and Row.

———. (1992). *School choice*. New York: Carnegie Foundation for the Advancement of Teaching.

Bracey, G. W. (1997). *Setting the record straight: Responses to misconceptions about public education in the United States*. Alexandria, VA: Association for Supervision and Curriculum Development.

———. (2002, November 30). Old whine, new battles. *The American Prospect*.

Bradbury, B. and Jantti, M. (1999). Child Poverty Across Industrialized Nations. Economic and Social Policy Series, No. 71, September 1999.

Bronner, E. (1962). *William Penn's holy experiment*. New York: Temple University.

Brooks, C. (2000, March). In the twilight zone between black and white: Japanese American resettlement and community in Chicago, 1942–1945. *Journal of American History 86*(4), 1655–1688.

Brunbaugh, Martin G. (ed). *The Life and Works of Christopher Dock*, Philadelphia: J.P. Lippincott Co, 1908: 18-20.

Bruner, J. (1996). *The culture of education*. Cambridge, MA: Harvard University Press.

Brunsma, D. and Rockquemoro,(1999). Effects of Student Uniforms on Attendance, Behavioral Problems, Substance Abuse and Academic Achievement. *Journal of Educational Research*, 92 (1) 53-62.

Bullock, A. A. and Hawk, P. (2000). *Developing a teaching portfolio* (2nd ed.). Upper Saddle River, NJ: Pearson.

Burns, J. A. (1969). *The principles, origins and establishment of the Catholic school system in the United States*. New York: Arno.

Burton, W. (1852). *The district school as it was*. Boston: T. R. Marvin.

Bushweller, K. (1998). Probing the Roots and Prevention of Youth Violence. *American School Board Journal*, 85 (12) A8-A12.

Calhoon, P. (1988). Mediator magic. *Educational Leadership, 45*(4), 92–93.

Canter, L., and Canter, M. (1976). *Assertive discipline*. Seal Beach, CA: Canter & Associates.

———. (1993). *Succeeding with difficult students*. Seal Beach, CA: Canter & Associates.

Carroll, H., Jr., Embree, A., Mellon, K., Schrier, A., & Taylor, A. (1961). *The development of civilization: A documentary history of politics, society and thought* (Vol. 1). Chicago: Scott Foresman.

Children's Defense Fund, (1998). *The State of America's Children. Yearbook*, 1998, Author.

Choice, District to District. (2002, December 5). *The News and Observer*.

Clifford, J. C. (1989). Man/Woman/Teacher: Gender, family and career. In D. Warren (Ed.), *American educational history: American teachers: Histories of a profession at work* (pp. 293–343). New York: Macmillan.

Cobo, Father B. (1983). *History of the Inca Empire: An Account of the Indians' Customs and their Origin* (Roland Hamilton, Trans.). Austin, TX: University of Texas Press.

Cohen, S. (1974a). *A documentary history of education—Vol. 3. U. S. Bureau of Education, 1895* (pp. 1290–1291). New York: Random House.

———. (1974b). *A history of colonial education 1607–1776*. New York: Wiley.

———. (1974c). *Education in the United States: A documentary history* (Vol. 2, pp. 997 –998). New York: Random House.

———. (1974d). *Education in the United States: A documentary history* (Vol. 3). New York: Random House.

Coons, J. E., Clune, W. H., & Sugarman, S. (1970). *Private wealth and public education*. Cambridge, MA: Harvard University Press.

Coto-Thorner, G. (1967). *Tropico in Manhattan*. San Juan, de Puerto Rico: Editorial Cordellera.

Cornell, S. (1988). *The Return of the Native: American Indian Political Resurgence*. New York: Oxford University Press.

Counts, G. (1932, April). Dare progressive education be progressive? (Vol. 9). *Progressive Education, 4*, 257–263.

Craven, W. (1949). *The Southern colonies in the seventeenth century, 1607–1689*. Baton Rouge: Louisiana State University.

Cruz, J. (1998). *Identity and power: Puerto Rican politics and the challenge of ethnicity*. Philadelphia: Temple University Press.

Cumberland County Schools. (2001). *Teacher incentive plan*. Fayetteville, NC.

Daniels, Roger. (2002). *Coming to America, Second Edition*. New York: HarperCollins.

De Bono, E. 1985. *Six Thinking Hats*. Boston: Little, Brown & Co.

De Diaz Cansecio, M. R. (1999). *A history of the Inca realm*. Cambridge, MA: Cambridge University Press.

DeBord, K. (1997). National Network for Child Care – NNCC. Focus on Kids: The effects of Divorce on Children. Raleigh, NC: North Carolina Cooperative Extension Service.

DeStafano, J., & Foley, E. (2003, April 16). The human resource factor. *Education Week.*

Dewey, J. (1899). *The school and society.* Chicago: University of Chicago Press.

———. (1916). *Democracy and education: An introduction to the philosophy of education.* New York: Macmillan.

Dewey, J., & Dewey, E. (1915). *Schools of to-morrow.* New York: E. P. Dutton.

Dickinson, D. K., & Tabors, P. O. (1991). Early literacy: Linkages between home, school, and literacy achievement at age five. *Journal of Research in Childhood Education, 6*(1), 30–46.

Diouf, S. A. (1998). *Servants of Allah: African Muslims enslaved in the Americas.* New York: New York University Press.

Dowling-Sendor, B. (2002, July) School law: Searching for the right balance. *American School Board Journal, 189,* 7.

Draper, A. S. (1895). Organization for city schools systems. *Report of the Committee of Fifteen.* Washington, D.C.: National Education Association.

Dreikurs, R., & Cassel, P. (1972). *Discipline without tears.* New York: Hawthorn.

Dworkin, M. (1959). *Dewey on education.* New York: Teachers College Press.

Education Week. (1982, May 26). Supreme Court's Decision in North Haven v. Bell.

Elliot, J. H. (2006). *Empires of the Atlantic world: Britain and Spain in America, 1492–1830.* New Haven, CT: Yale University Press.

Ellis, D. M., Frost, J. A., Syrett, H. C., & Carman, H. J. (1957). A short history of New York State. Ithaca, NY: Cornell University Press.

Elmore, E. W. (1923, January). Squads for discipline. *American Physical Education Review, 28,* 25–26.

Engel et al. v. Vitale Jr. et al., 370 U.S. 421–460 (1962).

Fears, D. (2001, July 18). Schools' racial isolation growing. *The Washington Post,* p. A3.

Female degrees. (1835, March 14). *Republican and Journal.* Springfield, MA.

Fernandez, R. (1996). *The disenchanted island: Puerto Rico and the United States in the twentieth century.* Westport, CT: Praeger.

Finkelstein, B. (1989). *Governing the young: Teacher behavior in popular primary schools in nineteenth century United States.* New York: Falmer Press.

Fischer, L., Schimmel, D., and Kelly, C. (1973). *The civil rights of teachers.* New York: Harper and Row.

———. (1999). *Teachers and the law.* New York: Longman.

Fish, S. (1993, November) Reverse racism, or how the pot got to call the kettle black. *The Atlantic.*

Fisher, C. W. and Berliner, D. C. (Eds.). (1885). Time and timing. *Perspectives on instructional time.* New York: Longman.

Foner, E. (1988). *Reconstruction: America's unfinished revolution 1863–1877.* New York: Harper and Row.

Ford, P. L. (Ed.). (1962). *The New England primer: A history of its origin and development.* New York: Teachers College Press. Original published 1867.

Freedmen's Bureau. (1865–1869) Records of the assistant commissioner for the District of Columbia. Washington, DC: National Archives Microfilm.

Frye, E. (1999). *One thousand instant words.* Laguna Beach, CA: Author.

Fuller, E. (1971) *Prudence Crandall.* Middletown, CT: Wesleyan University Press.

Gandy, K. (2003, Spring). Save affirmative action. *National NOW Times.*

Gardner, H. (1983). *Frames of mind: The theory of multiple intelligences.* New York: Basic Books.

———. (1995). Multiple intelligences: As a catalyst. *English Journal, 84*(8), 16–26.

———. (1999) *Intelligence reframed: Multiple intelligences for the 21st century.* New York: Basic Books.

Gibbon, E. (1909). *Decline and fall of the Roman Empire* (2nd ed.). In J. B. Bury, .(Ed.), Vol 4 (London).

Gibbs, N. It's Only Me. *Time,* March 19, 2002, p.12.

Gibson, P. (1989). Gay Male and Lesbian Youth Suicide. In M. Feinlieb (ed.) *Report of the Secretary's Task Force on Youth Suicide.* Washington D.C. Department of Health and Human Services. 3-143.

Ginott, H. (1965). *Between parent and child.* New York: Avon.

———. (1971). *Teacher and child.* New York: Macmillan.

Giroux, H. (1985). Teachers as transformative individuals. *Social Education, 49,* 376–379.

Glasser, W. (1965). *Reality therapy: A new approach to psychiatry.* New York: Harper and Row.
———. (1969). *Schools without failure.* New York: Harper and Row.
GLSEN, New York and Youth Pride, Inc., Providence RI.
Goleman, D. (1996, May/June). Emotional intelligence: Why it can matter more than IQ. *Learning,* 49–50.
Gomez, M. (2005). *Black crescent: African Muslims in the Americas and reversing sail: A history of the African diaspora.* Cambridge: Cambridge University Press.
Gomez, M. (Ed.). (2006). *A persistent call and response: Diasporic Africa reconsidered.* New York: New York University Press.
Goodman, K. (1986). *What is whole in whole language?* Portsmouth, NH: Heinemann.
Gracenin, D. (1993). On Their Own Terms. *The Executive Educator* 15 (10) 31-34.
Grant, C.A. and Sleeter, C.E. (2007) *Doing Multicultural Education for Achievement and Equity.* New York: Routledge.
Gray, W. and Monroe, M. (1956). *(The new) fun with Dick and Jane.* Chicago: Scott, Foresman.
Greene, M. (1988). *The dialect of freedom.* New York: Teachers College Press.
Griscom, John. An account of Pestalozzi's school, October 1818 in Frederick Binder (1970) *Education in the History of Western Civilization, Selected Readings.* (New York: MacMillan, Co.).
Guilday, P. (ed.). (1932). *The national pastorals of the American hierarchy, 1792–1919.* Washington, DC:
Harrow, A. J. (1972). *A taxonomy of the psychomotor domain.* New York: David McKay.
Henri, F. (1975). *Black migration: Movement northward, 1900–1920.* New York: Doubleday.
Herbart, J. (1904). *An introduction to Herbart's science and practice of education* (H. M. Felkin & E. Felkin, Trans.). Boston: D.C. Heath.
Hewett, E. C. (1884). *A treatise on pedagogy for young teachers.* Cincinnati, OH: Van Antwerp, Bragg.
Higham, J. (1988). *Strangers in the land: Patterns of American nativism, 1860–1925.* New Brunswick, NJ: Rutgers University Press.
Hillway, T. (1964). *American education: An introduction through readings.* Boston: Houghton Mifflin.
Hirsch, E. D. Jr. (1987). *Cultural literacy.* Boston: Houghton Mifflin.
———. (1993). The Core Knowledge Curriculum –What's Behind its Success? *Educational Leadership* 50 (8):23-25.
Holland, A., & Andre, T. (1987, Winter). Participation in extracurricular activities in secondary school: What is known, what needs to be known. *Review of Educational Research, 57*(4), 437–466.
Holmer, R. (2005). *The Aztec book of destiny.* North Charleston, SC: BookSurge.
Hunter, M. (1994). *Enhancing teaching.* New York: Macmillan.
Institute for Social Research. (1998). *Monitoring the Future.* Ann Arbor, MI: University of Michigan.
Jackson, P. (1968). *Life in classrooms.* New York: Holt, Reinhart and Winston.
James, W. (1950/1980). *Principles of psychology.* New York: Dover.
Jefferson, T. Notes on the State of Virginia, in Crusade Against Ignorance, ed. Gordon C. Lee (New York: Teachers College, Columbia University, 1961).
Jencks, C. (1994). *The homeless.* Cambridge, MA: Harvard University Press.
Johnson, C. (1963). *Old-time schools and school-books.* New York: Dover.
Johnson, D. and Johnson, R. (1989). *Cooperation and competition: Theory and research.* Edina, MN: Interaction Book.
———. (1991). Classroom instruction and co-operative learning. In H. C. Waxman & H. J. Walberg (Eds.), *Effective teaching: Current research* (pp. 277–293). Berkeley, CA: McCutchan.
Jones, F. (1987). *Positive classroom discipline.* New York: McGraw-Hill.
Kaestle, C. (Ed.). (1973). *Joseph Lancaster and the monitorial school movement: A documentary history.* New York: Teachers College Press.
———. (1983). *Pillars of the republic: Common schools and American society, 1780–1860.* New York: Hill and Wang.
Kaiser Family Foundation. (2005). Teen sexual activity fact sheet.
Kaufman, P. W. (1984). *Women teachers on the frontier.* New Haven, CT: Yale University Press.
Keller, B. (2000, August 2). School finance case draws to a close in New York. *Education Week.*
Kilpatrick, W. H. (Ed.). (1933). *The educational frontier.* New York: D. Appleton Century.
Kohn, A. (1996). *Beyond discipline: From compliance to community.* Alexandria, VA: Association for Supervision and Curriculum Development.

Kounin, J. (1971). *Discipline and group management in classrooms.* New York: Holt, Rinehart & Winston.

Kozol, J. (1992, September 21). Whittle and the privateers. *The Nation,* 272–278.

Krathwohl, D., Bloom, B., and Masia, B. (1956). *Taxonomy of educational objectives. Handbook II: Affective domain.* New York: David McKay.

Lambert, N. and McCombs, B. (Eds.). (1998). *How students learn: Reforming schools through learner-centered education.* Washington, DC: American Psychological Association.

Landry D., Kaeser, L., and Richards, C. (1999). Abstinence Promotion and the Provision of Information About Contraception in Public School District Sexuality Education Policies. *Family Planning Perspectives,* 31, 280-286.

Langdon, C. (1999). *The fifth Phi Delta Kappa poll of teachers' attitudes towards the public schools. Phi Delta Kappan.*

Larson, B. and Keiper, T. (2007) *Instructional strategies for middle and high school.* New York: Routledge.

Leach, P. (1995). *Children First.* New York: Viking.

Lee, D. and Garrett, J. (2005, July). *Academic freedom in the middle and secondary school classroom.* The Clearinghouse,

Leon-Portilla, M. (1990). *Aztec thought and culture: A study of the ancient Nahuati mind.* Norman, OK: University of Oklahoma Press.

Lerner, G. (1977). *The female experience: An American documentary.* Oxford, England: Oxford University Press.

Life Magazine. (1958, March 24, 31; April 7, 14, 21) The crisis in education.

Lightfoot, S. L. (1983). *The Good High School.* New York: Basic Books.

Locke, J. (1705/1968). Some thoughts concerning education. In J. Axtell (Ed.), *The educational writings of John Locke.* Cambridge, England: Cambridge University Press.

Louis Harris and Associates. (1996). *Students voice their opinion on their education, teachers and schools.* Part II of the Metropolitan Life survey of the American teacher. New York: Author.

Males, M. (1996). *The Scapegoat Generation: America's War on Adolescents.* Monroe, Maine: Common Courage Press.

Maria Montessori.Martin, J. (1985). Reclaiming a conversation. In *The Ideal of the Educated Woman* (pp. 1–7). New Haven, CT: Yale University Press.

Martin, Michael. (2000). Does Zero Mean Zero? Balancing Policy with Procedure in the Fight Against Weapons at School. *American School Board Journal,* 187, 3.

McCluskey, N. (Ed.). (1964). To the honorable board of aldermen of the City of New York. *Catholic education in America: A documentary history* (pp. 66–77). New York: Teachers College Press.

McCombs, B. (1991). *Metacognition and motivation in higher level thinking.* Paper presented at the annual meeting of the American Educational Research Association, Chicago, IL.

McCormick, G. and McCormick, C. (1992). Authentic multicultural activities: Avoiding pseudo-multiculturalism. *Childhood Education,* 68, 140–144.

McGuffey, W. (1836/1982). *The eclectic first reader.* Cincinnati, OH: Mott Media.

———. (1879/1962). *Fifth eclectic reader.* New York: Signet Classics.

McIntosh, J. (1996). *U.S.A. Suicide: 1994 Official Final Data. Washington,* DC: American Association of Suicidology.

Meltzer, M. (Ed.). (1967). *In their own words: A history of the American negro, 1916–1966.* New York: Thomas Y. Crowell.

Menacker, J. and Pascarella, E. (1983). How aware are educators of Supreme Court decisions that affect them? *Phi Delta Kappan,* 64(6), 424–426.

Methodist University. (2006–2007). Department of Education, Requirements for Admission into Teacher Education.

Mirandola, G. P. (1961). Oration on the Dignity of Man, in T*he Renaissance Philosophy of Man.* Cassier, F., ed. (Chicago: Phoenix Books): 224-225.

Morgan, H. (1995). *Historical perspectives on the education of Black children.* Westport, CT: Praeger.

Myrdal, G. (1944). *An American dilemma: The Negro problem.* New York: Harper and Row.

National assessment of educational progress. (2006). National Center for Education Statistics. Washington, DC: Institute of Education Sciences.

National Board for Professional Teaching Standards. (1991). *Toward high and rigorous teaching standards for the teaching profession: A summary* (2nd ed.). Detroit, MI: Author.

National Board for Professional Teaching Standards. (1994). *What teachers should know and be able to do*. Detroit, MI: Author.

National Center for Educational Statistics. (2003–2004). *Schools and staffing survey*. Washington, DC: U.S. Department of Education.

National Commission on Excellence in Education. (1983). A nation at risk: The imperative for educational reform. Washington, DC: U.S. Government Printing Office.

National Education Association (NEA). (2003). *Estimates of school statistics, 2000–2001*. Author.

National Education Association. (2006, January 6). NEA president calls Florida Supreme Court decision resounding rejection of school voucher plans. Washington, DC: Author.

Nebraska Farmer. (1915/1999, September). Rules for 1915 female teachers.

New American Schools Development Corporation. (1991). Designs for a new generation of American schools. Arlington, VA: Author.

Nielsen, W. (1972). *The big foundations*. New York: Columbia University Press.

Nieto, S. (1996). *Affirming diversity*, New York: Longman. The Nation's Report Card. (2006).

Northend, C. (1853). *The teacher and the parent: Treatise upon common school education: Containing practical suggestions to teachers and parents*. Boston: Jenks, Hickling and Swan.

Nuhfer, E. B. (2005, September). De Bono's red hat on Krathwohl's head: Irrational means to rational ends. *National Teaching and Learning Forum*, 14(5), 7–11.

Office of Special Education and Rehabilitative Services. (2006). Washington, DC: U. S. Department of Education..

Ozmon, H. and Craver, S. (1995). *Philosophical foundations of education*. Upper Saddle River, NJ: Prentice Hall.

Parker, F. (1883). *Notes on teaching*. New York: E. L. Kellogg.

Parkerson, D. H. and Parkerson, J. (1998). *The emergence of the common school in the U.S. countryside*. Lewiston, NY: Edwin Mellen Press.

———. (2001). *Transitions in American education: A social history of teaching*. New York: RoutledgeFalmer.

Parkerson, J. (1989). *The Curriculum of the Home*. Ed.D. Dissertation, University of South Carolina.

Pavur, C., S. J. (2005). *The ratio studiorum: The official plan for Jesuit education*. St. Louis, MO: The Institute of Jesuit Sources.

Perez, L. A. Jr. (2001). *On becoming Cuban: Identity, nationality, and culture*. New York: HarperCollins.

Pestalozzi, J. (1894). *Leonard and Gertrude and how Gertrude teaches her children* (E. Cooke, Ed., & L. E. Holland & F. C. Turner, Trans.). London: Routledge and Kegan Hall.

Pierson, M., & Rittenmeyer, S. (2001, May/June). Updated survey revisits random drug testing. *Illinois School Board Journal*.

Pipher, M. (1994). *Reviving Ophelia: Saving the Selves of Adolescent Girls*, New York: Ballantine Books.

Portes, A. and Rumbaut, R. G. (1996). *Immigrant America: A portrait* (2nd ed.). Berkley: University of California Press.

Portner, J. (1993). Prevention Efforts in Junior High Found Not to Curb Drug Use in High School. *Education Week*, 12 (40) 9.

———. (2000). Complex Set of Ills Spur Rising Teen Suicide Rate. *Education Week*, 19 (31) 1,22–31.

Prince, H. (1997, Spring). Michigan's school finance reform initial pupil equity results. *Journal of Education Finance*, 22(4), 394–409.

Purkey, W. and Novak, J. (1996). *Inviting school success: A self-concept to teaching, learning, and democratic practice*. Belmont, CA: Wadsworth.

Rafferty, Y. (1995, Spring). The Legal Rights and Educational Problems of Homeless Children and Youth. Educational Evaluation and Policy Analysis, 39–61.

Raths, L., Harmin, M., and Simon, S. (1966). *Values and teaching*. Columbus, OH: Charles Merrill.

Ravitch, D. (2000). *Left back: A century of failed school reforms*. New York: Simon and Schuster.

Reed, B. and Railsback, J. (2003). *Strategies and resources for mainstream teachers of English language learners*. Northwest Regional Educational Laboratories—Equity Center.

Reilly, W. E. (Ed.). (1990). *Sarah Jane Foster: Teacher of the freedmen—A diary and letters*. Charlottesville: University Press of Virginia.

Report on Violence in the Schools: 2000, Justice Policy Institute (Washington, D.C.). *Republican and Journal.* (March 14, 1835). Springfield, Massachusetts.

Roberts, J. M. (1995) *A Concise History of the World.* New York: Oxford University Press.

Roderick, T. (1988). Johnny can learn to negotiate. *Educational Leadership, 45*(4), 86–91.

Rogg, E. M. (1974). *The assimilation of Cuban exiles: The role of community and class.* New York: Aberdeen Press.

Rothstein, S. W. (Ed.). (1995). *Class, culture and race in American schools: A handbook.* Westport, CT: Greenwood Press.

Rotter, J. (1966). Generalized expectancies for internal versus external control of reinforcements. *(Psychological Monographs, 80,*(Whole No. 609)).

Rousseau, J. (1974). *Emile* (B. Foxley, Trans.). London: Everyman's Library.

Rudolph, F. (Ed.). (1965). *Essays on education in the early republic.* Cambridge, MA: Belknap Press.

Rush, B. Plan for the Establishment of Public Schools and the Diffusion of Knowledge in Philadelphia, Pennsylvania, 1786, in *Essays on Education in the early Republic,* ed. Fredrick Rudolph (Cambridge: Belknap Press of Harvard University Press, 1965).

Sadker, M. and Sadker, D. (1995). *Failing at fairness: How America's schools cheat girls.* New York: Touchstone Press.

Sadker, M., Sadker, D., and Klein, S. (1992). *The issue of gender in elementary and secondary education.* In G. Grant (Ed.), *Review of research in education.* Washington, DC: American Association of University Women.

Sagor, R. (1996). Building Resiliency in Students. *Educational Leadership* 54 (1) 8–43.

Salend, S. J. (2005). *Creating inclusive classrooms: Effective and reflective practices* (5th ed.). Upper Saddle River, NJ: Merrill/Prentice Hall.

Sandham, J. (2001). Home sweet school. *Education Week, 19*(20), 24–29.

Sauter, R. (1995). Standing up to violence. *Phi Delta Kappan, 76,* K1–K12.

Schwab, J. (1973). The practical 3: Translation into curriculum. *School Review, 81,* 501–522.

Schwab, J. and Schwartz, H. (1984, Winter). Schwab's "practical 4" and its corroboration in recent history. *Curriculum Inquiry, 14*(4), 437–463.

Schwartz, S. (1987). *A mixed multitude: The struggle for tolerance in colonial Pennsylvania.* New York: New York University Press.

Scott, E. C. and Branch, G. (August, 13, 2002) "Intelligent Design" Not Accepted by Most Scientists, *School Board News.*

Sears, J. T. (1991, September). Helping students understand and accept sexual diversity. *Educational Leadership,49*(1), 54–56.

Sears, J. T. and Williams, W. L. (1997) *Overcoming Heterosexim and Homophobia.* New York: Columbia University Press.

Sebring, P. and Bryk, A. (2000). School leadership and the bottom-line. *Phi Delta Kappan, 81*(6), 440–443.

Sellers, C. (1991). *The market revolution.* Oxford, England: Oxford University Press.

Sernett, M. C. (1997). *Bound for the promised land.* Durham, NC: Duke University Press.

Sherman, M. (2007, May 30). High court rules for Goodyear in pay fight. *Daily Reflector,* A-8.

Siegel, Barry. (1992). Parents Get a Lesson in Equality. *Los Angeles Times* (Washington edition) April, 13. A1, A18-19.

Silber, K. (1960). *Pestalozzi: The man and his work.* London: Routledge and Kegan Hall.

Silberman, C. (1970). *Crisis in the classroom: The remaking of American education.* New York: Random House.

Simon, W. (1978). *A time for truth.* New York: McGraw Hill.

Sizer, T. (1984). *Horace's compromise.* New York: Houghton Mifflin.

Skerry, P. (1993) *Mexican Americans: The Ambivalent Minority.* New York: Free Press.

Skinner, B. F. (1951). *Science and human behavior.* Boston: Houghton Mifflin.

———. (1971). *Beyond freedom and dignity.* New York: Knopf.

———. (1974). *Walden two.* New York: Macmillan.

Slavin, R. (1988) Cooperative revolution catches fire. *School Administrator, 45*(1), 9–13.

Spring, J. (1990). *The American school, 1642–1990: Varieties of historical interpretation of the foundations and development of American education* (2nd ed.). New York: Longman.

———. (2000). *American education.* Boston: McGraw Hill.

Takaki, R. (1993). *A different mirror: A history of multicultural America.* Boston: Little, Brown.

Tateishi, J. (1999). An oral history of life in the Japanese American detention camps. In K. Yamane (Ed.), *And Justice for All.* Seattle: University of Washington Press.

Thorndike, E. (1913). *Educational psychology*. New York: Teachers College, Columbia University Press.

Teacher salary incentives (2002, August 30). *Daily Reflector*.

Trelease, J. (1995). *The read-aloud handbook* (4th ed.). New York: Penguin.

Tyler, Ralph. (1949). *Basic Principles of Curriculum and Instruction*. Chicago: University of Chicago Press.

———. (1977). Desirable content for a curriculum development syllabus today. In A. Molnar and J.A. Zahorik, eds., *Curriculum Theory*: 36-44. Washington, D.C.: Association for Supervision and Curriculum Development.

Ulich, R. (1950). *History of educational thought*. New York: American Book.

U.S. Bureau of the Census. (1961). *Historical Statistics of the U.S.* Washington, D.C.: Author

U.S. Bureau of the Census. (1997). *Poverty Rate: Below the Poverty Line*. Washington D.C.: Author.

U.S. Bureau of Census, (1997, 1998, 2000). Statistics. Washington, D.C. Author.

U.S. Bureau of Census (1999). Current Population Survey.

U.S. Bureau of the Census. (2000a). *Historical poverty tables*. Washington, DC: Author.

U.S. Bureau of the Census. (2000b). *Statistics on population*. Washington, DC: Author.

U.S. Bureau of the Census. (2001) *Statistical abstract of the United States*. Washington, DC: Author.

U.S. Bureau of the Census. (2005). *Statistics*. Washington, DC: Author

U.S. Bureau of Education. (1871). *Annual report of the Commissioner of Education for 1870* (pp. 437–438). Washington, DC:

U.S. Bureau of Education. (1895). *Report of the Commissioner of Education: 1892–1893*. Washington, DC: Author.

U.S. Department of Commerce. (2002). *Characteristics of the population below the poverty level, 1970–2000*.

U.S. Department of Education. (1996). *Schools and staffing survey 1993–94*. Washington, DC: National Center of Educational Statistics.

U.S. Department of Education. National Center for Educational Statistics, (1998). Fast Response Survey System, "Principal/School Disciplinarian Survey on School Violence." FRSS 63.

U.S. Department of Education Web site. (2002). http://www.nclb.gov/next/overview/index.html

U.S. Department of Education. (2005). National Center of Education Statistics, National Household Education Survey.

U.S Department of Human Services, National Center on Child Abuse and Neglect. (1996). *Child Maltreatment 1994. Reports from the States to the National Center on Child Abuse and Neglect*. Washington DC: U.S. Government Printing Office.

U.S Department of Human Services, National Center on Child Abuse and Neglect. (1996). *Child Maltreatment 1994. Reports from the States to the National Center on Child Abuse and Neglect*. Washington DC: U.S. Government Printing Office.

U.S. Department of Labor. (2002). *United States selected occupations, national compensation survey*.

U.S. News and World Report. (1995). 24.

U.S. Senate, 97th Congress, 1st Session. (1985, January 28). *Hearing before the Committee on Labor and Human Resources: William Bennett of North Carolina, to be Secretary, Department of Education*.

Verstegen, D. (1994) The New Wave of School Finance Litigation. *Phi Delta Kappan*, November, vol 76:3 243-250.

Villegas, A. (1991). *Culturally responsive pedagogy for the 1990s and beyond*. Princeton, NJ: Educational Testing Service.

Walsh, W. (1998, October 14). Edison Project spares no cost in wooing prospective clients. *Education Week, 1*, 16.

Ward, L. F. (1935). *Young Ward's diary* (V. J. Stern, Ed.). New York: G.P. Putman's Son.

Webster, N. On the Education of Youth in America, in *Essays on Education in the early Republic*, ed. Fredrick Rudolph (Cambridge: Belknap Press of Harvard University Press, 1965).

Wegyln, M. (1996). *Years of infamy: The untold story of America's concentration camps*. Seattle: University of Washington Press.

White, K. (1999). Girls' sports: The best of times, the worst of times. *Education Week, 19*(7), 6.

Wilder, L. (1971) *These happy golden years*. New York: Harper Trophy.

Williams, H. A. (2005). *Self taught*. Chapel Hill: University of North Carolina Press.

Williams, J. R. (Ed). (1900). *Philip Vickers Fithian, journal and letters, 1769–1774*. Princeton, NJ: The University Library.

Willingham, W., & Cole, N. (1997). *Gender and fair assessment*. Mahwah, NJ: Erlbaum.

Wilson, T. (1994). *Navajo: Walking in beauty*. San Francisco: Chronicle Books.

Wittmer, J., & Myrick, R. D. (1989). The teacher as facilitator. Minneapolis, MN: Educational Media.

Woody, T. (1929). *A history of women's education in the United States* (Vol. 1). New York: The Science Press.

———. (1969). *Early Quaker education in Pennsylvania*.

Yudof, M., Kip, D., & Levin, B. (1992). *Education policy and the law* (3rd ed.). St. Paul. MN: West.

Internet Sites

American Alliance for Health, Physical Education, Recreation and Dance (AAHPERD): http://www.aahperd.org

American Association of Suicidology: http://www.suicidology.org

American Council on the Teaching of Foreign Languages: http://www.actfl.org

American Bar Association: http://www.abanet.org/publiced/lawday/studsurvey2000.html

American Federation of Teachers: http://www.aft.org/about/mission.htm

American Library Association, Banned Books: http://www.ala.org/ala/oif/bannedbooksweek/bbwlinks/100mostfrequently.htm

A Nation at Risk: http://www.ed.gov/pubs/NatAtRisk/recomm.html

Anti-Defamation League, Religious Freedom: http://adl.org/issue_religious_freedom/create/creationism2.asp

Association for Childhood Education International: http://www.acei.org

Association for Curriculum & Supervision Development: http://www.ascd.org/portal/site/ascd

Association for Educational Communications and Technology: http://www.aect.org

Association for Supervision and Curriculum Development—contains relevant research and practical ideas for teachers to implement in the classroom: http://www.ascd.org

Beaufort County Schools, North Carolina—has a description of the schools and the organization in the county: http://www.beaufort.k12.nc/bcs/organization.htm

Blackwell Museum of History of Education, Northern Illinois University—has books, artifacts, and photographs pertaining to American education. There is an extensive online collection: http://www.cedu.niu.edu/blackwell/books.html

Boston College: http://www.bc.edu

Boston College, Law School, Law Review: http://www.bc.edu/bc_org and http://www.bc.edu/cgi-bin/print_hit_bold.cgi/

Bucknell University, Hortonville School District v. Hortonville Education Association (1976): http://www.bucknell.edu/x10170.xml

Centers for Disease Control and Prevention: http://www.cdc.gov/hiv

Centers for Disease Control and Prevention Suicide Fact Sheet: http://www.cdc.gov/ncipc/dvp/suicide/

Civil Rights issues, legislation, and court rulings: http://www.146.186.233.120/civilrights

Clearinghouse on Reading, English and Communication, Indiana University—contains information on reading research, phonics, whole language, and teaching strategies: http://www.indiana.edu/~reading

Columbia University Encyclopedia online—contains information on a number of course cases, including the Bakke Reverse Discrimination case www.infoplease.com/ce6/history/A0841421.html

Conflict Resolution: http://www.resolutioneducation.com/http://www.crinfo.org/v3-menu-education.cfm

Consortium for Policy Research in Education (CPRE): http://www.wcer.wisc.edu/cpre/

Cooperative Learning Web site (University of Minnesota): http://www.clcrc.com

Cornell University Law School—site documents landmark Supreme Court decisions: http://www.supct.law.cornell.edu

Council of Chief State School Officers—this organization is involved with the creation of the INTASC Standards. Contains much information regarding INTASC: http://www.ccsso.org/intascst.html and http://www.ccsso.org/content/pdfs/StateTeacherPolicyFramework.pdf

Council of Exceptional Children: http://www.cec.sped.org

Cumberland County Schools, North Carolina: http://www.Ccs.k12.nc.us

D'Nealian Handwriting—includes information about methods and products: http://www.dnealian.com/lessons.html

Drug Abuse Resistance Education (DARE; 1995)—describes the DARE school program: http://www.ncjrs.gov/pdffiles/darefs.pdf

Department of Defense Schools, U.S. military—contains information regarding job opportunities on military bases: http://www.militaryconnection.com

Department of Education, Indiana—has detailed descriptions of the curriculum contents for the public schools. http://www.doe.state.in.us/publications/res_middleschool.html

Department of Public Education, Minnesota: http://www.educationminnesota.org

Department of Public Instruction, North Carolina: http://www.dpi.state.nc.us

Duke University, Law School: http://www.law.duke.edu/curriculum

Educational Law Center site—lists the Abbott v. Burke case and the important decision to provide more funding for schools with special needs children: http://www.edlawcenter.org/elcpublic/abbottvburke/aboutabbott.htm

Education Place: http://www.eduplace.com/ss/act/story.html

Education, Queensland Government, Students with Disabilities: http://education.qld.gov.au/curriculum/learning/students/disabilities/resources/information

Education Week, Online Newspaper and Research Center: www.edweek.org/ew/newstory.cfm/slug=42drug_web.h21

Emory University School of Law: http://www.law.emory.edu

Fact Sheet compiled by GLSEN, New York, NY and Youth Pride, Inc., Providence, RI http://members.tripod.com/~twood/guide.html#Statistics

Ferris State University, School of Education: http://www.ferris.edu/htmls/academics/center/Teaching_and_Learning_Tips/T_LHome.htm

First Amendment Center: http://www.firstamendmentcenter.org

Freedom Forum Organization—contains information regarding the news and freedom of speech: http://www.freedomforum.org/templates/document.asp

Health, Mental Health, and Safety Guidelines for Schools: http://www.nationalguidelines.org/guideline.cfm?guideNum=3-10

Holland & Knight Law Firm: http://www.hklaw.com

Home School Foundation—lists information supporting home schooling: http://www.home-schoolfoundation.org

Houston County Schools, Georgia—contains information related to the schools in Houston County, Georgia, including the dress code: http://www.hcbe.net/dresscode.html

Indiana University, Drug Education and Issues: http://www.drugs.indiana.edu/issues/suspicionless.html and http://www.drugs.indiana.edu/laws/vernonia.html

Internet Archive: http://www.archive.org/search.php?query=Andrew%20Draper

Internet in-Service on children and Divorce: http://www.hec.ohio-state.edu/famlife/divorce/index.htm

Interstate New Teacher Assessment and Support Consortium (INTASC)—site contains the standards for INTASC that are supported by the Council of Chief State School Officers: http://www.ccsso.org/projects/Interstate_New_Teacher_Assessment and_Support_Consortium/

International Reading Association (IRA): http://www.reading.org

Kentucky Educational Reform Act—lists efforts the state Kentucky has made to improve education: http://www.wku.edu/library/kera/orgs.htm

Lambda Legal Website—an organization devoted to promoting equality: http://www.lambdalegal.org

Leadership University: http://www.leaderu.com/real

Learning Disabilities Online: http://www.ldonline.org/ldbasics

Legal site for the San Antonio Rodriquez Case regarding equity: http://www.hrcr.org/safrica/equality/San_antonio_rodriguez.html

Military Connection: http://www.militaryconnection.com/

Milken Family Foundation, http://www.mff.org/presentation

Music Teachers National Association (MTNA): http://www.mtna.org

National Art Education Association (NAEA): http://www.naea.org

National Association of State Boards of Education: http://www.nasbe.org/Educational_Issues/New_Information/Policy_Updates/10_09.html

National Association for the Education of Young Children (NAEYC): http://www.naeyc.org

National Board for Professional Teacher Standards: http://www.nbpts.org

National Commission on Teaching and America's Future: http://www.ncataf.org

National Council for the Accreditation of Teacher Education—the site lists standards and procedures for the national accreditation of schools, colleges, and departments of education: http://www.ncate.org

National Council for the Social Studies (NCSS): http://www.ncss.org

National Council of Teachers of English (NCTE): http://www.ncte.org

National Council of Teachers of Mathematics (NCTM): http://www.nctm.org

National Education Association: http://www.nea.org; http://www.nea.org/aboutnea/code.htm and http://www.nea.org/futureteachers

National Education Association—Parents page: http://www.nea.org/parents.index.html

National Education Association—Read Across America Program: http://www.nea.org/readacross

National Parent Teacher Association: http://www.pta.org

National Parent Teacher Association Standards for Parent/Family Involvement Program: http://www.pta.org/programs/invstand

National Science Teachers Association (NSTA): http://www.nsta.org

No Child Left Behind—government site that lists the law and the school requirements: http://www.nclb.gov/next/overview/index.html

North Carolina Character Education Partnership, part of the Public Schools of North Carolina Web site—has ideas for implementing character education in the classroom: http://www.ncpublicschools.org/nccep/cumberland/schools.html

North Carolina Public Schools—has a detailed Web site regarding school organization at the state level: http://www.ncpublicschools.org/about_dpi

Northern Illinois University, Library—regarding teachers' right to strike, comments by Orville Bergren: http://www.lib.niu.edu/ipo/1977/ii770414.html

Northwest Regional Educational Laboratories—Equity Center: http://www.nwrel.org/request/2003may/resources.html

Northwest Regional Educational Laboratories—Mainstreaming: http://www.nwrel.org/request/2003may/resources.html

Ohio State University, College of Education: http://www.coe.ohio-state.edu

Open Court Resources—designed to assist teachers using the phonics based Open Court Reading Program, McGraw Hill. Has lesson plans, theme based unit plans, and free resources: http://www.opencourtresources.com

OYEZ, U.S. Supreme Court Media: http://www.oyez.org/cases/1960-1969/1961/1961_468/

Phi Delta Kappan: http://www.pdkintl.org/kappan/kappan.htm

Polk County Public Schools, Florida—has curriculum links that describe skills and concepts to be mastered by grade level: http://www.polk-fl.net/

Praxis Series, Registration and Tests at a Glance:http://www.ets.org/portal/site

Praxis I—Registration and Preparation:http://www.teachingandlearning.org

Praxis online test practice: http://www.ets.org/praxis/taags

Praxis Tests, Registration, and Test Information: http://www.ets.org/portal/site/ets

Regional Resource and Federal Centers—lists information for education sites that focus on specific topics, such as special education: http://www.rrfcnetwork.org/

School Integration in the United States: http://www.watson.org/~lisa/blackhistory/school-integration

Sex Education in America: A View from Inside the Nation's Classrooms, Kaiser Family Foundation, 2000: Menlo Park, CA: http://www.kff.org

Sex Education: Curricula and Programs, Advocates for Youth (November 2002: Washington, DC: http://www.advocatesforyouth.org/publications/factsheet/fssexcur.htm

Southeastern Louisiana University, School of Education: http://www2.selu.edu/Academics/Education/TEC/basal.htm

Suicide Prevention Online: http://www.samaritans.org

Thinkquest, information regarding school discipline: http://library.thinkquest.org/J002606/Discipline.html

U.S. Department of Education, Office for Civil Rights, 2002 Elementary and Secondary School Civil Rights Compliance Report: http://www.stophitting.com/disatschool/statesBanning.php

University of Colorado, School of Education, Student Teaching Observation Report:http://www.colorado.edu/education/students/studentteach/pdfs/ST_Obs_C.pdf/

University of Missouri, Kansas City School of Law—site lists important court decisions: http://www.law.umkc.edu/faculty/projects/ftrials/conlaw/goss.html

University of North Texas, Department of Communication Studies—contains information regarding the First Amendment Freedom Speech issue: http://www.comm.unt.edu

Villanova University School of Law, Women's Law Forum: http://vls.law.vill.edu/publications/womenslawforum/Comments/Spring%202001/stanleyvusc.html

Virginia Uribe, Fairfax High School, Los Angeles Unified School District, founder and director of PROJECT 10: http://www.members.tripod.com/~twood/guide

Webster University, information about Maria Montessori: http://www.webster.edu/~woolflm/montessori2.html/

West Virginia University, School of Education, working with Impaired Students: http://www.as.wvu.edu/~scidis/vision.html and http://www.as.wvu.edu/~scidis/hearing.html

White House Drug Policy, U.S. Government, Department of Justice: www.WhitehouseDrugPolicy.gov

Youth Pride, Inc.: http://www.members.tripod.com/~twood/guide

Index